Methods in
FIELD
EPIDEMIOLOGY

Pia D. M. MacDonald, PhD, MPH, CPH

Research Associate Professor
Department of Epidemiology
Director
UNC Center for Public Health Preparedness
North Carolina Institute for Public Health
Gillings School of Global Public Health
University of North Carolina at Chapel Hill
Chapel Hill, North Carolina

BARTLETT
LEARNING

World Headquarters

Jones & Bartlett Learning
5 Wall Street
Burlington, MA 01803
978-443-5000
info@jblearning.com
www.jblearning.com

Jones & Bartlett Learning Canada
6339 Ormindale Way
Mississauga, Ontario L5V 1J2
Canada

Jones & Bartlett Learning International
Barb House, Barb Mews
London W6 7PA
United Kingdom

Jones & Bartlett Learning books and products are available through most bookstores and online booksellers. To contact Jones & Bartlett Learning directly, call 800-832-0034, fax 978-443-8000, or visit our website, www.jblearning.com.

Substantial discounts on bulk quantities of Jones & Bartlett Learning publications are available to corporations, professional associations, and other qualified organizations. For details and specific discount information, contact the special sales department at Jones & Bartlett Learning via the above contact information or send an email to specialsales@jblearning.com.

Production Credits

Publisher: Michael Brown
Editorial Assistant: Teresa Reilly
Production Manager: Tracey McCrea
Director of Production: Amy Rose
Production Editor: Tiffany Sliter
Marketing Manager: Jody Sullivan
Manufacturing and Inventory Control Supervisor: Amy Bacus
Cover and Title Page Design: Kristin E. Parker
Composition: Cenveo Publisher Services
Cover and Title Page Image: © szefei/ShutterStock, Inc.
Printing and Binding: Malloy, Inc.
Cover Printing: Malloy, Inc.

Library of Congress Cataloging-in-Publication Data

MacDonald, Pia D. M.
    Methods in field epidemiology / Pia D. M. MacDonald.
        p. ; cm.
    Includes bibliographical references and index.
    ISBN-13: 978-0-7637-8459-1 (pbk.)
    ISBN-10: 0-7637-8459-1 (pbk.)
    1. Clinical epidemiology—Methodology. I. Title.
    [DNLM: 1. Epidemiologic Methods. 2. Disease Outbreaks. WA 950]
    RA652.2.C55M33 2012
    614.4—dc23   2011012723

6048
Printed in the United States of America
15 14 13 12 11   10 9 8 7 6 5 4 3 2 1

Dedication

To my husband, Daniel, and my parents, Gillan and Donald.
In memory of my brother, Ian MacDonald, who provided
unwavering support of my endeavors during his lifetime.

CONTENTS

PREFACE

The genesis of this book occurred while I was a Centers for Disease Control and Prevention Epidemic Intelligence Service (EIS) officer assigned to the North Carolina Division of Public Health. I was in the midst of my first outbreak investigation and turned searchingly to the only field epidemiology textbook available at the time for specific guidance. I found the book fell short in describing with enough detail the many aspects of conducting an outbreak investigation. I needed more direction and instructions on how to carry out the important components that make up an outbreak investigation. The scope of this book took root during those two years as an EIS officer. Writing a book felt daunting, but I was compelled to work on this gap in the literature. First, I launched the periodical *Focus on Field Epidemiology* (available at http://cphp.sph.unc.edu/focus/index.htm). Each issue was designed to guide an epidemiologist through a facet of an outbreak investigation and other related topics by providing hands-on, practical instructions and examples to illustrate points. Later, I developed a graduate-level online course at the University of North Carolina at Chapel Hill called Methods in Field Epidemiology. As I thought through the course content and the trouble students and practitioners had with certain concepts, many more ideas came to me in terms of content for a textbook on this topic.

This book has been adapted from materials developed for other purposes. To write each chapter, we started with pieces that were developed for *Focus on Field Epidemiology* and the course Methods in Field Epidemiology, as well as other UNC Center for Public Health Preparedness training materials. These works were developed by teams and the individuals listed as contributors worked on the materials used in writing the chapter text. Any errors are mine. All contributors have reviewed the materials and acknowledged their contributions to the content.

The target audience for this book is students and public health practitioners alike. The book covers many topics and is accompanied by numerous examples to illustrate the concepts. It can be used in academic courses that include topics such as outbreak investigations, applied epidemiology, and using epidemiology in public health practice.

Furthermore, it will be useful to practitioners who seek more direction and guidance to the methods used in field epidemiology, especially outbreak investigation. The chapters stand alone, generally, and follow the process that would be involved in an outbreak investigation. Additional chapters cover specific types of investigation such as forensic epidemiology, contact tracing, and environmental investigations, and resources that might be useful during investigations.

The focus of this book is applied epidemiology and how it is used in public health practice. It is not intended to replace a basic epidemiology textbook, but does go into great depth about using epidemiology in the context of applied public health such as outbreak investigation. Moreover, it is not intended to replace existing procedures or guidelines in local, state, or federal health departments. Instead, it should be used as a resource for training staff and providing further background on specific and sometimes complicated topics. This book is no substitute for experience and great mentorship.

I like to think of myself as a practicing epidemiologist. I borrow that term from physicians who, for their whole lives, say they "practice" medicine. The great thing about saying you practice a profession is that it implies you are constantly learning and building your skills. Epidemiology is much like medicine in that way. There is always more to learn, and experience is the best teacher, particularly when it is gained working as part of a team. I have learned a lot from many collaborators and colleagues. I hope this book is useful to you and helps you to keep learning, practicing, and protecting the public's health in whatever capacity you can.

ACKNOWLEDGMENTS

This book was written from materials developed for other purposes, including *Focus on Field Epidemiology* (available at http://cphp.sph.unc.edu/), a series of newsletters designed to guide an epidemiologist through facets of outbreaks investigations and other related topics by providing hands-on, practical instructions and examples to illustrate points; Methods in Field Epidemiology, a graduate-level online course at the University of North Carolina at Chapel Hill; and other training materials developed at the UNC Center for Public Health Preparedness (http://cphp.sph.unc.edu/). These source materials were developed by teams, and thus I have many contributors to acknowledge here and on each of the chapters, including: Laura Alexander, Lauren Bradley, Meredith Davis, Jennifer Horney, Morgan Johnson, Sandra McCoy, Sally Mountcastle, Amy Nelson, Sarah Pfau, David Rice, Matthew Simon, Cynthia Snider, Jeanette and Paul Stehr-Green, Michelle Torok, Andrew Voetsch, and Rachel Wilfert. I am very thankful to all the contributors for giving generous time to review their affiliated chapters. Additionally, I want to thank Sarah Pfau and Gene Matthews, who charitably reviewed Chapter 14 on the topic of forensic epidemiology. Lorraine Alexander was instrumental in developing the *Focus on Field Epidemiology* periodical. Furthermore, I am very grateful to the Council to Improve Foodborne Outbreak Response (CIFOR) for allowing us to reprint a section of their *Guidelines for Foodborne Disease Outbreak Response* about the agencies that become involved in foodborne disease investigations. It is the best review of this topic I have ever seen. I wholeheartedly thank David Rice, whose help with writing and editing this work was instrumental. His persistence and commitment to seeing the book completed is greatly appreciated. I want to thank my father, Donald MacDonald, whose unrelenting enthusiasm for this project was often greater than my own, and my mother, Gillan MacDonald, who has forever been supportive of all that I do, big and small. Finally, I want to thank my husband, Daniel Rodríguez, for his constant encouragement for this work.

CONTRIBUTORS

Laura C. Alexander, MPH
UNC Center for Public Health Preparedness
UNC Gillings School of Global Public Health
Chapel Hill, NC

Lauren N. Bradley, MHS
UNC Center for Public Health Preparedness
UNC Gillings School of Global Public Health
Chapel Hill, NC

Meredith K. Davis, MPH, CPH
UNC Center for Public Health Preparedness
UNC Gillings School of Global Public Health
Chapel Hill, NC

Jennifer A. Horney, PhD, MA, MPH, CPH
Research Assistant Professor
Department of Epidemiology
UNC Center for Public Health Preparedness
UNC Gillings School of Global Public Health
Chapel Hill, NC

Morgan L. Johnson, MPH
Emergency Management Training Coordinator
New York City Department of Health & Mental
    Hygiene
New York, NY

Pia D. M. MacDonald, PhD, MPH, CPH
Research Associate Professor
Department of Epidemiology
UNC Center for Public Health Preparedness

UNC Gillings School of Global Public Health
Chapel Hill, NC

Sandra I. McCoy, PhD, MPH
Institute of Business and Economic Research
University of California, Berkeley
Berkeley, CA

Sally B. Mountcastle, PhD, MSPH
Adjunct Assistant Professor
Department of Preventive Medicine &
    Public Health
University of Kansas Medical Center
Kansas City, KS

Amy L. Nelson, PhD, MPH, CPH
UNC Center for Public Health Preparedness
UNC Gillings School of Global Public Health
Chapel Hill, NC

Sarah Pfau, JD, MPH
Chapel Hill, NC

David B. Rice, MA
UNC Center for Public Health Preparedness
UNC Gillings School of Global Public Health
Chapel Hill, NC

Matthew C. Simon, MA
UNC Center for Public Health Preparedness
UNC Gillings School of Global Public Health
Chapel Hill, NC

Cynthia J. Snider, PhD, MHS
UNC Center for Public Health Preparedness
UNC Gillings School of Global Public Health
Chapel Hill, NC

Jeanette K. Stehr-Green, MD
Clinical Assistant Professor
Department of Epidemiology
University of Washington School of
   Public Health
Seattle, WA

Paul A. Stehr-Green, DrPH, MPH
Affiliate Associate Professor
Department of Epidemiology
University of Washington School of
   Public Health
Seattle, WA

Michelle R. Torok, PhD, MPH
UNC Center for Public Health Preparedness
UNC Gillings School of Global Public Health
Chapel Hill, NC

Andrew C. Voetsch, PhD
UNC Center for Public Health Preparedness
UNC Gillings School of Global Public Health
Chapel Hill, NC

Rachel Wilfert, MD, MPH, CPH
Research Associate for Training and Education
UNC Center for Public Health Preparedness
UNC Gillings School of Global Public Health
Chapel Hill, NC

Reviewers

Rosemary M. Caron, PhD, MPH
Associate Professor
Department of Health Management
 and Policy
University of New Hampshire
Durham, NH

Heather Henson-Ramsey, DVM, PhD
Division of Natural Sciences
 and Mathematics
Lewis-Clark State College
Lewiston, ID

Katherine W. Reeves, PhD, MPH
University of Massachusetts Amherst
Amherst, MA

Timothy Forde, PhD, MPH
Associate Director
Science Education Programs
Oak Ridge Associated Universities
Oak Ridge, TN

Kacey C. Ernst, PhD, MPH
Assistant Professor of Epidemiology
College of Public Health
University of Arizona
Tuscon, AZ

Sara S. Plaspohl, DrPH, MHS, CIM, CIP
Instructor
Department of Health Sciences
Armstrong Atlantic State University
Savannah, GA

H. Eduardo Velasco, MD, PhD, MSc
Professor
School of Community Health and Policy
Morgan State University
Baltimore, MD

About the Author

Dr. Pia D. M. MacDonald is a research associate professor in the Department of Epidemiology at the University of North Carolina Gillings School of Global Public Health (UNC SPH) and is the director of the UNC Center for Public Health Preparedness, the North Carolina Preparedness and Emergency Response Research Center, and the Certificate in Field Epidemiology Program in the North Carolina Institute for Public Health at UNC SPH. At UNC SPH, she leads the Team Epi-Aid program that provides graduate students with the opportunity to gain applied public health experience by assisting with outbreak investigations and other public health emergencies, while at the same time providing North Carolina's local and state health departments with needed surge capacity.

Dr. MacDonald received a PhD in epidemiological sciences from the University of Michigan in Ann Arbor and an MPH in infectious disease epidemiology from Yale University and is certified in public health. From 2000 to 2002, Dr. MacDonald was an Epidemic Intelligence Service officer with the Centers for Disease Control and Prevention (CDC) assigned to the North Carolina Division of Public Health, Communicable Disease Branch.

During Dr. MacDonald's tenure with the CDC, she worked on a variety of infectious disease outbreak investigations. These included outbreaks of human and canine blastomycosis, histoplasmosis among adventure travelers to Nicaragua, tuberculosis in an inner city social network, and Streptococcal disease. She was also involved in many foodborne disease outbreak investigations, among them listeriosis in the Hispanic community associated with noncommercial Mexican-style fresh cheese, statewide *Salmonella* Enteriditis associated with eggs from a certain multi-state distributor, gastrointestinal illness associated with *Staphylococcus aureus* contaminated food at a wedding, restaurant-associated *Salmonella* Heidelberg, and gastrointestinal illness associated with *Clostridium perfringens* at a large company picnic. Through the Team Epi-Aid program she has continued to be involved in outbreak investigations in collaboration with state and local health departments such as hepatitis B, HIV, foodborne diseases, influenza, and SARS.

Dr. MacDonald's work is focused on infectious disease surveillance, outbreak investigation, foodborne disease epidemiology, public health systems research, and public health workforce epidemiologic capacity development. She has authored or co-authored many scientific publications on these topics.

Chapter 1

Introduction

Pia D. M. MacDonald
Sandra I. McCoy

Learning Objectives
By the end of this chapter, the reader will be able to:

- Define epidemiology.
- Describe how applied epidemiology is related to public health practice.
- List the conditions that require field epidemiology.
- List programs that include field epidemiology training.

Epidemiology is the study of the distribution and determinants of disease, risk factors and exposures, and health status in specified populations to improve population health. Epidemiology can be used to study the health risks associated with specific exposures, it can be used as a tool to identify and help control epidemics, and it can monitor population rates of disease and exposures.

Applied epidemiology is the application of epidemiologic methods to public health practice. It is based on five core ideas that seek to (1) synthesize the results of etiologic studies to assess cause; (2) describe disease and risk factor patterns to set priorities; (3) evaluate public health programs, laws, and policies; (4) measure the patterns and outcomes of health care; and (5) communicate epidemiologic findings.[1] In contrast to academic epidemiology, applied epidemiology is closely linked to public health practice and typically has widespread application in the community.

Historically, applied epidemiology was the mainstay of epidemiologic inquiry. British epidemiology in the nineteenth century was primarily a practice-oriented field, with few epidemiologists engaging in research.[2] Notably, many of epidemiology's heroes—including John Snow, who implemented public health measures in response to an 1854 cholera outbreak in London; Ignaz Semmelweis, who found that maternal mortality could be reduced by hand washing in obstetric clinics; and Joseph Goldberger, who established that a nutritional deficiency was the cause of pellagra—are admired for their thoughtful application of epidemiologic knowledge to public health intervention.[3,4] It was not until after World War I, however, that epidemiology was adopted as an academic science in prominent universities, where etiologic research was the primary goal.[2] Over time, the discipline has broadened to include epidemiologists with primary interests in methodology, statistics, genetics, and molecular biology.

The tension between academic and applied epidemiology is well documented in the epidemiologic literature. Some believe that epidemiology is external to public health practice and that its extension into advocacy and policymaking compromises the validity and objectivity of the science.[5,6] Others view making policy recommendations, implementing public health interventions, and participating as an advocate as *responsibilities* of the epidemiologist.[3,7] Still others argue that this tension between the desire to conduct objective science and the social responsibility to improve the public's health is *essential*—overemphasizing either of these components places epidemiology at risk of neglecting to improve the health of the public.[8] Considering that epidemiology has always been interdisciplinary in nature and inclusive of emerging methodologies, this diverse range of viewpoints is characteristic of modern epidemiology. Indeed, epidemiology finds strength in its integrative nature and willingness to accept new methods, fields of inquiry, and scientific perspectives.

The principal areas of applied epidemiology include public health surveillance, cluster and outbreak investigations, survey sampling, risk assessment, and bioterrorism preparedness—skills that apply to students in all areas of epidemiology, not simply those who focus on infectious diseases. For example, while methods such as outbreak investigation are generally taught in the context of infectious diseases, practicing epidemiologists know that some conditions that may be originally suspected to have infectious origins can turn out to have noninfectious causes (e.g., environmental and industrial contaminants and toxins). Further, epidemiologists in all focus areas may use data from surveillance programs and registries that require sophisticated statistical analysis. Clusters of chronic disease and occupational injury can be investigated with field methodology. Finally, survey design, sampling, and implementation are critical skills to collect valid and reliable data across all subject areas.

The term *field epidemiology* is used to describe the application of epidemiology under a set of general conditions that include an unexpected public health problem that demands a timely response, a time-constrained investigation due to the need for quick interventions, and the need for epidemiologists to work in the field to solve the problem.[9] Although epidemiologic investigations in the field share many similarities with planned epidemiologic studies, they differ in a few important ways. Field investigations often start without a clear hypothesis and require the use of descriptive studies to generate hypotheses; analytic studies are then conducted to test the hypotheses. Field investigations are undertaken when urgent public health problems emerge and there is an immediate need to protect the community's health and attend to their concerns. These aspects of the investigation require that epidemiologists do more than simply collect and analyze data: They must also take public health action, and they must act in a timely fashion. In fact, action must often be taken before the causal agent is definitively identified. Therefore, in field investigations epidemiologists must decide when they have sufficient data to take action rather than wait until they have all the answers (from extensive data collection).[9]

There are many opportunities for applied epidemiologic learning experiences external to academic epidemiology in the United States. Of particular note are the Centers for

Disease Control and Prevention's (CDC's) Epidemic Intelligence Service (EIS), the CDC's and Council of State and Territorial Epidemiologists' (CSTE's) Applied Epidemiology Fellowship Program, and the numerous fellowship programs managed by the Association of Schools of Public Health. These kinds of applied programs have strengthened the public health workforce, made important contributions to the literature, and rapidly responded to evolving public health needs.[10,11]

These programs have a limited number of positions open on an annual basis, however, and all of them are directed at students who have completed their degrees. The EIS program accepts physicians, doctoral-level scientists, medical professionals with a master of public health (MPH) or equivalent degree, and veterinarians with an MPH (or equivalent degree) or public health experience. The CSTE Fellowship Program requires an MPH, master of science in public health, master of science in epidemiology, or an equivalent degree or advanced degree in a health-related field. Some EIS-like programs are also available in certain states, including California and Florida, that require a master's or doctoral degree in a health-related field (and some academic course requirements). For medical and veterinary students, the CDC offers an Epidemiology Elective Program for fourth-year students to do a six- to eight-week rotation at the CDC to gain a public health perspective during their clinical training.

Globally, additional field epidemiology training programs are available. Canada offers a two-year Canadian Field Epidemiology program. The European Centre for Disease Prevention and Control sponsors the two-year European Programme for Intervention Epidemiology Training (EPIET) program, and other countries offer field epidemiology training programs that bear similarities to the EIS program. The Training Programs in Epidemiology and Public Health Interventions Network (TEPHINET) provide information on field epidemiology training programs worldwide.

While this book is not exhaustive, the topics covered here are relevant to anyone engaged in an epidemiologic field investigation. Its coverage begins with a look at surveillance, which underpins many investigations; continues with the basic components of an investigation and specific types of investigation in which an epidemiologist might become involved, such as forensic epidemiology, contact tracing, and environmental investigations; and concludes with resources that might come into play during investigations, such as public health laboratories, the incident command system, and geographic information systems.

This book does assume some knowledge of the vocabulary used in medicine, public health, and epidemiology, although we have tried to define many of the technical terms when they are first mentioned. A reader may benefit from an accompanying dictionary of epidemiology and a medical dictionary. Following is a list of other resources that may be helpful:

- Chin J, ed. *Control of Communicable Diseases Manual*. 19th ed. Washington, DC: American Public Health Association; 2008.
- Porta M, ed. *A Dictionary of Epidemiology*. 5th ed. New York, NY: Oxford University Press; 2008.

These sources are available online:

- Beaglehole R, Bonita R, Kjellström T. *Basic Epidemiology*. Geneva, Switzerland: World Health Organization; 1993. http://whqlibdoc.who.int/publications/9241544465.pdf
- Council to Improve Foodborne Outbreak Response (CIFOR). *Guidelines for Foodborne Disease Outbreak Response*. Atlanta, GA: Council of State and Territorial Epidemiologists; 2009. http://www.cifor.us/documents/CIFORGuidelinesforFoodborneDiseaseOutbreakResponse-updated.pdf
- Pickering LK, ed. *Red Book: 2009 Report of the Committee on Infectious Diseases*. 28th ed. Elk Grove Village, IL: American Academy of Pediatrics; 2009. http://aapredbook.aappublications.org/current.dtl

References

1. Brownson R, Hoehner C. Epidemiology, a foundation of public health. In: Brownson R, Petitti D, eds. *Applied Epidemiology: Theory to Practice*. New York, NY: Oxford University Press; 2006:3–29.
2. Amsterdamska O. Demarcating epidemiology. *Sci Technol Hum Val*. 2005;30:17–51.
3. Weed DL, Mink PJ. Roles and responsibilities of epidemiologists. *Ann Epidemiol*. 2002;12(2):67–72.
4. Noakes TD, Borresen J, Hew-Butler T, et al. Semmelweis and the aetiology of puerperal sepsis 160 years on: An historical review. *Epidemiol Infect*. 2008;136(1):1–9.
5. Rothman KJ, Poole C. Science and policy making. *Am J Public Health*. 1985;75(4):340–1.
6. Savitz DA, Poole C, Miller WC. Reassessing the role of epidemiology in public health. *Am J Public Health*. 1999;89(8):1158–61.
7. Parascandola M. Objectivity and the neutral expert. *J Epidemiol Commun H*. 2003;57(1):3–4.
8. Morabia A. Epidemiology and bacteriology in 1900: Who is the handmaid of whom? *J Epidemiol Commun H*. 1998;52(10):617–8.
9. Gregg M. *Field Epidemiology*. 2nd ed. New York, NY: Oxford University Press; 2002.
10. Thacker SB, Buffington J. Applied epidemiology for the 21st century. *Int J Epidemiol*. 2001;30(2):320–325.
11. Moolenaar RL, Thacker SB. Evaluation of field training in the epidemic intelligence service: publications and job choices. *Am J Prev Med*. 2004;26(4):299–306.

Chapter 2

Introduction to Outbreak Investigations

Jeanette K. Stehr-Green
Paul A. Stehr-Green
Andrew C. Voetsch
Pia D. M. MacDonald

Learning Objectives

By the end of this chapter, the reader will be able to:

- Define the terms "epidemic," "outbreak," "case," and "cluster" from an epidemiological perspective.
- Describe factors that are used to determine the existence of an outbreak.
- List several ways that outbreaks are detected.
- Explain why it is important to investigate outbreaks.
- List and describe the basic components of an outbreak investigation.
- Describe how John Snow followed the processes of an outbreak investigation in his groundbreaking study of London's 1854 cholera outbreak.

Introduction

The terms "outbreak" and "epidemic" have become part of the world's general vocabulary, used broadly and frequently to describe health, financial, and social maladies—"an epidemic of obesity among our children," "an outbreak of corporate corruption," "an epidemic of failed marriages." The word "outbreak" gets our attention and indicates that something is awry. But what is an outbreak from an epidemiologic point of view, and how do we determine if an event or observation represents an outbreak? In this chapter, we define the key terms associated with outbreak investigations, discuss the importance of investigating outbreaks, outline the basic processes of an outbreak investigation, and describe how the pioneering epidemiologist John Snow followed these processes in his 1854 investigation of a cholera outbreak in London.

What Is an Outbreak?

To understand the concept of an outbreak, first we need to understand the epidemiological definitions of a few basic terms.

Outbreaks and Epidemics

An outbreak is an increase—often sudden—in the observed number of cases of a disease or health problem compared with the expected number for a given place or among a specific group of people over a particular period of time.[1] The definition of "epidemic" is essentially identical to that of "outbreak": "[t]he occurrence in a community or region of cases of an illness, specific health-related behavior, or other health-related events clearly in excess of normal expectancy."[2] The term "outbreak" may be used interchangeably with "epidemic," although public health officials often prefer "outbreak" to describe a localized epidemic, meaning one that is limited to a village, town, or specific institution. Investigators determine whether an epidemic (or outbreak) is taking place (or has taken place) by determining whether the number of cases of a certain disease—in a certain area, among a specific population, during a certain time of the year—is significantly greater than usual.[2]

If an outbreak or epidemic occurs over a very wide area, affecting a large proportion of the population in several countries or continents, the Director-General of the World Health Organization (WHO) has the responsibility to declare it a "pandemic" (*pan* = all and *demos* = people).[3] An example that predates the founding of WHO is the influenza pandemic of 1918, which killed an estimated 50 million people as it swept through North America, Europe, Asia, Africa, Brazil, and the South Pacific.[4] More recent examples of globe-spanning epidemics include the "Asian flu" pandemic of 1957–1958, the "Hong Kong flu" pandemic of 1968, and the emergence of influenza A (H1N1), which the WHO declared a pandemic in June 2009.[5] While infection with human immunodeficiency virus (HIV) is sometimes referred to as a "global epidemic" rather than a pandemic, an estimated 33 million people around the world were living with HIV in 2007.[6]

Declaring the existence of a pandemic can be controversial. When the global outbreak of H1N1 in 2009 turned out to be not as severe as expected, for example, some critics accused WHO of exaggerating the dangers of the virus under pressure from drug companies. In response, WHO announced early in 2010 that it would review the way it dealt with the outbreak once the pandemic had subsided.[7]

A health department may be called upon to investigate a wide variety of unusual health events, such as outbreaks due to food poisoning, geographic clusters of cancer, or a mysterious rash illness in a school. Although this book focuses mainly on infectious diseases, be aware that the terms "outbreak" and "epidemic" do not pertain only to communicable diseases. That is, these terms can be applied to noninfectious diseases such as cancers, nutritional deficiencies, smoking, or low-birth-weight babies. (We address investigating noncommunicable disease events in Chapter 13.) To suspect an epidemic or outbreak, public health officials need simply see an increase in the number of cases above what is expected for a given group for a given period of time.

Case

In epidemiology, the term "case" describes the particular disease, health disorder, or condition under investigation; it is also often used to describe a person in a population or study group who is identified as having the disease, disorder, or condition.[2] (In case-control studies, which are discussed in Chapter 7, cases may also be referred to as "patients in the case group" or "case patients."[8]) Investigators classify cases or case patients based on the case definition they develop as they explore a potential outbreak. A case definition takes into account the signs and symptoms of the disease or condition, as well as important epidemiologic characteristics of the patient—the "what, who, where, and when" of a disease outbreak. (Case definitions are described in detail in Chapter 4.) The epidemiological definition of a case is not the same as the normal clinical definition that physicians or other healthcare providers might use, although it may be similar.

Cluster

Outbreak investigations often begin when investigators identify a suspected cluster of cases of a disease. A cluster is a geographical or temporal collection of cases that seem to be greater than the expected number for the given place and/or time. The many challenges of an outbreak investigation often begin with determining whether a suspected cluster is a true cluster.

When Does a Number of Cases Become an Outbreak?

Understanding these terms leads us to the first hurdle of an outbreak investigation— determining whether an outbreak is under way. This task is more complicated than simply counting cases. Potential outbreaks may be true outbreaks with a common cause, or they may be unrelated cases of the same disease. In general, the key determinant that an outbreak is under way is whether the number of cases is "unusually high" or falls within the expected range of cases for that population at that time of year. Before declaring an outbreak, investigators must take many factors into account:

- The etiologic agent
- The size and composition of the population
- The previous occurrence of the disease in the community
- The season

The *etiologic agent* is the pathogen that is causing the disease. Investigators need to know the agent's identity, and they need to determine whether it is rare or common. When a disease is relatively common, such as genital herpes or seasonal influenza, there may need to be a very large number of cases or the cases may need to be uniquely related before public health officials will consider them to represent an outbreak. In contrast, for rare diseases such as botulism, polio, smallpox, or anthrax, health officials may treat even a single case as an outbreak and embark on urgent health action. For example:

- Public health officials may act promptly when a single case of botulism is reported, by ordering the recall of contaminated commercial products or the destruction of contaminated home-canned goods, so as to prevent other people from becoming ill.[9]

- Although polio was eliminated in the United States in 1994, it continues to afflict children in Asia and Africa; U.S. public health officials remain vigilant for its return to this country, knowing that new cases of the disease are just a plane ride away.[10]

- A single case of smallpox would cause a worldwide alarm: The disease has not been diagnosed in the United States since 1949, and the last naturally occurring case in the world was in Somalia in 1977. Officials remain concerned that laboratory stocks of the virus that causes smallpox could be used as an agent of bioterrorism.[11]

- Four cases of inhalational anthrax detected in 2001 were the first confirmed cases of anthrax associated with intentional exposure in the United States. (Humans generally become infected when they come into direct contact with *Bacillus anthracis* spores from infected animals.) The discovery that anthrax had been used in a suspected case of bioterrorism led to a widespread criminal investigation and a rapid public health response to detect and treat additional cases.[12]

The *size and composition of the population* is another important factor in determining whether an outbreak is under way. Investigators need to learn quickly how many and which groups of people are becoming ill. Size matters: Obviously, 1,000 cases of influenza are likely to be of more concern in a community of 50,000 than in a city of 500,000. Likewise, an increase in the number of cases of a given disease must be considered in relation to changes in population size. For example, a college town is likely to have more reports of disease when school is in session than during the summer break or over the winter holidays. The make-up of a population is also important. Population characteristics such as age distribution and socioeconomic status can influence disease rates. For example, researchers who studied an increase in cases of tuberculosis in New York City from 1984 to 1992 found a strong association between poverty and tuberculosis.[13]

Previous occurrence of a disease in the community is a third factor in determining whether an outbreak is under way. Before investigators decide whether a certain number of cases constitutes an outbreak, they must know whether and how often the disease has been diagnosed in the community in the past. For example, if 51 cases of a disease are confirmed in one month in a county that averages 12 cases of the disease each month, and there are no errors in laboratory identification or reporting procedures, then it is likely the 51 cases represent an outbreak.

The *season* is the final determinant. Because the incidence of many types of infectious disease rises and falls seasonally, investigators must take the time of year into account when they explore a potential outbreak. The same number of cases of influenza, for example, might be "expected" for winter but "greater than expected" for summer.

Sometimes it is a relatively simple matter for investigators to determine whether a cluster of cases is an outbreak, but often it is not. For example, public health officials might suspect that a number of cases of severe respiratory illness signals an influenza outbreak. Upon closer examination, however, one case might be a severe cold, another might be bronchitis, a third might be pneumonia, and so on. Many people might be ill, but there would be no evidence of a specific outbreak. Apparent outbreaks of gastrointestinal illness can also be difficult to confirm. If everyone at the company picnic develops diarrhea, it may be relatively easy to determine that everyone who ate the potato salad got ill. If the cases are more widely scattered, however, or if the agent that caused people to become ill is not readily apparent, additional epidemiological detective work might be necessary. In a suspected outbreak of gastrointestinal illness, for example, investigators might need to order laboratory tests for diarrhea-causing pathogens and interview case patients to identify possible common exposures.

How Are Potential Outbreaks Detected?

Public health officials identify potential outbreaks in a variety of ways—through surveillance or health information systems, clinical laboratories, affected citizens, and astute healthcare providers, for example.

As discussed in Chapter 3, outbreaks are often detected through the routine and timely analysis of health information systems such as disease surveillance systems managed by state and local health departments. Health department staff may detect increases or unusual patterns of disease from weekly tabulations of case reports by time and place. Hospital administrators may discover an increased number of possible hospital-acquired infections through a weekly analysis of microbiologic isolates from patients by organism and ward or unit.

Members of affected groups are another important reporting source for apparent clusters of both infectious and noninfectious disease. A local citizen may call a health department to report that he and several co-workers came down with severe gastroenteritis after attending a banquet several nights earlier. Similarly, a community member may call to express concern that several cases of cancer diagnosed among her neighbors seem more than coincidental.

Nonetheless, many outbreaks come to the attention of public health officials because an alert clinician, infection control nurse, or clinical laboratory worker recognizes an unusual pattern of disease and notifies the health department.[14] Here is an example:

> In September 2002, a gastroenterologist contacted the Nebraska Health and Human Services System after seeing four patients who had recently been diagnosed with hepatitis C virus infection. Each patient had been treated at the same hematology/oncology clinic. A preliminary investigation revealed that 10 clinic patients had recently been diagnosed with hepatitis C virus infection, and that a

healthcare worker who administered medication infusions had repeatedly used the same syringe to draw blood from patients' catheters and catheter-flushing solution from saline bags that were used for several patients. This incident was one of several healthcare-related viral hepatitis outbreaks discovered in the United States between 2000 and 2002 because clinicians suspected that infections were healthcare related and contacted public health authorities.[15]

Physicians are not the only healthcare providers who might pinpoint potential outbreaks. Outbreaks have been detected thanks to reports from microbiologists, school nurses, and pharmacists, to name just a few of these sources. Early indications of a new disease, acquired immunodeficiency syndrome (AIDS), surfaced in 1981 when the Centers for Disease Control and Prevention (CDC) Drug Service received increased requests for pentamidine, a medication used to treat a rare form of pneumonia. (Due to the rarity of this illness at that time, the CDC Drug Service was one of the few sources for this drug in the United States.) Investigation of these requests led to a growing awareness of multiple emerging health problems among homosexual males in several major metropolitan areas. Investigation of the syndrome determined it was caused by infection with HIV.[16]

Sometimes reports from various members of the health community converge to bring an outbreak to light. In 1993, for example, the health department in Milwaukee, Wisconsin, identified a large community-wide outbreak of cryptosporidiosis—a parasitic disease characterized by severe diarrhea, cramps, and stomach upset—after receiving reports from multiple sources throughout the city. Pharmacists reported difficulty keeping over-the-counter and prescription antidiarrheal medications in stock. Clinical laboratories reported a significant increase in demand for the media used to perform routine stool cultures, resulting in requests to other labs and the Wisconsin State Laboratory of Hygiene for additional supplies. The local water authority was deluged by complaints from customers about increased water turbidity and water that tasted and smelled unpleasant. Many school nurses noted increased absences of students for diarrheal illnesses, and individual citizens jammed health department telephone lines with concerns about a diarrheal illness sweeping across their community. Before long, the health department had identified the largest waterborne outbreak of cryptosporidiosis reported in the United States—a public health emergency that affected more than 400,000 people.[17]

Most health departments have routine procedures for handling calls from healthcare providers and the public regarding potential disease outbreaks and clusters. These procedures focus on characterizing the problem—that is, determining the "what," "who," "when," "where," and "why" (or "how"):

- *What* is the problem? Is there a clinical description of the illness, including signs and symptoms, diagnosis, and duration? Was a physician consulted? Were any tests performed or any treatments provided?
- *Who* is ill and what are those individuals' characteristics (e.g., name, age, occupation)?
- *When* did the affected persons become ill?

- *Where* are the affected persons located, including residential or work locations?
- *Why* (and *how*) do patients think they became ill? What are the relevant risk factors, suspected exposures, and suspected modes of transmission? Are there clues based on who did and did not become ill?

Accurate data collection during these initial reports is critical and can be the key to the timely recognition and investigation of an outbreak.

Why Investigate Outbreaks?

It is important to investigate disease outbreaks for many reasons. Perhaps the most immediate and important motivation is that people might still be getting sick from the same cause. To prevent additional cases, investigators need to identify and eliminate the source of the problem.[14]

Here are two examples of how a thorough investigation can characterize a health problem and allow public health officials to take appropriate actions to control the problem or keep it from happening again.

Example 1

From May 1 to October 15, 2010, a multistate outbreak of *Salmonella enteritidis* associated with shell eggs caused an estimated 1,813 cases of illness across the United States. Epidemiologic investigations in 11 states identified 29 restaurants or event clusters where more than one person had eaten before becoming ill with the outbreak strain. Additional investigation of several of these clusters traced the infections to contaminated shell eggs from one of two firms in Iowa: Wright County Egg and Hillandale Farms of Iowa. Eggs from both firms were shipped to distribution centers in several states and later distributed nationwide.

Wright County Egg conducted a nationwide voluntary recall of shell eggs in August, and later expanded the recall. Hillandale Farms of Iowa also conducted a nationwide voluntary recall. The U.S. Food and Drug Administration (FDA) posted lists of the brand names under which the eggs were packaged and pointed out identifying information on the packaging. Consumers were advised not to eat any potentially contaminated eggs they had purchased but to return them to the place of purchase for a full refund.[18]

Example 2

When the Minnesota Department of Health conducted a case-control study of an outbreak of *Salmonella* cases in the state in 1994, officials found that 11 of 15 confirmed cases had eaten Schwan's ice cream. They did not discover any other risk factors. Recognizing that the outbreak could be far reaching, the Department of Health announced its existence to the public and began a full-scale investigation. Investigators carried out national surveillance and interviewed customers who had eaten the implicated manufacturer's products. They compared the steps in the manufacture of tainted ice cream with those of products that were not known to be associated with the infections. They obtained and tested cultures from ice cream samples, the ice cream plant, and the tanker trucks that carried the ice cream "premix" to the plants.

Upon completing their studies, the investigators estimated that 224,000 people had been infected across the country, and concluded that the outbreak was most likely caused by the contamination of pasteurized ice cream premix when it was transported in trucks that had previously carried nonpasteurized liquid eggs containing *Salmonella enteritidis*. They recommended steps to prevent similar outbreaks in the future. Based on their field-work, the investigators characterized the disease as follows:

What: Infection with *Salmonella enteritidis*

Who: 224,000 people

When: September and October 2004, within a week of consuming Schwan's ice cream

Where: Nationwide (United States)

Why: Consumption of Schwan's ice cream made with contaminated premix[19]

There are several other good reasons why public health officials should investigate outbreaks. Notably, outbreak investigations may identify risk factors associated with infection that urgently need to be contained or that are preventable in the future. Epidemiologic investigations of *Escherichia coli* O157:H7 outbreaks, for example, have identified consumption of foods such as pink ("rare") hamburger meat,[20] unpasteurized apple juice,[21] or alfalfa sprouts[22] that consumers may avoid to reduce their risk of illness.

Outbreak investigations can also identify new pathogens that infect people. The strains of HIV-1 that caused the global epidemic of AIDS have been characterized as Group M viruses, for example, but a new strain was identified in the mid-1990s that was not detected consistently by standard HIV diagnostic tests. A case in the United States involving the new type, HIV-1 Group O, was reported in Los Angeles in 1996. The patient was a woman who had come to the United States from Africa, where most of the relatively small number of infections with this type have been detected.[23] Other examples include the Ebola virus, which was discovered in 1976 when investigators searched for the cause of a new type of viral hemorrhagic fever in Africa,[24] and the severe acute respiratory syndrome–associated coronavirus, which was discovered in 2003.[25]

Moreover, outbreak investigations can provide new research insights into a disease, even if no new cases are occurring. The investigation into the first cluster of human monkeypox cases in the United States in 2003, for example, revealed an unusual transmission route: Humans contracted the disease from pet prairie dogs that had been housed or transported with African rodents. Investigators associated 35 confirmed cases reported in five Midwestern states with prairie dogs obtained from an Illinois animal distributor, or from animal distributors who purchased prairie dogs from the Illinois distributor. All of the prairie dogs that transmitted monkeypox to humans appeared to have been infected through contact with Gambian giant rats and dormice that originated in Ghana.

These investigations led to public health strategies to control the outbreak, including banning importation and prohibiting movement of the implicated animal species, enhancing restrictions on intrastate animal shipment and trade, instituting premise quarantine, and euthanizing infected animals. Some potentially exposed persons also received pre- and post-exposure vaccination with smallpox vaccine.[26] (Because the monkeypox virus is related to the virus that causes smallpox, the smallpox vaccine can protect people from getting monkeypox as well as smallpox.)

Finally, outbreak investigations provide opportunities for public health practitioners to practice the process and methods of epidemiologic investigation that are essential to protect the public health. These same skills are likely to prove valuable when practitioners are called into action after a hurricane or flood, or asked to respond to an act of bioterrorism. Training and assistance in disease outbreak investigations are available from state and federal agencies, such as the CDC, but novice investigators will also benefit immensely from working alongside more experienced practitioners on outbreak investigations. Similar to physicians who "practice" medicine for the duration of their careers, implying that their skills continue to grow with experience, public health practitioners continue to hone their practice skills primarily with experience.

The Components of an Outbreak Investigation

Once they identify an outbreak, investigators should take a systematic approach, such as the process detailed in Table 2-1. Although we list the components of the process sequentially here, these steps often occur simultaneously or may be repeated as new information is received or uncovered. Some outbreak investigations may require only a phone call or two to complete; others, as we shall see, may involve assembling a multidisciplinary

TABLE 2-1   **The Basic Components of an Outbreak Investigation**

1. Verify the diagnosis and confirm the outbreak
2. Define a case and conduct case finding
3. Tabulate and orient data: time, place, and person
4. Take immediate control measures
5. Formulate and test hypothesis
6. Plan and execute additional studies
7. Implement and evaluate control measures
8. Communicate findings

outbreak investigation team and collaborating with state and federal health agencies, law enforcement agencies, and others. Likewise, some investigations may require few resources in terms of time and money; others may be lengthy and expensive.

1. Verify the Diagnosis and Confirm the Outbreak

As discussed earlier in this chapter, the first essential step is to confirm the existence of an outbreak. This effort may require investigators to learn as much as possible about a specific disease, and to review existing surveillance baseline data to determine whether a suspected cluster of cases exceeds the expected number of cases. Confirming any diagnosis with a laboratory is another important early step, especially if the pathogen that is making people ill is new or unusual. Confirming that an outbreak is under way may also require reviewing medical records, talking with healthcare providers, and even talking with patients themselves. Depending on the scope of the investigation, it may be necessary to assemble a multidisciplinary outbreak investigation team and gather necessary equipment and supplies to collect clinical or environmental samples.

2. Define a Case and Conduct Case Finding

The investigation team should create a case definition and begin to identify cases that may be associated with the outbreak. The case definition may evolve as the investigation continues—early on, it might be designed broadly to identify as many cases as possible; later, the definition might be narrowed to exclude false positives (people originally thought to be part of the outbreak but who are not included as investigators receive more information).

3. Tabulate and Orient Data: Time, Place, Person

Investigators should organize information collected from medical records or patient interviews in a line listing and summarize it according to person, place, and time—that is, who is getting sick, where, and when. "Who, where, and when" are the central questions investigators must answer before they can develop and test hypotheses about the cause of the outbreak.

4. Take Immediate Control Measures

If at any point the team identifies an obvious source of contamination, the health department (and other agencies involved in the investigation) should take immediate control measures. Making public announcements about steps people can take to minimize their risk of infection and instituting plant closings or product recalls are examples of public health actions in response to outbreaks. Acting on information that can safeguard the public's health is a core responsibility of public health practitioners.

5. Formulate and Test Hypotheses

As team members gather and organize information, they should develop hypotheses about the cause of the outbreak. For example, investigators may find useful clues by researching previous outbreaks and studying the epidemiology and microbiology of the pathogen. They can gain additional insight by interviewing case patients. Conducting analytic studies such as retrospective cohort studies or case-control studies will allow the team to test one or more hypotheses.

6. Plan and Execute Additional Studies

In parallel to the epidemiologic investigation, an environmental investigation may be undertaken that includes environmental sampling. In a foodborne outbreak investigation, for example, the team should collect and test food and beverage samples as soon as possible.

7. Implement and Evaluate Control Measures

During the later stages of an outbreak investigation, the investigation team may work with government regulators, industry, and health educators to undertake control measures to prevent further illness and future outbreaks. The team should design mechanisms to evaluate the short- and long-term success of the investigation, summarize the investigation, and prepare and disseminate specific recommendations.

8. Communicate Findings

At the conclusion of the study, or earlier if necessary and appropriate, the team should prepare health promotion messages for the general public. Communication—both among team members and with the public—is essential for the success of an outbreak investigation, and the news media can be helpful in presenting information to the public.[27] The team should agree on the information to be released, and should appoint one member of the team to act as the point of contact for media inquiries.

In the coming chapters, we discuss each component of the outbreak investigation process in detail. First, however, we walk through the process, using one of the earliest and most famous historical outbreak investigations as an example. (Other well-known investigations can be found in Berton Roueche's collection, *The Medical Detectives*.[28])

Snow on Cholera

> The most terrible outbreak of cholera which ever occurred in this kingdom, is probably that which took place in Broad Street, Golden Square, and the adjoining streets, a few weeks ago. Within two hundred and fifty yards of the spot where Cambridge Street joins Broad Street, there were upwards of five hundred fatal attacks of cholera in ten days. The mortality in this limited area probably equals any that was ever caused in this country, even by the plague: and it was much more sudden, as the greater number of cases terminated in a few hours.[29]

Thus begins *On the Mode of Communication of Cholera*, Dr. John Snow's description of his investigation of the 1854 cholera outbreak in London, which is often cited as the first instance of modern infectious disease epidemiology. Using the principles of outbreak investigation outlined in the preceding section, Snow determined that the outbreak of the deadly disease was caused by fecal contamination of the water supply. More specifically, he used an analytic study design to determine which of the local water supply companies was responsible for the contamination, and convinced authorities to take action to control the outbreak.

The following case study outlines the outbreak investigation process, using Snow's experiences as examples.

1. Verify the Diagnosis and Confirm the Outbreak

Cholera is an acute, diarrheal illness that is often mild or without symptoms, but in 5% of patients it can be severe, characterized by profuse watery diarrhea, vomiting, and leg cramps. Rapid loss of body fluids leads to dehydration and shock; without treatment, death can occur within hours. The microbiological etiology of the disease, *Vibrio cholerae*, was unknown to Snow at the time. (Coincidentally, Filippo Pacini had identified *V. cholerae* during an outbreak in Florence one year earlier, in 1853. Pacini's discovery was confirmed and made widely known by Robert Koch in 1884.) Having studied several cholera outbreaks, Snow hurried to Broad Street when he learned of the new outbreak.

> There were a few cases of cholera in the neighborhood of Broad Street, Golden Square, in the latter part of August; and the so-called outbreak, which commenced in the night between the 31st August and the 1st September, was, as in all similar instances, only a violent increase of the malady. As soon as I became acquainted with the situation and extent of this irruption of cholera, I suspected some contamination of the water of the much-frequented street-pump in Broad Street, near the end of Cambridge Street.[29]

2. Define a Case and Conduct Case Finding

Snow defined a case as a death from cholera. Although he did not use microbiological confirmation in his case definition, death from watery diarrhea during the London outbreak was a reasonable case definition. His case definition was highly sensitive (meaning it would include most cholera cases), but it was also highly nonspecific (meaning it would not exclude noncholera diarrheal deaths). This definition enabled Snow to verify that a severe outbreak of cholera was taking place. He conducted case finding through mortality records by contacting medical practitioners in the neighborhoods around Golden Square.

> I requested permission, therefore, to take a list, at the General Register Office, of the deaths from cholera, registered during the week ending 2nd September, in the subdistricts of Golden Square, Berwick Street, and St. Ann's, Soho, which was kindly granted. Eighty-nine deaths from cholera were registered, during the

week, in the three subdistricts. Of these, only six occurred in the four first days of the week; four occurred on Thursday, the 31st August; and the remaining seventy-nine on Friday and Saturday.[29]

Figure 2-1 shows cholera deaths in Golden Square during the outbreak.

3. Tabulate and Orient the Information: Person, Place, Time

To pinpoint the "who, when, and where" of the outbreak, Snow created a line listing of cases, including the age, gender, and address of each patient. He plotted his cases on a map and observed that they occurred in proximity to the pump on Broad Street. This information suggested that the case patients could have been infected from water at the pump, and that it was a point-source outbreak.

> On proceeding to the spot, I found that nearly all the deaths had taken place within a short distance of the pump. There were only ten deaths in houses situated decidedly nearer to another street pump. In five of these cases the families of the deceased persons informed me that they always sent to the pump in Broad Street, as they preferred the water to that of the pump which was nearer. In three other cases, the deceased were children who went to school near the pump in Broad Street. Two of them were known to drink the water; and the parents of the third think it probable that it did so. The other two deaths, beyond the district which this pump supplies, represent only the amount of mortality from cholera that was occurring before the irruption took place.[29]

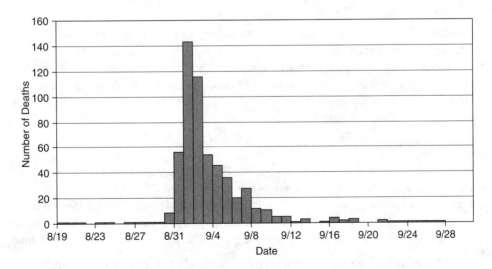

Figure 2-1   Cholera deaths in the Golden Square Section of London, 1854

Data from: Snow J. *On the Mode of Communication of Cholera.* 2nd ed. London, England: John Churchill, New Burlington Street; 1855.

4. Take Immediate Control Measures

Snow suspected the Broad Street pump was the source of the cholera. In a now famous symbol of public health action, he called for the removal of the pump handle from the well so that people could not access the contaminated water.

> I had an interview with the Board of Guardians of St. James's parish, on the evening of Thursday, 7th September, and represented the above circumstances to them. In consequence of what I said, the handle of the pump was removed on the following day.[29]

5. Formulate and Test Hypotheses

Although Snow was convinced that drinking from the Broad Street well was making people ill, he found additional evidence of the association among a group of persons who were not exposed to the well water.

> There is a Brewery in Broad Street, near to the pump, and on perceiving that no brewer's men were registered as having died of cholera, I called on Mr. Huggins, the proprietor. He informed me that there were above seventy workmen employed in the brewery, and that none of them had suffered from cholera,—at least in a severe form,—only two having been indisposed, and that not seriously, at the time the disease prevailed. The men are allowed a certain quantity of malt liquor, and Mr. Huggins believes they do not drink water at all; and he is quite certain that the workmen never obtained water from the pump in the street. There is a deep well in the brewery, in addition to the New River water.[29]

Present-day epidemiologists would have conducted an analytic study at this phase—for example, a case-control study using case patients and persons without disease at the brewery as a comparison group. However, based in part on the evidence provided by the brewers, Snow concluded "that there had been no particular outbreak or increase of cholera, in this part of London, except among the persons who were in the habit of drinking the water of the above-mentioned pump-well."[29]

6. Plan and Execute Additional Studies

Snow suspected that a previous cholera outbreak in 1848 was associated with the London water supply. He further suspected a single supplier of water, the Southwark and Vauxhall Company, was associated with the contamination. To test his hypothesis, Snow compared the mortality rate due to cholera (number of cholera deaths per 10,000 households) between two companies that supplied water in a single geographic area south of the River Thames.

> The experiment, too, was on the grandest scale. No fewer than three hundred thousand people of both sexes, of every age and occupation, and of every rank and station, from gentlefolks down to the very poor, were divided into two groups without their choice, and, in most cases, without their knowledge; one group

being supplied with water containing the sewage of London, and, amongst it, whatever might have come from the cholera patients, the other group having water quite free from such impurity.[29]

The resulting study implicated the Southwark and Vauxhall Company, which had drawn its water from the downstream section of the River Thames, which was more heavily contaminated with sewage. Compared to the water supply companies in the rest of London, customers of Southwark and Vauxhall were nearly six times more likely to die from cholera than the general population; customers of Lambeth were less likely to die from cholera than the general population (Table 2-2).

7. Implement and Evaluate Control Measures

Snow concluded *On the Mode of Communication of Cholera* with 12 specific recommendations to prevent illness. These included prevention of transmission by medical practitioners, isolation of patients, treatment of the water supply, suggested water sources for London, disposal of human waste, and quarantine of persons suspected to have been exposed in foreign countries.

8. Communicate Findings

Snow shared his findings with members of the medical profession and government officials in Parliament.

> After the Registrar-General alluded, in the "Weekly Return" of 14th October last, to the very conclusive investigation of the effects of polluted water in the south districts of London, there was a leading article, in nearly all the medical periodicals, [*Medical Times and Gazette, Lancet,* and *Association Journal*] fully admitting the influence of the water on the mortality from cholera. It may therefore be safely concluded that this influence is pretty generally admitted by the profession.[29]

TABLE 2-2 **Comparison of the Cholera Mortality Rate per 10,000 Households by Water Source in London, 1848**

Water Supply	Households	Deaths	Deaths/10,000 Households	Rate Ratio (95% CI*)
Southwark and Vauxhall	40,046	1,263	315	5.7 (5.3–6.1)
Lambeth	26,107	98	37	0.7 (0.6–0.8)
Rest of London	256,423	1,422	55	1.0 (referent)

*CI = confidence interval

Source: Snow J. *On the Mode of Communication of Cholera.* 2nd ed. London: John Churchill, New Burlington Street; 1855.

Summary

In epidemiology, the terms "epidemic" and "outbreak" describe an increase in the observed number of cases of a disease or health problem compared with the expected number for a given place or among a specific group of people over a particular period of time. ("Outbreak" is often used to describe a localized epidemic.) Public health practitioners may be called upon to investigate outbreaks due to food poisoning, geographic clusters of cancer, or a mysterious illness in a school. Outbreak investigations often begin with information from surveillance or health information systems, clinical laboratories, affected citizens, or astute healthcare providers about a suspicious number of cases of a disease or health problem. To determine whether a potential outbreak is a true outbreak, investigators gather such information as what pathogen is causing the infection, who is becoming ill, and where and when the cases are occurring.

When an outbreak is detected, a thorough investigation can allow public health practitioners to take actions to control the outbreak and prevent additional people from becoming ill. Outbreak investigations can also identify risk factors associated with outbreaks, discover emerging pathogens, and provide new research insights. Taking part in investigations also gives practitioners important experience. Outbreak investigators typically follow an eight-step process. Investigators may carry out these activities simultaneously, or they may repeat some of them as more information comes to light. John Snow's *On the Mode of Communication of Cholera*, published in 1855, is a classic example of the process of an outbreak investigation.

References

1. Gregg M. *Field Epidemiology*. 3rd ed. New York, NY: Oxford University Press; 2008.
2. Porta M, ed. *A Dictionary of Epidemiology*. 5th ed. New York, NY: Oxford University Press; 2008.
3. Current WHO phase of pandemic alert for avian influenza H5N1. World Health Organization website: http://www.who.int/csr/disease/avian_influenza/phase/en/index.html. Accessed June 15, 2010.
4. Taubenberger JK, Morens DM. 1918 influenza: The mother of all pandemics. *Emerg Infect Dis*. 2006;12(1). http://www.cdc.gov/ncidod/EID/vol12no01/05-0979.htm. Accessed June 15, 2010.
5. Influenza A (H1N1) pandemic alert phase 6 declared, of moderate severity. World Health Organization website: http://www.euro.who.int/en/what-we-publish/information-for-the-media/sections/press-releases/2009/06/influenza-a-h1n1-who-announces-pandemic-alert-phase-6,-of-moderate-severity. Accessed June 15, 2010.
6. UNAIDS. *Report on the Global AIDS Epidemic*. Geneva, Switzerland: World Health Organization; 2009. UNAIDS Publication Series. http://www.unaids.org/en/media/unaids/contentassets/dataimport/pub/globalreport/2008/jc1510_2008globalreport_en.zip. Accessed May 11, 2011.
7. Lynn, J. WHO to review its handling of H1N1 flu pandemic. Reuters. January 12, 2010. http://www.reuters.com/article/idUSTRE5BL2ZT20100112. Accessed January 21, 2011.
8. *JAMA & Archives* Journals. *AMA Manual of Style: A Guide for Authors and Editors*. 10th ed. New York, NY: Oxford University Press; 2007.
9. Botulism. Centers for Disease Control and Prevention website: http://emergency.cdc.gov/agent/botulism/. Accessed September 28, 2010.

10. Centers for Disease Control and Prevention. Notice to Readers: 50th Anniversary of the First Effective Polio Vaccine—April 12, 2005. *Morb Mortal Weekly Rep.* 2005;54(13):335-6.

11. Smallpox Disease Overview. Updated 2004; reviewed 2007. Centers for Disease Control and Prevention website: http://www.bt.cdc.gov/agent/smallpox/overview/disease-facts.asp. Accessed September 9, 2010.

12. Centers for Disease Control and Prevention. Update: Investigation of anthrax associated with intentional exposure and interim public health guidelines, October 2001. *Morb Mortal Weekly Rep.* 2001;50(41):889-93.

13. Barr RG, Diez-Roux AV, Knirsch CA, et al. Neighborhood poverty and the resurgence of tuberculosis in New York City, 1984-1992. *Am J Public Health.* 2001;91(9):1487-93.

14. Reingold AL. Outbreak investigations—A perspective. *Emerg Infect Dis.* 1998;4(1). Updated 2005. http://www.cdc.gov/ncidod/eid/vol4no1/reingold.htm. Accessed September 9, 2010.

15. Centers for Disease Control and Prevention. Transmission of hepatitis B and C viruses in outpatient settings—New York, Oklahoma, and Nebraska, 2000-2002. *Morb Mortal Weekly Rep.* 2003;52(38):901-6.

16. Centers for Disease Control Task Force on Kaposi's Sarcoma and Opportunistic Infections. *N Engl J Med.* 1982;306:248-52.

17. Proctor ME, Blair KA, Davis JP. Surveillance data for waterborne illness detection: An assessment following a massive waterborne outbreak of *Cryptosporidium* infection. *Epidemiol Infect.* 1998;120:43-54.

18. Investigation update: Multistate outbreak of human *Salmonella enteritidis* infections associated with shell eggs. Centers for Disease Control and Prevention website: http://www.cdc.gov/print.do?url=http%3A//www.cdc.gov/salmonella/enteritidis/. Accessed October 29, 2010.

19. Hennessy TW, Hedberg CW, Slutsker L, et al. A national outbreak of *Salmonella enteritidis* infections from ice cream. *N Engl J Med.* 1996;334(20):1281-6.

20. Kassenborg HG, Hedberg CW, Hoekstra M. Farm visits and undercooked hamburgers as major risk factors for sporadic *Escherichia coli* O157:H7 infection: Data from a case-control study in 5 FoodNet sites. *Clin Infect Dis.* 2004;38(suppl):S271-8.

21. Centers for Disease Control and Prevention. Outbreak of *Escherichia coli* O157:H7 infections associated with drinking unpasteurized commercial apple juice—British Columbia, California, Colorado, and Washington, October 1996. *Morb Mortal Weekly Rep.* 1996;45(44):975.

22. Centers for Disease Control and Prevention. Outbreaks of *Escherichia coli* O157:H7 infection associated with eating alfalfa sprouts—Michigan and Virginia, June-July 1997. *Morb Mortal Weekly Rep.* 1997;46(32):741-4.

23. Centers for Disease Control and Prevention. Identification of HIV-1 Group O infection—Los Angeles County, California, 1996. *Morb Mortal Weekly Rep.* 1996;45(26):561-5.

24. Bowen ETW, Platt GS, Lloyd G, et al. Viral haemorrhagic fever in southern Sudan and northern Zaire: Preliminary studies on the aetiologic agent. *Lancet.* 1977;1:571-3.

25. Marra MA, Jones SJM, Astell CR, et al. The genome sequence of the SARS-associated coronavirus. *Science.* 2003;300(5624):1399-1404.

26. Centers for Disease Control and Prevention. Update: Multistate outbreak of monkeypox—Illinois, Indiana, Kansas, Missouri, Ohio, and Wisconsin, 2003. *Morb Mortal Weekly Rep.* 2003;52(27):642-6.

27. Garrett L. Understanding media's response to epidemics. *Public Health Rep.* 2001;116 (suppl 2):87-91.

28. Roueche B. *The Medical Detectives.* New York, NY: Truman Talley Books/Plume; 1991.

29. Snow J. *On the Mode of Communication of Cholera.* 2nd ed. London: John Churchill, New Burlington Street; 1855. http://www.ph.ucla.edu/epi/snow/snowbook.html.

Chapter 3

Public Health Surveillance

Cynthia J. Snider
Pia D. M. MacDonald

Learning Objectives
By the end of this chapter, the reader will be able to:

- Define public health surveillance.
- Describe the different types of surveillance.
- Recognize the different categories of surveillance.
- Understand the uses of surveillance data.
- List the different sources of surveillance data.

Introduction

The focus of this book is on field epidemiology, which involves investigating perceived public health threats. But how do we know what constitutes a threat to public health? In the United States, field investigators have access to a number of resources that can help them determine whether a public health threat is real. Sometimes these resources may provide the necessary data to conduct an investigation without leaving the office. Moreover, they can help investigators decide when to implement control measures as well as help them monitor and evaluate the effectiveness of control measures. Before embarking on a field investigation, investigators should familiarize themselves with these resources, which are collectively known as public health surveillance data.

In this chapter, we define public health surveillance, describe the types and categories of surveillance, and review the uses of public health surveillance data. We conclude the chapter by providing a brief overview of the various sources of public health surveillance data and examples of how they were used to aid field investigations.

What Is Public Health Surveillance?

Public health surveillance has been defined as the "ongoing, systematic collection, analysis, interpretation, and dissemination of data regarding a health-related event for use in public health action to reduce morbidity and mortality and to improve health."[1]

Two important points relevant for our discussion of field epidemiology are raised by the descriptors "ongoing" and "systematic collection."

First, ongoing, or routinely, collected data on health-related events are available for field investigators to use. By "ongoing," we mean daily, monthly, or yearly acquisition of data—any schedule qualifies as long as there is a routine to the collection of the data. Even the decennial collection of the U.S. Census is routine data collection. One-time surveys are informative but would not be considered surveillance data because the data are not collected in an "ongoing" manner. The routine collection of data provides an understanding of the health conditions, and changes in the health conditions, of the population from which the data were collected. Depending on how the data were collected, investigators may be able to generalize these findings to a larger population.

"Systematic collection" indicates the data are collected in a standardized manner across various locations; in other words, the data are collected in the same, uniform manner. If five people were told to collect information on Mr. Smith, for example, but were provided no instructions, they would compile five different summaries of Mr. Smith.

Standardization in data collection is important to ensure that three criteria are met:

- All necessary and pertinent information are collected.
- Data are collected using the same format.
- The same definitions are used.

Standardization is also time efficient; it reduces time spent on data cleaning (e.g., reformatting) and data entry. Finally, standardization is critical for making comparisons when the collected data are analyzed.

Other descriptors in the definition of public health surveillance—"analysis," "interpretation," and "dissemination of data"—are also relevant, as data that are not analyzed, interpreted, or disseminated yield very little value for public health practice. Surveillance data can be useful to the investigator in several ways. First, the published report will be of value. What is the prevalence of obesity in Alabama? How many people died from seasonal influenza in the United States in 2009? What is the baseline rate of leptospirosis in Hawaii? These questions can be and have been answered using public health surveillance data. More importantly, surveillance data can be used by the field investigator to identify, investigate, control, and prevent public health threats. Clusters of cancers and birth defects, infectious disease outbreaks, and the obesity epidemic can all be investigated using public health surveillance data.

A point of clarification may be necessary in any discussion of public health surveillance systems. Advances in technology have led to the development of health information systems that are used in clinical and laboratory settings as a means of entering, storing, and reviewing patient information. Public health surveillance systems may be viewed in a similar light, as public health officials enter, store, and review public health data. Yet these systems are quite different in their functions. Data from health information systems are used for medical and administrative purposes such as billing and insurance, whereas public health surveillance data are used in various activities to improve the health and well-being of communities.

Public health surveillance was introduced as a means of capturing information on infectious diseases, but over time systems have evolved to capture information on noninfectious diseases such as cardiovascular disease, injury, and birth defects.[2] Likewise, field investigations have expanded over the years to include noninfectious disease threats. Increased birth defects in Love Canal, New York; hurricane-related carbon monoxide poisonings; and risk of breast cancer from oral contraceptive use are just a few examples of public health threats resulting from noninfectious diseases.[3-6]

Types of Public Health Surveillance

The three types of public health surveillance systems are: passive, active, and enhanced-passive (Figure 3-1). As depicted in Figure 3-1, two general populations are involved in surveillance: organizations that provide public health data (e.g., healthcare providers, hospitals, and laboratories) and public health agencies. The flow of action between these populations differs among the three types of public health surveillance.

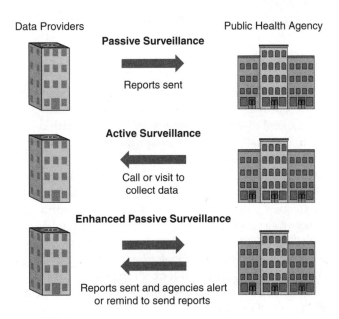

Figure 3-1   Three types of surveillance

Passive Surveillance

Passive surveillance is the sharing of health data between healthcare-related individuals such as physicians and infection control nurses and facilities such as hospitals, clinics, and laboratories with public health agencies.[2] Healthcare-related individuals and facilities collect data on their patients, including demographic, clinical, and laboratory information, to help them provide appropriate diagnosis and treatment. Given that these data are already collected and available, pertinent information is then shared with public health agencies. Depending on the health condition, data may be shared immediately, weekly, or monthly with the appropriate public health agency, by fax, Internet, mail, or phone.

There is very little action necessary by public health agencies to perform surveillance via this method except to ensure timely sharing of information back to the data providers, such as feedback reports. This type of surveillance is inexpensive, as it requires few human and financial resources. However, compared to the other types of surveillance, data obtained from passive surveillance are more likely to be incomplete and missing records. If electronic reporting is unavailable, timeliness is a concern; it may take weeks or months for reports to arrive at public health offices and be entered in databases.

An example of a passive surveillance system is the CDC's Nationally Notifiable Disease Reporting System (NNDSS).[7] In 2010, there were almost 70 nationally notifiable (i.e., reportable) infectious diseases.[8] Each state and territory in the United States has a mandate requiring healthcare providers, clinics, hospitals, and laboratories to report all diagnoses of certain reportable diseases to their local or state/territorial health departments.

Active Surveillance

Active surveillance requires "active" involvement of public health agencies to collect health data. These agencies routinely contact their data sources (such as healthcare providers, hospitals, and laboratories) to acquire all reports of relevant health conditions.[2] Examples of routine contact include calling a healthcare provider to interview him or her or conducting a site visit to review medical records.

The drawback to active surveillance is that it can be expensive for public health agencies because it requires additional financial and human resources. It can also be time-intensive depending on the frequency of contacts—daily, weekly, or monthly. The benefit is that data collected from active surveillance are more likely to be complete, with fewer missing records. Active surveillance is often undertaken during field investigations when it is vital to identify all potentially affected individuals to ensure prompt diagnosis and proper treatment, especially if there is a potential for contacts to be affected.

An example of a surveillance system that conducts active surveillance is CDC's foodborne diseases active surveillance network (FoodNet).[9] State health departments involved in this network routinely contact their clinical laboratories to obtain information on all laboratory-confirmed illnesses of foodborne diseases such as *Escherichia coli* O157:H7 and *Salmonella*.

Enhanced-Passive Surveillance

The final type of surveillance is enhanced-passive surveillance, which is a combination of passive and active surveillance. It is considered passive surveillance because the reporting mechanism is based on data being shared by healthcare-related individuals and organizations with public health agencies; it is an enhancement to passive surveillance because public health agencies send notifications to healthcare providers and healthcare facilities to remind them to report data. Enhanced-passive surveillance is often instituted during an ongoing field investigation when investigators send alerts and notices to healthcare providers to remind them to report any confirmed illnesses.

Categories of Public Health Surveillance

This section provides a brief overview of six common categories of surveillance. It also addresses how each category of surveillance can be useful to investigators despite its limitations. Each of these categories can be combined with active or passive surveillance. For instance, surveillance systems may be "active, population based" or "passive, hospital based."

Population-Based Surveillance

Population-based surveillance entails the collection of health data that are representative of the target population. For instance, if the target population is the state of Wyoming, one option would be to collect data on health events from everyone who resides in Wyoming. Another option would be to collect data on health events from a random sample of individuals who live in the state.

An example of population-based surveillance is the Nationally Notifiable Diseases Surveillance System (NNDSS) mentioned earlier.[7] The Behavioral Risk Factor Surveillance System (BRFSS) is another example.[10] Surveys are conducted monthly at the state level to obtain information on risk behaviors, health practices, and access to healthcare services associated with injury and chronic health problems. Probability sampling is used to select households so that findings can be generalized to the state. The CDC then compiles this information to provide national-level statistics.

Population-based surveillance systems provide the best estimates of prevalence and patterns of disease in a population because they provide information on the entire target population. Nevertheless, there are certain disadvantages to population-based surveillance. This type of surveillance is more expensive to conduct than other categories of surveillance. Depending on how the data are collected, population-based surveillance may not capture all ill individuals. Individuals who do not seek medical care would not be captured by a surveillance system such as the NNDSS, for example—although the NNDSS would capture all illnesses requiring medical attention, regardless of the characteristics of the individual. Population-based surveillance may also miss subgroups. For instance, household surveys will not capture information from individuals who do not have a stable residence.

This omission can be problematic if the health condition is more prevalent in people without stable residences than in other persons.

Community-Based Surveillance

In community-based surveillance, community members detect and report illnesses that might otherwise not be reported to healthcare facilities. This type of surveillance is often conducted by volunteers who receive training on the health condition(s) from healthcare workers and healthcare facilities. If volunteers detect a condition, they report it to a designated healthcare professional or facility for proper diagnosis and treatment. Low- and middle-income countries often use community-based surveillance to track diseases such as malaria and dengue.

Community-based surveillance is especially useful for detecting individuals who do not seek medical attention. It can also build a healthcare network within the community where neighbors help one another. Finally, it can strengthen relations between the communities and local public health agencies by improving the health of the communities and the effectiveness of the local public health agencies. Even so, community-based surveillance has a number of limitations. A high rate of false positives—individuals diagnosed with a condition who do not really have the condition—may result if illnesses are not confirmed by a trained healthcare professional or laboratory testing. It can be time-consuming from a public health point of view. Public health officials need to monitor activities regularly to ensure they are carried out appropriately. These officials also need to make sure volunteers are effectively serving the community. Finally, not all health conditions are suitable for community-based surveillance. Health conditions of a sensitive nature, such as sexually transmitted diseases, are not ideal for community-based surveillance because of their associated social pressures and consequences.

Hospital-Based Surveillance

Health conditions that require the level of care and treatment provided by hospitals are often targeted for hospital-based surveillance. The National Electronic Injury Surveillance System (NEISS) organized by the U.S. Consumer Protection and Safety Commission (CPSC) is an example of a hospital-based surveillance system.[11] Within this system, select hospitals report all emergency room visits for nonfatal injuries to provide nationally representative estimates of injuries in the United States and its territories.

It is not advantageous to perform hospital-based surveillance on health conditions that cause mild illness, because individuals with these illnesses are not likely to seek medical care or require hospitalization. Thus the prevalence and incidence of a mild condition would be grossly underestimated by this type of surveillance. In addition to mild illnesses, there are some serious health events that might potentially lead to hospitalization that hospital-based surveillance does not track well. Myocardial infarctions (heart attacks) typically lead to hospitalization, for example, but the proportion of individuals who survive until hospital admission is small enough that it could produce an underestimation of the true incidence of the event.

Laboratory-Based Surveillance

Laboratories perform tests for bacteria, parasites, viruses, and other pathogens to provide healthcare providers with accurate diagnoses for their patients. Many states require laboratories to report positive results for pathogens that cause any of the diseases that are legally reportable. For some pathogens, isolates must be sent to public health laboratories for confirmation, serotyping, or antibiotic susceptibility. With advances in technology, the number of laboratories reporting results to public health agencies electronically is increasing. By reducing the time spent manually entering data into surveillance systems, electronic reporting is improving the timeliness of data availability for public health agencies.

The National Respiratory and Enteric Virus Surveillance System (NREVSS) is an example of a laboratory-based surveillance system.[12] Commercial laboratories and laboratories from collaborating hospitals, local and state public health departments, and universities provide information to NREVSS to monitor trends in respiratory and enteric viruses such as respiratory syncytial virus (RSV) and rotavirus.

In addition to helping public health officials track infectious diseases, laboratory data are valuable for noninfectious health conditions. States participating in the National Institute for Occupational Safety and Health's (NIOSH's) Adult Blood Lead Epidemiology and Surveillance (ABLES), for example, require laboratories to report adult blood levels to designated public health agencies.[13] Data collected through this system are then used to monitor trends in adult blood lead levels.

Laboratory-based surveillance has advantages and disadvantages. The major advantage is that laboratory tests are required to confirm the disease. However, information provided by laboratories is often limited to the patient's name and the test results. In addition, physicians must request that a specimen be tested. For gastrointestinal or respiratory illnesses, physicians may treat the patient directly and not confirm the diagnosis with a laboratory test, so these data would never enter the surveillance system. Likewise, laboratory-based surveillance is not beneficial when health conditions of interest represent syndromes that cannot be confirmed through the laboratory.[14] Finally, use of improper testing methods can lead to inaccurate diagnoses, resulting in inaccurate surveillance data.

School-Based Surveillance

For surveillance of health-related behavior or health conditions affecting children or adolescents, school-based surveillance is an option. Across most states and territories, school attendance is compulsory until the age of 16, making schools an ideal setting for surveillance. An example of school-based surveillance is the Youth Risk Behavior Surveillance System.[15,16] To understand health risk behaviors such as tobacco use and unhealthy diets among youths and young adults, school-based surveys are conducted every two years among a sample of ninth to twelfth graders.

An advantage of school-based surveillance is the ability to quickly identify the target population for research geared toward understanding the health and health behaviors of children and adolescents. However, school-based surveillance requires involvement of school officials and parental approval. Sensitive issues may also be difficult to include on surveys.

Sentinel-Based Surveillance

Some health conditions are not reportable, but have an important impact on public health.[2] Other conditions may be reportable, yet the quality of the data may be questionable. Under these circumstances, it may be possible to conduct surveillance among a sample of reporting sites. This practice is known as sentinel-based surveillance, and the reporting sites are referred to as sentinel sites. These sites may include a number of venues, including healthcare facilities or schools.

Sites are often selected because the information collected can be generalized to the larger target population. At the same time, site selection takes into account practical considerations, such as data quality, staff resources, technical resources, and specialties and skills. The advantage of sentinel surveillance can be its ability to collect high-quality data. However, sites must have staff members who are willing and available to collect appropriate data, collect specimens for testing, and report results to public health agencies in a timely manner. A tertiary hospital—a hospital dedicated to a particular specialty such as cancer or pediatrics—is a good choice for a sentinel site if the medical condition requires specialized care. A site may also be selected if the personnel have the technical skills or the facility has the equipment necessary to accurately diagnose a health condition.

Epidemiological considerations are also important in selecting a sentinel site. The geographic location is an important consideration, especially for capturing illnesses among a target population. For example, sentinel surveillance for the vectorborne disease plague should include sites located in high-risk areas where *Yersinia pestis* is found. Sites may also be chosen based on the population they serve. A public hospital serves the general population, for example, whereas a small private clinic would serve only a very specific subgroup of the general population.

The CDC's Emerging Infections Program (EIP) is an example of a sentinel surveillance program.[17] Health departments from 10 sites in the United States provide data to CDC on invasive bacterial diseases, foodborne diseases, influenza-related hospitalizations, and healthcare-associated infections. Information from these sites is approximately representative of the U.S. population and is used to make national estimates of the burden and incidence of the targeted diseases.

Sentinel surveillance is not restricted to obtaining information from humans; that is, data may also be collected from animals. West Nile virus (WNV) surveillance activities include chicken flocks as sentinel sites.[18] These flocks, which are located around the United States, are monitored regularly for serologic evidence of WNV infections. Data may also be collected from vectors that transmit the disease, such as ticks and fleas. WNV surveillance activities include placing mosquito traps at strategic locations to capture and test mosquitoes for the presence of WNV.[18]

The advantages of sentinel-based surveillance are that it is less expensive than population-based surveillance and that it can address specific public health questions. The disadvantage is that if sites are not selected properly, data may not be representative of the general population, thereby providing inaccurate estimates of the prevalence and incidence of health conditions.

Uses of Public Health Surveillance Data

Public health agencies use surveillance data for a number of reasons (Table 3-1). Our interest is in how surveillance data can be used by the investigator, so most of the discussion in this section focuses on the items shown in boldface in Table 3-1.

Establish the Baseline of Morbidity and Mortality

Imagine the local public health department learns that four individuals have been diagnosed with malaria in the past seven days in Palm Beach County, Florida.[19] Assume the individuals have never traveled outside the United States. Does this group of cases suggest a possible outbreak?

TABLE 3-1   Uses of Public Health Surveillance Data

1. **Establish the baseline of a health condition.**
2. **Understand trends and patterns of disease.**
3. **Detect outbreaks or emergence of new diseases.**
4. **Estimate the magnitude of a health problem.**
5. **Identify resources needed during and after public health emergencies.**
6. **Evaluate public health programs and control measures.**
7. Determine the natural history of disease.
8. Monitor changes in infectious agents.
9. Set research priorities.
10. Stimulate research.
11. Test hypotheses.
12. Inform research plans and implementation.
13. Support public health program planning.
14. Monitor changes in health practices.

Sources: Adapted from Thacker SB, Berkelman RL. Public health surveillance in the United States. *Epidemiol Rev.* 1988;10:164–190; Thacker SB. Historical development. In: Teutsch SM, Churchill RE, eds. *Principles and Practices of Public Health Surveillance.* 2nd ed. New York: Oxford University Press; 2000:1–16; Thacker SB, Birkhead, G.S. Surveillance. In: Gregg MB, ed. *Field Epidemiology.* 3rd ed. New York: Oxford University Press; 2008:38–64.

It is important for investigators to know which health conditions are affecting their communities. One of the most critical pieces of information provided by public health surveillance is baseline morbidity (illness) and mortality. Here "baseline" means the number of events that would be expected to occur under routine conditions. Illness and death are a part of life and will occur in the absence of triggers such as contaminated water sources or earthquakes. It is under these routine conditions that we establish the baseline. Another way of thinking about this issue is by asking the following question: How much illness or death normally occurs in a community?

The baseline is established by using data from previous time periods. One common measure is the five-year median—that is, the median number of a particular health event in the previous five years. Another measure is the five-year mean, which is the mean, or average, number of a particular event in the previous five years. The median is often preferred for public health surveillance purposes because it is less susceptible to extreme values than the mean. Another commonly used measure is the baseline rate—the number of events that occurs in a given population over a specified period. For instance, the baseline rate of tuberculosis in the United States in 2009 was 3.8 cases per 100,000 persons per year.[20]

Let us revisit our earlier question about malaria and Florida. Malaria was a problem in the southeastern United States; in fact, the CDC was originally established in Atlanta in 1946 to address this problem.[21] Since the mid-1950s, only a few cases of locally acquired malaria (i.e., airport, mother-to-child [congenital], or transfusion) have been reported. The five-year median of locally acquired malaria cases in the United States from 1998 to 2002 was five cases (range: two to five cases).[22-26] Hence the four reported malaria cases in Palm Beach County over one week would represent an increase in malaria cases that warrants further investigation.[19]

Understand Trends and Patterns over Time

Once the baseline rate of morbidity or mortality has been established, investigators can use surveillance data to monitor trends and patterns over time. Examining trends often leads to questions for hypothesis testing.

As an example, consider Figure 3-2, which depicts the death rates for the three leading causes of injury death in the United States from 1979 to 2007.[27] There appears to be a steady increase in the rate of death due to poisoning from 1979 to 1998. Assuming no poison prevention interventions were implemented during this time period, what could account for this steady increase?

By 2007, the rate of motor vehicle deaths appears to be similar to the rate of poisoning deaths. However, it is important to point out that in 1999, the International Classification of Diseases, tenth revision (ICD-10) codes replaced the previous ICD-9 codes.[27] Because the definitions for deaths associated with motor vehicles and poisonings changed, fewer deaths were attributed to motor vehicle collisions. Meanwhile, other changes led to more deaths being classified as poisonings. The changes in the definitions of these deaths

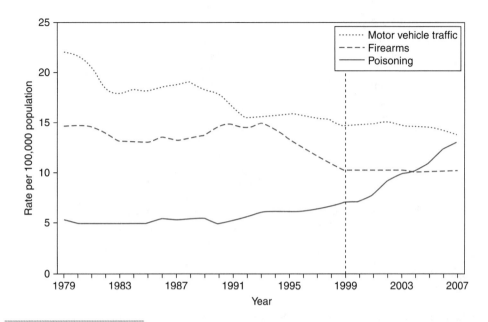

Figure 3-2   Death Rates for the Three Leading Causes of Injury Death in the United States, 1979–2007

Reproduced from: Centers for Disease Control and Prevention. QuickStats: Death Rates for the Three Leading Causes of Injury Death—United States, 1979-2007. *Morb Mortal Weekly Report.* 2009;59(30):957.

results in the appearance of a dramatic increase in poisoning deaths from 1999 to 2007; this effect is called a surveillance artifact. A surveillance artifact arises when changes in the number of reported events are caused by alterations in the conduct of surveillance activities rather than being a reflection of what is truly taking place in the population. Figure 3-2 highlights how changes in case definition can influence the number of events: More deaths met the new definition of poisoning, while fewer deaths met the definition of having a motor vehicle cause. Other potential sources of surveillance artifacts include the availability of new laboratory tests, improvements in reporting procedures, and increased healthcare provider awareness. To understand trends and patterns, investigators must know the data they are using.

Seasonality is an important trend for a number of infectious diseases, particularly respiratory and vectorborne diseases. Figure 3-3 highlights the seasonality of Lyme disease.[28] The summer months of May to August are high-risk months when tick populations are abundant and humans enjoy outdoor activities. Understanding seasonality trends is important because increases in reported cases may not represent a true outbreak, but rather reflect the natural occurrence of a health condition over the course of a year.

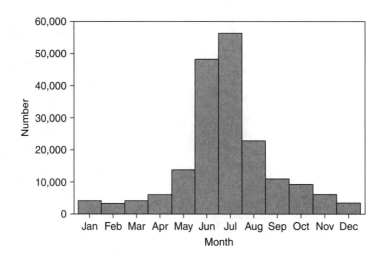

Figure 3-3 Number of Lyme disease cases reported by month of onset—United States, 1992–2006

Reproduced from: Bacon RM, Kugeler KJ, Mead PS. Surveillance for Lyme disease—United States, 1992–2006. *Morb Mortal Weekly Rep. Surveill Summ.* 2008;57(10):1–9.

A number of infectious diseases, especially viral diseases, show a cyclic periodicity in their occurrence. For example, during the pre-vaccine era, an outbreak of mumps would be reported every three years while increases in measles cases were reported every two years.[29-31] These cycles reflect a balance between susceptible and immune populations. As the number of individuals susceptible to disease grew larger than the number of immune individuals, outbreaks occurred and then subsided as individuals developed immunity.

Monitoring the trends of health conditions will influence whether investigators determine an event warrants further investigation. Trends can help clarify whether increased events represent a natural, predictable pattern of change in the incidence of a health condition, helping investigators to prioritize their time and resources.

Estimate the Magnitude of a Health Problem

Once we know which health conditions affect our communities, it is important to estimate the magnitude, or scope, of the health problem. This information will help guide allocation of limited resources to improve public health.

For example, smoking during pregnancy has been identified as a risk factor for adverse fetal development, including low birth weight and preterm birth.[32] Figure 3-4 shows the prevalence of smoking during the last three months of pregnancy in 26 study sites participating in the Pregnancy Risk Assessment Monitoring System (PRAMS) in 2005. It is clear that smoking during pregnancy remains a health problem despite education on its harm to the fetus.

Figure 3-4   Prevalence of smoking during pregnancy in Pregnancy Risk Assessment and Monitoring System sites, United States, 2005

Reproduced from: Tong VT, Jones JR, Dietz PM, D'Angelo D, Bombard JM. Trends in smoking before, during, and after pregnancy—Pregnancy Risk Assessment Monitoring System (PRAMS), United States, 31 sites, 2000-2005. *Morb Mortal Weekly Rep. Surveill Summ.* 2009;58(4):1-29.

The availability of quantitative evidence describing the magnitude of a health condition is important for investigators. It represents a source of feedback, by providing a measure for how well public health interventions and controls are working. As evidenced by Figure 3-4, it can also be used to describe the geographic distribution of the health condition. Furthermore, it aids in detecting new or emerging health conditions. Finally, quantitative evidence can be used to inform public health policies.

Detect Outbreaks or Emergence of New Diseases

It is often the notification from an astute healthcare provider to public health officials that triggers an outbreak investigation or the detection of a new disease. However, public health surveillance data can serve the same purpose. Later, once the baseline for a health condition is established, public health officials can use surveillance data to detect any substantial increases in the number of events that may represent an outbreak.

For example, in Figure 3-5, a dashed black line represents the historical average of dengue cases reported in Puerto Rico.[33] Using this historical average, public health professionals

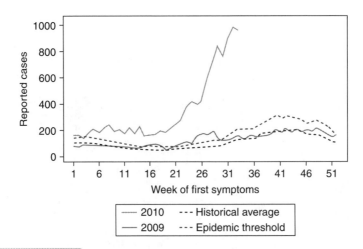

Figure 3-5 Suspected dengue cases reported in Puerto Rico, as of August 18, 2010

Reproduced from: Centers for Disease Control and Prevention Dengue Branch and Puerto Rico Department of Health. Dengue Surveillance Weekly Report. http://www.cdc.gov/dengue/resources/wklyrpt_eng/wklyrpt_eng.pdf. Accessed September 16, 2010, 2010.

were able to estimate the epidemic threshold for dengue at different time points throughout the year; this threshold is represented by the dotted blue line in Figure 3-5. These two pieces of information in the graph show that the number of suspected dengue cases (solid blue line) reported to the Puerto Rico Department of Health as of August 18, 2010, was above the epidemic threshold.[33] This outbreak appeared to have begun in early 2010, when the number of suspected cases was just above the epidemic threshold. However, the outbreak took hold by the fourth week of 2010, as demonstrated by a sudden increase in the number of cases during a period when the historical average and epidemic thresholds indicated the number of suspected dengue cases should have been decreasing.

The key to the effective use of surveillance data for the detection of events is the availability of high-quality data in a timely manner for analysis. Poor-quality data or delays in the availability of data make detection of events difficult.

Identify Needs During and After Public Health Emergencies

Areas affected by public health emergencies (either natural or human-made disasters) are vulnerable to a number of potential adverse health conditions, such as exacerbation of chronic pulmonary conditions due to fires or waterborne diseases due to flooding. Surveillance data can be used to monitor health conditions during and after public health emergencies, thereby allowing officials to quickly identify additional resources or education needed to control and prevent further morbidity and mortality.

During the latter part of the 2004 hurricane season, for example, the Florida Department of Health (FDOH) reviewed data collected from the Florida Poison Information Center Network (FPICN) to identify any health hazards that may have been associated with hurricanes.[4] In 2005, FDOH collaborated with FPICN to monitor daily reports during the hurricane season. Figure 3-6 summarizes the number of carbon monoxide (CO) exposures reported to FPICN in association with the timing of hurricane landfalls in 2005. Data for 2003 are also included to contrast the number of reported CO exposures when no hurricanes made landfall. After analyzing these data, FDOH alerted the public to the risk of CO exposure from improper use of gasoline-powered equipment, especially generators. The agency also shared findings with other public health authorities, including the CDC, which were able to provide notices and alerts to communities affected by Hurricane Katrina.[3]

Evaluate Programs and Control Measures

The goal of prevention programs and control measures is to reduce the burden of a health condition or to prevent deaths from this cause. Surveillance data can be used to assess how well these programs and measures are working.

For example, *Healthy People 2010* is a set of objectives established to improve the health of Americans.[34] Various programs have been designed around the *Healthy People 2010* indicators, and surveillance data have been used to monitor progress toward achieving these nationwide objectives. The goal of objective 19-2 is to "reduce the proportion of adults who are obese" to 15%.[35] Data from the 2009 BRFSS were used to assess the progress made by initiatives focused on reducing obesity in adults. Figure 3-7 shows the self-reported

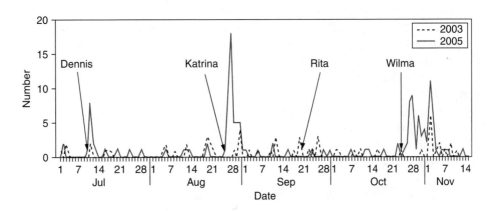

Figure 3-6 Number of reported carbon monoxide exposures and hurricane landfalls in Florida, July 1–November 14, 2003 and 2005

Reproduced from: Monitoring poison control center data to detect health hazards during hurricane season—Florida, 2003-2005. *Morb Mortal Weekly Rep.* 2006;55(15):426–8.

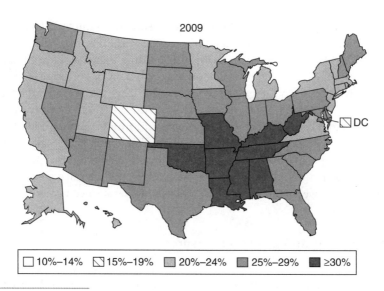

Figure 3-7   Self-reported prevalence of obesity among adults in the United States, 2009

Reproduced from: Vital signs: state-specific obesity prevalence among adults—United States, 2009. *Morb Mortal Weekly Rep.* 2010;59(30):951–5.

prevalence of obesity among adults in 2009.[36] The obesity epidemic affects much of the United States, with more than 25% of respondents classified as obese (body mass index [BMI] of 30 or higher based on self-reported height and weight) in more than 30 states. More importantly, none of the states reported less than 15% prevalence in obesity; only Colorado and Washington, DC, had prevalence estimates between 15% and 19%, indicating that the *Healthy People 2010* objective 19-2 would not be reached by 2010. In this situation, the data obtained through surveillance suggest that public health officials should reevaluate initiatives designed to control the obesity epidemic and identify more effective strategies.

Field investigators need to assess whether the control measures they have implemented have the desired effect of reducing morbidity and mortality. Surveillance data allow investigators to monitor the progress of their control measures and determine whether they need to reevaluate their efforts.

Other Uses of Public Health Surveillance Data

Following is a brief summary of other uses of public health surveillance data.

Follow the Natural History of Disease

Some diseases have short incubation periods, whereas others, such as cancer, can take years to develop. Certain diseases cause mild infection, while others are often fatal. Surveillance data provide an opportunity to characterize the natural history of a disease, from the early stages of infection to its resolution or long-term consequences.

Monitor Changes in Infectious Agents

All organisms adapt to their environments, and infectious agents are no exception. They can adapt to new hosts, become resistant to drug therapies, or expand geographically. Surveillance of diseases caused by pathogens such as *Mycobacterium tuberculosis* and *Staphylococcus aureus* has identified dangerous trends in resistance. Once these kinds of discoveries are made, the medical and public health community can use the information to identify new effective treatment therapies.

Set Research Priorities

Examining surveillance data can lead investigators to ask questions about the driving forces of trends, vulnerability of subgroups, and risk factors for an undesirable health event. Investigators can use the information they gather to set priorities for research that will inform improvements to public health services or policies.

Stimulate Research

Investigators often generate hypotheses from surveillance data, particularly data about the causes of a health condition and the vulnerability of certain subgroups to that condition. These hypotheses can stimulate public health officials to conduct research.

Test Hypotheses

Research can be an expensive endeavor. Depending on the research question, surveillance data may provide a more cost-effective, timely option to explore questions that investigators may be able to answer with existing data.

Inform Research Plans and Implementation

Reviewing surveillance data provides valuable information on how to conduct a study that will optimize limited time and resources. For example, if the incidence of a health condition of interest is low, investigators may decide to plan a study that will take longer than a study of a health condition that has a higher incidence.

Support Public Health Planning

Data from surveillance provides valuable quantitative evidence for action. Officials can use surveillance data to introduce or improve public health programs that efficiently target the most vulnerable populations with the limited available resources.

Monitor Changes in Health Practices

Access to medical care, vaccination coverage, and antibiotic use are important health practices that can influence the overall health of communities. Monitoring health practices such as these will highlight areas of improvement and identify practices that require corrective measures to improve public health.

Establishing and Evaluating Public Health Surveillance Systems

Establishing and evaluating public health surveillance systems are important activities carried out by public health authorities. As described in the previous section, implementation of a public health surveillance system yields many benefits. Meanwhile, evaluations of public health surveillance systems are critical to identify and correct problems with surveillance activities that could affect the quality of the collected data. Factors such as completeness (few missing data), representativeness (data accurately represent the occurrence and distribution of disease in the population), timeliness (limited delay between symptom onset and report to public health officials), reliability (disease information is always reported in the same manner), and validity (disease and other collected information are accurate) are all factors that can influence the quality of surveillance data. Surveillance systems that collect data that are incomplete, are unrepresentative, lack timeliness, or are unreliable or invalid are of no benefit to public health officials because analysis and interpretation of the data could lead to erroneous conclusions.

Poorly collected data cannot be remedied. For this reason, periodic evaluations of surveillance systems should be conducted. Unfortunately, these activities are resource- and time-intensive, often requiring a team of public health professionals to carry out. They should be conducted as part of routine public health surveillance efforts, rather than by a field epidemiologist about to launch a field investigation. To keep our discussion focused on field epidemiology, we will refrain from discussing how to establish or evaluate public health surveillance systems. Several publications listed in the References section for this chapter describe these topics in detail.[1, 37, 38]

Sources of Public Health Surveillance Data

Field investigations are both resource- and time-intensive. Before beginning any investigation, therefore, it is advantageous for investigators to explore any existing data that might help them answer the questions they are asking. Pertinent surveillance data may be available at the local, state, national, and even international levels. Investigators can obtain information from vital statistics, established surveillance systems for health-related events, registries, surveys, health-related data, and data on animals and vectors. This section highlights a few examples of data sources available at the national level.

Vital Statistics

Vital statistics on births, deaths, marriages, and divorces are collected in each state and territory of the United States.[35] Each locality is legally responsible for maintaining records and issuing certificates for all of these events. The CDC's National Center of Health Statistics (NCHS) then collects data from each of the jurisdictions for compilation and dissemination.

Because collection of the information is legally required, vital statistics data are generally complete, with very little missing information. Nevertheless, there may be a substantial time lag between when a health event occurs and when the corresponding data are available for use.[2] Furthermore, information available from vital statistics is limited and may need to be linked to other data sources to provide needed information. In addition, the validity of "cause of death" in death certificates may be questionable—the underlying condition that led to the fatal event often is not captured or recorded on the death certificate.[2] This inconsistency can lead to an underestimation of the impact of certain health conditions on mortality.

Nevertheless vital statistics data can be, and have been, used in field investigations. For example, investigators studying a cancer cluster in Randolph, Massachusetts, in the mid-1980s used a variety of data, including death certificates, to address whether there was an increase in the number of cancer cases in the Bartlett-Green Acres neighborhood.[38] In Florida, researchers used birth certificate records linked to infant death certificate records to assess whether there was an association between prepregnancy maternal obesity and infant death.[39]

Surveillance Systems for Health-Related Events

Data on an array of health-related events, such as infectious diseases, injury, adverse events, and birth defects, are collected and available through surveillance systems. The list in Table 3-2 is not exhaustive but includes several of the national-level surveillance systems.

A few systems, such as AERS, NHSN, and VAERS, collect data through voluntary reporting, but the majority of systems rely on mandatory reporting. Reporting of certain health-related events is mandated at the state level by legislation or regulation. Reportable events include both infectious and noninfectious diseases, such as measles and birth defects.[40] The Council of State and Territorial Epidemiologists (CSTE), state health departments, and CDC collaborate to generate a list of nationally notifiable diseases each year. Although a number of reportable health-related events exist, we will focus here on the nationally notifiable diseases that contribute to the CDC's NNDSS.

Infectious diseases reporting in the United States began in the late 1800s. By 1928, all states were reporting data on 29 infectious diseases to the national level.[7] Since then, the list of nationally notifiable diseases has been revised each year, so that it now includes almost 70 infectious diseases.[41] Reporting has also increased to include all 50 states, the District of Columbia, designated cities, and U.S. territories (we will refer to this group as "jurisdictions"). Reporting of health conditions from jurisdictions to the CDC is voluntary. At their discretion, jurisdictions may or may not report all of the nationally notifiable diseases.[40,42] Jurisdictions may also choose to conduct surveillance for health conditions that are endemic in their areas but are not readily found in other jurisdictions, such as dengue fever and leptospirosis. Hence there is jurisdiction-to-jurisdiction variability in the list of reportable conditions.[40]

Beginning in 2010, noninfectious conditions were added to the list of nationally notifiable diseases.[43] These conditions include cancers, elevated blood lead levels, acute pesticide-related illness, silicosis, and waterborne disease outbreaks.

TABLE 3-2 Names and Web Addresses of Surveillance Systems for Health-Related Events

Name	Web Address
Active Bacterial Core Surveillance (ABC)	http://www.cdc.gov/abcs/index.html
Adult Blood Level Epidemiology and Surveillance (ABLES)	http://www.cdc.gov/niosh/topics/ABLES/ables.html
Adverse Event Reporting System (AERS)	http://www.fda.gov/Drugs/GuidanceComplianceRegulatoryInformation/Surveillance/AdverseDrugEffects/default.htm
Fatality Analysis Reporting System (FARS)	http://www.nhtsa.gov/FARS
Foodborne Active Disease Surveillance Network (FoodNet)	http://www.cdc.gov/FoodNet/
Gonococcal Isolate Surveillance Project	http://www.cdc.gov/std/gisp/
Influenza Surveillance	http://www.cdc.gov/flu/weekly/fluactivitysurv.htm
Metropolitan Atlanta Congenital Defects Program	http://www.cdc.gov/ncbddd/bd/macdp.htm
National Antimicrobial Resistance Monitoring System (NARMS): Enteric Bacteria	http://www.cdc.gov/narms/index.htm
National Automotive Sampling System	http://www.nhtsa.gov/NASS
National Electronic Injury Surveillance System (NEISS)	http://www.cpsc.gov/library/neiss.html
National Fire Incident Reporting System	http://nfirs.fema.gov/
National Healthcare Safety Network (NHSN)	http://www.cdc.gov/nhsn/
National Notifiable Disease Surveillance System (NNDSS)	http://www.cdc.gov/ncphi/disss/nndss/nndsshis.htm
National Respiratory and Enteric Virus Surveillance System (NREVSS)	http://www.cdc.gov/surveillance/nrevss/
National Toxic Substance Incidents Program (NTSIP)	http://www.atsdr.cdc.gov/ntsip/index.html
National Tuberculosis Surveillance System	http://www.cdc.gov/tb/statistics/default.htm
Pregnancy Risk Assessment Monitoring System (PRAMS)	http://www.cdc.gov/prams/
Sentinel Event Notification Systems for Occupational Risks (SENSOR)	http://cdc.gov/niosh/docs/2004-146/appendix/ap-a/ap-a-17.html
Vaccine Adverse Event Reporting System	http://vaers.hhs.gov/index
Work-Related Lung Disease (WoRLD) Surveillance System	http://www2.cdc.gov/drds/WorldReportData/

Source: Adapted from Thacker SB, Birkhead GS. Surveillance. In: Gregg MB, ed. Field Epidemiology. 3rd ed. New York: Oxford University Press; 2008:38–64.

As discussed earlier, surveillance for reportable diseases comprises a population-based, passive surveillance system. Depending on the jurisdiction, healthcare providers, hospitals, infection control nurses, laboratories, and clinics may report illnesses to the local or state/territory health department. Standardized forms are used to provide patient contact information, demographics, signs and symptoms, laboratory testing and results, and patient outcome. For certain diseases such as hepatitis A or HIV, additional information on risk factors may also be collected. Laboratories, however, often do not have complete information on patients, especially commercial or reference laboratories. Thus these sources generally provide only the patient name, the name of the requesting facility, the name of the laboratory test, and the test results.

An advantage of using data from reportable disease surveillance systems is that, depending on the disease, such systems can provide a great deal of information, including geographic location, clinical profile, outcome, and risk factor information. The information gathered about diagnoses requiring laboratory confirmation is generally accurate, as is information about severe and rare diseases. Reportable disease surveillance systems have their drawbacks, however. In particular, passive surveillance systems are plagued by underreporting and missing information on case reports. Milder illnesses not requiring medical attention may be missed.[2] Finally, many reportable conditions may be underreported because physicians do not collect specimens for testing.

Investigators have used reportable disease surveillance systems both to detect outbreaks and to rule them out. In Arizona, for example, the incidence of coccidioidomycosis reported through the National Electronic Telecommunications Surveillance System (NETSS) increased by 186% from 1995 to 2001. An investigation concluded the increase was associated with seasonal peaks related to climate.[44] The Utah Department of Health implemented control measures after receiving eight case reports of cryptosporidiosis in late July 2007; the annual median number of cases between 2002 and 2006 was 16.[20] Eventually, a total of 1,902 laboratory-confirmed cases were identified. In an example of using surveillance systems to rule out additional cases of disease, officials implemented enhanced-passive surveillance in fall 2001 in Delaware, New Jersey, and Pennsylvania to identify suspect inhalational and cutaneous anthrax cases,[45] but no additional cases were identified.

Syndromic surveillance is another form of surveillance that has gained popularity in the United States in recent years. Historically, in resource-limited countries where laboratory testing is not readily available, public health officials have used clinical profiles, or syndromes, compatible with diseases such as malaria, polio, and diarrheal diseases, to inform prevention and control strategies. With the increased threat of bioterrorism, U.S. public health officials have reexamined the benefits of syndromic surveillance. Although the syndromes under surveillance vary by system, most are compatible with illnesses caused by pathogens that might be used in a biological terrorist event, such as anthrax, plague, and botulism. In syndromic surveillance, prediagnostic health-related data are used to conduct surveillance.[46]

In a number of states, mandates require certain health-related data be provided to public health officials to conduct syndromic surveillance. Data that have been used include emergency department data, ambulatory care data, poison control data, and sales of over-the-counter medications.[47] Similar to the situation with reportable conditions, jurisdictions have discretion in deciding which syndromes they will monitor.

To prepare for the possibility of a bioterrorist event, a few states have developed syndromic surveillance systems that utilize data from a number of sources to capture information on severe and milder illnesses in humans as well as animals. For example, the North Carolina Disease Event Tracking and Epidemiologic Collection Tool (NC DETECT) uses data from emergency departments, prehospital medical information system, the Carolinas Poison Center, select urgent care clinics, and the North Carolina State University College of Veterinary Medicine laboratories to look for suspicious patterns of disease.[48]

The detection of an outbreak of norovirus in 2006 demonstrates how investigators make use of syndromic surveillance.[49] The Texas Department of State Health Services detected an increase in cases of gastrointestinal illness through the state's emergency department data-based syndromic surveillance system. Further investigation identified outbreaks of norovirus in two nursing homes, which ultimately affected 43 staff and residents.

Registries

In addition to vital events such as births and deaths, other health conditions must be registered with state-level government authorities. These registries are often population based, collecting information from all individuals diagnosed with the health condition of interest. They represent a rich source of data that investigators can use to estimate the burden of particular health concerns, monitor trends, set research priorities, and evaluate prevention programs. Table 3-3 lists a few of the registries available at the national level in the United States.

Two programs—CDC's National Program of Cancer Registries (NPCR) and the National Cancer Institute's (NCI) Surveillance, Epidemiology, and End Results (SEER) system— collect data on all cancer cases and deaths in the United States.[50] Healthcare facilities and

---

TABLE 3-3 **Names and Web Addresses of Registries for Health-Related Events**

Name	Web Address
National Birth Defects Prevention Network	http://www.nbdpn.org/
National Birth Defects Registry	http://www.birthdefects.org/registry/
National Program of Cancer Registries (NPCR)	http://www.cdc.gov/cancer/npcr/
Surveillance and Epidemiology and End Results (SEER) system	http://seer.cancer.gov/

Source: Adapted from Thacker SB, Birkhead GS. Surveillance. In: Gregg MB, ed. *Field Epidemiology.* 3rd ed. New York: Oxford University Press; 2008:38–64.

facilities that provide cancer-related services are required to report all cancers to their state cancer registry. NPCR collects data from most states, cities, and territories (covering an estimated 96% of the U.S. population), while SEER collects data from a smaller number of registries, representing approximately 26% of the U.S. population. Combined, these programs collect information on cancers from the entire U.S. population (Figure 3-8).[51]

Another important health condition registered at the state level is birth defects, which represent the leading cause of infant mortality in the United States.[52] Forty-six states and Puerto Rico had established surveillance systems for monitoring birth defects as of 2009.[53] Although the registries vary from state to state, the majority collect population-based information on birth defects using a combination of active and passive surveillance. Sources of reports include delivery hospitals, pediatric and tertiary care facilities, vital statistics, physician reports, other state-based children registries (such as special needs and hearing screening), midwifery, prenatal care facilities, and Medicaid. Twenty-two of these state-based registries submit data to CDC's National Center on Birth Defects and Developmental Disabilities (NCBDDD), which compiles the data to provide national estimates of birth defects.[52]

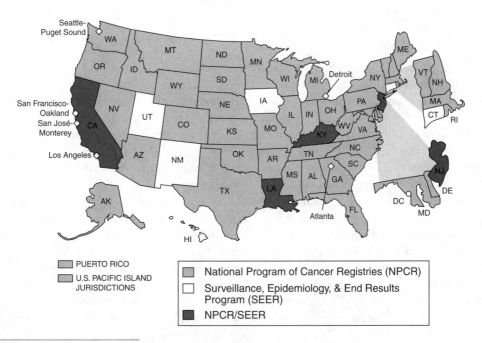

Figure 3-8   NPCR and SEER funded territories in the US

Reproduced from: Centers for Disease Control and Prevention. National Program of Cancer Registries. http://apps.nccd.cdc.gov/cancercontacts/npcr/contacts.asp. Accessed September 18, 2010.

An advantage of registries is that they are often population based, meaning that they capture all health conditions diagnosed within each jurisdiction and provide accurate estimates for the prevalence and incidence of the condition. Data from registries that gather data through active case ascertainment are typically high quality and complete, whereas registries that obtain data through passive surveillance may have incomplete or missing data. Another disadvantage of registries is that, depending on the jurisdiction, there may be no established registry. Existing state and territorial registries may go back only 5 to 20 years, making it difficult to explore questions from earlier time points.

Registries have been useful in epidemiologic investigations, especially in the investigation of noninfectious disease clusters. In the fall of 1989, a urologist in Phoenixville, Pennsylvania, became concerned about the increased number of invasive bladder cancers he was diagnosing.[54] As part of their study of the cancer cluster, investigators used data from the Pennsylvania Cancer Registry to estimate the baseline incidence rate of invasive bladder cancer. Likewise, investigators used data from SEER and the California Cancer Registry as part of an investigation into a cluster of childhood leukemia cases in Fallon, Nevada.[55] Finally, information from cancer registries was integral in the Selected Cancer Study, which explored the possible association of Agent Orange and several rare cancers among Vietnam War veterans.[56-58]

Routine Surveys

Surveys conducted routinely or periodically, especially for health-related behaviors and chronic diseases, are another source of surveillance data that public health officials use to estimate the burden of health conditions, monitor trends in health conditions and health practices, evaluate public health programs, and inform public health policies. Surveys are often completed by taking a sample of individuals from the target population; this target population may be a small community or the entire country. Data can be collected through interviews, medical exams, or clinical samples. Before using data from surveys to address any questions, investigators should take the time to learn how the data were collected. In addition, they should be aware that survey data collected from one community will not be generalizable to the national population. A few of the available surveys are listed in Table 3-4.

One example of a survey is BRFSS, a state-based system of health surveys established by the CDC in 1984.[10] All 50 states, the District of Columbia, Guam, Puerto Rico, and the U.S. Virgin Islands collect data monthly on topics related to chronic disease and injury such as health-risk behavior, preventive health practices, and access to health care. For several localities, the BRFSS is the only source of data on health behaviors. It is used to identify emerging health problems, establish and monitor health objectives such as those associated with *Healthy People 2010*, and support health-related legislature.

Another well-known survey used for surveillance is the National Health and Nutrition Examination Survey (NHANES), which is conducted by CDC's National Center for Health Statistics.[59] This survey was designed to collect health and nutritional measurements on adults and children in the United States. Face-to-face interviews and physical examinations are completed on a nationally representative sample of approximately 5,000 individuals

TABLE 3-4   Names and Web Addresses of Routine Surveys for Health-Related Events

Name	Web Address
Behavioral Risk Factor Surveillance System (BRFSS)	http://www.cdc.gov/brfss/
National Ambulatory Medical Care Survey (NAMCS)	http://www.cdc.gov/nchs/ahcd.htm
National Health and Nutrition Examination Survey (NHANES)	http://www.cdc.gov/nchs/nhanes.htm
National Health Interview Survey (NHIS)	http://www.cdc.gov/nchs/nhis.htm
National Hospital Ambulatory Medical Care Survey (NHAMCS)	http://www.cdc.gov/nchs/ahcd.htm
National Hospital Discharge Survey (NHDS)	http://www.cdc.gov/nchs/nhds.htm
National Immunization Survey (NIS)	http://www.cdc.gov/nis/
National Nursing Home Survey (NNHS)	http://www.cdc.gov/nchs/nnhs.htm
National Survey of Ambulatory Surgery (NSAS)	http://www.cdc.gov/nchs/nsas.htm
Youth Risk Behavior Surveillance System (YRBSS)	http://www.cdc.gov/HealthyYouth/yrbs/index.htm

Source: Adapted from Thacker SB, Birkhead GS. Surveillance. In: Gregg MB, ed. *Field Epidemiology*. 3rd ed. New York: Oxford University Press; 2008:38–64.

each year. Officials use the resulting data to estimate the burden of health conditions, establish national standards for health-related measurements such as weight and blood pressure, and conduct research that will inform public health policies and services.

Surveys are flexible enough to permit more questions to be added as new health concerns arise. They can become a burden for the respondent if too many questions are included, however. Depending on how the survey is administered (i.e., face-to-face, self-administered, or telephone), there is the possibility of a low response rate. Response bias may also be a problem, especially with face-to-face surveys on sensitive issues, which may lead some respondents to give a socially acceptable answer rather than the truth. Using telephones to complete interviews may be problematic: In certain populations, such as the homeless, many individuals may not own a landline or cellular phone.

Surveys have been used to monitor the obesity (BMI ≥ 30) epidemic in the United States. Both the BRFSS and NHANES have been used to monitor the spread of this epidemic.[36,60] Although the surveys measured BMI differently, both surveys found the prevalence of obesity has been growing in the United States.

Health-Related Data

Health-related data—that is, data from emergency rooms, ambulatory care, hospital discharge, and Medicare and Medicaid—can provide valuable surveillance data. Depending on the investigation, investigators may seek data from specific types of healthcare organizations, such as health maintenance organizations (HMOs) and Veterans Affairs (VA) hospitals. Information available from these sources typically includes patient demographics, diagnoses, procedures performed, medications provided, and discharge status. Health-related data can provide valuable information on potential outbreaks or the emergence of a new disease, changes in healthcare practices, and the burden of a health condition.

Pharmacies are another source of health-related data. By monitoring purchases of medications, it is possible to detect community-wide outbreaks that may necessitate palliative but not medical care. For instance, limited availability of antidiarrheal medication in pharmacies may indicate a gastrointestinal disease outbreak in the local community.

Data from poison control centers are another important source of health-related data. The American Association of Poison Control Centers compiles data from all poison control centers in the United States within the National Poison Data System.[61] Investigators can then use data from these sources to identify potential outbreaks associated with poisons and chemicals.

An advantage of using health-related data is that they often contain detailed information about the clinical manifestations of an outbreak. Because the information is used for the diagnosis and treatment of patients, it is generally comprehensive. Information on signs and symptoms collected by physicians can also be used to conduct syndromic surveillance.

A disadvantage of using health-related data is that such data typically do not contain risk factor information, which is important to an outbreak investigation. In addition, individuals who seek medical attention typically have a more severe form of illness, so the data are not representative of all individuals suffering from the same condition. Finally, inaccuracies in diagnostic coding—which often arise because the information is collected for administrative or billing purposes rather than public health surveillance—may be problematic for some health-related data.[2]

Investigators often utilize health-related data to provide more information on cases, identify additional cases, or even detect an outbreak. For example, from December 2002 to June 2003, four cases of acute idiopathic pulmonary hemorrhage (AIPH) were identified in Boston, Massachusetts; three occurred among inpatients at the same hospital.[62] As part of their investigation, public health officials reviewed hospital discharge data and admissions records for pediatric and neonatal intensive care units to identify additional cases. Investigators determined the infants had an underlying susceptibility that made them vulnerable to pulmonary bleeding. In a very different case, in 2003, poison control center data identified a gastrointestinal outbreak among a local community in northern Maine.[63] An investigation determined that coffee served at a church gathering had been intentionally contaminated with arsenic.

Animal and Vector Data

Zoonotic and vectorborne diseases can have a significant impact on human and animal health. An advantage of investigating these diseases is that surveillance can also be conducted in the animals and vectors themselves. Both wild and domestic animals can be monitored for illnesses, such avian influenza H5N1 and Eastern equine encephalitis (EEE). Animals can also be used to monitor illnesses caused by environmental contaminants before the detection of those diseases in humans, such as the use of canaries in mines.[2] Meanwhile, vectors such as mosquitoes and ticks can be captured and tested in laboratories to identify whether they are carrying pathogens that cause illnesses such as West Nile virus and Rocky Mountain spotted fever.

Several surveillance systems use animal and vector data. Reporting sources vary by disease but may include veterinary reports, sentinel sites involving susceptible animals such as horses or chickens, dead animal reports, and animal bait-and-catch methods. An example of a disease for which animal surveillance is conducted is rabies. Rabies is almost 100% fatal in humans if untreated and is spread to humans by the bite of an infected animal. Rabies in animals, both wild and domestic, is a nationally notifiable disease; jurisdictions report cases to CDC on a weekly basis.[64] Animals suspected to be infected with rabies are sent to a designated laboratory, such as a public health laboratory, for testing. Figure 3-9 highlights the geographic boundaries of terrestrial animal reservoirs for rabies in 2008.

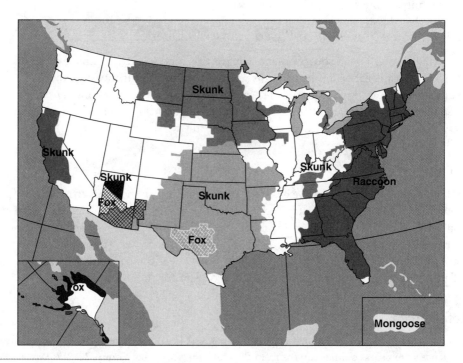

Figure 3-9   Geographic boundaries of terrestrial animal reservoirs for rabies, US, 2008

Reproduced from: CDC. Rabies—Wild Animal Surveillance. March 22, 2010. http://www.cdc.gov/rabies/location/usa/surveillance/wild_animals.html. Accessed September 18, 2010.

Human health data synthesized with animal or vector data provide a big picture of the impact of a disease, particularly the disease's geographic spread. This analysis enables public health officials to take a holistic approach when implementing prevention and control measures to reduce the risk of illness in humans. Similar to the drawbacks with other data sources, however, animal data are limited by underreporting. Veterinarians are busy and may be unable to send reports to public health veterinary officials. Meanwhile, illnesses involving domesticated animals that provide a source of income may not be reported out of financial concern. Finally, the inability to identify an appropriate location—near a breeding site, for example—or to use an appropriate trap will hinder the ability to capture vectors for testing.

A primary example of animal health and vector data used in conjunction with surveillance in humans is the West Nile virus epidemic that began in the United States in 1999.[65] Observations during the 1999 outbreak in the northeastern United States led the CDC to recommend surveillance activities in mosquito populations, sentinel birds, wild birds including dead crows, and susceptible animal populations such as horses.[18] Data were compiled and used to monitor the geographic spread of WNV and as early alerts for possible human illness.

Additional Resources: Web-Based Statistical Queries

Data from several of the sources mentioned in this section are available for public use. The CDC website, for example, contains web-based queries that investigators can use to obtain simple descriptive statistics. These queries address the wide-ranging online data for epidemiological research (http://wonder.cdc.gov/) and the web-based injury statistics query and reporting system (http://www.cdc.gov/injury/wisqars/index.html).

Summary

Epidemiologic investigators have a wealth of information at their fingertips in the form of public health surveillance data. In the United States, agencies at the federal, state, and local levels conduct surveillance for a variety of health conditions, including cancers, injuries, infectious diseases, deaths, and health-related behaviors. These data can provide needed quantitative evidence to support a field investigation. Investigators may use surveillance data as primary or secondary sources of data for the investigation.

References

1. German RR, Lee LM, Horan JM, et al. Updated guidelines for evaluating public health surveillance systems: Recommendations from the Guidelines Working Group. *MMWR Recomm Rep.* 2001;50(RR-13):1–35; quiz CE31–37.
2. Thacker SB, Birkhead GS. Surveillance. In: Gregg MB, ed. *Field Epidemiology.* 3rd ed. New York: Oxford University Press; 2008:38–64.
3. Carbon monoxide poisoning after hurricane Katrina—Alabama, Louisiana, and Mississippi, August–September 2005. *Morb Mortal Weekly Rep.* 2005;54(39):996–8.

4. Monitoring poison control center data to detect health hazards during hurricane season–Florida, 2003–2005. *Morb Mortal Weekly Rep.* 2006;55(15):426–8.

5. Elliott J. Lessons from Love Canal. *JAMA.* 1978;240(19):2033–4, 2040.

6. Long-term oral contraceptive use and the risk of breast cancer. The Centers for Disease Control Cancer and Steroid Hormone Study. *JAMA.* 1983;249(12):1591–5.

7. National Notifiable Diseases Surveillance System. January 25, 2010. Centers for Disease Control and Prevention website: http://www.cdc.gov/ncphi/disss/nndss/nndsshis.htm. Accessed September 7, 2010.

8. Nationally Notifiable Infectious Conditions–United States 2010. Updated July 21, 2010. Centers for Disease Control and Prevention website: http://www.cdc.gov/ncphi/disss/nndss/PHS/infdis2010.htm. Accessed September 19, 2010.

9. FoodNet: Foodborne Diseases Active Surveillance Network. Updated April 15, 2010. Centers for Disease and Control website: http://www.cdc.gov/FoodNet/index.htm. Accessed September 13, 2010.

10. Behavioral Risk Factor Surveillance System. Updated August 25, 2010. Centers for Disease Control and Prevention website: http://www.cdc.gov/brfss/. Accessed September 7, 2010.

11. National Electronic Injury Surveillance System (NEISS) On-line. U.S. Consumer Product Safety Commission website: http://www.cpsc.gov/library/neiss.html. Accessed September 18, 2010.

12. National Respiratory and Enteric Virus Surveillance System (NREVSS). Updated September 14, 2010. Centers for Disease Control and Prevention website: http://www.cdc.gov/surveillance/nrevss/. Accessed September 18, 2010.

13. Adult Blood Lead Epidemiology and Surveillance (ABLES). Updated May 4, 2010. Centers for Disease Control and Prevention website: http://www.cdc.gov/niosh/topics/ABLES/ables-description.html. Accessed September 29, 2010.

14. Istre G. Disease surveillance at the state and local levels. In: Halperin WBJE, Monson RR, eds. *Public Health Surveillance.* New York: Van Nostrand Reinhold; 1992:42–55.

15. Youth Risk Behavior Surveillance System. Centers for Disease Control and Prevention website: http://www.cdc.gov/HealthyYouth/yrbs/pdf/system_overview_yrbs.pdf. Accessed November 3, 2010.

16. YRBSS: Youth Risk Behavior Surveillance System. Updated September 10, 2010. Centers for Disease Control and Prevention website: http://www.cdc.gov/HealthyYouth/yrbs/index.htm. Accessed November 3, 2010.

17. Division of Emerging Infections and Surveillance Services (DEISS)–Emerging Infections Programs. Updated January 20, 2010. Centers for Disease Control and Prevention website: http://www.cdc.gov/ncpdcid/deiss/eip/index.html. Accessed September 18, 2010.

18. Guidelines for surveillance, prevention, and control of West Nile virus infection–United States. *Morb Mortal Weekly Rep.* 2000;49(2):25–28.

19. Local transmission of *Plasmodium vivax* malaria–Palm Beach County, Florida, 2003. *Morb Mortal Weekly Rep.* 2003;52(38):908–11.

20. Decrease in reported tuberculosis cases–United States, 2009. *Morb Mortal Weekly Rep.* 2010;59:289–94

21. Langmuir AD. Evolution of the concept of surveillance in the United States. *Proc R Soc Med.* 1971;64(6):681–4.

22. Causer LM, Newman RD, Barber AM, et al. Malaria surveillance–United States, 2000. *MMWR CDC Surveill Summ.* 2002;51(SS-5):9–21.

23. Filler S, Causer LM, Newman RD, et al. Malaria surveillance–United States, 2001. *MMWR Surveill Summ.* 2003;52(5):1–14.

24. Holtz TH, Kachur SP, MacArthur JR, et al. Malaria surveillance—United States, 1998. *MMWR CDC Surveill Summ.* 2001;50(5):1–20.

25. Newman RD, Barber AM, Roberts J, et al. Malaria surveillance—United States, 1999. *MMWR Surveill Summ.* 2002;51(1):15–28.

26. Shah S, Filler S, Causer LM, et al. Malaria surveillance—United States, 2002. *MMWR Surveill Summ.* 2004;53(1):21–34.

27. Centers for Disease Control and Prevention. QuickStats: Death rates for the three leading causes of injury death—United States, 1979–2007. *Morb Mortal Weekly Rep.* 2009;59(30):957.

28. Bacon RM, Kugeler KJ, Mead PS. Surveillance for Lyme disease—United States, 1992–2006. *MMWR Surveill Summ.* 2008;57(10):1–9.

29. Anderson RM, Grenfell BT, May RM. Oscillatory fluctuations in the incidence of infectious disease and the impact of vaccination: time series analysis. *J Hyg (Lond).* 1984;93(3): 587–608.

30. Barskey AE, Glasser JW, LeBaron CW. Mumps resurgences in the United States: A historical perspective on unexpected elements. *Vaccine.* 2009;27(44):6186–6195.

31. Noah ND. Cyclical patterns and predictability in infection. *Epidemiol Infect.* 1989;102(2): 175–90.

32. Tong VT, Jones JR, Dietz PM, et al. Trends in smoking before, during, and after pregnancy—Pregnancy Risk Assessment Monitoring System (PRAMS), United States, 31 sites, 2000–2005. *MMWR Surveill Summ.* 2009;58(4):1–29.

33. CDC Dengue Branch and Puerto Rico Department of Health: Dengue Surveillance Weekly Report. Centers for Disease Control and Prevention website: http://www.cdc.gov/dengue/resources/wklyrpt_eng/wklyrpt_eng.pdf. Accessed September 16, 2010, 2010.

34. *Healthy People 2010.* U.S. Department of Health and Human Services website: http://www.healthypeople.gov/. Accessed September 18, 2010.

35. *Healthy People 2010.* 19. Food and nutrition. U.S. Department of Health and Human Services website: http://www.healthypeople.gov/document/html/volume2/19nutrition.htm#_Toc490383122. Accessed September 17, 2010.

36. Centers for Disease Control and Prevention. Vital signs: State-specific obesity prevalence among adults—United States, 2009. *Morb Mortal Weekly Rep.* 2010;59(30):951–5.

37. Buehler JW, Hopkins RS, Overhage JM, et al. Framework for evaluating public health surveillance systems for early detection of outbreaks: Recommendations from the CDC Working Group. *MMWR Recomm Rep.* 2004;53(RR-5):1–11.

38. Romaguera RA, German RR, Klaucke DN. Evaluating public health surveillance. In: Teutsch SM, Churchill RE, eds. *Principles and Practice of Public Health Surveillance.* 2nd ed. New York: Oxford University Press; 2000:176–93.

39. National Vital Statistics System. Updated August 27, 2010. Centers for Disease Control and Prevention website: http://www.cdc.gov/nchs/nvss/about_nvss.htm. Accessed September 18, 2010.

40. Day R, Ware JH, Wartenberg D, et al. An investigation of a reported cancer cluster in Randolph, Massachusetts. *J Clin Epidemiol.* 1989;42(2):137–50.

41. Thompson DR, Clark CL, Wood B, et al. Maternal obesity and risk of infant death based on Florida birth records for 2004. *Public Health Rep.* 2008;123(4):487–93.

42. Koo D, Wetterhall SF. History and current status of the National Notifiable Diseases Surveillance System. *J Public Health Manag Pract.* 1996;2(4):4–10.

43. Centers for Disease Control and Prevention. Case definitions for infectious conditions under public health surveillance. *MMWR Recomm Rep.* 1997;46(RR-10):1–55.

44. Thacker SB, Berkelman RL. Public health surveillance in the United States. *Epidemiol Rev.* 1988;10:164–90.

45. Nationally Notifiable Non-infectious Conditions—United States 2010. Updated July 21, 2010. Centers for Disease Control and Prevention website: http://www.cdc.gov/ncphi/disss/nndss/PHS/non_infdis2010.htm. Accessed September 19, 2010.

46. Increase in coccidioidomycosis—Arizona, 1998–2001. *Morb Mortal Weekly Rep.* 2003;52(6):109–12.

47. Tan CG, Sandhu HS, Crawford DC, et al. Surveillance for anthrax cases associated with contaminated letters, New Jersey, Delaware, and Pennsylvania, 2001. *Emerg Infect Dis.* 2002;8(10):1073–7.

48. Syndromic surveillance: An applied approach to outbreak detection. Updated January 3, 2008. Centers for Disease Control and Prevention website: http://www.cdc.gov/ncphi/disss/nndss/syndromic.htm. Accessed September 18, 2010.

49. Syndromic surveillance: Reports from a national conference, 2004. *Morb Mortal Weekly Rep.* 2005;54(suppl):1–212.

50. NC DETECT. http://www.ncdetect.org/. Accessed September 18, 2010.

51. Guerrero AC, Shim T, Kemple S, et al. Norovirus outbreak detected by emergency department syndromic surveillance using RedBat. *Adv Dis Surveill.* 2007;4:165.

52. National Program of Cancer Registries (NPCR). Updated May 21, 2010. Centers for Disease Control and Prevention website: http://www.cdc.gov/cancer/npcr/. Accessed September 18, 2010.

53. Surveillance, Epidemiology, and End Result. National Cancer Institute website: http://seer.cancer.gov/. Accessed September 18, 2010.

54. National Center on Birth Defects and Developmental Disabilities. September 13, 2010 Centers for Disease Control and Prevention website: http://www.cdc.gov/ncbddd/index.html. Accessed September 18, 2010.

55. National Birth Defects Prevention Network. State birth defects surveillance program directory. *Birth Defects Research Part A.* 2009;85:1007–55.

56. Balbus-Kornfeld JM, Frumkin H. Investigation of a reported cluster of bladder cancer cases in the Pottstown/Phoenixville area of Pennsylvania. *Arch Environ Health.* 1992;47(4):285–91.

57. Steinmaus C, Lu M, Todd RL, et al. Probability estimates for the unique childhood leukemia cluster in Fallon, Nevada, and risks near other U.S. military aviation facilities. *Environ Health Perspect.* 2004;112(6):766–71.

58. The association of selected cancers with service in the US military in Vietnam. III. Hodgkin's disease, nasal cancer, nasopharyngeal cancer, and primary liver cancer. The Selected Cancers Cooperative Study Group. *Arch Intern Med.* 1990;150(12):2495–505.

59. The association of selected cancers with service in the US military in Vietnam. II. Soft-tissue and other sarcomas. The Selected Cancers Cooperative Study Group. *Arch Intern Med.* 1990;150(12):2485–92.

60. The association of selected cancers with service in the US military in Vietnam. I. Non-Hodgkin's lymphoma. The Selected Cancers Cooperative Study Group. *Arch Intern Med.* 1990;150(12):2473–83.

61. National Health and Nutrition Examination Survey. Updated September 2, 2010. Centers for Disease Control and Prevention website: http://www.cdc.gov/nchs/nhanes.htm. Accessed September 18, 2010.

62. Flegal KM, Carroll MD, Ogden CL, Curtin LR. Prevalence and trends in obesity among US adults, 1999–2008. *JAMA.* 20;303(3):235–41.

63. National Poison Data System. American Association of Poison Control Centers website: http://www.aapcc.org/dnn/NPDSPoisonData.aspx. Accessed September 18, 2010.

64. Investigation of acute idiopathic pulmonary hemorrhage among infants—Massachusetts, December 2002–June 2003. *Morb Mortal Weekly Rep.* 2004;53(35):817-20.

65. Wolkin AF, Patel M, Watson W, et al. Early detection of illness associated with poisonings of public health significance. *Ann Emerg Med.* 2006;47(2):170-6.

66. Rabies Surveillance Data in the United States. Updated March 22, 2010. Centers for Disease Control and Prevention website: http://www.cdc.gov/rabies/location/usa/surveillance/index.html. Accessed September 18, 2010.

67. Outbreak of West Nile-like viral encephalitis—New York, 1999. *Morb Mortal Weekly Rep.* 1999;48(38):845-9.

Chapter 4

Is a Potential Outbreak Real?

Amy L. Nelson
Jeanette K. Stehr-Green
Paul A. Stehr-Green
Pia D. M. MacDonald

Learning Objectives

By the end of this chapter, the reader will be able to:

- List and describe the five steps investigators follow to determine the existence of an outbreak.
- Describe the elements of a case definition and give an example of a case definition.
- Differentiate between active and passive case-finding techniques.
- List and describe the four categories of information to collect during case finding.
- Use a line listing to organize data.
- Calculate incidence rates.
- Cite examples of "artificial" and "real" reasons for an increase in cases.

Introduction

Some outbreaks are easy to detect: A gastrointestinal illness that strikes everyone who ate the potato salad at a company picnic is a classic example of an easily identified event among a small, well-defined group of people. Others can be more difficult to recognize, such as an increase in cases of a disease among apparently unrelated persons across a state, province, or country. To determine whether less apparent clusters of cases or events represent an outbreak, health departments often have to act quickly to collect, analyze, and interpret additional information.

As explained in Chapter 3, an outbreak is an increase—often sudden—in the observed number of cases of a disease or health problem compared with the expected number for a given place or among a specific group of people over a particular period of time.[1] Investigators can follow five steps to help them decide if an apparent increase in cases represents an outbreak (Figure 4-1). We describe each step in detail in this chapter.

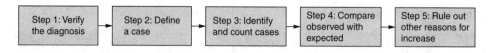

Figure 4-1   The steps to determine if reported cases represent an outbreak

Step 1. Verify the Diagnosis

To verify the diagnosis, investigators must do the following:

- Make sure the problem has been properly diagnosed.
- Make sure all of the cases have the same disease.
- Rule out laboratory or other errors.

Make Sure the Problem Has Been Properly Diagnosed

Investigators should review clinical findings and laboratory results to determine whether the cases likely have the same disease. The objective findings—signs of disease observed by the healthcare provider or the investigator—should be consistent with the diagnosis. Talking to the healthcare providers who evaluated the case patients, a qualified microbiologist, and even a few of the case patients can help investigators verify the diagnosis.

Make Sure All of the Cases Have the Same Disease

Identifying the genus and species of the causative agent alone may not always be enough to determine whether two individuals are suffering from the same disease. For example, outbreaks resulting from bacterial and viral pathogens are typically caused by a single strain (i.e., subtype) of the microorganism. Subtyping the bacterium or virus isolated from case-patient specimens—using laboratory tests such as serotyping, pulsed-field gel electrophoresis (PFGE), and genetic sequencing to group the microorganisms below the species level—can help investigators determine whether the case patients have the same disease and whether their diseases are related.

Rule Out Laboratory or Other Errors

If the outbreak involves infectious or toxic chemical agents, it is important to be certain that an increase in diagnosed cases is not the result of laboratory error. The investigation should always rely on standardized, proven laboratory tests, and laboratories should be able to verify that no contamination or other events occurred that might lead to erroneous agent identification. If the outbreak investigation team does not include a qualified laboratory professional, the team should work with one to ensure that the appropriate tests have been done correctly and that the laboratory findings are consistent with the clinical findings.[2]

Step 2. Define a Case

A case definition is a standard set of criteria that investigators in an epidemiologic investigation use to decide whether an individual should be classified as having the disease of interest. The case definition helps investigators count cases consistently over time and from place to place. It also helps investigators compare the observed number of cases of a disease with the expected number and decide whether they represent an outbreak.

A case definition includes both of the following elements:

- Clinical criteria and/or laboratory test results suggestive of the disease *and*
- Restrictions by time, place, and person

Clinical Criteria

Clinical criteria should be simple and objective, such as a fever greater than 101°F, x-ray evidence of pneumonia, three or more loose bowel movements within 24 hours, or a laboratory-confirmed *Salmonella* infection. If time is of the essence, investigators may not be able to wait for the results of laboratory tests; in this circumstance, they should be guided by the clinically accepted, usual presentation of the disease.[1]

Restrictions by Time, Place, and Person

Restrictions by time, place, and person refer to the circumstances around the outbreak. Their use increases the likelihood that cases of the disease that meet the case definition are associated with the outbreak under investigation.

Sensitivity Versus Specificity

A case definition can emphasize *sensitivity* (identifying all possible cases) or *specificity* (identifying only those cases with the illness under investigation that are associated with the outbreak under investigation). Investigators design a sensitive case definition when their goal is to include as many people as possible who truly have the disease in question, which increases the sensitivity (true positive rate); they use a specific case definition to exclude those individuals who truly do not have the disease, which increases the specificity (true negative rate).[1]

In general, investigations should begin with a "looser," or more sensitive, definition that risks mixing in a few false positives (people who really do not have the disease or condition of interest) along with as many true positives (people who really do have the disease or condition of interest) as possible. It is usually better to gather too much information than too little; having information about people who are not true cases is better than having to go back and find true case patients who were mistakenly ruled out earlier in the investigation. Likewise, gathering information from potential case patients about many possible exposures—even if the exposures turn out not to be related to the outbreak—is easier than trying to contact people a second time to ask more questions. As the investigators become more certain of the symptoms and the agent, the place of exposure, and the time frame, they can confidently narrow the case definition.

The case definition should be discriminating—that is, it should be able to distinguish individuals with the disease of interest from individuals with other diseases or no disease at all. The criteria should also be as objective as possible. This characteristic means that different investigators should be able to apply the same criteria and come up with the same results.

Here is a simple example of a case definition:

> On May 14, 1984, administrators at Hospital X became aware of a large number of absences due to a febrile gastrointestinal illness among nursing personnel. The outbreak occurred after "Nurses Appreciation Day" luncheons were held at the hospital on May 9-10. Reported symptoms included diarrhea (86%), abdominal cramps (85%), nausea (58%), subjective fever (40%), vomiting (17%), and bloody diarrhea (4%). *Salmonella* was identified in stool cultures from several ill nurses. Because only a few of the ill nurses had stool cultures performed, the clinical criteria included symptoms suggestive of infection with *Salmonella*. (Limiting cases to those with positive stool cultures would have excluded many true cases from the investigation, thereby limiting the power of the study to identify the source of the outbreak.) As a result, investigators selected the following clinical criteria for the case definition: either three or more loose stools in a 24-hour period *or* a combination of fever and nausea, vomiting, or abdominal cramps or stool culture that yielded *Salmonella*. (Investigators used "three or more loose stools in a 24-hour period" rather than "diarrhea" in their definition to distinguish between natural variations in bowel patterns and more serious symptoms due to an infection.) Because the investigators were focusing on the outbreak at the hospital, they also restricted cases by time, place, and person to include only nurses or nursing students with onset of symptoms from May 9-15 who were employed at Hospital X. The clinical criteria and restrictions increased the likelihood that cases that met the case definition were truly illnesses associated with the outbreak under investigation.[3]

Investigators often group all potential cases by placing each case into one of three categories:

- *Confirmed*: typical clinical features of the illness or agent, as well as either a laboratory test confirming the presence of the agent or an epidemiologic link to a laboratory-confirmed case
- *Probable*: typical clinical features of the illness or agent, but no laboratory confirmation or epidemiologic link
- *Possible*: fewer typical clinical features of the illness and no laboratory confirmation or epidemiologic link

It is important to note that a case definition differs from a clinical diagnosis. A case definition is used for epidemiologic purposes only, with the aim of ensuring that strict criteria are applied consistently to all potential cases of the disease. In contrast, a clinical diagnosis is used to make healthcare decisions for an individual patient; it is influenced by many factors, including the circumstances surrounding the illness or the patient's medical history. In some instances, patients may fit the case definition for a disease without having the related clinical diagnosis, and vice versa. This is particularly true for diseases for which a confirmatory diagnostic test is lacking.

Step 3. Identify and Count Cases

Case finding is critical to the success of an outbreak investigation. Cases that are reported to the health department often signal that an outbreak is under way, but they may represent only a small portion of the total number of outbreak-related cases and also may be different from other cases associated with the outbreak in some way. Some sick people may not seek care. Others may seek care but may not be reported. To understand the full scope of an outbreak including the size and geographic boundaries, investigators need to know exactly which types of people are getting the disease, when they became symptomatic, and where they may have been exposed. This information may help identify a potential exposure source, the cause of the outbreak, or both. Identifying this information may require getting out into the community and aggressively seeking out infected individuals; in some cases, it may also mean keeping an open mind and looking beyond easy conclusions about the source of an outbreak based on the initially reported cases.

Case finding at the beginning of an investigation provides critical information that helps the investigation team refine the case definition, determine the extent of the outbreak, and define the population of interest. The more information the team gathers at this stage of the investigation, the better it will be able to understand the epidemiology of the outbreak, determine the resources needed for a successful investigation, and develop appropriate control measures.

How to Find Cases

Just as it is important to begin an investigation with a broad case definition, it is best to cast a wide net when beginning to search for cases. Investigators can use two strategies to identify cases:

- *Active case finding* identifies cases through such methods as soliciting case reports and laboratory findings from healthcare facilities and laboratories, searching for cases in hospital discharge databases, screening exposed populations with diagnostic tests, and contacting other health departments, schools, nursing homes, and other facilities and institutions.

- *Passive case finding*, which is less aggressive and requires fewer resources, may involve examining existing county or state surveillance data to identify cases reported through communicable disease reporting systems, cancer registries, or other sources.

Here are some ways investigators find cases:

- *Seeking information from healthcare provider offices, clinics, hospitals, and laboratories.* Investigators might visit a local hospital emergency room and ask to review emergency room intake logs or the medical records of all patients seen during a certain period with the illness or with specific signs and symptoms. They might ask clinicians to request specimens from all patients who meet a clinical case definition, ask infection control practitioners to review the medical records of patients with a particular diagnosis, or ask a school nurse to provide the names of all students who were seen with a particular illness.

- *Querying the community through local television, radio, newspapers, or the Internet.* This method can be particularly effective if the outbreak involves a contaminated food product or a potential act of bioterrorism. In 1989, for example, the New Mexico Department of Health and Environment learned of three patients with eosinophilia and severe myalgia who had been taking oral preparations of L-tryptophan, an essential amino acid normally ingested as a constituent of dietary protein. Within two weeks, media publicity, including requests for cases to be reported to state health departments that were published in the CDC's *Morbidity and Mortality Weekly Report*, helped generate reports of 154 additional potential cases of a similar illness in 17 states and the District of Columbia.[4]

- *Examining records such as wedding invitation lists, guest books, credit card receipts, and customer lists.* In 2001, the first case of bioterrorism-related inhalational anthrax—the so-called index patient—traveled to North Carolina three days before he became ill, raising the possibility that exposure to *Bacillus anthracis* spores could have occurred in that state. To identify whether the index patient's exposure occurred naturally or was the result of bioterrorism, investigators visited hospital intensive care units, microbiology laboratories, and the offices of medical examiners and veterinarians, as well as places that the patient had visited. At one of these sites, a rural tourist park, investigators obtained credit card receipts and records of annual pass holders in case they needed to track approximately 700 park patrons who had visited the park on the same day as the index case.[5] (Investigators who use credit card receipts must tell the credit card holder how and why they obtained the information and how they will handle it. State laws vary on which information is to be held confidential in outbreak investigations.[6])

- *Interviewing every person in the affected population.* This method can be especially effective if an exposure has occurred in a defined population and setting. Investigators might query everyone who was at a church picnic, wedding, or school function; contact all the passengers who were on a cruise; or undertake a phone survey of people living in the affected community. Asking case patients if they know of anyone else who has become ill may help identify additional cases. Investigators can also take a random sample of individuals from the affected population to interview—a technique that is especially useful when the affected population is large.

- *Using multiple strategies to locate members of hard-to-reach populations.* During the investigation of an outbreak of tuberculosis at a large homeless shelter in Raleigh, North Carolina, for example, investigators used shelter sign-in sheets, dates of previous incarceration in the Wake County jail and state prison system, and employment records from three temporary labor agencies to identify men who had stayed at the shelter during the outbreak period. Eventually, 620 shelter residents and all shelter employees were screened for tuberculosis by using skin testing and chest radiographs. The investigation identified 16 patients with tuberculosis, in addition to the 9 members of the original outbreak cluster. The infected men were offered treatment, and the investigation team made recommendations to reduce the risk of future outbreaks.[7]

Investigators need to be creative, aggressive, and diligent in the search for possible cases, while balancing the resources expended—in terms of both time and cost—with the potential productivity of the source. They should always focus their efforts on those sources most likely to yield the largest number of cases. If a disease often leads to hospitalization, for example, discussions with staff and chart reviews at hospitals and emergency rooms are likely to be a good source of information. If the diagnosis requires laboratory confirmation, investigators should seek test results from clinical laboratories, both public and private.

Challenges in Case Finding

Even with the most active efforts, a number of factors are likely to make it difficult to identify or confirm all of the cases in an outbreak. First, not all laboratory specimens are routinely tested for certain pathogens. For example, *E. coli* O157:H7 testing is often not included in the standard panel of stool screens. If a healthcare provider does not request *E. coli* O157:H7 testing, the person examined could not be classified as a laboratory-confirmed case. (Such a patient could qualify as a probable or possible case, assuming that he or she had clinical features of the illness under investigation.)

Second, the spectrum of symptoms experienced by case patients might cause investigators to miss some cases. A patient exposed to the source of an outbreak of gastrointestinal illness who experiences only slight symptoms (such as abdominal cramping) might not seek medical attention and, therefore, would not be identified by a healthcare provider. Even if the outbreak is publicized in the media, the person might not connect his or her mild symptoms to the publicized outbreak. Similarly, some patients, even if seen by a healthcare provider, might not be associated with the outbreak illness if they do not have the typical clinical features of the illness.

Finally, the exposed population may be difficult to define or to trace. If, for example, a family vacationing from out of state ate at a restaurant involved in a foodborne disease outbreak, paid with cash, and drove away without meeting anyone in the community, investigators would not know to look for them.

Information to Collect During the Case-Finding Process

The precise information that investigators need to collect depends on the outbreak, but can generally be grouped into four categories:

- Identifying information
- Demographic information
- Clinical information
- Risk factor information[2]

Identifying information may include the name, address, phone number, date of birth, and contact information for the case patient. These data enable investigators to obtain further details about the case or exclude duplicate reports of the case. All identifying information must be kept confidential. One way to do so is to assign a number to each case patient; this number can then be used throughout the investigation instead of the case patient's name. The file containing personal identifiers and the assigned case number should be password protected or kept in a locked file cabinet.

Demographic information helps characterize the population at risk and includes age, sex, race, ethnicity, occupation, place of occupation, and travel history. The information required depends on the nature of the outbreak. For example, in an outbreak of diarrhea among children of preschool age, it would be important to ask whether a child attended a daycare program and, if so, the name of the facility.

Clinical information, such as symptoms, the date on which symptoms began, consultation with a healthcare provider (or not), and laboratory findings, allows investigators to verify that the case definition has been met, to characterize the disease, and to create an epidemic curve that plots the distribution of cases by time of onset (epidemic curves are discussed in more detail in Chapter 6). It also allows investigators to obtain further information from healthcare providers about the patient's diagnosis and patient specimens.

Risk factor information—those personal behaviors, environment exposures, or inborn or inherited characteristics that may link a person to a health-related condition—helps focus the investigation. In the preliminary stages of an investigation, investigators typically ask about general risk factors such as sources of water, contact with animals, contact with children, and recent international travel. Once investigators have generated hypotheses, they can collect more detailed information that will confirm or refute the hypotheses—in other words, they can test the hypothesis. The relevant risk factor information for each investigation depends on the type of outbreak. In an outbreak of *E. coli* O157:H7, for example, investigators initially might ask whether case patients had exposures associated with previous outbreaks of *E. coli* O157:H7 including consumption of ground beef or produce, exposure to recreational water, close contact with farm animals, or attending a daycare program. If preliminary analyses implicated beef consumption as a potential exposure, investigators would seek additional details, such as the date of purchase and the brand name of the beef, when they test their hypotheses.

The information initially collected from cases is usually obtained via a questionnaire or standard case report form. Examples of forms used in suspected foodborne disease outbreaks are available at http://www.cdc.gov/outbreaknet/references_resources/. Use of standardized core questions and data elements ensures that investigators are familiar with the questions to be asked and enhances data sharing and comparisons between investigators where appropriate.

Using a Line Listing to Organize Data

Line listings are tables that organize key information about each case in the outbreak. Each row in the line listing table represents a case. Each column represents such variables of interest as date of exposure or onset of illness, signs and symptoms, laboratory results, and demographic information. Organizing these data in a line listing provides investigators with an easy-to-review characterization of the population affected by the outbreak.

Investigators should add new cases to the list as they are identified, and update the entries as they obtain new information. Updating the line listing is a good way to categorize and track cases as the investigation progresses. For example, investigators can enter cases into the line listing as "possible," "probable," or "laboratory confirmed" and update them as more information becomes available (e.g., when a laboratory confirms a "probable" case). Because the data in the line listing will be used to create the graphs, tables, and maps to help investigators generate and test hypotheses, it is critical that these data are as accurate and complete as possible.

How to Create and Manage a Line Listing

Line listings can be written out on paper, although they are most often generated on a computer. Many health departments use commercial programs such as Microsoft Excel and Microsoft Access or free software such as Epi Info (http://www.cdc.gov/epiinfo/index.htm) for this purpose. These programs are easy to use and have the added benefit of allowing users to generate frequency distributions and epidemic curves.

TABLE 4-1 Example of a Line Listing for Gastrointestinal Illness

Case Number	Date of Symptom Onset	Signs/Symptoms			Labs	Demographics	
		Diarrhea	Vomiting	Fever >101°F	Positive Stool Culture	Age	Gender
1	1/2/04	1	1	?	1	19	M
2	1/5/04	0	1	0	0	17	M
3	1/2/04	0	1	0	1	23	F
4	1/7/04	1	1	1	1	18	?
5	1/1/04	?	1	1	1	18	F

1 = yes; 0 = no.

Table 4-1 provides an example of a simple line listing that might be used in the investigation of an outbreak of gastrointestinal illness.

Table 4-2 provides an example of a more detailed line listing that might be used in an investigation of an outbreak of hepatitis A.

The line listing typically includes the patient's name or identifying number and the date of symptom onset or specimen collection (depending on what information is available), as well as the components of the case definition. For example, for an investigation of an outbreak of acute hepatitis A, the CDC defines a case as follows:

- Clinical description: an acute illness with (1) discrete onset of symptoms and (2) jaundice or elevated serum aminotransferase levels
- Laboratory criteria for diagnosis: immunoglobulin M (IgM) antibody to hepatitis A virus (anti-HAV) positive[8]

For an investigation using this case definition, the line listing should include columns indicating the presence or absence of the discrete onset of symptoms, jaundice, and elevated aminotransferase levels. It should also indicate the presence or absence of IgM antibody to hepatitis A virus (anti-HAV) positive.

Line listings usually contain demographic information such as age and sex of the patient; they may also contain risk factor information such as drug use, meal at restaurant X, and sexual orientation. The information to include will depend on the nature of the outbreak. In the case of a hepatitis A outbreak, for example, relevant risk factor information includes drug use or sexual behavior. (In some other outbreaks, this kind of information would not be relevant.)

TABLE 4-2 Example of a line Listing for Acute Hepatitis A

Case Number	Report Date	Onset Date	Physician Diagnosis	Signs/Symptoms						Labs		Demographics	
				N	V	A	F	D	J	HAIgM	Other	Sex	Age
1	10/12/02	10/5/02	Hepatitis A	1	1	1	1	1	1	1	Low SGOT	M	37
2	10/12/02	10/4/02	Hepatitis A	1	0	1	1	1	1	1	Low ALT	M	62
3	10/13/02	10/4/02	Hepatitis A	1	0	1	1	1	1	1	Low SGOT	M	38
4	10/13/02	10/9/02	NA	0	0	0	0	?	0	NA	NA	F	44
5	10/15/02	10/13/02	Hepatitis A	1	1	1	1	1	0	1	HBsAg−	M	17
6	10/16/02	10/6/02	Hepatitis A	0	0	1	1	1	1	1	SGOT=240	F	43

N = nausea; V = vomiting; A = elevated aminotransferase; F = fever; D = discrete onset; J = jaundice; HAIgM = hepatitis A IgM antibody test; SGOT = serum glutamic oxaloacetic transaminase; ALT = alanine aminotransferase; HBsAg⁻ = hepatitis B surface antigen negative.

1 = yes; 0 = no; NA = not available.

Source: Adapted from Centers for Disease Control and Prevention. *Principles of Epidemiology in Public Health Practice*. 3rd ed. Atlanta, GA: Centers for Disease Control and Prevention; 2006.

Step 4. Compare Observed with Expected Cases

Typically, investigators compare the current number of cases of a disease—the observed number—with the number of cases seen during a similar period of time in the previous few weeks or months in the same population—the expected number. If there is a significant difference between the two numbers, an outbreak is likely to be occurring.

In the example presented in Figure 4-2, 51 cases of hepatitis A virus infection were reported in County X in May 2001. This is the observed number. Based on health department surveillance records (notifiable disease reports in which healthcare providers and laboratories report cases of selected diseases to the local or state health department), it appears that an average of 12 cases are reported each month. This is the expected number. Thus the 51 cases of hepatitis A in May 2001 are clearly in excess of the usual 12 for this community. In the absence of other factors, such as errors in laboratory identification or changes in reporting procedures, these cases very likely represent an outbreak.

When diseases are seasonal in nature—meaning the characteristic distribution of occurrence normally differs through the year—investigators must derive the expected number of cases from comparable time periods in previous years. For example, the reported cases of arboviral encephalitis, a viral infection spread by mosquitoes, increase during the summer months when mosquito activity increases. Because this disease is seasonal, investigators would compare incidence rates based on current case counts to incidence rates based on counts from the same month(s) in previous years to determine whether an outbreak of arboviral encephalitis is under way.

The following sources of data may help investigators determine the expected number of cases of a disease (see Chapter 3 for much more information on this topic):

- Health department surveillance records
- Hospital discharge records

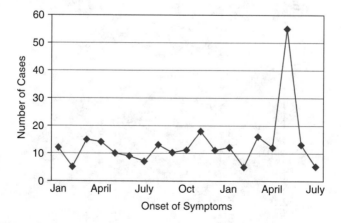

Figure 4-2 Hepatitis A cases by month of onset of symptoms, County X, January 2000 to June 2001

- Mortality statistics
- Surveys of healthcare providers to establish background or historical levels of disease
- Surveys of the community to establish background or historical levels of disease

Because case counts in the same population may not be readily available for previous time periods, investigators might need to base the expected number of cases on information from neighboring communities, the state, other states, or even the nation as a whole. If these other populations are not the same size and composition, a direct comparison of the number of cases might not be appropriate. For example, the investigator might reasonably expect a larger number of cases to occur in a larger population group compared with the number of cases observed in a smaller population group. If it is not possible to use the exact same population (or one of identical size and composition) to determine the expected number of cases, investigators need to take into account the relative magnitude of cases with respect to the size of the population at risk by calculating an incidence rate.

Calculating Incidence Rates

The incidence rate measures the probability of a new occurrence of a specific event in a defined population:

$$\text{Incidence rate} = \text{number of new events/population at risk}$$

The numerator is the number of events occurring during a given time period. The denominator is the size of the population at risk in the same time period. Time and place must always be specified when calculating the incidence rate. Only those people who are eligible to appear in the numerator should be counted in the denominator—for example, men should not be included in the denominator when calculating the rate of ovarian cancer.

Here is an example of how to calculate an incidence rate:

> In 1997, 109 laboratory-confirmed cases of salmonellosis occurred in Trinidad and Tobago. The population of Trinidad and Tobago was estimated to be 1,265,000 in mid-1997. What is the incidence of laboratory-confirmed salmonellosis in that country for 1997?

$$\text{Incidence (laboratory-confirmed salmonellosis)}$$
$$= 109 \text{ cases per } 1,265,000 \text{ people per year}$$
$$= 0.0000862 \text{ case per person per year}$$
$$= 8.6 \text{ cases per } 100,000 \text{ persons per year}[9]$$

Calculating the incidence rate is straightforward—divide the number of events by the population estimate. The resulting number can be very small and difficult to visualize, however, so investigators often calculate how many events would be expected among a larger group of people (typically 100,000) by multiplying by that larger number.

Making Rate Adjustments

In general, tabulating numbers of cases and incidence rates is useful when investigators want to compare observed cases of a disease with expected cases. But making appropriate comparisons can be complicated: Different age groups, races, ethnicities, and sexes have different inherent risks for particular diseases. For example, children have a higher rate of diarrheal illnesses, elderly individuals have a higher risk of hospital-acquired bloodstream infection, Hispanics and American Indians have higher rates of diabetes, and women are more likely to suffer from autoimmune disorders. Thus, when comparing "observed" and "expected" cases (or rates) of a particular disease using different populations, case numbers or even incidence rates may not be sufficient to determine if there is an excess of disease. In this circumstance, it might be necessary to compare "adjusted" rates (rates that take factors such as the age, race, or sex composition of the two populations into account) to determine whether an excess number of cases is actually present. Rates that do not take age, race, or sex composition into account are often referred to as "crude" rates.

Here is an example of a situation in which investigators would have to adjust rates to produce a meaningful comparison:

> Two counties in Washington State, Clallam and Clark, have crude death rates of 12.9 per 100,000 per year and 6.9 per 100,000 per year, respectively. The crude death rate in Clallam County appears to be almost twice that of Clark County, but does that make Clallam County an unsafe place to live? In fact, the crude rates are so divergent simply because Clallam County has an older population than Clark County. The median age in Clallam County is 43.8 years compared to 34.2 years in Clark. Twenty-two percent of the population in Clallam County is 65 years of age or older, compared to only 10% of the Clark County population. Because older individuals are at a higher risk of death, Clallam County has a higher death rate than Clark County. If you adjust the rates by taking into account the age distribution, the death rates for the two counties are actually very similar. Using the U.S. age distribution in 2000 as the standard, the age-adjusted death rates are 8.3 per 100,000 for Clallam County and 8.4 per 100,000 for Clark County.[10]

These adjusted rates do not represent a measure of the absolute burden of disease in those communities, but they do permit comparisons of the relative occurrence of a disease between or among different populations. For that reason, investigators should keep the age, race, ethnicity, and sex composition of populations in mind when comparing disease rates.

Once investigators have determined whether there is a difference between observed and expected cases or rates, they must decide whether the difference is meaningful. If 17 cases of a disease are reported each month on average, and there are 40 cases in a particular month, for example, those 23 additional cases appear to be a meaningful difference. But what if there are 18 cases—or 19 or 20—in a particular month? Are those case counts "different" from 17? Does the increase represent an outbreak, or is it due to random variation in incidence? Statistical techniques are available for formally assessing these differences, some of which are discussed in Chapter 9. Using them is particularly important when either the number of cases or the population size is small.

Step 5. Rule Out Other Reasons for an Increase in Cases

Even if the current number of cases exceeds the expected number, the excess may not necessarily be due to an outbreak. Investigators must rule out other reasons for an increase in case counts, such as changes in diagnostic or reporting procedures or population characteristics. Some investigators divide potential explanations for an increase in cases into "artificial" and "real" reasons. In an artificial increase, the increase does not reflect an actual change in the occurrence of the disease, but rather results from errors in diagnosis or data entry or changes in the completeness of reporting. For example, better surveillance results in a higher proportion of cases coming to the attention of public health officials. In a real increase, the increase in reported cases reflects a true increase in the occurrence of disease.

Even a true increase in numbers does not confirm an outbreak, however. The number of cases can increase, for example, because the size of the population at risk has increased, as when cases of a particular disease rise in a college town as the number of inhabitants increases during the school year. (In this situation, it is important to note that the incidence rate should not increase.) Similarly, changes in the characteristics of the population can lead to an increase in occurrence of disease if the changes result in a larger proportion of the population being at higher risk for developing a disease. For example, patients who undergo organ transplantation typically receive immunosuppressant drugs to prevent rejection of the transplanted organ. As a result, they are at a higher risk for developing hospital-acquired infections. If a hospital begins a new organ transplant program, administrators might anticipate an increase in hospital-acquired infections due to the change in characteristics of the patient population.

Table 4-3 summarizes some reasons why the observed number of cases might increase. Some of these reasons may become evident during earlier steps of the investigation. In any event, before investigators declare an increase to be either real or artificial, they should consider once again whether any of these factors may have affected the perceived case counts.

For example, in 1983, a medical laboratory in Los Angeles reported a large increase in diagnoses of intestinal amebiasis (infection with *Entamoeba histolytica*, shown in Figure 4-3). Thirty-eight cases were identified during a four-month period, compared with one *E. histolytica* infection per month before that period. A preliminary investigation failed to identify a common source of the infection. There had been no increase in the number of specimens examined and no clustering of cases in particular facilities. Most patients did not belong to groups recognized as being at high risk for acquiring amebiasis, such as male homosexuals, tourists to or immigrants from developing countries, or institutionalized persons.

TABLE 4-3 Possible Reasons for an Increase in the Observed Number of Cases

Possible Reasons for an Artificial Increase	Possible Reasons for an Real Increase
• Increased testing of laboratory specimens	• An increase in population size
• Initiation of new testing by the laboratory	• Changes in population characteristics
• Changes in reporting procedures	• An increase in rate of incidence due to random variation in incidence (i.e., chance)
• Increased interest in reporting	
• Laboratory error in identification	• A true outbreak
• Contamination of cultures	
• Errors in data entry	

To evaluate the accuracy of the *E. histolytica* diagnoses, investigators reexamined microbiologic slides from the patients. Specimens from only two patients contained *E. histolytica*. Specimens from 34 patients contained white blood cells (polymorphonuclear neutrophils and macrophages) that resemble *E. histolytica*. Two contained nonpathogenic protozoa. Recent changes in methods of slide preparation apparently led to the errors in diagnosis.[11] If investigators had followed the five steps of detecting an outbreak, they would have discovered the problem at Step 1, "Verifying the diagnosis."

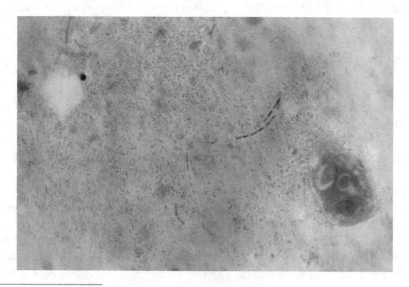

Figure 4-3   Entamoeba histolytica

Reproduced from: Centers for Disease Control and Prevention Public Health Image Library, ID# 10616.

In another example, after several wild migratory birds were confirmed to be infected with the highly pathogenic avian influenza A/H5N1 virus in Greece in February and March 2006, many patients went to local hospitals complaining about respiratory infections and expressing concern that they had been exposed to avian influenza. The majority of the patients were from northern Greece, where most of the birds infected with the avian influenza A/H5N1 cases were documented; many were admitted to the hospital and placed in isolation for observation. A case-control study of 26 potential patients found that while 85% met the clinical criteria of the case definition and 39% met the restrictions on time, place, or person in the case definition, none of the potential case patients actually were infected with avian influenza A/H5N1 as revealed by molecular testing. Investigators suggested that the pseudo-outbreak could be attributed to several causes, including increased awareness on the part of the general public about the illness, and poor interpretation of the case definition by clinicians.[12]

Mass Psychogenic Illness

When investigating potential outbreaks, investigators should keep in mind a phenomenon known as mass psychogenic illness (also known as mass hysteria and epidemic hysteria). This condition is marked by symptoms suggestive of organic illness, but without an identifiable cause, that occur among two or more people who share beliefs related to the source of those symptoms.

Outbreaks of mass psychogenic hysteria have been described in industrial settings and among schoolchildren, for example. Symptoms commonly include abdominal pain, headache, dizziness, fainting, nausea, and hyperventilation. More unusual symptoms include convulsions, seizures, laughing, and even hysterical dancing. In some instances, actual clinical illness in some group members may "spread" as anxiety spreads among individuals who observe those persons who were initially ill. These outbreaks can be socially and economically costly, resulting in school or business closings, emergency response expenses, and expensive investigations to identify and eliminate possible causes of the "outbreak."

Mass psychogenic illness is a diagnosis of exclusion. The investigator should always carefully consider whether the "real" cause of the illness is being overlooked. Certain clues identified early in the investigation, however, may suggest that an outbreak is psychogenic in nature:

- A number of persons experience a sudden onset of symptoms without the usual range in incubation period seen with most causative agents.
- Case patients display moderate to severe symptoms that are not the usual symptoms caused by the alleged contaminant.
- Symptoms among case patients resemble organic illness but lack an identifiable cause.
- Other groups sharing the same environment do not display the same symptoms.

- Physical proximity to the alleged contaminant is not related to illness.
- Females have a higher attack rate than males.
- The illness recurs when previously affected individuals congregate.
- Case patients display evidence of unusual physical or psychogenic stress.[13]

Examples of mass psychogenic illness have been well documented in the literature. For example, in October 2001, a nurse practitioner reported that five adolescent girls in a very conservative Old Order Amish religious community had developed a mysterious, life-threatening syndrome with neurologic features that included systemic weaknesses and anorexia. At the time when the girls became ill, substantial social conflict was occurring within their Amish community. The patients, who were aged 9 to 13, had thorough medical examinations that did not identify an organic cause. All five girls met the diagnostic criteria for conversion disorder, a psychiatric condition in which a person becomes blind or paralyzed or suffers other nervous system symptoms that cannot be explained. Four of the five girls were in good or improved health three months after the investigation. The investigators concluded that clinicians should be aware of the potential for outbreaks of psychogenic illness and should strive to develop effective intervention strategies, especially in cross-cultural settings.[14]

In another case, in November 1998, a teacher at a high school in Tennessee developed headache, nausea, shortness of breath, and dizziness soon after noticing a "gasoline-like" smell in her classroom. Authorities evacuated the school, and 80 students and 18 staff members checked into a nearby hospital's emergency room. Thirty-eight persons stayed in the hospital overnight. Five days later, after the school reopened, another 71 patients went to the emergency room complaining of headache, dizziness, nausea, and drowsiness. Several government agencies took part in an extensive investigation, but were unable to find a medical or environmental explanation for why people became sick. According to the results of a questionnaire administered a month after the incidents, becoming ill was closely associated with the individual being female, seeing someone else who was ill, learning that a classmate was ill, and reporting an unusual odor at the school. Investigators concluded that the illness had features of mass psychogenic hysteria, especially the widespread subjective symptoms that people believed had resulted from an environmental exposure to a toxic substance despite the lack of objective evidence of an environmental cause.[15]

Finally, during a 10- to 12-hour period in September 1998, an epidemic of respiratory symptoms took place among military recruits at a training center in San Diego, California. During the episode, temperatures were high (92–107°F), the Pollution Standards Index was relatively high, and brush fires were occurring in the area. After a group of recruits and their company instructor complained of cough and chest pain, officers and medical personnel suspected toxic gaseous exposure and evacuated more than 1,800 men from their barracks. Recruits complained of a wide variety of symptoms, mostly respiratory in nature, with approximately 1,000 personnel developing at least one new symptom after dinner. Several recruits underwent cardiopulmonary resuscitation, although physicians who examined them later believed they had hyperventilated and fainted. Ambulances evacuated 375 recruits for further medical evaluation, and at least 8 were admitted to a hospital. The county hazardous materials incident response team conducted an investigation, but found no significant toxic gas levels. Inspectors also found no obvious toxic exposures or discrepancies in sanitation in the base's galley. An epidemiologic investigation associated evidence of physical stress, mental stress, and awareness of rumors of odors, gases, or smoke with developing new symptoms and receiving further medical evaluation. The epidemic was distinctive because it took place in an all-male population and because so many people were involved.[16]

The point made earlier—that psychogenic illness is a diagnosis of exclusion—bears repeating. Outbreak investigators should rule out all potential causes of an outbreak before labeling it psychogenic. They should treat every potential case patient with respect, while being aware that in rare cases an outbreak truly lacks a causative agent.

Case Study: Determining Whether an Increase in Cases Represents an Outbreak

In June and July 1997, the Michigan Department of Community Health (MDCH) Bureau of Epidemiology noticed an increase in reports of *E. coli* O157:H7 infection from certain counties. According to notifiable disease records, 64 laboratory-confirmed cases of *E. coli* O157:H7 infection had onset of illness from June 15 to July 31, compared to 31 reported during the same period in 1996.

Do these cases represent an outbreak? Which steps would investigators take to make a decision? Which questions would they ask?

Step 1. Verify the Diagnosis

E. coli O157:H7 causes severe diarrhea (sometimes bloody) and abdominal cramps. A suspected case of *E. coli* O157:H7 infection is confirmed by detecting the bacterium in the stool. In Michigan, the MDCH laboratory confirmed the diagnosis of all *E. coli* O157:H7 isolates and performed pulsed field gel electrophoresis (PFGE) to determine whether the isolates might be related. The laboratory reported that all of the isolates were confirmed to be *E. coli* O157:H7, and PFGE subtyping showed that a number of the isolates had patterns that were indistinguishable.

Step 2. Define a Case

Investigators defined a case as follows:

Clinical Criteria

- Diarrhea (at least three loose stools in a 24-hour period) or abdominal cramps *and*
- A stool culture yielding *E. coli* O157:H7 with the same PFGE pattern as other isolates tested in the suspected outbreak

(continues)

Case Study: Determining Whether an Increase in Cases Represents an Outbreak (*continued*)

Restrictions on Person, Place, and Time

- Resident of Michigan *and*
- Onset of symptoms from June 15 to July 31, 1997

Step 3. Identify and Count Cases

Given that the case definition requires laboratory confirmation with PFGE subtyping, the best source for finding cases that meet the case definition was the state laboratory where PFGE subtyping was performed. Based on MDCH laboratories reports, 38 patients met the case definition for *E. coli* O157:H7 infection for this investigation.

Step 4. Compare Observed with Expected Cases

The PGFE pattern associated with the cases did not match any isolates from patients with *E. coli* O157:H7 infection diagnosed prior to May 1997 and only a few were identified in May. Therefore, the number of cases (38) identified in June and July of 1997 was larger than expected.

Step 5. Rule Out Other Reasons for an Increase in Cases

The initiation of new testing by a laboratory, laboratory error in identification, contamination of cultures, changes in reporting procedures, and increased interest in reporting are all potential reasons for an "artificial" increase in cases. Laboratories in Michigan have been doing testing for *E. coli* O157:H7 since the early 1990s, so initiation of new testing seemed an unlikely reason for the increase. The diagnosis was confirmed by the state laboratory, so an error in identification seemed equally unlikely. The isolates came from several different clinical laboratories, so it was fairly certain that contamination of cultures was not a problem. *E. coli* O157:H7 infection had been added to the list of notifiable diseases in Michigan in 1993, reporting procedures had not changed since 1993, and no recent training efforts or media events had occurred that might have increased interest in reporting, so changes in reporting procedures were also unlikely to explain the increase in cases.

　　Having followed all five steps carefully, a competent investigation team was likely to determine that the increase in cases of *E. coli* O157:H7 infection in Michigan in June 1997 represented an outbreak.

Source: Breuer T, Benkel DH, Shapiro RL, et al. A multistate outbreak of *Escherichia coli* O157:H7 infections linked to alfalfa sprouts grown from contaminated seeds. *Emerg Infect Dis*. 2001;7:977–82.

Summary

Accurate identification of an outbreak is critical, as delaying the investigation and control of a true outbreak could result in increased morbidity and mortality in the community. Likewise, extensive investigation of a false outbreak could result in a waste of time and money. By following the five steps of detecting an outbreak—verifying the diagnosis, defining a case, identifying and counting cases, comparing observed and expected cases, and ruling out other reasons for an increase in cases—investigators should be able to correctly decide whether an increase in cases represents an outbreak. Investigators can then choose the proper course of action, which may mean undertaking a full-fledged epidemiologic investigation and, possibly, environmental and laboratory-based studies as well.

References

1. Last, JM, ed. *A Dictionary of Epidemiology*. 3rd ed. New York, NY: Oxford University Press; 1995.
2. EXCITE! How to Investigate an Outbreak: Steps of an Outbreak Investigation. Updated October 2008. Centers for Disease Control and Prevention website: http://www.cdc.gov/excite/. Accessed May 24, 2010.
3. Tauxe RV, Hassan LF, Findeisen KO, et al. Salmonellosis in nurses: Lack of transmission to patients. *J Infect Dis*. 1988;157(2):370-3.
4. Centers for Disease Control and Prevention. Epidemiologic notes and reports eosinophilia-myalgia syndrome—New Mexico. *Morb Mortal Weekly Rep*. 1989;38(45):765-7.
5. Maillard J-M, Fischer M, McKee KT Jr, et al. First case of bioterrorism-related inhalational anthrax, Florida, 2001: North Carolina investigation. *Emerg Infect Dis*. 2002;8(10):1035-8. http://www.cdc.gov/ncidod/EID/vol8no10/02-0389.htm. Accessed May 24, 2010.
6. Dwyer DM, Groves C. Outbreak epidemiology. In: Nelson KE, Masters Williams C, Graham NMH, eds. *Infectious Disease Epidemiology: Theory and Practice*. Gaithersburg, MD: Aspen, 2001:119-48.
7. McElroy PD, Southwick KL, Fortenberry ER, et al. Outbreak of tuberculosis among homeless persons coinfected with human immunodeficiency Virus. *Clin Infect Dis*. 2003;36:1305-12.
8. Centers for Disease Control and Prevention. Summary of notifiable diseases—United States, 2001. *Morb Mortal Weekly Rep*. 2003;50(53):100-8.
9. *Salmonella* in the Caribbean (CB1117). Updated April 2008. Centers for Disease Control and Prevention website: http://www.cdc.gov/epicasestudies/computer_salmonella.html. Accessed May 13, 2011.
10. Death Data. Updated 2009. Washington State Department of Health Center for Health Statistics website: http://www.doh.wa.gov/EHSPHL/CHS/chs-data/death/dea_VD.htm. Accessed May 24, 2010.
11. Centers for Disease Control and Prevention. Epidemiologic notes and reports pseudo-outbreak of intestinal amebiasis—California. *Morb Mortal Weekly Rep*. 1985;34(9):125-6.
12. Spala G, Panagiotopoulos T, Mavroidi N, et al. A pseudo-outbreak of human A/H5N1 infections in Greece and its public health implications. *Euro Surveill*. 2006;11(11):658. http://www.eurosurveillance.org/ViewArticle.aspx?ArticleId=658. Accessed May 24, 2010.

13. Boss, LP. Epidemic hysteria: A review of the published literature. *Epidemiol Rev.* 1997; 19(2):233–43.

14. Cassady JD, Kirschke DL, Jones TF, et al. Case series: Outbreak of conversion disorder among Amish adolescent girls. *J Am Acad Child Adolesc Psychiatry.* 2005;44(3):291–7.

15. Jones TF, Craig AS, Hoy D, et al. Mass psychogenic illness attributed to toxic exposure at a high school. *N Engl J Med.* 2000;342(2):96–100.

16. Struewing JP, Gray GC. An epidemic of respiratory complaints exacerbated by mass psychogenic illness in a military recruit population. *Am J Epidemiol.* 1990;132(6):1120–9.

Chapter 5

Assembling and Equipping an Outbreak Investigation Team

Pia D. M. MacDonald
Andrew C. Voetsch

Learning Objectives
By the end of this chapter, the reader will be able to:

- Identify the potential members of an interdisciplinary outbreak investigation team.
- List the equipment and resources that an investigation team may require.
- Describe strategies for effective communication during an outbreak investigation.
- Identify potential collaborators in outbreak investigations and cite examples of collaboration during investigations.

Introduction

Once an outbreak has been confirmed and planning for the investigation is under way, the health department will select an investigation team leader. The team leader's duties will vary with the type, size, complexity, and severity of the outbreak. Typically, however, they include assembling the outbreak investigation team, making sure it has adequate resources, managing the investigation from start to finish, and reaching out to experts, other agencies, and the public as required. The ideal team leader combines public health expertise with communications and management skills. The team leader works quickly, efficiently, and collaboratively, and—perhaps most importantly—maintains his or her composure under pressure.

Successful outbreak investigations require a multidisciplinary approach with effective communication and collaboration. Like the team leader, the members of the investigation team must bring specific skills to the investigation. They must be flexible team players who are able to change course based on the evidence and who work well under tight deadlines. They must also work with a sense of urgency because people's lives may be at stake.

This chapter discusses the types of investigators who might become involved in an outbreak investigation, the roles they might play, and the equipment they typically need to carry out a successful investigation. It also considers the importance of communication and collaboration in outbreak investigations, concluding with an example of the many agencies that might take part in a foodborne disease outbreak investigation. In most states and many counties, outbreak response teams are using the Incident Command System (ICS) to coordinate their response to outbreaks; ICS is covered in detail in Chapter 16.

The Members of the Outbreak Investigation Team

Depending on the type of investigation and the available resources, an outbreak investigation team may include any or all of the members described in this section.

The *team leader* is responsible for assembling the team, presenting available information, outlining the plan for investigation, and assigning roles and responsibilities to the team members early in the investigation. This person is also responsible for communicating within his or her agency as well as with other agencies. The team leader should have experience in outbreak investigation and public health epidemiology. The outbreak setting or the microorganism that caused the outbreak may help determine who is best suited for the job. For example, a foodborne outbreak in a hospital cafeteria could be led by infection control personnel in the hospital, while an outbreak at a wedding reception would likely be the responsibility of the local health department. Depending on the size and organization of the health department, the team leader may be the local health director, a physician, a public health nurse, an epidemiologist, or an environmental health specialist.

Epidemiologists have expertise in various aspects of outbreak investigation, from designing studies and developing questionnaires to creating databases and conducting data analysis.

Clinicians—that is, health professionals who work with patients—are also important members of the outbreak team. During an outbreak of hepatitis A, for example, clinicians are needed to administer immunoglobulin or vaccine to people who have come into contact with infected individuals. Clinicians may also help collect clinical specimens from case patients, conduct interviews, and review patient charts. They may come to the team from the health department or the local medical community.[1]

Veterinarians provide expertise in animal reservoirs or vectors during zoonotic outbreaks in which disease is transmitted from animals to humans.

Microbiologists—usually at a local, state, or regional public health laboratory—can verify the diagnosis and classify pathogens to help refine a case definition. In a foodborne illness outbreak, for example, a microbiologist might test bacterial pathogens such as *Salmonella* or *Listeria monocytogenes*, compare the results to determine whether cases are related to the outbreak, and share them via national databases to learn whether the outbreak is widespread.[2]

Environmental health specialists or *sanitarians* help prevent foodborne outbreaks by inspecting food preparation facilities, providing health education, and training employees who handle food. Once an outbreak occurs, sanitarians are able to identify food safety issues that may have contributed to it, such as time and temperature violations in a food service establishment, and can make sure food and environmental samples are collected properly. Environmental health specialists may also help investigate disease outbreaks related to water contamination, chemical and radiological contamination, and airborne pathogens.

Interviewers will collect data, either in person or by telephone, during an analytic study. Interviewers can come from the ranks of health department personnel, including nurses and clerical support staff; personnel at some state agencies may already be trained to conduct telephone surveys.[3] In large outbreaks, state or federal personnel or students in medicine or public health may be recruited to conduct interviews. To have the best chance of getting honest answers, investigators in some cases may seek interviewers who are similar to the respondents in terms of age, gender, or race.[4] Regardless of the interviewers' professional backgrounds, they need to be trained in interviewing techniques and be familiar with the specific survey instrument.

Regulators from state or federal agencies may be included on the outbreak team to help facilitate identification of the source of contaminated food items and develop prevention strategies through enforcement of food safety regulations.

One team member should act as the *communications person* to make certain that the community receives clear and consistent messages about the health issues at stake. The communications person helps write news releases, manages media contacts, and may work on prevention activities related to the outbreak. Prompt, clear, effective communications are especially important if the outbreak is ongoing or if a suspected bioterrorism incident or other event has elevated public anxiety. In addition, the team should identify early on the person who will write a comprehensive outbreak investigation report.

Other personnel may not be included on the investigation team but may play critical roles in the investigation. Administrative staff may fulfill a number of support functions, for example, and legal counsel may be needed to prepare public health orders.

Equipping an Outbreak Investigation Team

The outbreak investigation team must be properly equipped. Depending on the type of investigation, the team may need specialized equipment, software, and Internet access to help them collect specimens, conduct environmental sampling, gather and organize information, and document their activities. Following are some of the materials the team may require.

Collecting Specimens and Samples

Many investigations require basic equipment for specimen collection, including rectal swabs or specimen cups to collect specimens, phlebotomy equipment for collecting blood samples, and a cooler to transport specimens. If the investigation requires environmental sampling, the required equipment might include the following items:

- Sterile sample containers
- Sterile and wrapped sample-collection implements
- Sterilizing and sanitizing agents
- Ice packs, thermometer, and insulated containers
- Labeling and sealing equipment
- Forms, such as sample collection and blank laboratory submission forms and chain-of-custody forms
- Disposable plastic gloves, hair restraints, laboratory coats, and other specialized clothing
- Personal protective equipment such as gloves and masks[5]

Before heading into the field, it is important to inform the laboratory that samples will be coming. It is also critical to ask for the laboratory's suggested methods for collecting, storing, and transporting samples.

Line Listings, Epidemic Curves, and Literature Searches

Software packages, including Microsoft Excel and Epi Info, can help investigators assemble line listings and create epidemic curves. Resources available on the Internet—the Centers for Disease Control and Prevention's (CDC's) *Morbidity and Mortality Weekly Report*, PubMed, Ovid, Lonesome Doc, and ProMED are a few—can facilitate literature searches that otherwise might require a trip to a health sciences library. (We explore many of these resources in Chapter 6.)

Documentation

The outbreak investigation team should not leave home without the proper documents. These items may include forms that can assist with pathogen identification, such as checklists for risk factors, clinical signs and symptoms, and epidemiology; templates that investigators can modify as needed for data collection; and administrative documentation. A few pertinent materials are noted here and shown in Figure 5-1 (and more can be found at http://www.cdc.gov/outbreaknet/references_resources/):

- Proof of employment with the health department
- Guides and materials (such as this book) about conducting an investigation
- Case reporting forms
- Summary case count forms
- Standard questionnaires for cases, contacts, and physician/healthcare workers (described in more detail in Chapters 6 and 7); some standard examples are available from the CDC (http://www.cdc.gov/outbreaknet/)

Location of Investigation _____   Date _____

____ Proof of employment with health department

____ Guides and materials about conducting an investigation

____ National/international case reporting form

____ National/international summary case count form

____ Standard questionnaire for cases

____ Standard questionnaire for contacts

____ Standard questionnaire for physician/healthcare workers

____ Line listing form

____ Data collection form for environmental/home investigation

____ Clinical sample collection form

____ Animal sample collection form

____ Environmental sample collection form

____ Educational and informational material for general public (IEC)

____ Budget request/documentation forms for travel, lodging, PPE, or other expenses

____ Reference documents on avian influenza

____ List of contacts locally and at the regional/national/international level

Figure 5-1   Sample checklist of documents needed for avian influenza outbreak investigation

- Line listing form (described in Chapter 4)
- Data collection form for environmental or home investigation
- Clinical sample, animal sample, and environmental sample collection forms
- Budget request and documentation forms
- Reference documents on the disease or condition of interest
- List of contacts

Communication in Outbreak Investigations

Effective communications are essential to the success of an outbreak investigation. The team leader should be skilled at coordinating communications within an interdisciplinary investigation team, within the agency, between the team and other agencies, and—in many cases—with the public. All members of the team should make sure they bring cell phones or other means to communicate in the field.[5]

Regular meetings, telephone calls, or conference calls are critical to the effective functioning of the outbreak team. The team leader should make task checklists and assign specific roles and responsibilities to team members. The leader should receive regular updates from team members to measure progress in the investigation, and he or she should use this information, in turn, to provide feedback and direction. Documenting the team's activities as the investigation continues can keep all team members up to date on the response and make it easier to draft the final report.

To share or receive critical information from other collaborators, the team leader should establish a point of contact at each agency involved in the outbreak investigation. Regular discussion—through phone calls, e-mails, or conference calls, for example—can assure that the investigation team receives timely laboratory reports, results of environmental studies, notices of food recalls, and other information it needs to complete its work. By sharing information appropriately, the investigation team can also help federal, state, and local health agencies, law enforcement, and other entities do their part to help control outbreaks.

In recent years, as the response to the severe acute respiratory syndrome (SARS) and other outbreaks have made clear, the Internet has become an important tool for sharing information about infectious and other disease diagnosis, treatment, and control.[6] Unfortunately, the Internet spreads rumor and misinformation as rapidly and widely as accurate and useful materials, so investigators should use the web with caution. Respected and well-sourced locations such as the CDC's and U.S. Food and Drug Administration's (FDA's) websites are generally good sources of accurate information. One effort to winnow reliable information from a vast sea of data is the World Health Organization's (WHO) outbreak verification system. WHO collects, collates, analyzes, and interprets data from this global network of formal and informal sources so that it can provide timely, accurate information about important disease outbreaks to those who need the information for action.[7,8]

Outbreak investigations do not always come to the attention of the media and the public, but investigators often have to field media requests and address public concerns. As an investigation is initiated and progresses, the investigation team should consider how to share information with public officials, the media, the general public, and the specific population affected by the outbreak. Members of the media can sometimes get the story wrong, but they can also be powerful allies, providing the public with important information about an investigation and disseminating timely information, such as consumer product recalls.[9] Media coverage of an outbreak can also be a good way to identify new cases. For public health officials, it is useful to maintain relationships with some local reporters. Establishing rapport with the media before a crisis develops can position public health practitioners to deliver timely and accurate stories to the public. As the team develops a communications plan to meet the demands of the investigation, the designated communications person should transmit a consistent message with correct information to the public and other constituencies.

Efficient use of information technology and social networks can make critical information available to the public almost instantaneously when the public health system mobilizes to limit the size of an outbreak. When more than 500 people in 43 states and Canada became ill in 2008–2009 after eating peanut products contaminated by *Salmonella typhimurium*, for example, the U.S. Department of Health and Human Services, the FDA, the CDC, and state and local health agencies mobilized quickly to provide consumers, healthcare providers, retailers, directors of institutions and food service establishments, and manufacturers with information that could help keep contaminated products off store shelves and out of consumers' pantries. The information the agencies compiled included a searchable database of peanut products that were included in widespread recalls, updates on the investigation, consumer advice, and other information. The information delivery systems included websites, 24/7 hotlines, and a host of social media tools, including blogs, Twitter posts, podcasts, RSS feeds, and social networking sites. An information technology tool called content syndication allowed CDC partners to display CDC health and safety information on their own websites. Interagency cooperation and robust information technology made it possible to disseminate information as soon as it became available, thereby enabling people to avoid buying or using products that might make them ill.[10,11]

In countries without widespread Internet access, older forms of technology can help outbreak investigation teams prevent further illness and death. When the Ugandan government asked for help investigating an outbreak of Ebola hemorrhagic fever in December 2007, for example, the CDC assembled a team that included 6 epidemiologists, 3 laboratory scientists, and a communications specialist. With 134 cases and 34 deaths already reported, public education was a critical priority of the communications effort. The CDC supported a social mobilization effort that included playing educational messages on local radio stations as many as 24 times per day in 3 languages.[12]

When an outbreak is caused by a new pathogen, attentive patients who use the Internet wisely may trigger bottom-up health communications efforts that lead to the detection and treatment of cases that might otherwise go unnoticed. In the spring of 1997, for example, California experienced eight outbreaks of diarrhea caused by *Cyclospora cayetanensis*, a coccidian parasite that was identified in 1993 but was not yet on the state's registry of notifiable diseases. When 30 of the 46 guests at a wedding reception who ate the mixed-berry dessert developed persistent diarrhea, several of the people who became ill read media accounts of a *Cyclospora* outbreak in Reno, Nevada; recognized the symptoms as similar to their own; and sought more information from the CDC website. Only after they took the information to their healthcare providers were the patients tested for *Cyclospora* and given appropriate treatment.[13]

Public health authorities may saturate a community with information in multiple formats to keep a localized outbreak from becoming widespread. When eight cases of malaria were diagnosed in Florida in 2003, for example, officials used the local community notification system to make reverse-911 calls to approximately 300,000 residents; distributed insect repellent, postcards, flyers, and posters in multiple languages; made public announcements through the media and to homeless shelters and schools; and notified local hospitals and physicians. Although nearly all cases of malaria diagnosed in the

United States are imported from other countries where the disease is endemic, a limited number of cases are also acquired through local mosquito-borne transmission. Prompt action, including intensive communications with the community, helps keep malaria from being reintroduced to the United States.[14]

If the outbreak investigation involves ethnic or religious minority groups, the communications plan must take into account cultural and religious differences. When an investigation linked a multistate outbreak of shigellosis in late 1986 and early 1987 to tradition-observant Jews belonging to several religious sects, for example, public health officials in New York City worked with community and religious leaders and physicians in Brooklyn to encourage improved sanitation and personal hygiene in schools and homes. Officials focused their efforts on encouraging hand washing with soap and water. They instituted control measures in late March 1987, in anticipation that a large number of people would visit religious communities to celebrate the Passover holiday during the third week of April. The implementation of hygienic controls resulted in a decrease in culture-confirmed cases of shigellosis, although cases continued to be reported above the expected background rates among the religious groups in Brooklyn.[15]

Collaboration in Outbreak Investigations

The effectiveness of an outbreak investigation team depends on people from many fields working together—public health specialists, laboratory workers, regulators, and other members of an interdisciplinary team can all make valuable contributions to the response. A small outbreak might be handled by one or two people in a single health department, whereas a more extensive occurrence could involve hundreds of people at multiple agencies. Whether the outbreak investigation team numbers one or many, the team leader must be able to identify, recruit, and work with the appropriate contact persons at whatever local, state, or federal agencies that can help.

Many factors—including the nature of the outbreak; the type of pathogen involved; the number and location of affected persons; and local and state rules about food safety, contact tracing, or quarantine—help determine the types of agencies that need to collaborate during an outbreak investigation.[5] Foodborne disease outbreaks, for example, often affect multiple jurisdictions. As a consequence, managing these outbreaks effectively may require coordination and cooperation among local, state, and federal public health agencies and other government agencies, such as the FDA.[16]

Unusual outbreak situations may call for collaboration with experts from outside public health. For example, when public health investigators in California associated ongoing cases of wound botulism with subcutaneous or intramuscular injection of "black tar" heroin, they called on the California Department of Alcohol and Drug Programs and drug enforcement officials with expertise in the drug subculture.[17] In cases where criminal activity is suspected or the public's safety is threatened, such as the intentional releases of anthrax in 2001, public health and law enforcement investigators from local, state, and federal agencies may need to work together. These partnerships may prove challenging, however.

The CDC and the Federal Bureau of Investigation (FBI) bring unique perspectives that add value to bioterrorism investigations, but the vastly different goals of epidemiologic and law enforcement studies require mutual understanding.[18] (Partnerships between public health and law enforcement are discussed in more detail in Chapter 14.)

Investigators in foodborne disease outbreaks may work closely with social services agencies, laboratory workers, nongovernmental organizations that serve ethnic populations, non-English-language media outlets, churches, football (soccer) leagues, environmental health experts, veterinarians, local businesses that serve ethnic shoppers, and disadvantaged or hard-to-reach segments of the population. When the Forsyth County Department of Public Health in North Carolina investigated an outbreak of listeriosis among Hispanic women in 2000–2001, for example, investigators collaborated with the county's Women, Infant, and Children (WIC) office and the state prenatal care program (Baby Love) to identify controls for a case-control study; with environmental health specialists to arrange inspections of case patients' homes, local markets, and dairy farms to identify possible sources of contamination and potential intervention strategies; and with laboratories to test milk and cheese samples for the *Listeria monocytogenes* bacterium that had the same molecular subtype (PFGE) patterns as the case patients' isolates. By the time of its conclusion, the investigation involved the North Carolina Division of Public Health, the North Carolina Departments of Agriculture and Consumer Services and Environment and Natural Resources, the FDA, the CDC, and veterinarians from North Carolina State University.[19]

When a foodborne disease outbreak crosses state lines, the investigation may involve food distributors and restaurant and grocery store chains as well as state and federal departments of health and agriculture. In 2008, epidemiological studies and molecular fingerprinting initially linked 49 cases of *Escherichia coli* O157:H7 infection in seven states to the same outbreak. The CDC and public health agencies across the country conducted surveillance activities to identify additional cases, while CDC and state laboratories, with the help of the CDC's PulseNet national molecular subtyping network, used advanced molecular testing to help determine the extent of the outbreak. State health and agriculture departments tested beef purchased at Kroger grocery stores and recovered from a restaurant in Georgia where several ill patients reported eating. When the CDC's OutbreakNet Team conducted a multistate case-control study in collaboration with health authorities in Ohio and Michigan, they found a significant association between illness and eating ground beef purchased at Kroger stores in those two states. Kroger announced recalls of ground beef, and Nebraska Beef recalled 5.3 million pounds of beef manufacturing trimmings and other products. The U.S. Department of Agriculture's Food Safety and Inspection Service (FSIS) posted information about the recalls on its website and provided e-mail and hotline services for consumers with food safety questions. Information about safe ways to prepare and handle ground beef was also made available on the FSIS and CDC websites.[20]

When infectious disease outbreaks cross international borders, government agencies, multilateral agencies, and nongovernmental agencies may work together to prevent further transmission and to provide high-quality diagnosis and treatment consistent with international standards of care. In January 2005, an outbreak of tuberculosis (TB), including multidrug-resistant TB, was detected among Hmong refugees from Laos who were living in or had recently immigrated to the United States from a camp in Thailand. The CDC collaborated with international partners to investigate the factors that led to the emergence and dissemination of TB among these refugees. The agency developed enhanced screening and treatment guidelines for Hmong refugees and worked with the U.S. Department of State, panel physicians, the International Organization for Migration, and other organizations to develop similar enhancements to general pre-immigration TB screening guidelines. Finally, the CDC contacted state and local health departments in areas where refugees had been resettled.[21]

If an epidemiological investigation rules out inadvertent contamination as the cause of an outbreak, law enforcement officials may join the investigation. In 1984, 751 people became ill with *Salmonella* gastroenteritis in a community in Oregon. Epidemiologic studies involving county, state, and federal public health agencies linked the illness to salad bars at 10 area restaurants, but failed to find a common source of contamination. Investigators initially ruled out criminal activity, but members of a local commune came forward to claim that the contamination was the test run of a plot to make voters ill and affect the outcome of local elections. (The forensic epidemiology investigation of this case is explored in Chapter 14.) Oregon state law enforcement officials and the FBI became involved, and further testing demonstrated that vials of *S. typhimurium* found at a commune laboratory matched the strain that caused the infections.[22]

Agency Roles in Foodborne Disease Outbreak Investigations

As the preceding examples demonstrate, many agencies can become involved if a disease outbreak is large or crosses state lines. The following excerpt from a Council to Improve Foodborne Outbreak Response (CIFOR) publication, *Guidelines for Foodborne Disease Outbreak Response*, details the roles and responsibilities of the many agencies that may become involved in a foodborne disease outbreak. Although CIFOR focuses exclusively on foodborne diseases, the number of players and their roles can be equally large and complex in other outbreak investigations.

3.1.1 Overview

A foodborne disease outbreak may be managed solely by a single local agency or may become the shared responsibility of multiple local, state, and federal agencies. The nature of the outbreak, including the type of pathogen, the suspected or implicated vehicle, the number and location of affected persons, the geographic jurisdictions involved and the local and state food-safety rules and laws will determine the types of agencies that need to be involved. Outbreak response will also be influenced by agencies' roles and responsibilities and typically available resources. Each agency's response plan should include its likely role in a foodborne disease outbreak investigation, staff (or positions) that may be involved, contact information for relevant external agencies, and communication and escalation procedures for working with those agencies.

Agency Roles in Foodborne Disease Outbreak Investigations (*continued*)

3.1.2 Local, State, and Federal Agencies

Across the country, state and local agencies differ widely in their organizational structure, responsibilities, and relationships. The sections below summarize typical responsibilities for agencies at the local and state levels. However, assignment of those responsibilities will vary depending on a particular state's organizational, legal, and regulatory structure; the distribution of responsibilities across different types of state and local agencies; and the size and capacity of the local agencies.

3.1.2.1 Local Health Agencies

Roles and Responsibilities

Conduct surveillance; receive complaints about potential foodborne diseases; maintain and routinely review log of complaints; routinely communicate with local health-care professionals; regulate food-service operations; routinely inspect food-service operations; investigate complaints; implement control measures to stop outbreaks; educate food workers on preventing outbreaks of foodborne disease; inform the public and the media; serve as liaison with local industry representatives and with the state and federal public health and food-safety regulatory agencies. May also provide advanced laboratory testing, including subtyping, such as molecular fingerprinting in PulseNet.

Resources

Vary by agency but may include expertise in epidemiologic and environmental outbreak investigation and response; and health information and promotion information for dissemination to the public. Extensive knowledge of local populations and community businesses, health-care providers and organizations, and other resources.

Contribution to Outbreak Investigation and Response

Detect foodborne diseases; identify local outbreaks; know about suspected facilities (e.g., facility inspection reports, previous complaints); support recall efforts; know affected communities; know local health-care professionals and diagnostic practices.

3.1.2.2 State Agencies: Health Department

Roles and Responsibilities

Conduct surveillance; identify local and statewide outbreaks; coordinate multijurisdictional outbreaks; provide advanced laboratory testing, including molecular fingerprinting in PulseNet; support or direct environmental, laboratory, and epidemiologic investigations with advanced expertise; provide health education and promotion materials; maintain tools for collecting and analyzing outbreak-associated information; provide public information; provide legal support for outbreak investigation and control; promote statewide policies to increase food safety; serve as liaison and coordinate communication with other state, local, and federal agencies; disseminate information to local agencies. May conduct investigations in local areas where there is no local health agency with jurisdiction.

(continues)

Agency Roles in Foodborne Disease Outbreak Investigations (*continued*)

Resources

Expertise in epidemiologic and environmental outbreak investigation and response (including traceback investigations); expertise in specific disease agents; advanced laboratory testing with expertise in microbial analyses and identification through their state laboratories; tools for collecting and analyzing outbreak-associated information; health information and promotion information (often in multiple languages) for dissemination to the public; additional staff to aid in outbreak investigations.

Contribution to Outbreak Investigation and Response

Epidemiologic, environmental, and laboratory support for local health agencies; coordination of multijurisdictional outbreaks.

3.1.2.3 State Agencies: Environmental Conservation or Quality

Note: These roles may be carried out by agencies with different names, including environmental health.

Roles and Responsibilities

Support or direct environmental testing; provide advanced laboratory testing of food or environmental samples; provide educational materials and public information about environmental and food safety; maintain tools for collecting and analyzing outbreak-associated information; promote statewide policies to increase food and environmental safety; serve as liaison with other state, local, and federal agencies; disseminate information to local agencies.

Resources

Expertise in environmental and food-safety investigation and response; advanced laboratory testing with expertise in microbial analyses and identification; additional staff to aid in outbreak investigations.

Contribution to Outbreak Investigation and Response

Environmental investigation and laboratory support for local health agencies.

3.1.2.4 State Agencies: Food-Safety Regulatory Authorities

Note: These roles may be carried out by agencies with different names, including Department of Agriculture, Food Protection, or Environmental Health.

Roles and Responsibilities

Ensure good manufacturing practices in commercial food operations; test dairy, meat, and food products for microbial contamination; inspect plant after an outbreak; coordinate food recalls carried out by industry; and stop sales of adulterated product within their jurisdiction. Conduct regulatory sanitation inspections at retail establishments such as grocery stores, supermarkets, and warehouses. Consult with health departments in outbreak investigations (e.g., with knowledge of food production and distribution and information provided by industry that may contribute

Agency Roles in Foodborne Disease Outbreak Investigations (*continued*)

to the success of the investigations) and to direct plant inspections by thoroughly understanding the epidemiologic, environmental, and laboratory data.

Resources

Expertise in food manufacturing and distribution; staff to conduct plant inspections and specialized testing of dairy, meat, and food products; expertise in regulatory tracebacks. Laboratory support, usually involving surveillance for food adulterants, including chemical, physical, and microbiologic adulterants and contaminants.

Contribution to Outbreak Investigation and Response

Support investigations that involve commercially distributed food products through consultation with health department investigators, plant inspections, traceback investigations, and food recalls.

3.1.2.5 Federal Agencies: Centers for Disease Control and Prevention

Roles and Responsibilities

Conducts or coordinates national surveillance for illnesses caused by pathogens commonly transmitted through food and for outbreaks of foodborne diseases of any cause; leads and supports the national surveillance networks, Public Health Laboratory Information System (PHLIS), Foodnet, PulseNet, EHS-Net, and CDC's electronic Foodborne Outbreak Reporting System (eFORS); maintains clinical, epidemiologic, and laboratory expertise in pathogens of public health importance; develops and implements better tools for public health surveillance; provides consultation, assistance, and leadership in outbreak investigations; improves and standardizes laboratory testing methods for foodborne disease organisms; provides advanced laboratory testing; facilitates coordination among jurisdictions within multijurisdictional outbreaks where appropriate; coordinates communication with other federal agencies; provides training in methods; coordinates and collaborates with international surveillance, communication, and training methods; regulates ships that travel to international ports.

Resources

Experts (or trainees) in clinical, epidemiologic, and environmental health aspects to assist with cluster evaluation and outbreak investigations; advanced laboratory capacity (including resources to develop new testing methodologies); surge capacity to assist in large outbreaks; tools for collecting and analyzing outbreak-associated information; training programs; educational materials for the public.

Contribution to Outbreak Investigation and Response

Assistance in single-jurisdiction outbreaks upon request of the jurisdiction; leadership, coordination, and logistics support and coordination for multijurisdictional outbreaks; centralized data collection and analysis for large multistate outbreaks; assistance in outbreaks from new or rare disease agents or from new modes of transmission of known disease agents; advanced laboratory testing; availability of additional personnel and other resources to aid local and state health agencies; conduit to other federal agencies.

(*continues*)

Agency Roles in Foodborne Disease Outbreak Investigations (*continued*)

3.1.2.6 Federal Agencies: Food and Drug Administration

Roles and Responsibilities

Regulates the safety of most foods (except meat, poultry, and pasteurized egg products, which are regulated by USDA's Food Safety and Inspection Service [FSIS]); regulates food additives and food labeling for FDA-regulated foods; oversees seafood and juice regulations for Hazard Analysis and Critical Control Point; oversees imported food products under FDA jurisdiction; conducts research into foodborne contaminants; inspects food-processing plants; conducts food industry postmarket surveillance and compliance; oversees regulatory traceback investigations and recalls of the food products it regulates; publishes the Food Code; regulates ships that travel interstate such as on rivers and intercoastal waters and trains and buses that travel interstate.

Resources

Twenty district offices located in five regions, providing coordination, field investigators, laboratory support, technical consultation, regulatory support, and media relations; policy, technical, and scientific support to foodborne disease outbreak investigations provided by FDA's Center for Food Safety and Applied Nutrition (CFSAN); education materials for the public.

Contribution to Outbreak Investigation and Response

Once an FDA-regulated product is strongly suspected as the cause of an outbreak, identification of product source and extent of its distribution; testing of product obtained from commerce or production; traceback and factory investigations; prevention of further exposure to contaminated product; and initiation of regulatory action, including requesting recalls if indicated; assistance to the Federal Bureau of Investigation (FBI) when deliberate contamination of food is suspected by providing technical, investigatory, and laboratory support for FDA-regulated products.

3.1.2.7 Federal Agencies: U.S. Department of Agriculture, Food Safety and Inspection Service

Roles and Responsibilities

Ensures the nation's commercial supply of meat, poultry, and pasteurized egg products is safe, wholesome, and correctly labeled and packaged through a national program of inspection, investigation, and enforcement; provides data analysis, advice, and recommendations on food safety; conducts microbiologic testing of meat and poultry products; responds to foodborne illnesses, intentional food contamination, and major threats to FSIS-regulated products, including overseeing recalls for contaminated meat and poultry products; conducts audits to determine the equivalency of foreign food-safety systems and re-inspecting imported meat, poultry, and egg products; develops public information and education programs for consumers.

Agency Roles in Foodborne Disease Outbreak Investigations (*continued*)

Resources

Approximately 7,600 inspection program personnel in more than 6,000 federally regulated establishments nationwide coordinated by 15 district offices; three field laboratories, including the Outbreaks Section of Eastern Laboratory in Athens, Georgia; field investigators with expertise in inspection, traceback, and enforcement; personnel with expertise in food-safety science; educational materials and guidance for consumers.

Contribution to Outbreak Investigation and Response

Assistance, traceback coordination, and epidemiologic consultation during investigations involving FSIS-regulated meat, poultry, and egg products; testing of product from commerce or production; ability to take enforcement and regulatory control actions against food manufacturers and distributors; assistance in working with international food manufacturers and distributors; consultation to public health and state agriculture agencies.

3.1.3 Other Agencies

Outbreaks can occur in facilities or communities managed by agencies that have some level of autonomy and operate their own public health programs. Such agencies include tribes, the military, and the U.S. Department of the Interior (National Park Service [NPS]). Local, state, and federal public health agencies need to understand the jurisdictional issues involved in outbreaks in these settings, these groups' resources, and establishment of relationships with them.

Outbreaks also can be associated with intentional contamination. If that is suspected, the FBI has a role in the investigation.

3.1.3.1 Tribes

Jurisdiction

Varies by tribal organization, but in general the tribes have complete sovereignty and are completely autonomous. Investigations may be conducted by tribal health staff, Indian Health Services (IHS) staff, or state or local health departments, but nontribal entities can become involved in an investigation only at the tribe's request. No legal requirement exists for reporting a foodborne disease outbreak to any public health officials. Control measures typically are implemented by IHS staff in cooperation with tribal government but can be implemented only when authorized by tribal government.

Relationships

Outbreaks may be detected by IHS staff or by tribal members and reported to IHS. IHS notifies the appropriate state and local health departments. Some tribes also may notify the local or state health department or CDC. State and local health department staff need to develop relationships with IHS public health staff, tribal health staff (if any), and tribal leadership in tribal areas within or adjacent to the public health agency's jurisdiction. During an outbreak,

(*continues*)

Agency Roles in Foodborne Disease Outbreak Investigations (*continued*)

communication should be ongoing not only between state or local health department and IHS but also directly with tribal government. IHS has developed tribal epidemiology centers to provide regional epidemiology capacity for multiple tribes. These centers are run by tribal boards and focus on health issues selected by the boards. They may become involved in outbreak investigations and are a good place to promote routine communication. IHS is a good source of information about coordinating public health issues with tribes.

Resources for Outbreak Investigation and Response

IHS has many public health staff, including sanitarians and public health nurses, at clinics on many tribal lands. These staff most likely would handle an outbreak and would request help from IHS, the state, or CDC if needed. Some tribes have public health staff, but most do not have public health laws or capacity to respond to outbreaks.

3.1.3.2 Military

Jurisdiction

Autonomous authority over all military bases, facilities (including food-production and food-service facilities and health-care service facilities), and vehicles. The particular branch of the military involved and the U.S. Department of Defense maintain public health responsibility.

Relationships

Military public health personnel communicate with local and state health agencies for outbreaks that might involve civilians. Local and state health agencies should establish communication with the public health staff of any military facilities within or adjacent to their jurisdiction before any outbreaks. Other branches of the military and other federal agencies communicate through the Foodborne Outbreak Response Coordinating Group.

Resources for Outbreak Investigation and Response

Military agencies conduct training in food safety and epidemiology; inspect and test food-production and food-processing facilities and delivered food products; and coordinate these programs with other military and federal agencies. Preventive Medicine and Environmental Health Officers in each branch direct and conduct epidemiologic investigations of foodborne disease outbreaks and make recommendations. Veterinary Officers conduct traceback investigations. The Department of Defense has officers trained in public health, environmental health, epidemiology, microbiology, toxicology, pathology, and food technology who can coordinate and support outbreak investigations.

3.1.3.3 National Park Service

Jurisdiction

Jurisdiction in National Parks is a function of the legislation designating the specific park. Three types of jurisdiction exist: (a) exclusive federal jurisdiction; (b) concurrent jurisdiction with state and local agencies; and (c) proprietary (owned by the federal government

Agency Roles in Foodborne Disease Outbreak Investigations (*continued*)

but sometimes operated by local entity and depending on support from local police, fire departments, and others for services).

Relationships

Notifies relevant local and state health departments of suspected outbreaks. Notifies the appropriate federal agency if a commercial product is suspected. Works closely with CDC. Relies on CDC or state health departments for laboratory testing. Local and state health agencies whose jurisdiction contains or is adjacent to a national park should establish communication with the NPS Office of Public Health before any outbreaks. Where appropriate, local and state health departments should include questions about visiting parks when they conduct interviews during an investigation and notify NPS if a park might be involved.

Resources for Outbreak Investigation and Response

Epidemiology expertise including a medical epidemiologist in the NPS Office of Public Health; U.S. Public Health Service staff assigned to NPS to conduct investigations (including regional public health consultants based around the country); park rangers who have extensive knowledge of their jurisdiction and the population that visits that jurisdiction; scientists in the NPS system with a wide range of expertise (e.g., veterinarians, water specialists); contractors who run park operations on behalf of NPS.

3.1.3.4 Other Federal Lands

Jurisdiction

NPS jurisdiction is described above. Public health jurisdiction on other types of federal land is not always easy to determine. On many federal lands (e.g., national forests, Bureau of Land Management land), state laws apply, but federal agencies may have overlapping jurisdiction. State laws generally do not apply to federal prisons. Each public health agency that contains federal lands within its jurisdiction should identify the responsible local, state, and federal agencies before an outbreak.

3.1.4 Industry: Food Manufacturers, Distributors, Retailers, and Trade Associations

Roles and Responsibilities

Growing, raising, processing, manufacturing, packaging, distributing, storing and selling food using practices that protect the public's health; withdrawing or recalling products from the market place when they have been identified as the source of a foodborne disease outbreak; communicating with the public about outbreaks associated with food products.

Resources

Knowledge of and information about product identities, formulations, processing practices, and distribution patterns to assist with outbreak hypothesis testing and product/ingredient tracing. Some industry members have expertise in microbiology and food-safety research.

(*continues*)

Summary

When an outbreak is confirmed, the health department selects an investigation team leader, who assembles an outbreak investigation team. The team for a simple outbreak investigation might include one or two members; more complex investigations may require a multidisciplinary team that includes epidemiologists, clinicians, microbiologists, environmental health specialists, and others. The type of investigation will dictate which resources the team requires—equipment to collect biological and environmental samples, case reporting forms and questionnaires, and epidemiological software packages may all be on the list. Communication is an essential component of the success of an investigation; a team leader must establish clear lines of communication among team members and between the team and other agencies. If the investigation team needs to communicate with public officials, the media, or the general public, a designated communications officer should deliver a consistent message with accurate information. The outbreak investigation team may work independently, or it may collaborate with state, local, and federal agencies; if criminal intent is suspected, local, state, or federal law enforcement agencies may become involved in the investigation.

References

1. France RM, Jahre JA. Policy for managing a community infectious disease outbreak. *Infect Control Hosp Epidemiol.* 1991;12(6):364–7.
2. Swaminathan B, Barrett TJ, Hunter SB, et al. PulseNet: The molecular subtyping network for foodborne bacterial disease surveillance, United States. *Emerg Infect Dis.* 2001;7(3):382–9.
3. Fox LM, Ocfemia MCB, Hunt DC, et al. Emergency survey methods in acute cryptosporidiosis outbreak. *Emerg Infect Dis.* 2005;11(5). http://www.cdc.gov/ncidod/EID/vol11no05/04-0871 .htm. Accessed June 2, 2010.
4. Gregg M. *Field Epidemiology.* 3rd ed. New York: Oxford University Press; 2008.

5. Council to Improve Foodborne Outbreak Response (CIFOR). *Guidelines for Foodborne Disease Outbreak Response.* Atlanta, GA: Council of State and Territorial Epidemiologists; 2009.

6. Drazen JM, Campion EW. SARS, the Internet, and the Journal. *N Engl J Med.* 2003;348 (20):2029.

7. Epidemic intelligence: Systematic event detection. World Health Organization website: http:// www.who.int/csr/alertresponse/epidemicintelligence/en/index.html. Accessed June 2, 2010.

8. Grein TW, Kamara K-BO, Rodier G, et al. Rumors of disease in the global village: Outbreak verification. *Emerg Infect Dis.* 2000;6(2). http://www.cdc.gov/ncidod/eid/vol6no2/grein.htm. Accessed June 2, 2010.

9. Reingold AL. Outbreak investigations—A perspective. *Emerg Infect Dis.* 1998;4(1). Updated February 23, 2010. http://www.cdc.gov/ncidod/eid/vol4no1/reingold.htm. Accessed June 2, 2010.

10. Investigation information for outbreak of *Salmonella typhimurium* infections, 2008–2009. Updated May 11, 2010. Centers for Disease Control and Prevention website: http://www.cdc .gov/salmonella/typhimurium/. Accessed June 2, 2010.

11. Centers for Disease Control and Prevention. Multistate outbreak of *Salmonella* infections associated with peanut butter and peanut butter–containing products—United States, 2008–2009. *Morb Mortal Weekly Rep.* 2009;58(Early Release):1-6.

12. No break in CDC outbreak investigations for the holidays. December 20, 2007. Centers for Disease Control and Prevention website: http://www.cdc.gov/news/2007/12/OutbreakInvestigation. html. Accessed June 2, 2010.

13. Mohle-Boetaini JC, Werner SB, Waterman SH, et al. The impact of health communication and enhanced laboratory-based surveillance on detection of cyclosporiasis outbreaks in California. *Emerg Infect Dis.* 2000;6(2). http://www.cdc.gov/ncidod/EID/vol6no2/mohle-boetani .htm. Accessed June 2, 2010.

14. Centers for Disease Control and Prevention. Locally acquired mosquito-transmitted malaria: A guide for investigations in the United States. *Morb Mortal Weekly Rep.* 2006;5(RR13):1-9.

15. Centers for Disease Control and Prevention. Multistate outbreak of *Shigella sonnei* gastroenteritis—United States. *Morb Mortal Weekly Rep.* 1987:36(27);448-9.

16. Sobel J, Griffin PM, Slutsker L, et al. Investigation of multistate foodborne disease outbreaks. *Public Health Rep* 2002;117(1):8-19.

17. Werner SB, Passaro D, McGee J, et al. Wound botulism in California, 1951-1998: Recent epidemic in heroin injectors. *Clin Infect Dis.* 2000;31(4):1018-24.

18. Butler JC, Cohen ML, Friedman CR, et al. Collaboration between public health and law enforcement: New paradigms and partnerships for bioterrorism planning and response. *Emerg Infect Dis.* 2002;8(10):1152-6.

19. Centers for Disease Control and Prevention. Outbreak of listeriosis associated with homemade Mexican-style cheese—North Carolina, October 2000–January 2001. *Morb Mortal Weekly Rep.* 2001;50(26):560-2.

20. Investigation of multistate outbreak of *E. coli* 0157:H7 infections. Updated July 18, 2008. Centers for Disease Control and Prevention website: http://www.cdc.gov/ecoli/june2008outbreak/. Accessed June 2, 2010.

21. Oeltmann JE, Varma JK, Ortega L, et al. Multidrug-resistant tuberculosis outbreak among US-bound Hmong refugees, Thailand, 2005. *Emerg Infect Dis.* 2008;14(10):1715-21.

22. Torok TJ, Tauxe RV, Wise RP, et al. A large community outbreak of salmonellosis caused by intentional contamination of restaurant salad bars. *JAMA.* 1997;278(5):389-95.

Chapter 6

Hypothesis Generation and Descriptive Epidemiology

Jeanette K. Stehr-Green
Paul A. Stehr-Green
Pia D. M. MacDonald

Learning Objectives

By the end of this chapter, the reader will be able to:

- List the three primary methods of hypothesis generation.
- Discuss how known information about a disease agent can be used to develop hypotheses about the source of an outbreak.
- List useful resources related to the epidemiology of infectious diseases.
- Describe the purpose of hypothesis-generating interviews.
- Identify areas of focus for hypothesis-generating interviews that are appropriate for the disease or condition under study.
- List the goals for interpreting hypothesis-generating interviews.
- Describe (and give examples) of the time, place, and person components of descriptive epidemiology.
- Review the steps for creating an epidemic curve.
- Given an epidemic curve and the incubation period for a disease, determine the likely period of exposure for a point-source outbreak.
- Describe the uses of a spot map.
- Explain measures of central tendency and attack rates.
- Compare and contrast descriptive and analytic epidemiology.

Introduction

Chapter 4 discussed the five steps that investigators should take to determine whether an outbreak is real. These steps focus on confirming that a particular disease is making a particular group of people ill in a particular place at a particular time; that the number of cases is greater than would otherwise be expected for that population in that time and place; and that no other factors, such as changes in reporting procedures, can explain the increase.

Once investigators are convinced that an outbreak is taking place, they then turn their attention to what is often the most difficult part of the investigation—locating its cause. Discovering what people ate, drank, inhaled, touched, or, in rare cases, imagined that made them ill allows investigators to take immediate steps to stop the outbreak (if it is still going on) and implement control measures to keep similar outbreaks from occurring in the future. The critical first step in this phase of the investigation is generating a hypothesis (or hypotheses)—in other words, developing an educated guess about the source of the outbreak.

To identify the sources or exposures that are most likely to have caused a disease or health problem, investigators will take the following steps:

1. Review known information and consider likely risk factors or exposures for the disease based on basic science and previous investigations

2. Carry out hypothesis-generating interviews to explore exposures and further identify commonalities among cases

3. Examine the descriptive epidemiology of the outbreak—the time, place, and person data—to characterize persons at risk and identify commonalities among cases

In this chapter, we examine these three methods of generating hypotheses about the source of a disease or health problem, beginning with the review of known information about the disease.

Review of Known Information on the Disease

Given the time pressures of most outbreak investigations, investigators may not think they have time to sit down with reference books or the Internet to help determine what is making people ill. This assumption may be erroneous: Reviewing the basic biology and epidemiology of a disease agent often helps identify potential sources of an outbreak early in an investigation. Investigators can supplement the information they gathered while determining the outbreak was real with readily available scientific and epidemiologic background materials to help them craft working hypotheses about its cause.

What Information Do Investigators Need to Gather?

As with other aspects of outbreak investigations, the information investigators need to gather will vary depending on the type of outbreak and the information they already have in hand. If, for example, investigators know that an outbreak of diarrhea is under way but do not know the organism that caused it, a literature review will show that *Cyclospora*, *Shigella*, *Salmonella*, norovirus, *Giardia*, and *Escherichia coli* O157:H7 are among the organisms that have been associated with past outbreaks of diarrhea. This information may help investigators narrow their list of possible etiologic agents and generate hypotheses about the source or mode of transmission.

If investigators have identified the causative agent, reviewing the microbiology, natural history, and ecological niche of the organism may also help guide the investigation. If the etiologic agent has been identified as *Blastomyces dermatitidis* (a fungus), for example, a literature review would reveal that past outbreaks have been associated with activities that occurred near recreational water, in nitrogen-rich soil.[1] This information may help identify potential exposure sites that are epidemiologically consistent with the current outbreak and are conducive to *B. dermatitidis* growth.

When investigators conduct literature searches or contact experts as part of the hypothesis-generating phase of an outbreak investigation, they typically look for all or some of the following information about the disease-causing agent:

- Reservoirs that harbor the agent
- The means by which the agent exits and enters the body
- The agent's mode(s) of transmission
- Any factors that increase resistance or susceptibility to the disease

The *reservoir* for an infectious or toxic agent is the "habitat" in which the agent normally lives and multiplies, on which it depends primarily for survival, and from which it can be transmitted to the target population. The reservoir may or may not be the source from which an agent is transferred directly to a host. An intermediary (or intermediaries), such as an insect vector or inanimate object—known as a "fomite"—may help the agent move from the reservoir to the host.

Reservoirs that harbor pathogens may include humans, animals, and the environment. Many common infectious diseases have human reservoirs, including sexually transmitted diseases, measles, mumps, streptococcal infection, and most respiratory pathogens. Infectious diseases that are transmissible under normal conditions from animals to humans (called zoonoses) include brucellosis (from cows and pigs), anthrax (from sheep), plague (from rodents), trichinosis (from swine and many wild animals), and rabies (from bats, raccoons, dogs, and other mammals). The environment, primarily soil and water, is also a reservoir for some infectious and toxic agents. For example, soil can be the source of arsenic and lead from smelting operations, and it can harbor fungal agents, such as those that cause histoplasmosis, which live and multiply in it. Pools of water, including those produced by cooling towers and evaporative condensers, have been identified as the primary source of the bacillus that causes Legionnaires' disease.

Infectious agents that have human and animal reservoirs must leave the reservoir to affect other targets. The *portal of exit* usually corresponds with the agent's location in the human or animal reservoir. Thus tubercle bacilli and influenza viruses exit via the respiratory tract, schistosomes through urine or feces, *Vibrio cholerae* in feces, *Sarcoptes scabiei* in scabies skin lesions, and enterovirus 70 (an agent of hemorrhagic conjunctivitis) in conjunctival secretions. Some bloodborne agents can exit by crossing the placenta (rubella, syphilis, *Toxoplasma*); others escape by way of the skin through cuts or needles (hepatitis B) or blood-sucking arthropods (malaria).

After an agent exits its reservoir, it may be transmitted to a susceptible host in numerous ways. In general, the modes of transmission are classified as direct or indirect:

- In *direct* transmission, the agent is transferred from a reservoir to a susceptible host by direct contact or droplet spread. Direct contact occurs through kissing, skin-to-skin contact, and sexual intercourse. Infectious mononucleosis ("kissing disease") and gonorrhea, for example, are spread from person to person by direct contact. Infectious organisms can also be transmitted from soil or vegetation to humans through direct contact. Hookworm, for example, is spread when a person comes into direct contact with contaminated soil. Droplet spread takes place when an infected person coughs or sneezes—sometimes even when he or she is talking. The droplets travel a short distance through the air to the mucous membranes of the mouth, nose, or eyes of persons who are nearby. Large droplet spread is believed to be the primary mode of transmission for influenza and other respiratory illnesses, for example.

- In *indirect* transmission, suspended air particles or animate (vector) or inanimate (vehicle) intermediaries carry the agent from a reservoir to a susceptible host. Suspended air particles include dust and droplet nuclei. Droplet nuclei are residues resulting from the evaporation of fluid from droplets emitted from an infected host; due to their small size, these particles may remain suspended in the air for long periods, be blown over great distances, and easily be inhaled into the lungs and exhaled. Airborne dust can carry infectious particles blown from the soil, as well as material that has settled on surfaces and is picked up by air currents. Legionnaires' disease and tuberculosis (bacterial), measles (viral), and histoplasmosis (fungal) are examples of infectious agents that are spread through airborne transmission.

A *vector* is an organism that transmits a pathogen or disease agent from one host to another. Most vectors are arthropods such as mosquitoes, fleas, and ticks. Depending on the disease, the agent may multiply or undergo physiologic changes in the vector. For example, the parasite that causes malaria (*Plasmodium* sp.) develops and grows within the mosquito, assuming a form that is able to infect humans.

In contrast to a vector, a *vehicle* is a nonliving object that indirectly transmits a pathogen or disease agent from one host to another. Vehicles include food, water, biologic products such as blood, and fomites—inanimate objects such as toys, handkerchiefs, bedding, or surgical scalpels. A vehicle may carry an agent passively, as when food or water carries hepatitis A virus. Alternatively, it may provide an environment in which the agent grows, multiplies, or produces toxin; *Clostridium botulinum* may thrive and produce toxins in improperly canned foods, for example.

An agent enters a susceptible host through a *portal of entry* that provides access to tissues in which the agent can multiply or a toxin can act. Organisms often use the same portal to enter a new host that they use to exit the source host. For example, influenza virus exits the respiratory tract of the source host and enters the respiratory tract of the new host. The route of transmission of many enteric (intestinal) pathogenic agents is described as "fecal–oral" because the organisms are shed in feces, carried on inadequately washed hands, and then transferred through a vehicle (such as food, water, or cooking utensil) to the mouth of a new host. Other potential portals of entry into the human body include the skin (scabies), mucous membranes (syphilis, trachoma), and blood (hepatitis B).

The *susceptibility* of a host ultimately determines whether an exposed person develops the disease. Susceptibility depends on genetic factors, specific acquired immunity (through vaccination, passive transfer of antibodies, or previous infection), and other factors that affect an individual's ability to resist infection or to fight off illness. Factors that defend against infection include the skin, mucous membranes, gastric acidity, cilia in the respiratory tract, the cough reflex, and nonspecific immune responses—that is, immune responses that do not rely on the development of antibodies, such as when macrophages and neutrophils engulf foreign substances. Factors that may increase susceptibility to illness include malnutrition, alcoholism, coexisting diseases, or therapy that impairs the nonspecific immune response.

Resources to Learn More About Diseases

Information on specific diseases that may be implicated in outbreaks is available from a variety of resources, including a large number of medical and public health textbooks. The following references systematically and succinctly provide information on a range of infectious diseases of public health interest.

Print Resources

These works are revised periodically to incorporate new diseases/disease groups and updated information about these diseases, and may be available online. The listing here refers to the most recent editions at the time of publication.

- Heymann DL, ed. *Control of Communicable Diseases Manual.* 19th ed. Washington, DC: American Public Health Association; 2008. This resource covers more than 500 infectious diseases, providing detailed information on identification, occurrence, reservoir, modes of transmission, incubation period and period of communicability, susceptibility and resistance, and methods of control.

- Pickering LK, ed. *Red Book: 2009 Report of the Committee on Infectious Diseases.* 28th ed. Elk Grove Village, IL: American Academy of Pediatrics; 2009. The *Red Book* focuses on the control of infectious diseases in children, with a greater emphasis on treatment measures for the individual patient.

Electronic Resources

Sources of electronic full-text information about diseases, pathogens, and outbreaks include the following:

- The *Centers for Disease Control and Prevention* (CDC) website (http://www.cdc.gov) contains a wealth of information on infectious diseases and outbreaks. Basic information on a variety of diseases is available in the "Diseases and Conditions" section (http://www.cdc.gov/DiseasesConditions/). The "A–Z index" (http://www.cdc.gov/az.do) is organized alphabetically by disease and includes patient information sheets, frequently asked questions, and healthcare provider information for some diseases. The CDC Online Newsroom (http://www.cdc.gov/media/) offers timely articles on health-related topics, and the "Data and Statistics" section (http://www.cdc.gov/DataStatistics/) provides surveillance, laboratory, and health statistics information.

- *Morbidity and Mortality Weekly Report* (*MMWR*; http://www.cdc.gov/mmwr) features public health information and recommendations, including timely material about disease outbreaks. Most reports come from state and territorial health departments. Some reports originally published in *MMWR* later appear in other journals, whereas others appear only in this weekly publication. Unlike most other journals, *MMWR* publishes reports quickly, so the information is relatively current. The website offers full-text access and a "search" function.

- *PubMed* (http://www.ncbi.nlm.nih.gov/PubMed) is a free service of the U.S. National Library of Medicine (NLM) and the National Institutes of Health (NIH) that comprises more than 19 million citations for biomedical articles from MEDLINE (NLM's literature database of life sciences and biomedical information) and life sciences journals. Citations may include links to full-text articles from PubMed Central or publisher websites (some free, others for a fee).

- *Ovid* (http://www.ovid.com/site/index.jsp) offers electronic medical, scientific, and academic research information for a fee. Investigators whose state or academic institutions have agreements with companies such as Ovid may have greater access to journal abstracts or full texts through the contracting company than through PubMed.

- *Loansome Doc* (http://www.nlm.nih.gov/loansomedoc/loansome_home.html) is an NLM service that offers full-text copies of articles. Fees and service charges may vary by location.

- *ProMED-mail* (http://fas.org/promed/) is a global electronic reporting system for outbreaks of infectious human, plant, and animal diseases.

Human Resources

Many resource people at local and state health departments and the federal government can help in a search for disease-specific information. The CDC and most state health departments have staff members with expertise in specific diseases or duty officers who cover a large number of diseases. These individuals can often provide the most recent information about a particular disease or a referral to an expert in the investigation or control of the disease.

Using Basic Information on Biology and Epidemiology to Initiate an Investigation

To illustrate how investigators can use basic information on the biology and epidemiology of a disease agent—reservoir, modes of transmission, and factors that increase host susceptibility and resistance—to initiate an investigation of a disease or other health problem and provide the first clues as to the source, we will examine an outbreak of *Escherichia coli* O157:H7 infection that was detected in Michigan in June and July 1997. Thirty-eight cases of *E. coli* O157:H7 infection with indistinguishable pulsed-field gel electrophoresis (PFGE) patterns were reported during a two-month period. The PFGE pattern had not been seen before May 1997, and only a few isolates of this strain were identified in May. Outbreak investigators defined a case as diarrhea and/or abdominal cramps in a resident of Michigan with onset of symptoms from June 15 to July 31 and a stool culture yielding *E. coli* O157:H7 with the outbreak strain PFGE pattern.[2]

As they prepared to investigate the outbreak, the investigators may have turned to the *Control of Communicable Diseases Manual* to learn about likely sources and risk factors for infection with *E. coli* O157:H7. They would have learned these and other useful facts:

- Although cattle are the most important reservoir of Shiga toxin-producing *E. coli*, people may also serve as a reservoir for person-to-person transmission. Sheep, goats, deer, and other ruminants may also carry this type of *E. coli*.

- The most common modes of transmission are eating food contaminated with the feces of cattle and other ruminants and coming into direct contact with animals or their environment. In the United States, serious outbreaks, including cases of hemorrhagic colitis, hemolytic-uremic syndrome (HUS), and some deaths, have followed from consumption of contaminated beef (usually undercooked hamburger meat), produce, and unpasteurized milk. Direct transmission takes place in families, childcare centers, and custodial institutions, and waterborne transmission takes place from contaminated drinking water and from recreational waters.

- The incubation period ranges from 2 to 10 days, with a median of 3 to 4 days.

- Adults typically excrete the pathogen for a week or less, but one-third of children excrete it for three weeks. Prolonged carriage is not commonly observed.

- The infectious dose is very low. Researchers know little about differences in susceptibility and immunity, but persons of all ages become infected. Those most frequently diagnosed with infection and at greatest risk of developing HUS are children younger than five years old. The risk of complications also appears to be higher among elderly individuals.[3]

Based on this information, the investigators would have decided to pay close attention to contaminated foods that patients might have ingested, particularly ground beef and raw cow's milk. Aware of the possibility of person-to-person spread and waterborne transmission, they might also have conducted a literature search and learned that *E. coli* O157:H7 had been transmitted through a variety of foods, including deer jerky (in which the deer were probably infected with *E. coli*) and produce items such as lettuce, unpasteurized apple cider, and unpasteurized apple juice that became contaminated with manure from cattle. This effort would have given the investigation team some ideas about possible sources for the *E. coli* O157:H7 infections in this outbreak; conversations with patients would have provided more valuable information.

Hypothesis-Generating Interviews

It is as important for investigators to speak directly with the people most affected by the outbreak as it is to review the literature and the basic science of the disease agent. To explore possible exposures, astute investigators undertake hypothesis-generating interviews with a limited number of case patients early in an outbreak investigation.

A well-structured hypothesis-generating interview will help investigators achieve the following goals:

- Identify potential sources of exposure
- Clarify the signs and symptoms of the disease
- Explore potential transmission routes
- Develop or refine the case definition, which will help determine which patients to include or rule out as the investigation proceeds
- Develop a demographic profile that helps identify the population at risk
- Gather information that will help them develop more detailed hypothesis-testing interviews

When done correctly, hypothesis-generating interviews help investigators target suspicious exposures more quickly and use limited investigation resources most wisely.

For investigators, it is important to recognize the distinction between hypothesis-generating interviews and a second type of interview that will take place later in the investigation—the hypothesis-testing interview. *Hypothesis-generating interviews* take place early in the investigation, and are used to identify the most suspect exposures associated with an outbreak. Because only case patients are interviewed, they are not designed to determine with certainty the cause of the outbreak. Once investigators have used hypothesis-generating interviews to help determine the most likely cause or causes of the outbreak, they conduct a second round of interviews as part of a more rigorous analytical study, such as a case-control study or a cohort study. These *hypothesis-testing interviews* typically focus on the most likely cause or causes of the outbreak, are more structured, include a larger number of cases, and, most significantly, involve a suitable comparison group of people who did not become ill. (Hypothesis-testing interviews are described in great detail in Chapter 8.)

Hypothesis-generating interviews are a critical part of the outbreak investigation. Skipping them could lead to a poorly designed analytic study that would jeopardize the investigation and the ability to implicate a factor or exposure as a cause of the outbreak.

This section explores which information investigators should collect in hypothesis-generating interviews, which and how many patients they should interview, how they should conduct the interviews, and what they should do with the information they collect. It concludes with a series of tips that can help the interviews proceed smoothly and effectively.

Which Information Is Collected in Hypothesis-Generating Interviews?

The information that investigators collect during hypothesis-generating interviews depends on the circumstances of the outbreak; the etiologic agent, including whether it is known or unknown; and clues that have already been gathered. Many investigators use a standardized questionnaire as a starting point. (Examples from Minnesota and Oregon are available on the CDC's OutbreakNet Team website at http://www.cdc.gov/outbreaknet/references_resources/.) Investigators may also ask colleagues who have conducted similar investigations to share questionnaires they have used.

In general, a questionnaire is usually designed to collect the following information:

- Basic demographic information about the case patient, such as age, sex, place of residence, and contact information
- Clinical details of the patient's illness, including symptoms, date of onset, duration, and severity
- Information about exposures that could conceivably cause or predispose the patient to illness, such as attendance at social gatherings, travel, contact with children in a childcare setting, contact with animals, and leisure activities such as swimming

Additional questions will depend on the type of illness and whether the etiologic agent is known or unknown.

Known or Suspected Agent

If a specific pathogen has been identified as the etiologic agent in an outbreak, the questions in the hypothesis-generating interview typically focus on known reservoirs and modes of transmission for that agent; they should examine both common and less common sources of exposure. The onset of illness and the incubation period for the disease under investigation will dictate the time period that the questions will cover.

If the etiologic agent can be spread through food or beverages, the investigator should take a food history covering the incubation period of the disease. Cases should be asked about the following items:

- Foods eaten in their home
- Foods eaten in the homes of friends and family
- Foods eaten at restaurants, fast-food establishments, and delis (and the names and addresses of each place the patient has eaten)
- The date and time of food consumption and any suspicious observations

The next two examples describe the questions that might be asked during hypothesis-generating interviews for two outbreaks, one associated with an infection that is often foodborne and one associated with an airborne infection.

Example: A Hypothetical Outbreak of Salmonellosis

Investigators conducting hypothesis-generating interviews in an outbreak of salmonellosis will begin developing questions based on their review of the basic science and epidemiology. The modes of transmission for salmonellosis include ingestion of contaminated food and water, transmission from person to person, and transmission from animal to person. Epidemics are usually traced to processed meat products, inadequately cooked poultry and poultry products, and uncooked or lightly cooked foods containing eggs, raw milk, and dairy products. The incubation period is usually 12 to 36 hours but ranges from 6 to 72 hours.[3]

To help narrow the possible sources of exposure, interviewers will typically seek the following exposure information from case patients for the three days before onset of illness in the case:

- A complete food history
- Sources of water (e.g., tap water, private well water, untreated surface water, bottled water, other)
- Exposure to other ill persons
- Exposure to animals
- Travel outside the immediate area

While investigators should focus on exposures that make sense based on the basic science and previous outbreaks, they should remember that limiting hypothesis-generating interviews to the most common sources of infection could cause them to miss something important. Pet turtles, iguanas, and chicks have been associated with infection with *Salmonella*. Komodo dragons at a zoo were found to be the source of one outbreak.[4] Several outbreaks of salmonellosis have been traced to raw fruits and vegetables that were contaminated during slicing. A number of years ago, an outbreak of *Salmonella muenchen* was associated with exposure to marijuana.[5] These multiple modes of transmission suggest that an investigator will want to think creatively based on all available clues.

Example: An Outbreak of Legionnaires' Disease

Investigators seeking the source of an outbreak of Legionnaires' disease know (or will learn) that epidemiological evidence supports airborne transmission of this disease, although other methods of spread are possible, including aspiration of water. They also know that human-made water supplies, such as cooling towers, are the primary sources for the disease.[3]

Investigators can find a sample legionellosis questionnaire at the CDC's A–Z Index (http://www.cdc.gov/legionella/index.htm). It will prompt them to ask patients whether they engaged in any of the following activities:

- Shopped at a grocery store where there were mister machines for the fruit and vegetables

- Shopped at department stores, shopping malls, or home improvement stores
- Visited a hospital or nursing home
- Traveled or stayed overnight somewhere other than the patient's usual residence
- Attended any conference or public gathering
- Had dental work performed
- Went to a health and fitness club
- Might have been exposed to aerosolized water at work

In an outbreak of Legionnaires' disease in Virginia in 1996, hypothesis-generating interviews determined that 14 of 15 patients had visited a large home-improvement center during the 2 weeks prior to their onset of illness. After collecting and culturing samples from water sources in the home-improvement center and conducting a case-control study with a more detailed questionnaire, investigators were able to pinpoint a whirlpool spa display as the cause of the outbreak.[6]

Unknown Agent

If the etiologic agent is not known, investigators may need to be more general and expansive in their questioning, focusing on clinical signs and symptoms and activities that may provide clues about the source of exposure, reservoir, mode of transmission, incubation period, and potential causative agents. If the patients in a suspected outbreak complain of fever, chills, headache, cough, and muscle aches, for example, investigators might ask about potential exposures known to cause Legionnaires' disease, pneumonia, severe acute respiratory illness (SARS), or other respiratory illnesses. If the symptoms include diarrhea, investigators may want to focus broadly on exposures known to cause a number of gastrointestinal infections. In either case, investigators likely will take the opportunity to collect appropriate specimens from patients during the hypothesis-generating interviews to determine the causative agent.

Who Is Interviewed?

The primary source of information in hypothesis-generating interviews is case patients. This group will provide most of the information on potential sources of exposure. If a case patient has died, is too sick to be interviewed, or is otherwise unavailable, interviewers may seek out a family member or friend. If the case patients are children, interviewers may need to interview their parents or guardians. To gather the most information, investigators seek to include a wide variety of case patients with different demographic characteristics in the interviews; at the same time, the patients selected for interviews should be "typical," with onset of symptoms around the middle of the outbreak. It is important to avoid cases that are outliers and may have been exposed by some other source or route, such as secondary spread from initial cases. The number of case patients interviewed will depend on the size of the outbreak. For a large outbreak, 8 to 10 is usually an appropriate number.

Interviewing healthcare providers may also be useful. In some communities, healthcare providers, laboratory workers, and clinical staff may know the patients and their families; they may know their behaviors and the places they visit. They may also be able to promptly pinpoint an outbreak to a certain neighborhood or gathering place.[7]

How Is the Information Collected?

Hypothesis-generating interviews are usually conducted in person, often in the case patient's home. If visiting patients in their homes is not practical, interviews may take place over the telephone. If investigators are focusing on common exposures, they may bring patients together at the health department or another site to interview them in a group setting.

Interviewers should collect information by asking closed-ended and open-ended questions. Close-ended questions produce data that are easier to standardize, tabulate, and analyze. Open-ended questions impose fewer limits, so respondents can express themselves freely, but they are more difficult to code and analyze. A thorough interview will incorporate both types of questions.[8] (Closed-ended and open-ended questions are covered in greater detail in Chapter 8.)

Hypothesis-generating interviews are most likely to yield useful information if the same person conducts all of them. If two or more interviewers compare notes, for example, they may fail to recognize an unusual finding that would be readily apparent to a single interviewer who had heard the same thing from several different interviewees.

What Do Investigators Do with the Information They Gather?

Once an investigator has completed the hypothesis-generating interviews, he or she must interpret what may be an avalanche of information. The goals of interpretation include these aims:

- Developing a consistent clinical picture of the illness
- Identifying a location that many of the patients visited or an activity of interest that many of them took part in
- Trimming the list of exposures to identify exposures of greatest suspicion

Obtaining a Complete Clinical Picture

Obtaining a complete clinical picture during these interviews is more important than most investigators realize, for a number of reasons. First, the details of a clinical examination might help determine the most likely etiologic agent, if it is not already known. Second, investigators can use this information to develop or further refine the case definition. Third, if the etiologic agent is unknown, the predominant signs and symptoms can help focus the subsequent study of exposures. Finally, if an interviewer determines that a patient does not have the disease under investigation, he or she can remove the individual from the case list.

Identifying Locations and Activities of Interest

It is very important to ask questions that help determine whether case patients visited the same locations, worked or went to school together, or engaged in other common activities that could have exposed them to the causative agent. The commonalities identified during these interviews can help investigators develop a list of possible exposures. For example, all of the patients may have engaged in these activities:

- Swum in the same pool
- Eaten strawberry cheesecake
- Worked on the same farm

Asking about activities of interest is always important, but learning what patients did that may have exposed them to the causative agent is especially important if the agent is unknown or is known but has a number of possible modes of transmission.

Trimming the List of Exposures

A critical function of hypothesis-generating interviews is to shorten the list of exposures of interest for use in subsequent studies. If none of the cases involved in the interviews reports a specific exposure, then it is no longer a viable hypothesis and can be dropped from subsequent study. If more than 50% of cases report an exposure, it should be studied further. If fewer than 50% of cases report an exposure, it still may be of interest, particularly if the exposure is unusual or difficult to recognize.

Interviewing Tips

By observing experienced interviewers, practicing, and increasing their knowledge of disease-causing agents, investigators can become good interviewers. Interviewing skills are discussed in much greater detail in Chapter 8; for now, note that the following tips may help novice interviewers:

- Be prepared. Review basic information about the etiologic agent before starting the interview. Do a literature search and talk to experts, if necessary.
- Identify yourself at the beginning of the interview and provide your credentials and affiliation.
- Explain the purpose of the interview and how long it is likely to take. (But be circumspect with comments about the outbreak—discussions about suspected sources or sources found in other similar outbreaks could bias the case and affect a respondent's memory of exposures or events.)
- Maintain a professional attitude, but be friendly.
- Exhibit concern for the respondent's well-being.

- Develop an organized approach. Create an outline so that the line of questioning is systematic, yet flexible enough to accommodate the respondent's responses to questions. Maintain control of the interview, but be a patient listener.

- Base the level of communication on the respondent's age, occupation, and education. Avoid medical terminology, jargon, or abbreviations.

- Word questions carefully. Respondents may be sensitive about certain subjects such as age, income, bowel habits, and alcohol or drug use.

- Record the information gathered during the interview. If possible, use a standardized form such as the Minnesota or Oregon questionnaire available at http://www.cdc.gov/outbreaknet/references_resources/.

- If necessary, ask respondents to use records to enhance their memory. Credit-card bills, bank statements, receipts, and itemized lists of purchases linked to grocery store loyalty cards are examples of records that can help a person remember when and where he or she ate at a restaurant, bought a food item at a grocery store, or visited a recreation area.

- When the interview is over, thank the respondent. Emphasize that his or her participation will make a positive contribution to the control and prevention of illness in the community.

- Provide the respondent with contact information in case he or she thinks of additional information later.

- Tell the respondent that he or she may be contacted again for further details as the investigation continues.

Hypothesis-Generating Interviews in the E. coli O157:H7
Infection Outbreak in Michigan

To further explore potential sources of the outbreak of *E. coli* O157:H7 infections in Michigan discussed earlier in this chapter, investigators undertook hypothesis-generating interviews, selecting 7 case patients from the 38 reported through July 15. The patients lived in four different counties and ranged in age from 5 to 69 years old. Three were female. Although the findings from the interviews are not available, they might have resulted in observations similar to these:

- Three of the case patients had eaten hamburger or ground beef in the week before becoming ill.

- No patients had drunk raw milk.

- Only one patient had traveled outside Michigan.

- No patients had had contact with farm animals.

- No restaurant or social event was identified in common.

- All of the patients had consumed salad.

- Six patients had eaten alfalfa sprouts.

This information would enable investigators to eliminate ground beef, raw milk, and animal contact—all common sources of *E. coli* O157:H7 infection—from further consideration. Because patients mentioned salads and alfalfa sprouts most frequently in hypothesis-generating interviews, the investigators decided to focus on these possible exposures in the hypothesis-testing interviews.[2]

Describing an Outbreak

As the example of the investigation of an outbreak of *E. coli* O157:H7 infections demonstrates, examining the biology and epidemiology of the disease and interviewing case patients narrows the search and provides a context for information that is gathered subsequent to the interviews. Investigators practice descriptive epidemiology to organize, present, and better understand the data they have gathered in the early stages of an outbreak investigation.

What Is Descriptive Epidemiology?

Descriptive epidemiology breaks down an outbreak or other health problem by time, place, and person. This approach is basic to any outbreak investigation, and it serves three critical functions: providing a systematic method for dissecting the health problem into its fundamental components; characterizing the problem so others can easily understand it; and providing clues, such as commonalities among cases, that can help generate testable hypotheses about the cause of the problem.

This section describes the three components of descriptive epidemiology, and explores the tools that outbreak investigators use to make the most effective use of the data they have collected in the early stages of an outbreak. It concludes by comparing descriptive epidemiology with analytic epidemiology, which will be the focus of the next stage of the investigation.

Time

Pinpointing when people became ill is a critical factor in understanding and controlling an outbreak. Disease rates change over time. Some changes, such as the development of chronic diseases, occur relatively slowly. Others, such as infectious disease outbreaks, happen very rapidly. Some changes take place regularly and can be predicted, such as seasonal trends in respiratory illnesses, foodborne diseases, and illnesses spread by mosquito vectors. Other changes are not predictable at all.

Investigators typically track time data on a line graph or histogram using a rectangular coordinate system—that is, a graph consisting of two axes, the *x*-axis (the horizontal axis) and the *y*-axis (the vertical axis), that intersect at right angles. Each axis is divided into equally spaced intervals, although the intervals for the two axes may differ. Together, the two axes form a grid upon which investigators can plot points demonstrating the relationship between the variable on the *x*-axis and the *y*-axis. In a graph of time data (Figure 6-1),

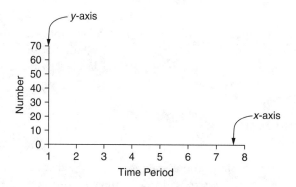

Figure 6-1 Drawing a line graph

the time periods of interest are on the *x*-axis and the number of cases or rate of the health problem during those time periods are on the *y*-axis.

Each point on the graph represents the number of cases or rate of disease for a particular time period. In the graph shown in Figure 6-2, 28 cases occurred during the first time period, and 61 cases occurred during the sixth time period.

Joining the points by a line makes it easier for readers to visualize trends over time. Graphs often identify the timing of events that investigators believe are related to the health problem, such as when an exposure occurred or control measures were implemented (Figure 6-3).

The units and intervals used on the *x*-axis—the time period of interest—depend on available data and the desired level of detail in the graph. The time period could be presented

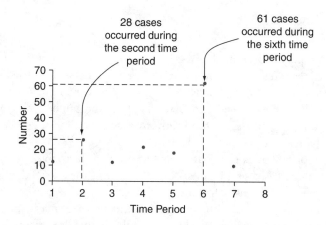

Figure 6-2 Drawing a line graph

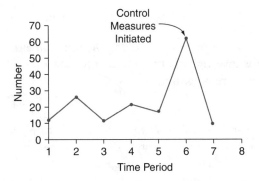

Figure 6-3   Drawing a line graph

in units of hours, days, weeks, months, quarters, or years. The units and intervals on the *y*-axis—the number or rate of cases—depend on the range of the data and the desired level of detail.

The shape of the graph will vary depending on the units and intervals used on each axis. For example, suppose two graphs, both based on the same data, show hospital-acquired infections at Hospital X over time (Figure 6-4). Each graph shows the rate of hospital-acquired infections (including surgical wound infections, pneumonias, urinary tract infections, and bloodstream infections) at Hospital X between 1998 and 2003. The first graph shows the number of infections by three-month periods; the second, by years. Despite containing the same information, the graphs look very different. One shows that hospital-acquired infections at Hospital X have remained relatively stable with no overall upward or downward trend over time, while the other highlights a large increase in cases (maybe even an outbreak) during a short period in 2000.

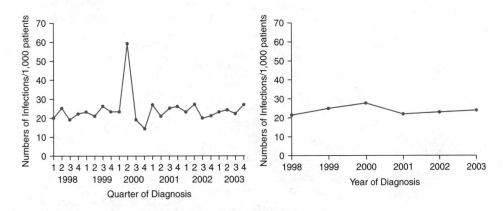

Figure 6-4   Hospital-acquired infections by quarter and by year of diagnosis, Hospital X, 1998–2003

The examples shown in Figure 6-4 demonstrate why investigators must create their graphs carefully. As these examples make plain, it is possible to present a very different picture of a given situation simply by changing the units on either the *x*- or *y*-axis. It is always a good idea for investigators to examine the data carefully and select the most appropriate layout when creating time graphs.

Epidemic Curves

The time graph used in an outbreak investigation is called an epidemic curve (or epi curve). While it is possible to create epidemic curves by hand, investigators often use a software program such as Epi Info (http://www.cdc.gov/epiinfo/) or Microsoft Excel to do the work.

An epidemic curve is often presented as a histogram. In a histogram, each case in the outbreak is represented by a box placed along the *x*-axis at the time that the case's symptoms began. If more than one case had onset of symptoms for a given time period, the boxes are stacked one atop the other. Sometimes cases with specific characteristics are represented using different-colored boxes. Cases among food handlers or secondary cases may be designated as a different color from the other cases, for example, or confirmed, probable, and suspected cases may be highlighted.

The unit of time and interval for the *x*-axis in an epidemic curve usually is based on the incubation period of the disease under investigation. As a general rule, the unit of time is set at roughly one-fourth of the average incubation period for the disease. For example, staphylococcal food poisoning has an incubation period of two to four hours. In an outbreak of staphylococcal food poisoning following a church supper, investigators would probably use an *x*-axis unit of 30 minutes to one hour, as shown in Figure 6-5.

In contrast, investigators would probably use an *x*-axis unit of 4 to 10 days to depict an outbreak of hepatitis A, which has a usual incubation period of 28 to 30 days. In the example shown in Figure 6-6, investigators used intervals of 4 days on the *x*-axis.

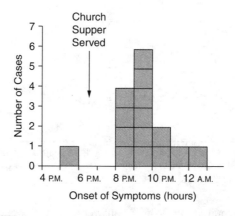

Figure 6-5   Onset of symptoms in an outbreak of staphylococcal food poisoning

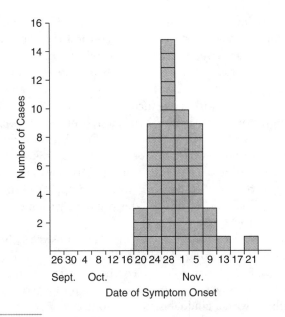

Figure 6-6   Onset of symptoms in an outbreak of hepatitis A

What to Remember When Creating an Epidemic Curve

1. Indicate the number of reported cases on the *y*-axis.

2. Indicate the date/time of symptom onset on the *x*-axis.

3. Choose an appropriate time interval for the *x*-axis, or try several to see which best represents the data.

4. Include pre-outbreak time on the *x*-axis to show the "baseline" disease level and to show visually when the outbreak began.

5. Label the *x*- and *y*-axes clearly.

6. Give the epi curve a descriptive, self-explanatory title.

7. Include more detailed information about the cases, if desired, such as geographic location or predominant symptom, by using different-colored boxes.

8. To be technically correct, make the bars touch each other (unless there are periods of time with no cases, in which circumstance there will be space between the bars).

What Epidemic Curves Tell Investigators About an Outbreak

The epidemic curve can provide a sense of the outbreak's magnitude and tell investigators whether the number of cases is still increasing or has already peaked. It can also identify outliers—cases that stand apart from the overall pattern, such as the first (index) case—thereby providing important clues about the source of the outbreak. The shape of an epidemic curve can also suggest the pattern of spread for an outbreak.

Point-source outbreaks share several common features: Persons are exposed to the same source of infection over a brief period of time, such as through a single meal or an event attended by all cases; the number of cases rises rapidly to a peak and falls off gradually; and the majority of cases occur within one incubation period. Figure 6-7 shows the typical shape of a point-source outbreak. In this hypothetical outbreak of cryptosporidiosis, a toddler at a childcare center was the source of infection for other children at the center for 1 day before being sent home with a case of diarrhea. This source case, called the index case, occurred about a week before the others, on the 11th day of the month. Subsequent cases started to appear on the 17th day, rose over 4 days, peaked on the 20th day, and then declined more gradually. Most of the cases occurred within one incubation period (average 7 days, range 1 to 12 days).

In a *continuous common-source outbreak,* persons are exposed to the same source but exposure is prolonged over a period of days, weeks, or longer, resulting in an epidemic curve that rises gradually and may plateau. The hypothetical example of a continuous common-source outbreak shown in Figure 6-8 depicts a prolonged occurrence of cases of a gastrointestinal illness with a gradual increase and decrease over an 11-day period.

A *propagated outbreak* does not have a common source, but instead spreads from person to person. In a classic propagated outbreak, such as an outbreak of influenza, the epidemic curve is a series of progressively taller peaks, each one incubation period apart from the last. Figure 6-9 demonstrates the pattern associated with person-to-person spread.

The shape of the epidemic curve in a real outbreak will rarely fit any of these descriptions exactly. This is particularly true of a propagated outbreak, as waves of cases overlap one another and obscure subsequent peaks or the peaks diminish with time. Nonetheless,

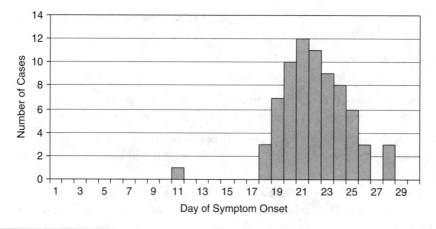

Figure 6-7   A point-source epidemic curve

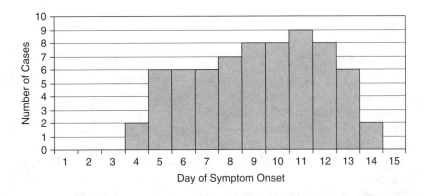

Figure 6-8 An epidemic curve from a continuous common-source exposure

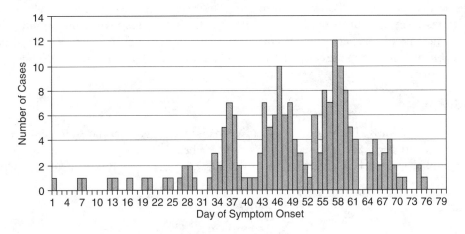

Figure 6-9 A propagated outbreak epidemic curve

the epidemic curve can provide investigators with a general sense of the pattern of spread of an outbreak.

An epidemic curve can also identify the most likely time period of exposure for a point-source outbreak of a known disease. To deduce this period from an epidemic curve, investigators should take the following steps:

1. Draw an epidemic curve.

2. Identify the peak of the outbreak on the curve and count back on the *x*-axis the average incubation period for the disease. If the curve does not obviously peak, select the median case. (The median case is the case that would be in the middle if the cases were listed in chronological order by date of onset of symptoms.)

3. Identify the earliest case and count back on the *x*-axis the minimum incubation period.

4. Identify the last case and count back on the *x*-axis the maximum incubation period.

Ideally, each of these resulting dates is similar and represents the most likely period of exposure. These techniques are not precise, however, and investigators usually widen the period of exposure by 10% to 20% on either side of these dates.

As an example, consider Figure 6-10, which shows the epidemic curve for a small outbreak of *E. coli* O157:H7 infection. The peak of the hypothetical outbreak occurred on December 10. To establish the most likely period of exposure, investigators would start by counting back the average incubation period for *E. coli* O157:H7 (3 to 4 days), from December 10 to December 6 or 7. Then they would establish a range by counting back the minimum incubation period (1 day) from December 8, the date the earliest case showed an onset of symptoms, and the maximum incubation period (8 days), from December 13, the date the last case had onset of symptoms. These steps establish the most likely period of exposure in this outbreak as December 5–7. To be safe, investigators might add a day on either end of this period, making it December 4–8. When they question cases about possible exposures to sources of *E. coli* O157:H7 infection, investigators will focus on this period.

Place

Investigators assess a health problem by place to discover its geographic extent and to seek important etiologic clues about it. For example, if a health problem is spread across a wide geographic area, such as an entire state or country, investigators might suspect that the

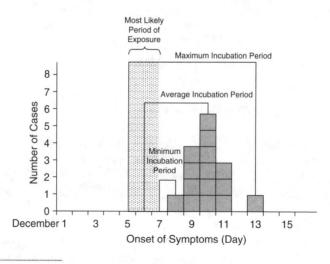

Figure 6-10   Onset of symptoms among cases of *E. coli* O157:H7 infection

source is a product with wide commercial distribution. In contrast, if a health problem is limited to a single neighborhood, it is more likely to be caused by a point source such as a contaminated water supply or tainted food served at a social event, person-to-person spread, or an illness caused by a product that is only sold locally.

Although place data can be organized in a table (as shown in Table 6-1), it is difficult to discern patterns from a table. It is often better to show place data pictorially, as in the examples shown later in this section.

Spot Maps

A spot map uses a symbol—a dot or an X—to indicate the location of each case. The location is a place that is potentially relevant to the health problem being investigated, such as the case's place of residence or work. Other sites may also be labeled, such as locations where investigators believe individuals may have been exposed to the causative factor.

Figure 6-11 depicts a spot map based on the information given in Table 6-1. The spot map provides a much different perspective on the geographic distribution of the problem, making it immediately apparent that the cases are clustered where the three states share a border.

TABLE 6-1 **Thyrotoxicosis Cases by County of Residence, Minnesota, South Dakota, and Iowa, February 1984 to August 1985**

County of Residence	Number of Cases
Minnesota	
Lincoln	7
Lyon	13
Murray	5
Nobles	18
Pipestone	10
Redwood	2
Rock	39
South Dakota	
Minnehaha	25
Iowa	
Lyon	1
Osceola	1
Total	121

Source: Adapted from Centers for Disease Control and Prevention Epidemiology Program Office. An epidemic of thyrotoxicosis. *Case Studies in Applied Epidemiology*, No. 873-703. http://www.cdc.gov/eis/casestudies/Xthyrotox.student.873-703.pdf. Accessed October 8, 2010.

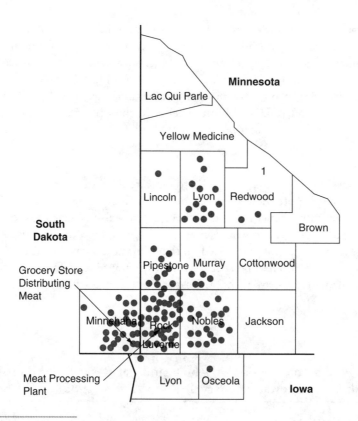

Figure 6-11 Spot map of thyrotoxicosis cases by county of residence, Minnesota, South Dakota, and Iowa, February 1984 to August 1985

Source: Adapted from: Centers for Disease Control and Prevention Epidemiology Program Office. An epidemic of thyrotoxicosis. *Case Studies in Applied Epidemiology,* No. 873-703. http://www.cdc.gov/eis/casestudies/Xthyrotox.student.873-703.pdf. Accessed October 8, 2010.

A spot map can be used to develop hypotheses about an outbreak but investigators must be aware of the limitations of spot mapping:

- The map shows numbers of cases, not rates. If the size of the population varies among areas being compared, the map can be misleading. An area map that shows area-specific attack rates can address this problem. Figure 6-12 shows an area map based on the data in the table and county population estimates.

- The location used on the map represents just one place the case might have been exposed. Affected individuals could have visited many places—their homes, places of work, homes of friends/family, stores—any of which might be a source of exposure.

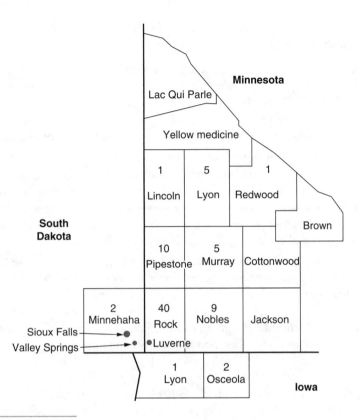

Figure 6-12   Area map of thyrotoxicosis cases (per 10,000 residents) by county of residence, Minnesota, South Dakota, and Iowa, February 1984 to August 1985

Source: Reproduced from Centers for Disease Control and Prevention Epidemiology Program Office. An epidemic of thyrotoxicosis. *Case Studies in Applied Epidemiology,* No. 873-703. http://www.cdc.gov/eis/casestudies/Xthyrotox.student.873-703.pdf. Accessed October 8, 2010.

Investigators can create spot maps by sticking pins in preprinted maps, drawing their own maps, or using geographic information system (GIS) software to store, manipulate, analyze, and display data in a geographic context. An example is the World Health Organization's HealthMapper (www.who.int/health_mapping/tools/healthmapper/en/index.html). We discuss maps and GIS in much greater detail in Chapter 15.

Person

Investigators study personal characteristics such as age, sex, and occupation that can influence an individual's susceptibility to a health problem and the chances that he or she was exposed to the agent causing the problem. A description of cases by personal characteristics may provide insight into the mode of spread, identify high-risk populations, and suggest risk factors for the health problem. For example:

- If the patients in a potentially foodborne outbreak are exclusively infants and their caregivers, investigators might suspect that the source was a food consumed only by babies and that their caregivers were infected by secondary spread; a food-borne outbreak affecting predominantly teenage and young adult males might point toward food from fast-food establishments as the source of infection.

- If the patients in an outbreak of respiratory infections all work at the same factory, investigators might suspect an airborne pathogen, such as *Legionella* bacteria, and order an environmental survey of the workplace. In contrast, if the patients are scattered over a wide area, investigators might look for other commonalities among them, such as attending a conference at the same hotel or shopping at the same home-improvement store.

- If an outbreak of hepatitis A is occurring only among men, investigators might seek additional information to determine whether having sex with men or using intravenous drugs are risk factors for infection. Likewise, if an outbreak of diarrhea caused by *E. coli* O157:H7 affects mostly women, as in the example of an outbreak in Michigan discussed throughout this chapter, investigators might suspect salad, alfalfa sprouts, or some other food that women are more likely than men to eat.

Occupation

For many health problems, occupation is another important personal characteristic; certain exposures and health problems are more prevalent in some job types. For example, health-care workers (e.g., physicians, nurses, aides, dentists, dental hygienists, operating room employees, laboratory technicians) are at increased risk for bloodborne illnesses;[9] workers in mines and foundries, in abrasive blasting operations, are at increased risk for silicosis.[10]

Other Personal Characteristics of Interest

Other personal characteristics of interest will be more specific to the disease under investigation and the setting of the outbreak. For example, in an outbreak centered in a school, investigators might characterize cases by grade or classroom and by student versus teacher. In an outbreak in a hospital, they might look at underlying medical diagnoses or treatments that could potentially increase the risk of certain exposures.

Population

As investigators gather personal information about the individuals affected by an outbreak, they begin to examine this information in an aggregated fashion to characterize the affected population. It can be very important, for example, to know if all of the case patients are very young or very old, if more women than men are affected, or if people who ate a certain food were more likely to become ill. Investigators use a variety of descriptive statistics to characterize the population they are studying.

Measures of Central Tendency

Measures of central tendency are a good example of the type of descriptive statistics commonly used in outbreak investigations. The four most commonly used measures of central tendency are as follows:

- Mean
- Median
- Mode
- Range

The *mean* is simply the arithmetic average. It is calculated by adding up all of the values and then dividing by the number of values. For example, if investigators wanted to calculate the mean age of 7 case patients in an outbreak investigation who were 7, 10, 8, 5, 5, 37, and 9 years of age, they would take the total of these values (81) and divide by the number of case patients (7). The mean, or average age, is 11.6 years.

The *median* is another measure of central tendency. It is the 50th percentile value or the value that divides a set of data into two halves. In other words, it is the value in the middle position of a set of measurements ordered from smallest to largest. Using the same example as in the previous paragraph, investigators would first rank the ages from youngest to oldest (i.e., 5, 5, 7, 8, 9, 10, 37). Because there are so few case patients, it is easy to see that the middle value, or median, is 8.

Compared to the mean, the median is less influenced by extreme values, because these values are not used to calculate the median. In this example, the case patient who is 37 years of age is quite a bit older than the rest of the cases. The mean age for these case patients is 11.6, but the median value is 8.

The following rules are used to identify the median in a set of values where the total number of values is equal to n:

- If the number of values is odd, the median value is the value with rank $(n+1)/2$. In our example, n is 7 and $(n+1)/2 = 4$. The fourth ordered value is 8.

- If the number of values is even, the median is the average of the two middle values— that is, the values with rank $(n/2)$ and $(n/2)+1$. (Again, it is important to remember to put the values in numerical order first, and then calculate the median.)

Another way to look at the center of a distribution of values is to look for the value that appears most frequently, called the *mode*. In our example data set (5, 5, 7, 8, 9, 10, 37), the mode would be 5, because it occurs twice, whereas the rest of the values occur only once. Depending on the data, there may be more than one modal value. For example, if investigators added someone to the study who was 10 years old there would be two values for the mode: 5 and 10.

Attack Rates

Another way to characterize the affected population before arriving at a hypothesis is to calculate attack rates. Some epidemiologists consider attack rates to be analytic epidemiology, but for the purposes of this book we will consider them as descriptive epidemiology—a useful tool to describe the population affected by an outbreak.

Attack rates are one of the most meaningful ways to examine the outbreak data for purposes of generating hypotheses. Investigators calculate attack rates by dividing the number of people in a population who become ill by the number of people who are at risk. These rates are useful for comparing the risk of disease in groups with different characteristics or exposures.

$$\text{Attack rate (AR)} = \frac{\text{Number of cases of a disease}}{\text{Number of people at risk (for a given period)}}$$

$$\text{Food-specific AR} = \frac{\text{Number of people who ate a food and became ill}}{\text{Number of people who ate that food}}$$

Investigators generally look for three situations when calculating attack rates in an outbreak:

- The attack rate is high among persons who had the exposure.
- The attack rate is low among persons who did not have the exposure.
- Most of the cases had the exposure, making the exposure a reasonable explanation for most or all cases.

Food-Specific Attack Rates

In a hypothetical example of gastrointestinal illness among wedding attendees, investigators calculated attack rates for those persons who ate a specific food item and those who did not by dividing the number of people who consumed an item and became ill by the total number of people who consumed the item, and then doing the same for persons who did not consume the food (Table 6-2).

TABLE 6-2   Food-Specific Attack Rates in an Outbreak of Gastrointestinal Illness

Item	Consumed Item			Did Not Consume Item		
	III	Total	AR (%)	III	Total	AR (%)
Chicken	12	46	26	17	29	59
Cake	26	43	61	20	32	63
Water	10	24	42	33	51	65
Green salad	42	54	78	3	21	14
Asparagus	4	6	67	42	69	61

The attack rate among those who consumed asparagus is relatively high (67%), but the attack rate among those who did not eat it is also fairly high (61%). Moreover, only four persons who consumed the asparagus became ill, so it probably is not the culprit. By comparison, the attack rate is high among those who consumed a green salad and is comparatively low among persons who did not eat the salad. Forty-two of the case patients ate the green salad, making it a reasonable explanation for the illness.

When the attack rate is high among both people who ate and who did not eat a specific food item, the food is not likely to be the source of infection. However, when the attack rate is high among people who *did* consume a specific food item and low among people who *did not* consume that food item, and many of the ill people consumed the food item in question, investigators should look closely at the causal relationship between the food item and illness.

Stratified Attack Rates

Investigators can also use a *stratified attack rate* to examine a particular characteristic of interest. Stratified attack rates can be calculated based on variables such as sex, age group, occupation, or race. For example, Table 6-3 shows sex-specific attack rates. Because women have a higher attack rate compared to men, the stratified attack rate might prompt investigators to consider an exposure that is common in women.

Pulling It All Together

We now return to the example of the *E. coli* O157:H7 outbreak in Michigan once again to demonstrate how investigators pool the information they have gathered to generate a hypothesis. In the Michigan investigation, the epidemic curve (Figure 6-13) showed that onset of illness among case patients occurred from mid-June to mid-July, with the largest number of cases occurring on June 22. Because the typical incubation period of *E. coli* O157:H7 infection is 3 to 4 days and the epidemic curve was relatively flat, investigators concluded that the outbreak likely had a continuous common source.

A spot map showing that case patients with *E. coli* O157:H7 infection resided in 10 different counties in Michigan (Figure 6-14) suggested that the source of the outbreak was disseminated across the state, decreasing the likelihood that the outbreak was due

TABLE 6-3 Stratified Attack Rates				
	Ill	Well	Total	Attack Rate (%)
Women	13	16	29	45
Men	5	27	32	16

Attack rate in women: 13/29 = 45%
Attack rate in men: 5/32 = 16%

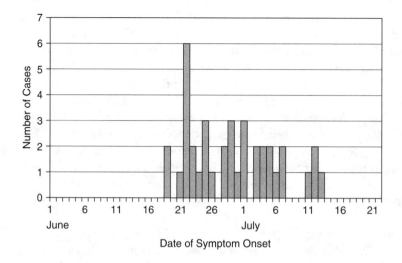

Figure 6-13 Cases of *E. coli* O157:H7 infection of the outbreak PFGE pattern by date of symptom onset, Michigan, 1997

Source: Adapted from Breuer T, Benkel DH, Shapiro RL, et al. A multistate outbreak of *Escherichia coli* O157:H7 infections linked to alfalfa sprouts grown from contaminated seeds. *Emerg Infect Dis.* 2007;7(6). http://www.cdc.gov/ncidod/eid/vol7no6/breuer.htm. Accessed August 23, 2010.

to a product sold locally, a common water supply, or person-to-person spread (although investigators could not absolutely rule out the latter at this point).

Twenty-six (68%) of the 38 case patients who met the case definition were female and 58% were between 20 and 59 years old (Table 6-4). The median age was 31 years, with a range of 2 to 76 years. From national surveillance data, the investigators knew that most cases of *E. coli* O157:H7 infection occur among children, and that men are more likely than women to be infected among adults. In the Michigan outbreak, nearly 70% of the cases were women, and the median age was 31 years. This demographic profile led investigators to hypothesize that produce might be responsible for the outbreak, rather than other commonly identified sources such as hamburger meat, unpasteurized milk, and contact with animals.

At this point in the investigation, laboratory tests had confirmed that the patients were infected with the same strain of *E. coli* O157:H7. Hypothesis-generating interviews had ruled out certain foods and pointed to salad and alfalfa sprouts as the most likely mode of transmission. Descriptive epidemiology had determined the time people became ill, the geographic range of the cases, the population affected by the outbreak, and the most likely type of outbreak. The investigators were ready to hypothesize that lettuce or alfalfa sprouts

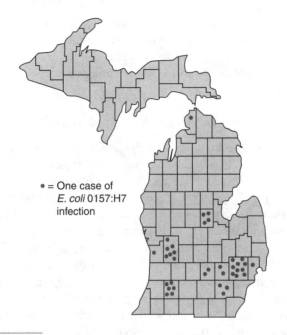

Figure 6-14   Cases of *E. coli* O157:H7 infection of the outbreak PFGE pattern by place of residence, Michigan, 1997

Source: Breuer T, Benkel DH, Shapiro RL, et al. Analysis of cases in a multistate outbreak of *Escherichia coli* O157:H7 infection in 1997. Unpublished raw data.

TABLE 6-4   Cases of *E. coli* O157:H7 Infection of the Outbreak PFGE Pattern by Age, Group, and Sex, Michigan, 1997

Age Group	Sex		Total
	Male	Female	
0–9	2 (17%)	2 (8%)	4 (11%)
10–19	2 (17%)	3 (11%)	5 (13%)
20–39	3 (25%)	9 (35%)	12 (32%)
40–59	2 (17%)	8 (31%)	10 (26%)
60+	3 (25%)	4 (15%)	7 (18%)

Source: Breuer T, Benkel DH, Shapiro RL, et al. Analysis of cases in a multistate outbreak of *Escherichia coli* O157:H7 infection in 1997. Unpublished raw data.

(or both) were the offending vehicles. Their next steps would be to carry out analytic studies that would confirm the hypothesis, and to order environmental and traceback studies that would determine where the tainted products were produced and sold. With that information in hand, investigators would be able to recommend control measures to prevent further infection and illness.[2]

Descriptive Epidemiology Versus Analytic Epidemiology

As we have seen in this chapter, descriptive epidemiology is very useful as investigators develop hypotheses about the source of a health problem. Unlike analytic epidemiology (which we explore in the following chapters), however, descriptive epidemiology cannot be used to draw conclusions, because it looks only at cases. The commonalities that descriptive epidemiology finds among cases may be related to the health problem, or they may be common in the population at large. Analytic epidemiology, which adds a comparison group to the mix, is necessary to test hypotheses about the source of a health problem and to understand the "how" and "why" of the problem. Descriptive epidemiology tells investigators that all of the guests who became ill at a wedding ate the cake; analytic epidemiology allows them to determine whether everyone else ate the cake as well, which would exclude contaminated cake as a possible source of infection. Both approaches, which are summarized in Table 6-5, are critical to the success of the outbreak investigation.

Summary

Once investigators have determined that an outbreak has taken place or is under way, their next task is to generate a hypothesis or hypotheses about the exposure that caused it. In this phase of the outbreak investigation, investigators review the basic science of the illness and reports of previous investigations into similar outbreaks, conduct hypothesis-generating interviews with case patients, and use the tools of descriptive epidemiology to delineate the time, place, and person characteristics of the outbreak—that is, *when* and *where* people became ill, and *what* patients have in common that might suggest how they became ill. In the outbreak of *E. coli* O157:H7 infection described in this chapter, investigators followed these steps to develop the hypothesis that eating contaminated salad or

TABLE 6-5 Comparison of Descriptive and Analytic Epidemiology

Descriptive Epidemiology	Analytic Epidemiology
Search for clues	Clues available
Formulate hypotheses	Test hypotheses
No comparison group	Comparison group
Answers: How much, who, what, when, where	Answers: How, why

alfalfa sprouts most likely caused the patients to become ill. Once they have developed a strong hypothesis, investigators use analytic epidemiology, with the inclusion of a comparison group, to test hypotheses and confirm the *how* and *why* of the outbreak. In the next chapters, we explore epidemiologic methods that are available to test these hypotheses.

References

1. Davies SF, Sarosi GA. Epidemiological and clinical features of pulmonary blastomycosis. *Semin Respir Infect.* 1997;12(3):206–18.
2. Breuer T, Benkel DH, Shapiro RL, et al. A multistate outbreak of *Escherichia coli* 0157:H7 infections linked to alfalfa sprouts grown from contaminated seeds. *Emerg Infect Dis.* 2007;7(6). http://www.cdc.gov/ncidod/eid/vol7no6/breuer.htm. Accessed August 23, 2010.
3. Heymann DL, ed. *Control of Communicable Diseases Manual.* 19th ed. Washington, DC: American Public Health Association; 2008.
4. Friedman CR, Torigian C, Shillam PJ, et al. An outbreak of salmonellosis among children attending a reptile exhibit at a zoo. *J Pediatr.* 1998;132:802–807.
5. Taylor DN, Wachsmuth IK, Shangkuan Y-H, et al. Salmonellosis associated with marijuana: A multistate outbreak traced by plasmid fingerprinting. *N Engl J Med.* 1982;306:1249.
6. Centers for Disease Control and Prevention. Legionnaires disease associated with a whirlpool spa display—Virginia, September–October 1996. *Morb Mortal Weekly Rep.* 1997;46(4):83–6.
7. U.S. Department of Health and Human Services. Principles of Epidemiology: An Introduction to Applied Epidemiology and Biostatistics, 2nd ed. Self-study course 3030-G. Lesson 6: Investigating an Outbreak. http://www.phppo.cdc.gov/PHTN/catalog/pdf-file/Epi_Course.pdf. Accessed October 8, 2010.
8. Cummings, SR, Stewart AL, Hulley SB. Designing questionnaires and data collection instruments. In Hulley SB, Cummings SR, Browner WS, et al., eds. *Designing Clinical Research*, 2nd ed. Philadelphia, PA: Lippincott Williams and Wilkins; 2001:231–45.
9. National Institute for Occupational Safety and Health. Worker Health Chartbook 2004. NIOSH Publication No. 2004-146. http://www.cdc.gov/niosh/docs/2004-146/ch2/ch2-2.asp.htm. Accessed on September 23, 2010.
10. National Institute for Occupation Safety and Health. Silicosis. NIOSH Publication No. 2004-108. http://www.cdc.gov/niosh/docs/2004-108/default.html. Accessed September 23, 2010.

Chapter 7

Epidemiological Studies in Outbreak Investigations

Jeanette K. Stehr-Green
Paul A. Stehr-Green
Pia D. M. MacDonald

Learning Objectives

By the end of this chapter, the reader will be able to:

- Describe the three types of analytic studies most commonly used in public health.

- List the strengths and weaknesses of each study type.

- Identify the best analytic study given an example of an outbreak.

- Describe the components of a case definition and cite examples of case definitions.

- Describe the most effective ways to identify and select cases for an analytic study.

- List ways to define and determine exposure status for an analytic study.

- Describe the function of a comparison group in an analytic study and discuss ways to identify a comparison group.

- List factors that can potentially affect the validity of an analytic study.

Introduction

Chapter 6 describes how to develop a hypothesis about the source of a health problem—such as an outbreak—based on the basic biology and epidemiology of the disease agent, the descriptive epidemiology of cases, and hypothesis-generating interviews. The resulting hypothesis will look something like this:

In a given population, a particular exposure leads to a particular outcome.

The "outcome of interest" can be a disease, injury, or death, or a healthy or unhealthy behavior. If the outcome is a disease, it can be either clinical (resulting in overt signs and symptoms) or subclinical (before signs and symptoms of the disease become apparent; detectable only through clinical examination or laboratory tests).

The "exposure of interest" is a factor that the investigator believes is linked to the outcome in some way, either by causing the disease or by affecting the likelihood of its occurrence. It can comprise exposure to a contaminant, a healthy or unhealthy behavior, a medical treatment (use of antibiotics or a surgical treatment, for example), or a characteristic of the host (the person or population with the exposure of interest) such as age, gender, genetic make-up, or underlying illnesses.

In the outbreak explored in Chapter 6, for example, investigators developed the following hypothesis:

> In a given population (38 patients in Michigan who became ill in June 1997), a particular exposure (eating contaminated salad or alfalfa sprouts) most likely caused a particular outcome (illness from *E. coli* O157:H7 infection).[1]

Once an investigator develops a hypothesis, the next step is to evaluate its credibility. In most instances, investigators use an analytic study to test a hypothesis. An analytic study compares observed data from a group of interest (people with either the exposure or the outcome of interest) with expected data from a comparison group. The comparison group provides a baseline of how much exposure or how much disease investigators might expect to find in the population under study (the "expected data") if an outbreak were not occurring. Comparing the two groups allows investigators to quantify the relationship between an exposure and an outcome, test hypotheses about causal relationships, and try to rule out the role of chance.

Investigators commonly use one of three types of studies to test hypotheses about public health problems such as outbreaks: cohort studies, case-control studies, or cross-sectional studies. We will examine each of these study types in this chapter. First, however, we discuss a study design that most investigators will probably never use in public health practice—an experimental study. The experimental study design sets the standard for epidemiologic research.

In an experimental study design (Figure 7-1), investigators attempt to change the outcome of interest among participants by manipulating the exposure of interest while controlling other factors that could be related to the outcome. Strict enrollment criteria determine which participants will be enrolled in the study. These criteria are established, in part, to make the participants more homogeneous; they include such factors as age group, disease stage, or having no risk factors for poor outcomes or side effects due to the exposure. Participants are then randomly assigned into exposure groups (exposure versus no exposure, or high-level exposure versus low-level exposure, for example). Investigators closely monitor participant exposure and outcome status over time using strict definitions. At the conclusion of the study, investigators compare the occurrence of the outcome(s) of interest among participants with different exposures and draw conclusions about the relationship between the exposure and the outcome.

One experimental study design is a randomized controlled therapeutic trial. In this type of study, patients with a particular disease are randomly assigned to a new treatment or the standard course of treatment. Investigators follow the patients to learn whether their illness improves (or is cured) and which side effects they experience. They compare the

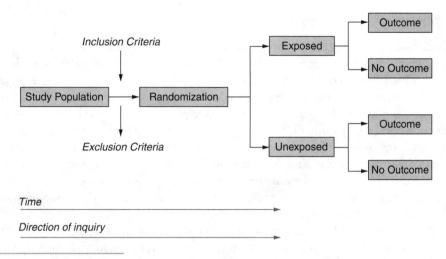

Figure 7-1   Design of an experimental study

outcomes of the two exposure groups to determine whether the new treatment offers any advantage over the standard course of treatment. An example would be a clinical trial in which patients with schizophrenia are randomly selected to receive either dipyridamo-leone (a new-generation therapy) or olanzapine (a standard therapy).

Experimental studies are considered the "gold standard" in epidemiology for at least two reasons. First, because enrollment criteria are strict and participants are randomly assigned to exposure groups, there is a good chance that the groups will be comparable on all factors possibly related to the outcome—except the exposure of interest, of course. Making the two groups as similar as possible increases the likelihood that differences in outcomes among the groups will be attributable to differences in the exposure of interest, rather than reflecting other differences between the groups. Second, because investigators follow participants closely using strict criteria and definitions, it is less likely that they will misclassify either the exposure or the outcome status of any given participant. In other words, participants labeled as having the exposure of interest will be very likely to have the exposure; participants labeled as having the outcome of interest will be very likely to have the outcome. Accurately determining exposure and outcome status increases the chances of detecting a difference in outcomes among exposure groups, if one exists.

Even though experimental studies are the gold standard for epidemiologic studies, investigators rarely conduct such experiments when they investigate outbreaks and other applied public health problems, for several reasons. First, investigators usually cannot assign exposures to health problems; the exposures have generally already occurred through genetics, choice, or circumstance. Second, because most of the exposures of interest studied in public health have a negative impact on the subject's physical or mental health, it would be unethical to expose individuals to them.

Observational Studies

Analytic studies of outbreaks and other public health problems take a different tack: They are almost always observational studies. An observational study is an epidemiological study in which the investigator does not intervene.[2] Instead of manipulating exposures (as in an experimental study design), in most cases the investigator in an observational study examines exposures or outcomes that have already occurred. He or she selects a group of people (the "group of interest") who already have either the exposure of interest or the outcome of interest, and compares the group of interest to another group (the "comparison group") whose members have not had the exposure or have not developed the outcome of interest. The investigator then draws conclusions about the relationship between the exposure and the outcome by comparing the people in the group of interest with the people in the comparison group.

Compared to the gold standard of experimental studies, observational studies have two major shortcomings. First, it is difficult to identify the appropriate comparison group. In an experimental study, participants are drawn from the same pool of patients and are randomly assigned to exposure groups. Careful randomization increases the probability that the groups are comparable at the start of the study, so that differences in outcomes accurately reflect differences in exposures. The same is not true in an observational study. As investigators observe and select people with (or without) the exposure or with (or without) the outcome for inclusion in the study, the potential exists that the groups will not be comparable with respect to a number of other factors besides the exposure or the outcome. Differences with respect to these other factors could affect the observed exposure–outcome relationship and lead investigators to draw erroneous conclusions based on study findings.

The second shortcoming shared by observational studies is the difficulty in determining exposure and/or outcome status among participants. In an experimental study, investigators monitor exposure and outcome over time, as they occur. They use strict classification criteria and collect information solely for the purposes of the study. In contrast, with the exception of prospective cohort studies, observational studies look back at events that have already taken place. Exposure could have occurred days, months, or years before the study. It may have been intermittent, unapparent, or otherwise difficult to recognize. The participant's knowledge of the outcome or hypotheses under investigation, or the disease experience itself, could affect his or her recollection of the exposure. All of these factors increase the likelihood that exposures will be misclassified. Similarly, the outcome may be misclassified if the outcome criteria are too loose or vague or if the methods used to find cases or determine outcome are insensitive or inconsistently applied. Errors in design and method can also influence the observed exposure–outcome relationship.

Depending on the specifics of a particular observational study (regardless of study type), these weaknesses may occur to a greater or lesser extent. Investigators should keep them in mind, along with the strengths of any particular study.

Cohort Studies

Of all the observational studies, the approach of the cohort study (Figure 7-2) most closely resembles an experimental study design. In a cohort study, the investigator selects study participants from the at-risk population who have not yet developed the outcome of interest. Study participants are divided into two groups—exposed and not exposed. The investigator can then compare the occurrence of outcome in the exposed and unexposed groups.

Cohort studies can be undertaken prospectively or retrospectively. In a prospective cohort study, participants who are alike in many ways but differ by a certain characteristic are enrolled into the study and followed for a specified time period to determine whether they develop the outcome of interest. An example might be a group of female nurses, some of whom smoke and some of whom do not, who are studied over time for the occurrence of lung cancer.[3] In a retrospective cohort study, investigators work backward: They identify participants based on their characteristics in the past and then trace their subsequent disease experience until some defined point in the more recent past or until the present time (or occasionally into the future).[4] A classic example is reconstructing what people might have eaten at the church picnic that made them ill; another example might be monitoring children who have been exposed to the chickenpox virus to see who contracts the illness. Retrospective studies rely on historical exposure information obtained from interviews, medical records, environmental and laboratory testing, and other sources. Prospective cohort studies are rarely used to investigate public health problems that require quick action to identify the source of the problem and implement control measures, but investigators often use retrospective cohort studies.

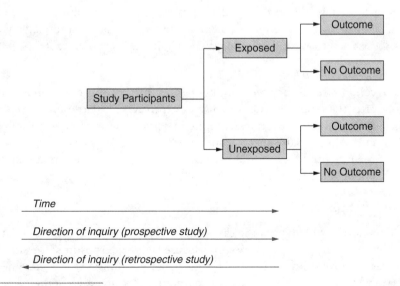

Figure 7-2   Design of a cohort study

Consider this example of a retrospective cohort study: The composition of the influenza vaccine used in the 2003–2004 influenza season was not well matched to the influenza virus that ultimately circulated that year. To determine the effectiveness of the 2003–2004 influenza vaccine, investigators conducted a retrospective cohort study of children enrolled in Kaiser Permanente Colorado. Children who were 6 to 23 months of age and had received two influenza vaccinations (the exposure of interest) were compared with children who had received no influenza vaccinations. Investigators examined the medical records (both inpatient and outpatient) of both groups for healthcare provider visits for the outcomes of interest—influenza-like illness, pneumonia, and influenza—using specific International Classification of Diseases (ICD) coding of the visit in the patient's medical chart to identify outcomes of interest. (Diagnoses did not have to be laboratory confirmed.) The investigators then compared the risk of developing any of these illnesses between fully vaccinated children and children who received no vaccinations.

This investigation was a cohort study because participants were enrolled based on their exposure status—vaccination versus no vaccination. It was retrospective because subjects were enrolled into the study after the exposure—receiving or not receiving the influenza vaccine. Investigators determined outcome status by using medical records, looking for healthcare provider visits that noted influenza-like illnesses.[5]

Strengths of Cohort Studies

Cohort studies are well suited to examine health effects following a relatively rare exposure. Each person with the exposure can be enrolled into the study and followed over time. Because entrance into a cohort study begins with exposure status, as opposed to outcome status, a cohort study allows investigators to monitor the occurrence of multiple outcomes that may result from a particular exposure. Finally, in a cohort study, investigators can directly measure the absolute risk of an outcome. A cohort study can answer the question, "What is the risk of developing disease X, if one is exposed to it?"

Weaknesses of Cohort Studies

Prospective cohort studies may require long periods of time if the outcome of interest occurs long after the exposure. They can also be expensive. The latter problem is magnified if the outcome of interest is rare, requiring investigators to follow larger numbers of exposed persons. Also, because entrance into a cohort study is based on exposure status, investigators cannot use a cohort study to examine multiple exposures that may be associated with an outcome.

Case-Control Studies

The second analytic study type is the case-control study (Figure 7-3). In contrast to the cohort study, in which participants are enrolled based on their exposure status, the investigator in a case-control study selects study participants according to their outcome status, regardless of whether they have the exposure of interest. The investigator then determines the prior occurrence of the exposure of interest, comparing individuals who had the

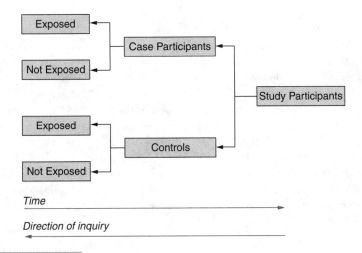

Figure 7-3 Design of a case-control study

outcome (cases) with individuals who did not (controls). Case-control studies rely on historical exposure information obtained through interviews, medical charts, environmental testing results, and other similar records. Because case-control studies are conceptually simple and usually can be completed relatively quickly, investigators frequently use them to investigate acute infectious disease outbreaks and other public health problems.

The companion study to the retrospective cohort study described previously provides a good example of a case-control study. To determine the effectiveness of the 2003-2004 influenza vaccine, investigators conducted a case-control study among persons aged 50 to 64 years. Cases—people who had influenza—were selected from the list of patients with laboratory-confirmed influenza reported to the Colorado Department of Public Health and Environment from November 1 to December 31, 2003. Controls—people who did not have influenza—were recruited through random-digit dialing using the same area code as the patients. During telephone interviews, investigators collected information on demographics, vaccination, and illness from both cases and controls. Investigators then compared the exposure—receiving or not receiving the vaccination—between cases and controls.

This investigation was a case-control study because participants were enrolled into the study based on their outcome status—whether they developed laboratory-confirmed influenza. Investigators interviewed patients to determine prior occurrence of the exposure—influenza vaccination.[5]

Strengths of Case-Control Studies
Case-control studies are ideal for studying outcomes that occur infrequently. Investigators can pointedly search for individuals with the outcome of interest and enroll them

> ## The Public Health Impact of Observational Studies
>
> While the Colorado vaccination studies were cited here as simple examples of cohort and case-control studies, it is interesting to note the public health impact of the two studies. The Kaiser Permanente Colorado cohort study demonstrated that the influenza vaccine had a 25% to 49% efficacy in preventing non-laboratory-confirmed influenza, and the Colorado Department of Public Health and Environment case-control study demonstrated that it had a 38% to 52% efficacy in preventing laboratory-confirmed influenza. Although these rates were substantially less than the 70% to 90% efficacy of the influenza vaccine in years when vaccine and circulating influenza viral strains are well matched, both studies showed substantial health benefits resulting from the vaccine. These studies supported public health recommendations to continue influenza vaccination efforts in 2004 despite a suboptimal match between the predominant circulating influenza and vaccine viral strains.[5]

into the study. (In situations of very rare health outcomes, however, the identification and enrollment of an adequate number of cases could still be problematic.) Because entrance into a case-control study begins with outcome status, as opposed to exposure status, a case-control study allows investigators to examine the relationship between multiple exposures and the outcome of interest. Finally, case-control studies typically provide a greater statistical power to detect differences between the group of interest and the comparison group, if they exist, compared to cohort and cross-sectional studies with the same number of subjects.

Weaknesses of Case-Control Studies

People are enrolled in case-control studies based on their outcome status, so investigators cannot use this type of study to examine multiple outcomes that may be associated with an exposure. In addition, it is not easy for investigators to use the results of case-control studies to calculate the absolute risk of an outcome given an exposure—that is, the observed or calculated probability that an event will take place in the population being studied.[2]

Cross-Sectional Studies

In a cross-sectional study (Figure 7-4), the investigator defines the population to be studied and then collects information from members of the population about their exposure status and outcome status. Subjects are enrolled into the study because they are members of the at-risk population, not because of their exposure or outcome status. Investigators can then compare individuals with and without exposures of interest to determine which participants also have the selected outcomes of interest. Investigators often use cross-sectional studies to determine the prevalence of an exposure or an outcome in a population of interest—in particular, chronic diseases and related risk factors.

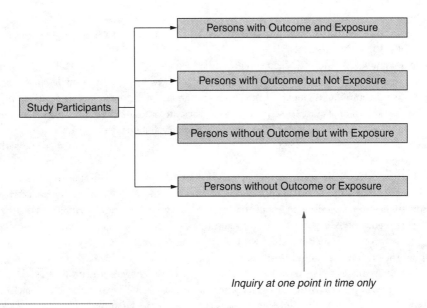

Figure 7-4   Design of a cross-sectional study

A cross-sectional study is essentially a survey. One well-known survey is the Behavioral Risk Factor Surveillance System (BRFSS), a state-based, random-digit-dialed telephone survey of the U.S. civilian, noninstitutionalized population aged 18 years and older. It covers demographic characteristics such as age, sex, education, and income; illnesses such as previous diagnosis of diabetes, high blood pressure, or asthma; and health-related habits such as smoking, consumption of alcohol, and use of preventive healthcare services. By providing prevalence estimates of risk factors and health conditions, the BRFSS helps guide direct public health education and other control/intervention programs.

Strengths of Cross-Sectional Studies
Cross-sectional studies are usually the most economical study type because investigators can examine multiple outcomes and multiple exposures through one effort. The data from this type of study, like the data obtained through cohort studies, are often useful for estimating absolute risk of outcome occurrence for a given exposure.

Weaknesses of Cross-Sectional Studies
Because investigators determine exposure and outcome status at the same time in a cross-sectional study, it is often difficult to assess the reasons for apparent associations between exposure and outcome or to determine cause and effect (which requires observations over time). This study design also has the lowest statistical power for the same number of subjects of all the study designs discussed so far.

A Small Controversy: Retrospective Cohort Studies Versus Cross-Sectional Studies

When a point-source outbreak occurs in a well-defined group of people—attendees at a church supper, guests at a wedding reception, or passengers on a cruise ship, for example—investigators will frequently enroll all members of the group into an analytic study and, in one concerted effort, question them about exposures (e.g., what they ate or drank during the event) and signs and symptoms of illness (e.g., vomiting, diarrhea, abdominal pain). To try to determine the source of the outbreak, investigators compare the development of illness among people with and without selected exposures.

This approach is commonly used in acute infectious disease outbreaks, but has a small controversy attached to it. Some epidemiologists consider these studies to be "retrospective cohort studies" because all members of the group were well before they assembled as a group and were then exposed to something that causes illness. Thus analyses to identify the source of the problem compare group members with and without the exposure, as opposed to with and without the outcome, as would be the approach of a case-control study. Other epidemiologists consider these studies to be "cross-sectional studies" because subjects are enrolled based on their "membership" in a particular population, not because of their exposure or outcome status; information on exposure and outcome status is collected at the same time.

For the purposes of this book, we will call these studies "retrospective cohort studies," reserving the term "cross-sectional study" for traditional chronic disease surveys that estimate the prevalence of a health problem and associated risk factors. Investigators should be aware of this disagreement when conducting a study or reading about a study undertaken by others, however: The methods and approach may be the same, but the label may be different.

Case Series

A fourth type of observational study, the case series, is less widely used than the cohort, case-control, and cross-sectional designs, but it has its place. As implied by the name, a case series studies case patients—the people who have developed the outcome of interest. Unlike the other observational studies, in a case series these individuals serve as their own comparison group. Investigators examine different time periods in the life of each case enrolled in the series for the occurrence of the outcome of interest. Investigators typically focus on time periods before the exposure of interest (the "unexposed time period") and after the exposure of interest (the "exposed time period"). They analyze the data by comparing the occurrence of the outcome of interest during the different time periods. Because cases serve as their own comparison group in a case series, the groups compared are relatively equivalent; that is, they are comparable on all factors possibly related to the exposure or outcome.

The case series approach has been used in examining adverse events related to vaccination. For example, in 1998, the U.S. Food and Drug Administration (FDA) licensed a vaccine against rotavirus, the most common cause of severe gastroenteritis worldwide. Over the next 10 months, 15 cases of intussusception were reported among infants who had received the vaccine. (Intussusception is a form of bowel obstruction in which one segment of bowel becomes enfolded within another segment like a collapsed telescope.) Ultimately, more than 400 cases of intussusception were reported.

Investigators used a case series approach to determine whether most cases of intussusception occurred shortly after vaccination or whether they were distributed more uniformly over a longer time period. They examined the occurrence of intussusception among cases for the following time periods for each case: 3 to 7 days after vaccination, 8 to 14 days after vaccination, and 15 to 21 days after vaccination. The occurrence of intussusception in each of these time periods was individually compared to the occurrence of intussusception in these same infants for a selected time period before vaccination. Through this analysis, researchers confirmed that the greatest risk of intussusception was observed 3 to 7 days after vaccination. On July 16, 1998, the Centers for Disease Control and Prevention (CDC) recommended suspension of use of the vaccine.[6]

When to Use Which Study Approach

When does an outbreak investigation team use each of the three major observational study types (cohort, case-control, and cross-sectional studies)? This is not an easy decision. Here are a few questions investigators can ask to help guide the decision (see also Table 7-1):

- What is already known about the exposure–outcome relationship? If little is known and multiple exposures are of interest, then a cross-sectional or case-control study is likely the best choice. Investigators often use cross-sectional studies to generate hypotheses before undertaking a more in-depth study.

- How common is the outcome of interest? If it is rare, a case-control study would allow investigators to search pointedly for cases and enroll as many people with the outcome as possible into the study.

- How common is the exposure of interest? If it is rare, investigators would likely elect to conduct a cohort study, which would allow them to search pointedly for exposed persons and enroll as many exposed persons as possible in the study.

- What is the proposed time period between exposure and outcome? How soon are the results of the study needed? If the disease takes a long time to develop and investigators need answers quickly so they can implement intervention or control measures, they would be unlikely to choose a prospective cohort study. A case-control, retrospective cohort, or cross-sectional design could be executed more quickly.

TABLE 7-1   The Strengths and Weaknesses of Experimental Study Types

Study Type	Strengths	Weaknesses	Best Use
Cohort	• Good for study of rare exposures • Can examine multiple outcomes • Provides most direct measurement of absolute risk	• Higher cost • Long time to complete • Can study only single exposures	• When exposure is rare • When outcome is common • When the population at risk is well defined
Case-control	• Good for study of rare diseases • Can examine multiple exposures • Most statistical power	• Cannot examine multiple outcomes • Cannot easily be used to calculate absolute risk	• When outcome is rare • If outcome has a long latency • When exposure is common • When the population at risk is not well defined
Cross-sectional	• Economical • Can examine multiple exposures and outcomes • May be used to calculate absolute risk	• Not easy to assess reasons for associations • Least statistical power	• As a first step for a more in-depth study

- Do investigators have access to a particular study population or existing data? If a disease registry or surveillance system provides access to cases, a case-control study might make more sense. If a registry of people with a particular exposure exists, or if a means to identify people with a particular exposure is available, a cohort study might be the better choice.

- Is the population at risk well defined? If the population at risk is well defined (e.g., guests at a wedding, patrons from a restaurant, workers at a factory), then either a cohort or case-control study can be undertaken. If the population at risk is not well defined, a case-control study should be undertaken.

- What are the budget and resources available to the study? A prospective cohort study is likely to be the most expensive approach, a cross-sectional study the least expensive, and a case-control or retrospective cohort study somewhere in between.

How to Select a Study Type: Some Examples

Problem 1

A nationwide epidemic of a new disease, eosinophilia myalgia syndrome (EMS), was recognized after a physician in New Mexico and a consultant in Minnesota saw three patients with severe muscle pain and a marked increase in eosinophils, a type of white blood cell. All three patients had been taking a food supplement called L-tryptophan. An announcement about the cases led to reports of more than 250 additional cases of EMS from 37 states. Previous exposure to L-tryptophan was unknown for these cases. Investigators hypothesized that L-tryptophan was the cause of this new disease.

Best Choice of Study for Problem 1

The population at risk for this new illness was not known. With only a few hundred cases of EMS identified across the United States, it was also relatively rare. Although exposure to L-tryptophan was reported for the initial cases, it was only one of many exposures investigators would probably have wanted to examine. A case-control study would probably have been the best choice for this investigation.[7]

Problem 2

On May 20, 1996, the chief medical officer of the Ontario Health Department notified the Texas Department of Health about *Cyclospora* infections in three Canadian businessmen. The three men were among 28 participants from three U.S. states and Canada who attended a meeting at a private club in Houston on May 9–10. Meals served during the meeting were prepared at the restaurant operated by the private club. Members of the restaurant staff suggested that other attendees at the meeting had also become ill.

Best Choice of Study for Problem 2

Because the *Cyclospora* outbreak was associated with a business meeting that involved a small, well-defined group of attendees, investigators decided to use a cohort study to identify the source. Because they initiated the study after the exposures leading to the outbreak and relied on the collection of historical exposure information, it was a retrospective cohort study.[8] (Recall that some epidemiologists might call this a cross-sectional study.)

Problem 3

Congenital rubella syndrome results from infection with rubella virus before birth and is characterized by multiple birth defects (e.g., abnormally small head and eyes, cataracts, glaucoma, cardiovascular defects, hearing loss), mental retardation, and fetal loss. Because the measles–mumps–rubella (MMR) vaccine contains attenuated live viruses, the Advisory Committee on Immunization Practices (ACIP) recommended that pregnant women not be vaccinated with MMR during early pregnancy for fear of possible congenital rubella syndrome. This recommendation was largely based on theory, however; no controlled studies had been undertaken. (Women who were pregnant but did not know they were pregnant and were vaccinated with MMR were reported to the CDC and included in a registry.)

Best Choice of Study for Problem 3

The best type of study to examine the relationship between MMR vaccination during early pregnancy and congenital rubella syndrome is a retrospective cohort study. Given the ACIP recommendations, the exposure of interest—MMR vaccination—was likely to be rare in this population. Pregnant women exposed to the vaccine and reported to CDC could become the exposed group for the cohort study. Pregnant women who did not receive the MMR vaccine could serve as a comparison group. Investigators could then follow both groups over time for congenital rubella syndrome in the offspring of that pregnancy. The follow-up period would probably need to last for several years: Although moderate and severe cases of congenital rubella syndrome are usually diagnosed shortly after birth, mild cases might not be detected for months or years.[9]

Problem 4

Each year, more than 30,000 deaths among persons 65 years of age and older are attributed to complications of influenza infection. The single best way to protect against influenza is to be vaccinated each fall. The CDC recommends that (among other high-risk persons) all people 65 and older should be vaccinated; however, many people in this age group fail to be vaccinated. Information is needed to better target public health education campaigns to encourage influenza vaccination.

Best Choice of Study for Problem 4

The ideal type of study to estimate influenza vaccine coverage in persons 65 years and older and to characterize people in this age group who do (or do not) get vaccinated is a traditional cross-sectional study—that is, a survey. Because the population of interest is persons 65 years and older, investigators would enroll people from this age group into the study and collect information on whether the person was vaccinated that year, as well as personal or demographic characteristics that might influence whether he or she decided to get vaccinated against influenza. The investigators could then compare individuals who did get vaccinated with those who did not and identify characteristics associated with vaccination, such as income, education, and access to health care. In 2004 and 2005, for example, the BRFSS (described earlier in the discussion of cross-sectional studies) included the question, "During the past 12 months, have you had a flu shot?"[10]

Problem 5

On September 28, 2002, a cruise ship embarked with 1,984 passengers and 941 crew members for a 7-day round-trip cruise from Florida to the Caribbean. By October 1, at least 70 passengers (4%) and 2 crew members (0.2%) had reported an acute gastrointestinal illness suggestive of norovirus infection. On October 3, CDC investigators boarded the ship to conduct an epidemiologic investigation.

Best Choice of Study for Problem 5

Either a cohort study or a case-control study would have been appropriate to investigate the source of this norovirus outbreak. The population at risk was well defined, consisting of cruise ship passengers and crew, who presumably were well and unexposed at the time they boarded the ship. These characteristics support the choice of a cohort study. Given the large number of individuals involved, however, a cohort study would have been costly and taken a long time—a significant consideration when passengers were due to disembark in one day. Investigators could have selected a random sample of the cohort, which would have been an easier undertaking. However, the outcome was seemingly rare—only 70 cases or approximately 4% of the individuals onboard—and a random sample would have captured fewer cases, decreasing the power of the study to find a source of the outbreak.

A case-control study would have allowed investigators to limit the number of subjects involved in the study, include a sufficient number of cases to assure adequate study power, and focus efforts on the smaller number of subjects to get higher participation/response rates. A case-control study also could be executed more quickly than a cohort study. Given the impending disembarkation of passengers, a case-control study would appear to have been the most cost-effective study type for this situation.[11]

When to Use More Than One Study

In the studies of influenza vaccine efficacy mentioned earlier in the chapter (i.e., the Kaiser Permanente Colorado cohort study and the Colorado Department of Public Health and Environment case-control study), investigators examined the same hypothesis using different study designs and populations. This practice is not uncommon. Investigators frequently approach a public health problem from different angles, depending on the resources and study populations available to them.

Study Details

Selecting a study type is just the beginning. To design and carry out a successful analytic study, investigators need to perform the following steps:

- Define the outcome of interest and find people with that outcome (or determine whether study participants have the outcome of interest)
- Establish the criteria for exposure and find people with that exposure (or determine whether study participants have been exposed or not)
- Identify the appropriate comparison group and recruit members of the group to participate in the study

Bad decisions at this stage could have serious consequences. At a minimum, they could limit the ultimate interpretation of the study findings or invalidate the results. At worst, they could result in erroneous conclusions about the problem and lead to ineffective (or even harmful) control measures.

Defining the Outcome

Discriminating between people with and without the outcome of interest is critical to the success of an analytical study. If the study hinges on comparing cases with controls and some of the controls are really cases or some of the cases are really controls, investigators might draw erroneous conclusions about the relationship between the exposure and the outcome. Developing an effective case definition is the best way to make sure investigators select their cases accurately.

As discussed in Chapter 4, a case definition is a standard set of criteria used to decide whether an individual should be classified as having an outcome of interest. The components of a case definition include clinical criteria, such as signs, symptoms, and results of laboratory tests, and restrictions by time, place, and person.

The criteria included in a case definition should be discriminating, so investigators are able to distinguish people with the outcome of interest from people with other diseases or no illness at all. They should also be as objective as possible and not open to interpretation. Thus different investigators should be able to apply the same criteria and reach the same outcome classification.

The case definition for an analytic study should never include exposures that the investigators wish to study (i.e., hypotheses on the source of the problem that investigators wish to test); if the case definition does not exclude exposures they plan to study, then every individual who meets the case definition will have the exposure. In these circumstances, the study will not be able to examine the association between the outcome of interest and the exposure because, by definition, all of the "cases" will have both.

In most case definitions, some people who truly have the outcome of interest will not meet the case definition (i.e., *false negatives*) and some people without the outcome will meet the case definition (i.e., *false positives*). The *sensitivity* and *specificity* of the case definition will determine whether the study leans toward limiting the number of false negatives (i.e., including as many cases as possible) or excluding as many false positives as possible. A sensitive case definition will capture a large proportion of people who truly have the outcome. A specific case definition will exclude a large proportion of people who do not have the outcome of interest. Patients meeting a specific case definition will be very likely to have the outcome of interest.

Both sensitive and specific case definitions have shortcomings. If the case definition used in an analytic study is too sensitive, it is likely to misclassify people who do not have the outcome of interest as case patients. Such misclassification errors can obscure the association between an exposure and an outcome and lead to erroneous conclusions. The effect usually, but not always, is toward finding no association between the exposure and the outcome of interest, thereby underestimating the true exposure–outcome relationship. Conversely, if the case definition is too specific, it will exclude true cases from the study. A decrease in the number of cases will decrease the statistical power of the study and the investigator's ability to find differences between the group of interest and the comparison group. Furthermore, excluding true cases may lead to a selection bias if some systematic difference exists between cases that meet the case definition and cases that do not.

Should the case definition for an analytic study be sensitive or specific? Investigators will likely base their decision on the outcome of interest, the means typically used to diagnose it, the stage of the investigation, and the circumstances surrounding the investigation. Ideally, the investigator will strike a balance between capturing as many cases as possible and excluding as many individuals as possible who do not have the outcome of interest. Because this aim is not always easy to achieve, some investigators apply both a more sensitive case definition and a more specific case definition when they analyze the information they have collected, and compare the results to determine the impact of misclassification that results from using a more sensitive case definition.

Here is an example: In a 2004 outbreak of histoplasmosis at an agricultural processing plant in Nebraska investigators defined cases in two ways:

Case Definition 1 (More Sensitive)

Clinical Criteria

- Fever *and*
- One of the following: headache, cough, chest pain, or shortness of breath

Restrictions by Person, Place, and Time

- Plant A worker *and*
- Onset of symptoms since January 1, 2004

Case Definition 2 (More Specific)

Clinical Criteria

- Fever *and*
- One of the following: headache, cough, chest pain, or shortness of breath *and*
- Histoplasmosis complement fixation titer of 1:32 or greater, or presence of an h or m band by immunodiffusion test

Restrictions by Person, Place, and Time

- Plant A worker *and*
- Onset of symptoms between January 7 and January 25, 2004

One hundred eight workers met the first case definition. Forty-four (41%) of the cases reported exposure to a particular building complex ("building complex X") compared with 141 (23%) of the controls (odds ratio = 2.8, $P < .0001$).

Eighteen workers met the second case definition. Twelve (67%) of these cases reported exposure to building complex X compared to 8 (26%) of 31 controls (odds ratio = 5.8, $P = .005$).

Using either case definition, illness was associated with building complex X, although the association was stronger with the more specific case definition. This finding suggests there was some misclassification of cases using the more sensitive case definition. However, the number of cases decreased from 44 to 18 using the more specific case definition.[12]

Case Identification and Selection

Accurately determining the outcome status and including a representative sample of people with the outcome of interest is of paramount importance in analytic studies. If the cases included in a study are not representative of all cases—only hospitalized patients, patients at risk for poor outcomes, or secondary cases are included, for example—or if investigators have inconsistently identified those who develop the outcome, the study may be biased. Investigators must be diligent about how they identify and select cases for an analytic study. Bias can jeopardize the validity of the study findings or, at least, make it more difficult to generalize the results.

So how do investigators identify cases? If the outcome affects a clearly identifiable at-risk population, such as people attending a picnic or workers in a particular building, finding cases will be relatively self-evident and easy. The investigators will interview or screen all of the people in the group and determine whether they have the outcome of interest. Investigators should carefully follow both exposed and unexposed participants to see whether they develop the outcome.

In contrast, if the population at risk is unknown or widely dispersed, investigators may need to search actively for cases. Here are some case-finding approaches:

- Contact physicians, hospitals, and emergency rooms; describe signs and symptoms suggestive of the outcome; and ask that all similar cases be reported.

- Contact laboratories that do testing related to the outcome and ask to be notified of patients with positive tests.

- Review medical records for hospitalized patients with a particular discharge diagnosis.

- Review death certificates for selected causes of death.

- Examine disease-specific registries.

- Talk with cases to identify other people with similar health problems.

- Notify the public through news media—newspapers, radio, television, Internet—and ask that people who may have had the outcome or exposure of interest see their healthcare providers.

Of course, once they have identified possible cases, investigators need to confirm who is a case patient and who is not by carefully and systematically applying the case definition without regard to the exposure status of the individual.

Defining the Exposure

Determining an individual's "exposure status"—that is, whether the person has been exposed to the suspected cause of disease—is as important as determining whether the person is a case patient. Both require investigators to develop and consistently apply a standard set of criteria to classify individuals. When exposure is a discrete event, such as eating a particular food at a picnic, defining exposure status can be relatively straightforward. However, when exposure is prolonged or difficult to quantify, investigators may need to apply a more complex definition of exposure that takes disease latency periods into account.

The following types of criteria are often used to determine exposure status:

- Estimates of the level of exposure in the person's environment
- History of a one-time, occasional, or routine occupational, recreational, or other activity that puts the person at risk of exposure
- Physical signs characteristic of exposure
- Laboratory tests that directly quantify concentrations, metabolites, or physiologic markers of exposure in such biologic specimens as whole blood, serum, urine, or saliva
- Restrictions by time, place, and person

Here are some examples of criteria for exposure:

- For an outbreak of gastroenteritis following a church picnic, the definition of exposure is based on each individual's recollection of foods eaten at the supper.
- For an outbreak of *E. coli* O157:H7 associated with a water park, the definition of exposure is based on whether the individual swam at the park during days when routine water sampling found elevated levels of fecal coliforms (i.e., bacteria often found in sewage or human waste).
- For a study of risk factors associated with meningococcal meningitis, the definition of exposure to a carrier is determined by a culture of the nose and throat of household contacts for *Meningococcal meningitides*.
- For a study of the impact of genital herpes on the progression of HIV infection, the definition of exposure is based on serologic evidence of infection with herpes simplex types 1 and 2.

Investigators sometimes use more than one measure of exposure to determine exposure status. For example, if the church picnic took place at a campground with a lake, both eating the potato salad and swimming in the lake might be criteria for exposure. Thus investigators would query guests who became ill about the food they ate and whether they swam in the lake.

When investigators develop a set of exposure criteria for an analytic study, they follow the same guidelines as they do when they develop a case definition. The criteria should be discriminating (i.e., able to distinguish people with the exposure from people without it), as objective as possible, and not open to interpretation. Different investigators should be able to apply the same criteria and come up with the same exposure classifications. Moreover, the characteristics of the outcome(s) that the study is designed to examine—the hypothesis or hypotheses to be tested—should never be part of the definition of an exposure.

As with case definitions, exposure criteria can be made more sensitive, so as to identify the maximum number of persons who may have been exposed, or more specific, so as to include only those persons who definitely had the exposure of interest. The decision to use a sensitive versus a specific definition should be based on the exposure, the stage of the investigation, and the circumstances surrounding the investigation.

Choosing a Comparison Group

Use of a comparison group is the hallmark of an analytic study. The comparison group provides a baseline of what to expect in the group of interest, whether they were selected because of their outcome status or because of their exposure status. In a case-control study, the comparison group provides the expected prevalence of the exposure of interest in the community. In a cohort study, it provides the expected incidence of the outcome of interest. By comparing the "observed data" in the group of interest with the "expected data" in the comparison group, investigators can quantify the relationship between exposure and outcome and test the statistical significance of various hypotheses.

Choosing a suitable comparison group is often the most difficult decision in designing a study. The key is to select a comparison group that is representative of the population from which the group of interest is derived on all relevant factors that predict both exposure and outcome. In some studies, all that is necessary is a random selection of other members in the community—that is, members who do not have the outcome or the exposure under investigation, depending on which kind of study investigators are undertaking. To truly reflect the target population from which the group of interest came, however, the comparison group in some studies may need to share certain characteristics with the group of interest. The process in which these commonalities are assured is called matching.

Matching

Matching is covered in more detail in Chapter 9, but this section provides an example to help readers understand the occasional need to match.

Suppose investigators want to undertake a cohort study to examine the association between breastfeeding (the exposure of interest) and the incidence of infant diarrhea (the outcome of interest) in an underdeveloped country. It is to be an observational study; that is, investigators will not randomly assign babies to be breastfed or not, but rather will observe the outcome among babies whose mothers decide whether to breastfeed on their own. Investigators cannot randomly select breastfed and nonbreastfed babies from the community, because babies who are breastfed and those who are not are likely to be dissimilar with respect to factors that predict both exposure and disease. Children from households with lower socioeconomic status are more likely to be breastfed than children from households with higher socioeconomic status, for example, and they are more likely to develop infant diarrhea due to a variety of factors other than breastfeeding, such as overcrowding, lack of access to potable water, and coexistent health conditions.

To undertake a valid study of the association between breastfeeding and infant diarrhea, investigators need to match study subjects on socioeconomic status. Conducting a study that does not control for socioeconomic status could conceal a positive effect of breastfeeding, because breastfeeding and childhood diarrhea are both more common among participants from a lower socioeconomic status.

Other Things to Consider in the Selection of Comparison Groups
Investigators should be aware of two other factors as they select comparison groups for analytic studies.

First, as noted in the earlier discussion of the different study types, the comparison group in a case-control study (the controls) should not have the outcome of interest. Likewise, in a cohort study, the comparison group should not have the exposure of interest. To make sure potential members of the comparison group do not have the outcomes or exposures of interest, investigators may need only to question individuals about past exposures or symptoms suggestive of the outcome. Sometimes, however, it may be necessary to undertake special testing or examinations to make this determination. For example, in the investigation of an outbreak of thyrotoxicosis in Minnesota, South Dakota, and Iowa discussed in Chapter 6, a high proportion of cases were asymptomatic—that is, the individuals were affected but did not have symptoms of thyrotoxicosis. To be sure that potential controls were not asymptomatic cases, investigators tested their thyroid function before enrolling them into the study.[13]

Second, while the comparison group in a case-control study should not have the outcome of interest and the comparison group in a cohort study should not have the exposure of interest, the comparison group in a case-control study should have the *potential* of developing the outcome of interest and the comparison group in a cohort study should have the *potential* of having the exposure of interest. For example, investigators who are seeking to determine the source of an outbreak of hepatitis A virus infection among customers at a restaurant would exclude those who had been vaccinated against hepatitis A from being controls. Even if they are exposed to the source of the outbreak, these previously vaccinated individuals will be unlikely to develop hepatitis A. They are not at risk for the outcome and, therefore, would not be good controls.

Sample Size

Making a decision about the sample size—that is, how many members from the group of interest and the comparison group to include—is another important task as investigators plan a study. Investigators typically select the sample size based on how reliable they need the results to be, although in practice they often have to choose between an ideal sample size and the expected cost of the study. The size of the sample should be big enough to accomplish the purpose but not so big that it draws resources away from other aspects of the study.[14]

Investigators can use a number of widely available sample size formulas to help. Sample size is discussed in more detail in Chapter 9, but this section briefly covers the parameters used in the formulas and offers some guidelines for coming up with a workable sample size.

Sample Size Formulas
Sample-size selection formulas are based on parameters such as these:

- The number of cases
- The estimated magnitude of association between the exposure and the outcome (see Chapter 9 for measures of association)
- The proportion of the general population that is exposed to the factor
- The desired level of significance—the probability that if a difference is found, it is due to chance alone
- The desired statistical power—the probability that if a real difference exists, it is detected

The quantitative nature of these formulas suggests there is one right answer to the question about sample size. This is not the case, however. Because the investigator sets the values of many of the parameters included in the formula based on his or her perspectives on the study and the study's goals, different investigators may come up with different sample sizes for the same study using the same formula.

The guidance that these calculations provide is important in the ultimate interpretation of the study results and can even help decide whether a study is worth doing at all. Investigators should carefully calculate the desired sample size for each study or consult a statistician who can perform these calculations.

Guidelines for Determining Sample Size
The following guidelines may help investigators set the sample size for a study:

- The bigger the sample size, the easier it will be to find an association between an exposure and an outcome.
- In a large study (50 or more cases or exposed persons), one member of the comparison group per member of the group of interest will usually suffice.
- In smaller studies, it may be necessary to select two, three, or four comparison group members for each member of the group of interest.
- Selecting more than four members of the comparison group per member of the group of interest will rarely increase the chances of finding an association between an exposure and an outcome.

Validity

A study is valid if its results reflect the truth. More specifically, it is valid if the inference drawn from it, especially generalizations that extend beyond the sample included in the study, is warranted when the study methods, the study sample's representativeness, and the nature of the population from which it is drawn are taken into account.[2] Many factors affect the validity of an epidemiologic study. Foreknowledge of these factors can help investigators minimize or avoid problems that could invalidate the results of a study.

In general, study findings may not be valid for any of three reasons:

- Random error (chance)
- Bias
- Confounding

Random Error

Random error is the tendency to produce results that differ from the truth due to chance alone. It can be caused by individual biological variation, sampling error, and measurement errors.

- Individual biological variation results from the inherent genetic differences between people and differences in their responses to environmental exposures.
- Sampling error occurs as part of the process of selecting study participants from a larger population.
- Measurement errors result from imprecise measurement procedures.

Random error can never be eliminated, but it can be reduced by using adequate sample sizes and carefully measuring exposure and outcome.

Bias

Bias is the tendency to produce results that differ in a systematic manner from the truth. (By "systematic," we mean that the error occurs with some pattern; for example, it is more likely to occur in persons with certain exposure–outcome characteristics.) Although many forms of bias exist—and authors tend to use different terms for similar types of bias—outbreak investigations will be most concerned with two types, selection bias and information bias.

Selection bias occurs when there is a systematic difference between the characteristics of the people selected to participate in the study and those not selected or between the study groups (e.g., exposed and unexposed persons). An obvious source of selection bias in healthcare research occurs when participants select themselves for a study either because they are unwell or because they are particularly worried about an exposure. Another source of selection bias is when the outcome under investigation itself makes people unavailable to participate in a study because they have died or are too sick to participate.

A well-known, if nonepidemiologic, example of selection bias is found in the annals of U.S. presidential history. Before the 1936 U.S. presidential election, the *Literary Digest* published the results of a poll forecasting that Alfred E. Landon would defeat Franklin Delano Roosevelt by 57% to 43%. When election day came, however, Roosevelt won in a landslide.

What went wrong? Some observers say the sample was at fault: The *Digest* sent its straw ballots to its own subscribers and lists of telephone and automobile owners, who were both wealthier and more likely to vote for Landon than the population as a whole. Others agreed with Maurice Bryson, who argued in an article published in *The American Statistician* in 1976 that the real source of bias was not the initial sample, but *voluntary response*: The *Digest* had mailed out 10 million surveys, but only 2.3 million people returned theirs.[15] Several years later, Peverill Squire, using information George Gallup gathered in a 1937 survey of people who had been on the *Digest's* mailing list, argued that both arguments had merit: Owners of cars and telephones were less supportive of Roosevelt than those who did not have either, but still came out strongly in favor of him; and persons who said they received the straw vote ballot as opposed to those who responded to the ballot went for Roosevelt by 55% to 44%.[16] Two years after the election the *Digest* was out of business, and Gallup, Elmo Roper, and others had built enduring polling organizations based on more scientific sampling procedures.

Information bias occurs when there are systematic errors in classification of outcome or exposure status. Information bias may arise when investigators use different interviewing or diagnostic techniques for people with certain exposure–outcome characteristics. It may also occur when members of these groups remember things differently. For example, people with the outcome of interest may be more likely than controls to recall a past exposure, especially if it is widely known to be associated with the outcome under investigation.

Addressing Selection and Information Bias

It is too late to correct selection and information bias during the analytic phase of a study. Even better, however, investigators can minimize (and even eliminate) bias by taking specific actions during the design and execution phase of a study. These steps include developing clear and scientifically sound definitions of exposure and outcome with the appropriate balance between sensitivity and specificity, searching diligently for members of the group of interest and the comparison group, including a representative sample from these two groups in the study, following up meticulously with participants to determine exposure and outcome status, and consistently applying exposure and outcome definitions.

Confounding

Confounding can occur when another exposure exists in the study population that is associated with both the outcome and exposure of interest. A problem arises if two conditions are met:

1. The other exposure is unequally distributed between the group of interest and the comparison group.

2. The effects of the two exposures have not been separated and investigators incorrectly conclude that the effect is due to one rather than the other.

Confounding can have a dramatic impact on study results, possibly even reversing an apparent association between the outcome and the exposure of interest from being a risk factor to being protective. In the study of breastfeeding and infant diarrhea described earlier in this chapter, for example, socioeconomic status is a confounder: It is associated with both the exposure and the outcome of interest. If the effect of socioeconomic status is not addressed in some manner, the positive association between the exposure of interest (breastfeeding) and the outcome of interest (infant diarrhea) will likely be obscured.

If investigators are aware of the likely confounders, it is relatively easy to deal with this issue in the selection of study subjects. Investigators can match study subjects on potential confounders or restrict the group of interest and the comparison group to those with a particular characteristic. Stratified analysis or various multivariate techniques (discussed in Chapter 9) can also address confounding during the analysis of the study results. Dealing with unknown confounders is more difficult, and may be best handled by randomization of study subjects. Of course, this is not possible in most public health studies.

Summary

The three types of analytic studies most commonly used to investigate outbreaks and other public health problems are cohort, case-control, and cross-sectional studies. Each study type has its strengths and weaknesses and apparent best uses. Deciding which study type to use in a particular investigation may seem to be a cut-and-dried task, but often it is not. Different investigators will approach a problem from different angles depending on available resources, time, and study populations. All studies, regardless of type, will have inherent strengths and weaknesses.

Identifying the etiologic agent, source, and vehicle of the outbreak requires investigators to exercise sound professional judgment and to know which methodological approaches are available, how to gauge the relative strengths and weaknesses of each, and how to apply these methods in real-life settings. In designing a study, investigators should carefully select exposure and outcome criteria based on the stage of the investigation, the means typically used to diagnose the disease or determine whether exposure has occurred, and the circumstances under which the study is occurring. Similarly, investigators should select study subjects, including a comparison group, to avoid—or at least minimize—the introduction of bias, misclassification, and confounding influences.

References

1. Centers for Disease Control and Prevention. Outbreaks of *Escherichia coli* 0157:H7 infection associated with eating alfalfa sprouts—Michigan and Virginia, June–July 1997. *Morb Mortal Weekly Rep.* 1997;46(32):741–4.
2. Last, JM, ed. *A Dictionary of Epidemiology.* 3rd ed. New York: Oxford University Press; 1995.
3. Prospective Cohort Study. Dictionary of cancer terms. National Cancer Institute website: http://www.cancer.gov/dictionary/?CdrID=286693. Accessed January 26, 2011.

4. Kelsey JL, Whittemore AS, Evans AS, et al. *Methods in Observational Epidemiology*. 2nd ed. New York: Oxford University Press; 1996.

5. Centers for Disease Control and Prevention. Assessment of the effectiveness of the 2003–04 influenza vaccine among children and adults—Colorado, 2003. *Morb Mortal Weekly Rep.* 2004;53(31):707–30.

6. Centers for Disease Control and Prevention. Intussusception among recipients of rotavirus vaccine—United States, 1998–1999. *Morb Mortal Weekly Rep.* 1999;48(27):577–81.

7. Centers for Disease Control and Prevention. Epidemiological notes and reports eosinophilia-myalgia syndrome and L-tryptophan–containing products—New Mexico, Minnesota, Oregon, and New York, 1989. *Morb Mortal Weekly Rep.* 1989;38(46):785–8.

8. Texas Department of Health. Outbreaks of *Cyclospora* infection. *Dis Prevent News.* 1997;57(11):1–4.

9. Centers for Disease Control and Prevention. Notice to readers: Revised ACIP recommendation for avoiding pregnancy after receiving a rubella-containing vaccine. *Morb Mortal Weekly Rep.* 2001;50(49):1117.

10. Centers for Disease Control and Prevention. Influenza and pneumococcal vaccination coverage among persons aged ≥65 years—United States, 2004–2005. *Morb Mortal Weekly Rep.* 2006;55(39):1065–8.

11. Centers for Disease Control and Prevention. Outbreaks of gastroenteritis associated with norovirus on cruise ships—United States, 2002. *Morb Mortal Weekly Rep.* 2002;51(49):1112–5.

12. Centers for Disease Control and Prevention. Outbreak of histoplasmosis among industrial plant workers—Nebraska, 2004. *Morb Mortal Weekly Rep.* 2004;53(43):1020–2.

13. Hedberg CW, Fishbein DB, Janssen RS, et al. An outbreak of thyrotoxicosis caused by the consumption of bovine thyroid gland in ground beef. *N Engl J Med.* 1987;316:993–8.

14. Gregg M. *Field Epidemiology*. 3rd ed. New York: Oxford University Press; 2008.

15. Bryson MC. The *Literary Digest* poll: Making of a statistical myth. *Am Statistician.* 1976;30(4):184–5.

16. Squire P. Why the 1936 *Literary Digest* poll failed. *Publ Opin Q.* 1988;(52):125–33.

Chapter 8

Hypothesis-Testing Interviews

Jeanette K. Stehr-Green
Paul A. Stehr-Green
Amy L. Nelson

Learning Objectives
By the end of this chapter, the reader will be able to:

- Describe the steps to develop a questionnaire for an epidemiologic study.

- List the five categories of information typically included in a questionnaire and give examples of each.

- Describe the three general types of questions and identify the best situation in which to use each type.

- List five considerations for wording questions.

- Given a hypothesis about the source of an outbreak, develop a questionnaire outline.

- List the primary methods for administering a questionnaire and the advantages and disadvantages of each method.

- List five tips for effective interviewing.

- Discuss the ethical and privacy concerns related to conducting hypothesis-testing interviews.

- Identify three ways to protect the confidentiality of a respondent.

Introduction

The key to a successful epidemiologic study is having a solid understanding—or at least a well-informed guess—about what is behind the problem being investigated. Before designing a study, creating a questionnaire, or beginning data collection, investigators should know who is being affected by the problem and how widespread it is. They should have narrowed down the possible source of the problem and have some sense of the contributing factors. If the team members do not know what they are looking for, they are unlikely to find it.

An apt analogy is locating a city on a map or looking up a word in the dictionary. Without some idea about where the city is located (for instance, in which state or general part of the country) or how the word is spelled (at least the first letter or two), it will be difficult to find. Consider trying to find Sequim (pronounced "Skwim," in one syllable) on a map of the United States without knowing it is located in Washington state, or finding the word "psychology" in *Webster's Unabridged Dictionary* without knowing that it starts with a "p". Without some prior knowledge, the search may be long or entirely fruitless.

An epidemiologic study is subject to similar limitations. If investigators do not know enough about the problem they face, they will not ask the right questions in the right way. And if they do not ask the right questions in the right way, they are unlikely to get answers that are meaningful and useful.

This chapter focuses on effective information gathering as part of an epidemiologic study (such as a case-control or cohort study). It explores how to create a questionnaire—which information to collect, how to write and organize the questions, and how to administer the questionnaire. The chapter concludes with a brief discussion of important things for interviewers to consider as they plan for interviews—most notably, measures to protect human subjects.

Developing a Questionnaire

Investigators should follow these steps when they develop a questionnaire:

1. Identify the leading hypothesis about the source of the problem.
2. Identify the information needed to test the hypothesis.
3. Identify the information needed for the logistics of the study.
4. Write the questions to collect this information.
5. Organize the questions into questionnaire format.
6. Determine how the information gathered will be managed.
7. Test the questionnaire.
8. Revise the questionnaire.
9. Administer the questionnaire (after training interviewers).

Novice investigators may be surprised to learn that writing the questions is not the first item on this list. In fact, writing the questions first is one of the most common errors in questionnaire development. Novice investigators may be anxious to get started and they often know which kinds of questions they ought to ask, based on previous experiences. So they start writing down questions as fast as they can, or they get on the computer and cut and paste questions from questionnaires used in other studies. In reality, before they write the first question, it is very important for investigators to understand what they are looking for—the hypothesis they want to test—and the information they need to prove or disprove the hypothesis. Only then can they write effective questions.

We will walk through the steps of writing, organizing, and administering a questionnaire in this section.

Identify the Leading Hypothesis

Beginning with the leading hypothesis allows investigators to identify the information they need to test the hypothesis and account for any factors that might confound the results. In the *Escherichia coli* O157:H7 outbreak discussed in Chapter 4, for example, investigators conducted hypothesis-generating interviews that helped identify consumption of contaminated alfalfa sprouts or salad as the most likely cause of illness.[1] Keeping the hypothesis in mind allowed them to design a well-structured questionnaire that focused on when people were likely infected, what they ate, where they ate it, and where the food came from, as well as other activities and risk factors that would help prove or disprove the hypothesis.

Identify the Information Needed to Test the Hypothesis

After identifying the leading hypothesis, but before writing questions and organizing them into a questionnaire, investigators must identify the information they need. Because a hypothesis is a carefully constructed supposition about the relationship between an exposure and a disease or health event, there are specific areas of information that should be defined for collection of information to effectively test the hypothesis:

- One or more proposed exposures
- One or more health outcomes of interest
- Boundaries on the person/population at risk (i.e., who was exposed or developed the outcome of interest)
- Boundaries on place (i.e., where the exposure or outcome of interest occurred)
- Boundaries on time (i.e., when the exposure or outcome of interest occurred)

To collect information to address these components of testing a hypothesis, investigators often collect information in several categories: demographic information to define the population and the place; exposure or risk factor information to define the exposures being investigated, including place and time; and clinical information to define the health outcome of interest, including place and time.

Demographic information characterizes the at-risk population by age, sex, highest educational level attained, location, and other identifying information. Such information is useful in describing the problem under investigation. It is also important in the search for possible confounders, or factors that can distort the apparent exposure–disease relationship. Demographic categories such as age, sex, educational level, and location can be confounders; investigators need to evaluate them to determine whether demographic and other factors affect the relationship they see—or think they see—between an exposure and a disease in a study.

Clinical information includes signs and symptoms of the disease, date of onset of illness, receipt of medical care or treatment, and results of laboratory testing. This information allows investigators to characterize the illness, decide who has the outcome of interest, and chart the time course of the problem. Determining who has developed the outcome of interest is critical in a cohort or cross-sectional study. It will also be important in a case-control study, as investigators need to verify the outcome status of participants. It is not uncommon to find out that some cases do not meet the case definition or that some individuals considered as controls do not fit the control criteria.

Exposure or risk factor information is used to explore the hypothesis under investigation. This information will likely be the focus of the questionnaire for an analytic study, such as a case-control or cohort study. The data collected will be very specific for the problem under investigation and will reflect the hypothesis about the source of the problem. Exposure or risk factor information often includes the following items:

- Exposure (or not) of the respondent to the factor of interest
- Route of exposure
- Amount of exposure
- Timing of exposure
- Other details of exposure, such as the brand and source of a contaminated food

As an example, let's return to the *E. coli* O157:H7 outbreak that was detected in Michigan in June 1997 and the leading hypothesis that people became ill from contaminated alfalfa sprouts or salads.[1] What information do investigators need to explore and test this hypothesis? Obviously, it is important to know if the respondent ate either of these items. In addition, investigators want to know when people ate the alfalfa sprouts or salads, as eating these items before or after the period of interest is unlikely to be of concern. Because a dosage effect might affect the outcome, it is also important to know how much was eaten. Even a small number of *E. coli* O157:H7 organisms can lead to infection, however, so exploring the amount eaten is unlikely to be of great interest in this outbreak, but it might be of concern with other pathogens. Finally, if alfalfa sprouts or salads are the cause of the outbreak, produce from a particular source might be the cause of the problem. Therefore, investigators need to learn where the respondent bought or ate these items and if they can trace them to a particular producer or distributor. Table 8-1 summarizes these pieces of information.

Identify the Information Needed for the Logistics of the Study

Identifying information includes the respondent's name or other personal identifiers, address, and telephone number. This information is important for the logistics of the study. It is used to identify the subject and allows investigators to update the questionnaire as more information becomes available. Identifying information can be used to link the questionnaire to other records, such as laboratory results or other questionnaires. It also can prevent duplicate entry of records if an individual is interviewed twice during a study or if questionnaires get mixed up during data entry.

The *source of the information* is the individual supplying the information as well as the person receiving it (i.e., the interviewer). Identifying the person supplying the information

TABLE 8-1   Information Needed to Test Hypotheses for an Investigation of *E. coli* O157:H7 Infection in Michigan

Leading Hypotheses on Vehicle of Transmission

Consumption of alfalfa sprouts
Consumption of salads

Information to Test Hypotheses

Did you eat either of these items?
When did you eat them?
How much did you eat?
Where did you buy them?
Were they from a particular producer or distributor?

Source: Adapted from Breuer T, Benkel DH, Shapiro RL, et al. A multistate outbreak of *Escherichia coli* O157:H7 infections linked to alfalfa sprouts grown from contaminated seeds. *Emerg Infect Dis.* 2007;7(6). http://www.cdc.gov/ncidod/eid/vol7no6/breuer.htm. Accessed August 23, 2010.

provides some insight into the information's validity. Is the person providing the information the study subject or a surrogate such as the subject's spouse or parent? In most situations, the actual subject of the study will provide better information than others who speak on behalf of the subject, although if the affected individuals are infants, children, or deceased persons someone else will have to speak for them. Identifying the interviewer is also important. If any questions are left unanswered, the handwriting is illegible, or some responses are nonsensical, the interviewer might be able to help correct these problems. Tracking the interviewer can also help identify a more serious problem: An inadequately trained interviewer may consistently misread a question, interpret a question inappropriately, or misquote a respondent's answers. Analyzing the data and stratifying the information by interviewer may reveal patterns suggesting this very problem. If interviewers are properly trained, this problem will be greatly minimized, but investigators must take the possibility into account.

Writing the Questions

After identifying the leading hypothesis and determining the information they need to test the hypothesis or for the logistics of the study, investigators can begin writing questions. The questions on an epidemiologic questionnaire are typically arranged into five categories of information:

- Identifying information
- Demographic information

- Clinical information
- Exposure or risk factor information
- Source of information

Whoever writes the questionnaire will determine the exact format and wording of the questions included based on his or her knowledge of the problem—that is, the hypothesis being tested, the kind of information to be collected, and the affected population. Each epidemiologic investigation will have different requirements, but we can make some generalizations about what types of questions to ask and how to construct them.

Types of Questions

Investigators use three types of questions in questionnaires for epidemiologic studies:

- Open-ended questions
- Fill-in-the-blank questions
- Closed-ended questions:
  - With categorical response options
  - With ordinal response options

Open-ended questions allow the respondent to say whatever he or she desires, rather than requiring a response based on a specific list of choices; the possible responses are limitless. Open-ended questions give the respondent the opportunity to express his or her own perspectives about a subject. They are useful in characterizing attitudes, beliefs, and behaviors. (They are also useful during hypothesis generation, when investigators know little about a problem and the range of potential responses to a question is largely unknown.) From the investigator's perspective, however, analyzing open-ended questions can be difficult and time-consuming. Unless the investigator intends to supply only a narrative report of the responses, he or she must read, categorize, and code every response. As a result, investigators tend to limit their use of this question type, particularly in studies involving large numbers of subjects.

As an example of how open-ended questions work, consider the survey that the Centers for Medicare & Medicaid Services (CMS) undertakes each year. Among other things, the survey seeks to determine influenza vaccination rates among Medicare beneficiaries and most frequently cited reasons for not receiving influenza vaccine. Respondents are asked, "Did you have a flu shot for last winter? Those who respond "No" are then asked, "Why didn't you get a flu shot for last winter?" Respondents are free to give any reason or reasons. The following responses are fictitious but might be similar to the answers given by some respondents:

- I did not get the vaccine because I had read a report in the newspaper that it could make you sick. Some of these illnesses are minor, like pain or redness where the vaccine is injected or a slight fever, but others are serious. In fact, the report said that some people developed a disease called Guillain-Barré syndrome due to the flu vaccine, and one elderly man died.

- I have macular degeneration and don't drive. I have a difficult time getting to the doctor's and I have to ask my friend to drive me. My doctor said I should get vaccinated in October and I wrote it on the calendar, but I didn't want to impose on my friend. She is so busy and her husband is quite ill. Anyway, because I don't get out much—just to church and the grocery store—I don't think I need the vaccination.

- I got flu the last time I got the flu shot. I started feeling bad as I was driving home from the clinic. I felt kind of achy and then my throat got scratchy. I was laid up in bed for days. My doctor tells me I should get the flu shot every year but I won't make that mistake again.

To determine the primary reasons that a respondent did not get vaccinated against influenza, the interviewers then coded each response into one of the following categories:

A. Did not know the shot was needed

B. Shot could cause flu

C. Shot could have side effects or cause disease

D. Didn't think it would prevent the flu/could cause flu anyway

E. Flu not serious/would not get flu anyway/not at risk

F. Doctor did not recommend the shot

G. Doctor recommended against getting shot/allergic to shot/medical reasons

H. Don't like shots or needles/concerns about soreness or rash/local reactions

I. Inconvenient to get shot/unable to get to location

J. Did not think about it/forgot/missed it

K. Cost of shot/not worth the money

L. Had shot before/didn't need it again

M. Other (specify)

N. Refused

O. Don't know[2]

As you can imagine, it would take a fair amount of time to code these data. Thus, in general, investigators should use this type of question only when it is absolutely necessary.

Fill-in-the-blank questions, like open-ended questions, do not provide any response choices. With fill-in-the-blanks, however, it is expected that the response will be relatively short, such as one or two words. These questions should be used when the possible response categories are numerous and the question measures a simple respondent attribute, such as age, educational level, or place of residence; when collecting a date, such as birth date, date of onset of illness, or date of exposure; or when quantifying something specific, such as a number of visits to a healthcare provider. Fill-in-the-blanks do not work well when longer, more involved responses are expected. Some examples of fill-in-the blank questions follow:

In which county do you live? _____ (DK = don't know; R = refused)

What is your date of birth? _____ (mm/dd/yyyy) (DK = don't know; R = refused)

When did you receive your pneumonia vaccination? _____ (mm/dd/yyyy) (DK = don't know; R = refused)

How many times did you see your healthcare provider in the last year? _____ (DK = don't know; R = refused)

Like open-ended questions, fill-in-the-blank questions often require that the investigator categorize and code the responses. However, because the responses are generally short, the burden is not as great as with open-ended questions.

Close-ended questions have response choices from which the respondent must choose. They are used when possible responses are known and the range is relatively narrow (that is, responses can be provided to respondents in a short list). Unlike open-ended and fill-in-the-blank questions, closed-ended questions do not require the investigator to categorize and code the responses. They do require him or her to satisfy the following conditions:

- Anticipate the most likely responses to the question
- Present the responses as a list of mutually exclusive choices
- State the responses in a clear and concise manner that respondents can easily understand

Close-ended questions can be either categorical or ordinal (although the difference between the two may not be evident until the data are analyzed). In categorical close-ended questions, the available responses fit into categories that have no particular order or inherent numerical value with respect to each other. For example, the following question is used on the Centers for Disease Control and Prevention's (CDC's) Behavioral Risk Factor Surveillance System (BRFSS) questionnaire.

Which one or more of the following would you say is your race?

1. White
2. Black or African American
3. Asian
4. Native Hawaiian or other Pacific Islander
5. American Indian or Alaska Native
6. Other [specify]_____
7. Refused[3]

In this example, the responses do not have any numerical relationship to each other. "White" bears no quantitative relationship to "Black or African American," which bears no quantitative relationship to "Asian," and so on.

In ordinal close-ended questions, the available responses tend to describe a range of choices along a continuum and to have a numerical value with respect to one another. For example, in seeking information about a respondent's education level, the BRFSS uses the following ordinal close-ended question:

What is the highest grade or year of school you completed?

1. Never attended school or only attended kindergarten
2. Grades 1 through 8 (Elementary)
3. Grades 9 through 11 (Some high school)
4. Grade 12 or GED (High school graduate)
5. College 1 year to 3 years (Some college or technical school)
6. College 4 years or more (College graduate)
7. Refused

Clearly, the numbered responses are related to one another with respect to the level of education a respondent has had: The lower-numbered responses suggest less formal education and the higher-numbered responses suggest more formal education.

All three question types—open-ended, fill-in-the-blank, and close-ended—have their place. Investigators select which type to use based on the kind of information they wish to collect and their expectations and prior knowledge of that information. Early in an investigation, when investigators may know little about the problem, they are more likely to use open-ended questions. As they gather more information, they should be able to anticipate possible responses and, therefore, become more likely to use close-ended questions.

Wording the Questions

Choosing the type of question is just the first step in creating the question. Investigators need to take great care with the specific wording and the response categories (if applicable). Following are a few guidelines to consider when writing questions for an epidemiologic study:

- Use language that the respondents can understand. Avoid technical jargon, slang, and abbreviations. Depending on the level of education of respondents, investigators might need to further simplify the language. For example:

  Use: Has a physician or other healthcare provider measured your blood pressure to determine if you have high blood pressure?

  Not: Have you been evaluated for hypertension?

- If the questionnaire is translated from one language to another, investigators should test it with native speakers. A good test is to have the translated questionnaire "back-translated"—that is, translated from the language intended for use with the respondents into the language used by the investigators. Back-translation allows the investigators to see or hear what the respondents will be reading or hearing and may reveal potential problems.

- Limit each question to a single idea. Combining questions can result in unclear or conflicting responses. For example:

  Use: Have you had vomiting? Have you had diarrhea as defined by three or more loose stools in a 24-hour period?

  Not: Have you had vomiting and diarrhea?

- Word each question as precisely as possible. Avoid words with vaguely defined meanings, leaving as little to the respondent's interpretation as possible. Exercise caution with general adjectives and adverbs that may have different meanings to different people, such as "big," "bad," and "nicely."

  Use: Have you had three or more loose stools in any 24-hour period between April 25 and May 1?

  Not: Did you have severe diarrhea?

- Do not phrase questions in a way that suggests a response—that is, as a leading question—or implies a value judgment. How respondents perceive the interviewer's attitude can influence the responses they provide. For example:

  Use: Has your child been immunized against measles?

  Not: Childhood immunizations are important ways parents can protect their children against serious diseases. Has your child been immunized against measles?

- Avoid double negatives. For example:

  Use: Do you always buckle your seat belt while riding in a car?

  Not: Do you never go in a car without buckling your seat belt?

- Always include a "Don't know" or "Refused" category with potential responses. This option will help distinguish between respondents who do not answer a question because they do not remember the answer, choose not to answer, or just skipped the question.

- When creating the responses for a close-ended question, be sure that the categories cover all potential responses and are mutually exclusive (that is, they do not overlap). Each response should fit into one and only one category. For example:

Which of the following age categories do you fit into?

  A. 1–20 years

  B. 20–40 years

  C. 40–60 years

  D. Greater than or equal to 60 years

  E. Don't know

  F. Refused

These categories do not have a place for an infant younger than one year of age. Also, they are not mutually exclusive because they fail to indicate whether someone who is 40 years old would fit into category B or C; there are similar problems for people aged 20 or 60 years. The following categories are clearer:

A. Less than 20 years

B. 20–39 years

C. 40–59 years

D. 60 years or older

E. Don't know

F. Refused

Organize the Questions into Questionnaire Format

Once investigators know the categories of information collected in an epidemiologic questionnaire and the general types of questions, they can turn their attention to assembling the questions into a questionnaire. This section includes a number of thoughts about what makes a good questionnaire and helps it flow smoothly.

Introduce the Questionnaire

Each questionnaire should begin with an introduction. The introduction serves several purposes. It allows investigators to identify the organization sponsoring the study and explain the purpose of the study. Both pieces of information will lend credence to the undertaking and increase the likelihood that the respondent will participate and answer honestly. To avoid biasing the respondent, the introduction should not provide too much information about the investigation, such as the suspected source of the problem. Investigators can and should explain the purpose of the study in general terms to help the respondent understand the importance of the interview and his or her part in the investigation. The introduction should also include information about how long the interview is likely to take and reassurance that the respondent's answers will be held in the strictest of confidence.

Here is an example of the introduction to a study questionnaire, taken from a sample questionnaire on the CDC's OutbreakNet website (http://www.cdc.gov/outbreaknet/toolkit/standard_ques.pdf):

> Hello. My name is _____ and I'm calling from the _____ State Health Department. I'm calling because there have been several cases of _____ in our community and we are working to identify the source of infection, so we can prevent additional illness in the community. We understand that you are one of the people who had this illness. I would like to ask you some questions about your illness and foods that you ate before becoming ill, that will help us in this work. This will take about ____ minutes. Can we go ahead?

Manage the Length of the Questionnaire

In general, a questionnaire should be as short as possible and should focus on the hypothesis being tested in the study. Two important reasons to limit the length of a questionnaire are the resources needed to administer it and the willingness of respondents to complete it. Asking a great number of questions may also lead to another problem, called "multiple comparisons": Comparing the study group and the control group on too many factors can increase the likelihood that investigators will find a statistical association between an exposure and the disease under investigation due to chance alone.

Ask Only Essential Questions

Investigators need to prioritize the questions to include in the questionnaire, focusing on the leading hypothesis and the discrete pieces of information needed to evaluate it. Only then should they try to strike a balance between evaluating the hypothesis and taking advantage of the opportunities that access to the study population permits. The questionnaire should include only questions that are important to resolving the health problem, rather than also including questions whose answers are just interesting to know.

Organize the Questionnaire

When investigators lay out a questionnaire, they should organize the questions to help the interviewer develop rapport with the respondent. The best means to do so depends largely on the nature of the questionnaire, the problem being explored, and the persons being interviewed. When designing a questionnaire, investigators may want to use these formatting tips:

- Group together similar types of information or topics.
- Ask more general questions first, followed by more specific questions.
- Lead with the least sensitive questions, leaving the most personal or potentially threatening questions—those regarding sexual habits, religious beliefs, political orientation, or income—for last, when the respondent may be more comfortable with the interviewer.
- Ask the most important questions—those relating to the leading hypothesis—first.

Regardless of which approach investigators take, the questionnaire should be logical and well organized. It should also be easy to read and complete. Instructions for the questionnaire or specific questions should be clearly stated. Questions and pages should be numbered. Each page should include an identifying code for the respondent. Responses to questions, or the space for recording responses, should be clearly separated from the questions.

Include Skip Patterns

The questionnaire should include "skip patterns" to avoid asking irrelevant questions. A skip pattern usually begins with a screening question that tells the interviewer whether subsequent questions pertain to a particular respondent. If they do, the interviewer reads the questions. If not, the interviewer is instructed to skip over the questions and continue with the next set.

Here is an example of a skip pattern. Questions 1, 2, and 4 are screening questions.

1. In the last 7 days, did you eat any lettuce? This includes lettuce in a salad or in combination with any other food item such as sandwiches or tacos.

    Yes   No   Don't know   Refused

If no, skip to Question 6.

2. Did you eat any lettuce bought as a head of lettuce?

    Yes   No   Don't know   Refused

If no, skip to Question 4.

3. Did you eat any of the following lettuce bought as a head or loose leaves (not precut or in a special bag):

a. Iceberg?	Yes	No	Don't know	Refused
b. Romaine?	Yes	No	Don't know	Refused
c. Leaf lettuce?	Yes	No	Don't know	Refused
d. Bibb lettuce?	Yes	No	Don't know	Refused
e. Boston lettuce?	Yes	No	Don't know	Refused

4. Was any of the lettuce mixed lettuce? This lettuce can be pre-bagged, or it can be picked from a bin, so that you use tongs to put it into a bag yourself. It is sometimes called "spring" or "mesclun" mix.

    Yes   No   Don't know   Refused

If no, skip to Question 6.

5. Was the type of lettuce mix called:

a. Italian?	Yes	No	Don't know	Refused
b. Caesar?	Yes	No	Don't know	Refused
c. Garden?	Yes	No	Don't know	Refused
d. Riviera?	Yes	No	Don't know	Refused
f. Ranch?	Yes	No	Don't know	Refused
g. European?	Yes	No	Don't know	Refused
h. American mix?	Yes	No	Don't know	Refused
i. Spring mix?	Yes	No	Don't know	Refused
j. Mesclun mix?	Yes	No	Don't know	Refused
k. California?	Yes	No	Don't know	Refused
l. Santa Barbara?	Yes	No	Don't know	Refused
m. A shredded mix?	Yes	No	Don't know	Refused

6. In the last 7 days, did you eat sprouts, such as alfalfa or bean sprouts? These may have been eaten as part of a salad or as part of any other food item such as sandwiches or tacos.

    Yes   No   Don't know   Refused

As you can see, use of skip patterns can prevent a respondent from listening to and having to answer many questions that do not pertain to him or her. They can save time and are less wearing on the patience of the respondent. Skip patterns should always be clearly marked and easy to follow.

Depending on how investigators plan to code their data and enter it into an electronic file, they may have to consider the physical layout of the questionnaire. It may be necessary, for instance, to line up blanks or boxes for recording responses, or to display codes for responses. Most computer-based software packages for data entry reduce the need for coding, however, so it may not be necessary to establish a strict format for a questionnaire. In most cases, the electronic copy of the questionnaire can look exactly like the paper copy, or the computer can manipulate codes and store them in whatever format investigators select.

Include an Ending Statement

The questionnaire should conclude with an ending statement. The interviewer should thank the respondent for his or her input and time, and provide the respondent with a means to contact the interviewer or the study investigators if he or she has questions or remembers additional information pertinent to the investigation. Providing a contact number will also reassure the respondent that the interview was part of a legitimate undertaking.

Here are two examples of language to include in an ending statement:

- That was my last question. I realize that I have asked you a lot of questions. Do you have any questions or comments for me?

- Thank you very much for your time and cooperation. Your assistance with this investigation may help us prevent further cases of _____ in the community. If you think of something else and want to reach us, please leave a message for [NAME OF PRIMARY INVESTIGATOR] at xxx-xxx-xxxx and we will get back to you.

Determine How the Information Will Be Managed

If investigators plan to enter the questions and answers from their outbreak investigation questionnaire into an electronic database, they need to think about how they will arrange the raw data (i.e., the answers from a questionnaire) into ready-to-analyze data. Several types of questions—open-ended, fill-in-the-blank, and close-ended—may have been asked. The answers to each of these questions are variables that must be assigned a value, coded, and possibly grouped or categorized so that investigators can analyze the information. Thinking about how they will code the responses while designing their questionnaire, before any data are gathered, will help investigators collect the data in a format they can use.

Coding

Coding is the process of translating the information gathered from questionnaires or other investigations into something that can be analyzed, typically using a computer program. Coding involves assigning a value to the information obtained from a questionnaire; often that value is given a label. In addition to helping organize data, coding can make the data more consistent. For example, if investigators have asked participants to indicate their gender, the answers might include "Male," "Female," or "M," "F," and so on. Coding will avoid such inconsistencies.

A common coding system (code and label) for dichotomous variables is this:

0 = No

1 = Yes

In this system, the number 1 is the value assigned, and "Yes" is the label or meaning of that value.

Some investigators prefer to use a system of ones and twos:

1 = No

2 = Yes

This distinction brings out an important point in coding: When investigators assign a value to a piece of information, they must also make it clear what that value means. In the first example given in this section, 1 = Yes; in the second example, 1 = No. Either way is fine, as long as it is clear how the data are coded. One way to make it clear is to create a data dictionary as a separate file to accompany the data set.

Similarly, we might code the dichotomous variable for sex:

0 = Female

1 = Male

Many analysis software packages allow users to attach a label to variable values. The computer automatically labels the zeros as male and the ones as female in the previous example. This type of labeling can make it easier to understand the output, as shown here:

Without Label: Variable SEX Frequency Percent

0 21 60%

1 14 40%

With Label: Variable SEX Frequency Percent

Male 21 60%

Female 14 40%

The coding process is similar for other categorical variables. For the variable "education," we might code the responses as follows:

0 = Did not graduate from high school

1 = High school graduate

2 = Some college or post–high school education

3 = College graduate

It is important to be consistent in numbering for ordinal categorical variables, because the value of the code assigned has significance. The higher the code in the preceding example, the more educated the respondent. This variable could have also been coded in reverse order, so that 0 = College graduate and 3 = Did not graduate from high school. In this case, the higher the code, the less educated the respondent. Either way is acceptable, as long as investigators remember the coding when interpreting the analysis.

The following is an example of bad coding:

0 = Some college or post–high school education

1 = High school graduate

2 = College graduate

3 = Did not graduate from high school

The data has an inherent order, but the coding in this example does not follow that order. This is not appropriate coding for an ordinal categorical variable.

For a nominal categorical variable, however, the order makes no difference. Although we code each category with a number, the number does not represent a numerical value. For example, for the variable "reside" (meaning place of residence), the following responses would be appropriate:

1 = Northeast

2 = South

3 = Northwest

4 = Midwest

5 = Southwest

It doesn't matter how these categories are ordered. Midwest can be coded as 4, 2, or 5, because there is not an ordered value associated with each response.

Coding continuous variables is straightforward. If someone gives his or her age as 37 years, it is entered into the database as 37. Alternatively, investigators might decide to use age *categories* in their analysis instead of the data they collected in years. Creating categories from a continuous variable is a common practice, and is easily done using analysis software. With a software package, investigators can break down a continuous variable such as age into categories by creating an ordinal categorical variable, such as the following:

AGECAT

1 = 0–9 years old

2 = 10–19 years old

3 = 20–39 years old

4 = 40–49 years old

5 = 50-59 years old

6 = 60 years or older

Investigators should create ordinal categorical variables based on the characteristics of the population under study. If the ages of the people in the study are clustered around a certain point, it is appropriate to use narrow categories, such as 60-61 years old, 62-63 years old, and so on. If the ages vary widely, larger categories, such as 10-year or 20-year increments, may work better.

Other situations that may require categorical code responses include fill-in-the-blank questions, open-ended questions, and questions that offer an "other (specify)" option. Because answers to open-ended questions (e.g., "Why did you choose not to see a doctor about this illness?") will likely vary from respondent to respondent, these types of questions can be difficult to analyze. One way to make them manageable is to group responses with similar themes. For the preceding question, responses of "Didn't feel sick enough to see a doctor," "Symptoms stopped," and "The illness didn't last very long" could all be grouped together as "The illness was not severe."

Finally, it is necessary to code "Don't know" responses. Typically, "Don't know" is coded as 9.

Test the Questionnaire

No matter how careful investigators are in developing questionnaires and phrasing each question, sometimes what seems like a clear question to a public health specialist may baffle the respondent. It is good practice—and often a critical step—to allow others to review the questionnaire and provide comments, and to pre-test a questionnaire before administering it to the intended group of respondents. Pre-testing is also referred to as "pilot testing" or "field testing."

The pre-test helps investigators assess all aspects of the questionnaire, including clarity, wording, sequence, format, and instructions. It can also help investigators determine the time required and resources needed to complete the interviews. Here is a list of questions a pre-test of a questionnaire can help answer:

- Are all of the words easy to understand?
- Do all respondents interpret the questions the same way?

- Are skip patterns followed correctly?
- Does any part of the questionnaire suggest bias on the interviewer's part?
- Does the questionnaire create a positive impression that motivates people to respond?
- Do the responses seem appropriate and consistent with the intent for the question?
- Is each question yielding the intended information?
- How long did it take to complete the questionnaire?

When pre-testing a questionnaire, investigators should administer it to people similar to the target group of respondents, albeit not to the people who will be included in the study. Using individuals familiar with the disease under investigation or the study might provide misleading results.

Revise the Questionnaire

The final step before administering the questionnaire is to revise it based on comments from colleagues and the pre-test, if one has been conducted. This phase of development is the last chance for investigators to make sure that the questionnaire is well designed to get exactly the information needed as efficiently as possible. If investigators incorporate feedback from colleagues and knowledge gained from pre-tests, they can be more confident that they are asking the right questions. They can also be sure they have worded and organized the questions so that respondents are most likely to understand them and to provide truly useful answers. Investigators should be prepared to revise the questionnaire until its administration goes smoothly and all concerns about the questionnaire are resolved.

Administering the Questionnaire

A study questionnaire is merely an instrument. The questionnaire must be properly administered to ensure the validity and reliability of the information collected. To make sure the questionnaire is administered properly, investigators must select the best format to use, train interviewers if necessary, and take steps to protect the rights and welfare of the respondents.

Format

Two general formats of questionnaire administration are distinguished: A questionnaire can be administered by an interviewer or self-administered (or some combination of the two). In an interviewer-administered questionnaire, the interviewer reads the questionnaire to the respondent, including instructions and potential response categories, if appropriate, and records the responses. Such an interview can take place in person or by telephone. In a self-administered questionnaire, the respondent reads the questionnaire and records his or her own responses. A self-administered questionnaire can be either paper or computer based.

Strengths and Weaknesses of Interviewer-Administered Versus Self-Administered Questionnaires

Each form of questionnaire administration has its advantages and disadvantages. In interviewer-administered questionnaires, the interviewer can explain or clarify items in the questionnaire. He or she can ensure that respondents complete all items on the questionnaire and, if necessary, prompt the respondent. Interviewer-administered questionnaires can also use more complex designs, such as skip patterns, than self-administered questionnaires, although computer-assisted self-administered questionnaires can often be programmed to follow predetermined skip patterns and provide some of the prompts that an interviewer might provide. Interviewer-administered questionnaires tend to have higher response rates than self-administered questions, with more accurate recording of responses. Moreover, face-to-face interviews tend to have higher response rates than telephone interviews.

On the downside, interviewer-administered questionnaires are more costly and more time consuming to administer than self-administered questionnaires. They require interviewers to locate subjects and arrange a time to meet and/or talk. Interviewer-administered questionnaires may seem less anonymous to respondents than self-administered questionnaires. As a result, respondents may be less honest in their responses—some may be more likely to give answers they think the interviewer wants to hear. Finally, the interviewer-administered questionnaire carries a risk that the interviewer will interject his or her own feelings or interpretations as he or she reads the questions to respondents or records their answers.

Selection of Which Type of Questionnaire to Use

When they decide which type of questionnaire to use, investigators should weigh the relative advantages and disadvantages of each format. They should also consider the available resources—financial and staff—and determine how quickly they need to complete the interviews. They should also keep in mind that the form of administration they select will affect the instructions provided to respondents and the physical layout of the questionnaire.

Training Interviewers

If investigators decide to use interviewers to collect the study information, they have yet another step to undertake: training the interviewers. To be effective, interviewers need to know the questionnaire thoroughly (especially the intent of the questions), the way in which it is laid out, and its skip patterns. They need to be able to pronounce the words in the questionnaire and move from question to question in a smooth and effortless manner. Interviewers also need to be trained to record responses in the format the study designers have selected.

Training interviewers is critical to good questionnaire administration. An excellent way to begin training is to read through the questionnaire as a group, allow interviewers to ask questions about the questionnaire, and then have them practice administering the questionnaire to others. Interviewers can also benefit from watching a more experienced interviewer complete an interview. Some investigators begin the training of interviewers while the questionnaire is still in development, so they can use feedback from the interviewers to improve the questionnaire. Following are some general rules for effective interviews:

- Verify that the respondent is the person who has been selected for the interview.
- If another person accompanies the respondent, confirm that the respondent wants the other person to be present during the interview.
- Direct any gestures to the respondent, not his or her companion.
- Ask a translator who is trained in administering the questionnaire to ask the questions if the interviewer does not speak the respondent's native language.
- Seek to put the respondent at ease by reading the questions in a friendly, natural manner.
- If a participant does not want to answer a question, move on to the next question. (If the respondent seems confused rather than reluctant, the interviewer can ask if he or she is being clear.)
- Speak at a moderate rate, deliberately and distinctly.
- Read questions in the exact order they appear.
- Read every question word for word.
- Do not skip questions (unless the questionnaire includes skip patterns); an interviewer should never assume he or she knows an answer.
- Never hurry the interview. Be supportive and patient.
- Remain objective. Indicating surprise, pleasure, or disapproval at anything the respondent says might affect the respondent's answers.
- Probe if necessary and appropriate. For example, if the respondent seems not to understand the question or gives an answer that does not make sense, the interviewer may need to provide more information or ask the respondent to answer in more detail.
- Never offer a personal interpretation of questions.
- Review the questionnaire at the end of the interview to make sure that all appropriate questions have been answered. It is better to identify missing information during the interview than to have to contact the respondent again after the interview is concluded.

Interviewing is a skill. Like any other skill, it can be learned and improved with practice. People have different levels of natural ability, but with good instruction and sufficient practice, most people can become effective interviewers.

Human Subjects and Ethical Considerations

Investigators are responsible for protecting the rights and welfare of the people whom they recruit to participate in their studies. This responsibility affects many aspects of an epidemiologic investigation, not just data collection. This section touches on the main points briefly as they affect questionnaire development and administration.

Respondents' Rights

Respondents have a right to know what the purpose of a study is, who is sponsoring the study, and how or why they are being asked to participate. Investigators should inform respondents that their participation is voluntary and that they may refuse to answer any question or quit the interview at any time without penalty. Investigators should inform respondents that their responses will be held in the strictest of confidence and will be used only for the purposes of the study.

Although it is acceptable to encourage people to participate in a study or complete a questionnaire, they should not be pressured in an offensive way. More than two follow-up contacts may be seen as undue pressure. Once a person has refused to participate in a study or complete any part of a questionnaire, the investigators should honor that refusal.

Privacy

Investigators should do everything in their power to ensure the privacy of each respondent and the confidentiality of his or her responses. To facilitate this outcome, investigators should take the following steps:

- Administer the questionnaire in a private setting in which conversations cannot be overheard.
- Interview the respondent alone, unless the presence of another person is required, and then only with the explicit permission of the respondent.
- Do not share information gained from an interview, except with others who need to know for the purposes of the investigation and as allowed by law.
- Keep completed or partially completed questionnaires out of the sight of others, ideally in a locked filing cabinet or desk drawer (or in password-protected files).
- Consider removing identifying information from the completed forms once the information is no longer needed for the logistics of the study.
- Follow all federal, state, or institutional requirements to protect respondents' confidentiality.

The Health Insurance Portability and Accountability Act (HIPAA) established national standards for the electronic exchange, privacy, and security of certain health information. In particular, the HIPAA Privacy Rule limits the use and disclosure of individually iden-tifiable health information without authorization by the individual. HIPAA recognizes, however, the need for public health authorities and others responsible for ensuring public health and safety to have access to protected health information to carry out their public health mission. For this reason, public health officials are permitted, in general, to collect health data for the purpose of investigating threats to the health and safety of the public without an individual's authorization. Nonetheless, investigators should make sure that their studies (and the associated data collection) fall under the provisions of HIPPA and comply with all applicable requirements.

Protecting the confidentiality of respondents is critical. Respondents who do not feel that the information they provide will be protected from inappropriate use may decide not to participate in the study or may not provide honest answers.

Minority Considerations

Awareness and acceptance of cultural differences is an integral part of any investigation. Investigators in an outbreak investigation may interact with individuals or groups who are culturally, ethnically, or linguistically diverse; physically or psychologically diverse; or financially, socially, or historically diverse. The individuals in any study may also have differing educational backgrounds and literacy levels. Public health practitioners have certain legal and ethical responsibilities that they must satisfy when they seek to interview persons from cultures other than their own.

Title VI of the Civil Rights Act of 1964 prohibits discrimination by government agencies that receive federal funding, which includes failing to provide materials in languages other than English in certain situations. If a study subject cannot speak English or would prefer to complete the questionnaire in his or her primary language, a spouse, child, or friend may be able to translate for the subject. In general, however, if the study involves respondents with limited or no English skills, interpreters and translators should be available. The website of the Federal Interagency Working Group on Limited English Proficiency (http://www.lep.gov/) has additional information and resources on this topic.

Beyond making sure the study subject can understand and answer all the questions, it is important for investigators to understand, appreciate, and respect the cultural differences and similarities within, among, and between diverse groups. In practice, meeting this requirement means making sure questionnaires are prepared with cultural differences and sensitivities in mind, and interviewers are appropriately trained for the population or populations they will be interviewing. Like developing a strong hypothesis and writing short, focused questionnaires, thinking in advance about cultural differences is another way in which investigators can ensure the success of their hypothesis-testing interviews.

Summary

The most important steps in constructing a questionnaire for an outbreak investigation are to carefully frame and refine the hypothesis under investigation and to decide which information is needed to test it. With this understanding in place, investigators can develop a series of open-ended, fill-in-the-blank, and close-ended questions to obtain the needed information, paying careful attention to the specific wording and organization of the questionnaire. Following this time-tested approach, investigators are more likely to get the right information from the right people at the right time.

Developing and administering a questionnaire for an epidemiologic study comes with many challenges and great responsibilities—including the investigators' legal and ethical responsibilities to the people they want to study. The form of questionnaire administration (interviewer administered versus self-administered), interviewing techniques, and human subjects and ethical considerations will all affect the outcome of the study, including the response rate and the completeness and accuracy of the information obtained. Likewise, these factors will affect the resources required to undertake the study. Decisions about the administration of a questionnaire are critical and cannot be undervalued. If investigators make the correct decisions, the questionnaire will provide some of the answers they seek.

Sources of More Information on Writing Questions and Organizing Questionnaires

The CDC's OutbreakNet Team: Foodborne Disease Surveillance and Outbreak Investigation Toolkit (http://www.cdc.gov/outbreaknet/references_resources/) includes standard questionnaires for hypothesis-generating and hypothesis-testing interviews for foodborne disease outbreaks. Investigators may want to use these materials as templates for their own questionnaires.

The CDC also provides a tutorial, titled "Using Epi Info in an Outbreak Investigation, Advanced Analysis & Mapping" (http://www.cdc.gov/globalhealth/FETP/pdf/Cholera_020806_508.pdf), that includes instructions on entering questions into Epi Info.

References

1. Breuer T, Benkel DH, Shapiro RL, et al. A multistate outbreak of *Escherichia coli* 0157:H7 infections linked to alfalfa sprouts grown from contaminated seeds. *Emerg Infect Dis.* 2007;7(6). http://www.cdc.gov/ncidod/eid/vol7no6/breuer.htm. Accessed August 23, 2010.
2. Main study—round 16 community component HS. Health status and functioning. US Department of Health and Human Services website: http://www.cms.hhs.gov/MCBS/Downloads/1996_CBQ_hs.pdf. Accessed June 24, 2010.
3. 2008 Behavioral Risk Factor Surveillance System Questionnaire, December 31, 2007. Centers for Disease Control and Prevention website: http://www.cdc.gov/BRFSS/questionnaires/pdf-ques/2008brfss.pdf. Accessed September 28, 2010.

Chapter 9

Data Analysis

Amy L. Nelson
Meredith K. Davis

Learning Objectives
By the end of this chapter, the reader will be able to:

- Define measures of association, identify the measures of association most commonly used in cohort and case-control studies, and calculate and interpret the relative risk (risk ratio) and the odds ratio.

- Describe the role of confidence intervals for measures of association.

- Name several statistical programs that epidemiologists use to calculate confidence intervals.

- Identify formal statistical tests that epidemiologists use to determine whether the results of an analytical study are statistically significant, and identify which tests are used with categorical and continuous data.

- Describe how the *P*-value is used to determine the statistical significance for measures of association.

- Define confounders, name the most common ways to control for confounding, and explain how to use stratification, matching, and logistic regression to control for confounding.

- Explain why investigators sometimes have to plan and conduct additional analytic studies.

Introduction

At this point in an outbreak investigation, investigators have done their homework and their fieldwork. They have developed a hypothesis about why the case patients became ill, carried out an epidemiological study to test their hypothesis, and carefully entered their data. Now it is time to determine whether the data support the hypothesis. In the outbreak of *Escherichia coli* O157:H7 infection described in previous chapters, for example, investigators developed the hypothesis that eating contaminated salads or alfalfa sprouts most likely caused the patients to become ill and designed a case-control study. Then they were ready to apply some of the statistical methods described in this chapter to test the hypothesis.[1]

This chapter discusses the major steps in data analysis, including cleaning data, calculating measures of association and confidence intervals, and carrying out statistical tests such as chi-square and analysis of variance (ANOVA), focusing on the two analytic studies most commonly used in outbreak investigations: the case-control study and the cohort study. The chapter then examines confounders, including how to control for them. It concludes with a brief discussion of why it is sometimes necessary to conduct additional analytic studies.

Data Cleaning

Investigators should always remember that the conclusions they draw from an outbreak investigation are only as good as the data they collect and record. Data cleaning—the process of examining each variable in the data set individually—involves tasks such as checking for accuracy, consistency, and completeness, and getting to know the basic descriptive findings of the data. Analyzing data without *knowing* the data can lead to inaccurate conclusions. This section examines two common problems that investigators address during data cleaning—namely, outliers and missing values.

Outliers

Properly identifying and understanding outliers is an important step in analyzing descriptive data. Cases at the very beginning or end of an outbreak are the most obvious outliers, but investigators should also pay close attention to any observations that vary so widely from the rest of the data that they seem to be in error or to have come from a different population. The first thing that investigators should do when considering outliers is to make sure they are not mistakes due to data collection, coding, or entry errors. For example, if there is only one 1-year-old patient or one 95-year-old patient, and the remaining case patients range in age from 10 to 60 years old, investigators should confirm that the outlying values for age have been accurately recorded or calculated and entered into the database.

If an outlier is not an error, it may provide important information about the outbreak. For example, an outlying case may represent the source of the outbreak, a case exposed earlier than the others, a case exposed later than the others, a case with a long incubation period, or an unrelated case. Correctly determining which outliers are important trends in the outbreak and which are errors will pay big dividends when investigators analyze the data.

Missing Values

Data cleaning also reveals which variables have missing values, and sometimes why those values may be missing. Investigators can often determine which missing values are expected—for example, children are likely to have a missing value for occupation and persons not seen by a healthcare provider are unlikely to have laboratory results. Creating frequency distributions—that is, lists showing the number of times each value appears—can reveal outliers and how many values are missing for each variable.

TABLE 9-1   Data Cleaning: Frequency Distributions

Date Output Missing	Frequency	Percentage	Cumulative Percentage
	29	38.7%	38.7%
4/18/40 3:00 P.M.	1	1.3%	40.0%
4/18/40 9:00 P.M.	1	1.3%	41.3%
4/18/40 9:15 P.M.	1	1.3%	42.7%
4/18/40 9:30 P.M.	2	2.7%	45.3%
4/18/40 9:45 P.M.	2	2.7%	48.0%
4/18/40 10:00 P.M.	1	1.3%	49.3%
4/18/40 10:15 P.M.	1	1.3%	50.7%
4/18/40 10:30 P.M.	4	5.3%	56.0%
4/18/40 11:00 P.M.	5	6.7%	62.7%
4/18/40 11:30 P.M.	2	2.7%	65.3%
4/19/40 12:00 A.M.	2	2.7%	68.0%
4/19/40 12:30 A.M.	7	9.3%	77.3%
4/19/40 1:00 A.M.	10	13.3%	90.7%
4/19/40 2:00 A.M.	3	4.0%	94.7%
4/19/40 2:15 A.M.	1	1.3%	96.0%
4/19/40 2:30 A.M.	2	2.8%	98.7%
4/19/40 10:30 A.M.	1	1.3%	100.0%
Total	75	100.0%	100.0%

Suppose a frequency table (Table 9-1) for the variable representing the date of onset of illness shows that 29 of 75 records (almost 40%) are missing data for the date of onset of illness. Because 40% is a significant percentage, investigators might try to obtain these dates. If completing the data set is not possible, they will know that this variable—date of illness onset—may not be very reliable.

Cleaning data throughout the investigation helps investigators understand and manage outliers, missing values, and other problems, and it better acquaints them with the data. With a clean data set, they are ready to determine that an outbreak is real and move on to generating and testing hypotheses.

Measures of Association

In an outbreak investigation, investigators collect information on exposure and disease so as to identify risk factors for disease and measure the extent to which they may have caused or contributed to the outbreak. Measures of association are used to describe the strength or degree of the connection between two variables, such as between an exposure and a disease.[2] In the *E. coli* outbreak in Michigan and Virginia, for example, the investigators wanted to determine whether eating salads or alfalfa (the exposure) was strongly associated with diarrhea (the disease). The two measures of association used most often are the relative risk, or risk ratio (RR), and the odds ratio (OR). The decision to calculate a risk ratio or an odds ratio depends on the study design. In a cohort study, which compares the risk for an exposed group to the risk for an unexposed group, the risk ratio is used. In a case-control study, which compares diseased and nondiseased groups, the odds ratio is the ratio of choice. An odds ratio—the odds of exposure among cases divided by the odds of exposure among controls—provides a rough estimate of the risk ratio.

Risk Ratio

Risk of disease is the fundamental measure in epidemiology. Conceptually, risk is the probability that a person in a given population or group will develop disease. Mathematically, risk is the proportion of people in a population who develop disease, calculated by dividing the number of new cases by the number of people in the population (or group) as a whole.

A risk ratio compares the risk between two populations or groups. Investigators calculate a risk ratio by calculating the risk of disease in the exposed group, and then separately calculating the risk of disease in the unexposed group. In Table 9-2, for example, the risk of disease among the exposed group is $A/(A + B)$ and the risk of disease in the unexposed group is $C/(C + D)$. The risk ratio is the ratio of the risk in the exposed group to the risk in the unexposed group; it is shown at the bottom of the table. Investigators often use tables such as Table 9-2, known as 2×2 tables, to calculate measures of association. In a cohort study with multiple exposures, for example, investigators would create multiple 2×2 tables and calculate a risk ratio for the association between each different potential exposure and the disease. There might be one 2×2 table and risk ratio for having eaten potato salad, for example, and another 2×2 table and risk ratio for having eaten ham.

A risk ratio is interpreted as follows:

- If the exposure is not associated with the illness, RR = 1
- If the exposure is positively associated with the illness, RR > 1
- If the exposure is negatively associated with the illness (indicating a potential protective effect of the exposure), RR < 1

TABLE 9-2 2×2 **Table for Calculating a Risk Ratio**

	Ill	Not Ill	Total
Exposed	A	B	A + B
Unexposed	C	D	C + D
Risk Ratio		$\dfrac{[A/(A+B)]}{[C/(C+D)]}$	

TABLE 9-3   Calculating the Risk Ratio for Alfalfa Sprouts Consumption in a Hypothetical Outbreak of *Salmonella*

	Ill	Well	Total
Ate alfalfa sprouts	43	11	54
Did not eat alfalfa sprouts	3	18	21
Total	46	29	75

$$RR = \frac{[A/(A + B)]}{[C/(C + D)]} = \frac{(43/54)}{(3/21)} = 5.6$$

Table 9-3 shows a 2 × 2 table for a hypothetical outbreak of *Salmonella* with consumption of alfalfa sprouts as the potential exposure. Investigators calculate the risk ratio as the risk in the exposed group (43/54) divided by the risk in the unexposed group (3/21). The resulting risk ratio is 5.6. It indicates that persons who ate alfalfa sprouts were 5.6 times more likely to become ill than those who did not eat alfalfa sprouts.

Odds Ratio

In a case-control study, investigators compare people with the disease and people without the disease, instead of people who were exposed or not exposed, as in a cohort study. Because the entire population at risk is not included in a case-control study (by design), it is impossible to determine the risk in the exposed and unexposed groups and directly calculate the risk ratio. Instead, investigators use another measure of association, the odds ratio, to estimate the risk ratio. The odds ratio can be calculated from information in a 2 × 2 table (Table 9-4). It is generated by first calculating the odds that a case was exposed (A/C) and the odds that a control was exposed (B/D) and then taking their ratio: (A/C)/(B/D), which simplifies to (A × D)/(B × C). In any given investigation, investigators might use more than one 2 × 2 table and calculate more than one odds ratio to examine the relationship between multiple exposures and the illness.

In the hypothetical outbreak of hepatitis A shown in Table 9-5, the exposure is having eaten at restaurant X in April 2010. Investigators conducted a case-control study and

TABLE 9-4   Calculating an Odds Ratio

	Cases	Controls
Exposed	A	B
Unexposed	C	D
Odds Ratio	$\dfrac{(A/C)}{(B/D)} = \dfrac{(A \times D)}{(B \times C)}$	

TABLE 9-5 Calculating the Odds Ratio for Exposure to Restaurant X in a Hypothetical Outbreak of Hepatitis A, April 2010

	Case	Control	Total
Ate at restaurant X	60	25	85
Did not eat at restaurant X	18	55	73
Total	78	80	158

$$OR = \frac{(A/C)}{(B/D)} = \frac{(A \times D)}{(B \times C)} = \frac{(60/18)}{(25/55)} = \frac{(60 \times 55)}{(18 \times 25)} = 7.3$$

generated an odds ratio of 7.3, meaning the odds of having eaten at restaurant X in April 2010 were more than 7 times greater among persons with hepatitis A than among persons without hepatitis A.

The odds ratio is interpreted in the same way as a risk ratio:

- If the exposure is not associated with the illness, OR = 1
- If the exposure is positively associated with the illness, OR > 1
- If the exposure is negatively associated with the illness (indicating a potential protective effect of the exposure), OR < 1

Confidence Intervals

When investigators calculate an estimate (such as risk or odds) or a measure of association (such as a risk ratio or an odds ratio), the number they come up with is called a point estimate. Once investigators determine the odds ratio or risk ratio, they need to assess how precise the estimate is. Precision is an important factor in field epidemiology studies; because field conditions may not be ideal for scientific research, the precision of a measure of association can help investigators interpret the measure of association.

To describe the precision of the estimate, investigators begin by calculating the *confidence interval* (CI) around the odds ratio. The confidence interval includes a lower limit and an upper limit around the point estimate. The narrower the confidence interval, the more precise the point estimate.[3] The point estimate will usually be near the middle value of the confidence interval. For example, in a study with an odds ratio of 1.9, the confidence interval may be in the range of 1.1 to 2.7. The interpretation is as follows: Of 100 confidence intervals constructed in this way, 95 will contain the true point estimate. In practice, this is considered to mean that there is a 95% probability that the true estimate lies within this interval.

An analogy can help explain confidence intervals. Suppose investigators are interested in knowing the percentage of green marbles in a bag of 500 red, green, and blue marbles, but they do not have the time to count every marble. They decide to shake up the bag and select 50 marbles to give themselves an idea, or an estimate, of the percentage of green marbles in the bag. In the sample of 50 marbles, they find 15 green marbles, 10 red marbles, and 25 blue marbles. Based on this sample, the investigators can conclude that 30% (15 out of 50) of the marbles in the bag are green. In this example, 30% is the point estimate. Do the investigators feel confident in stating that 30% of the marbles are green? They might have some uncertainty about this statement, because they did not count all the marbles and there is a chance that the actual percentage of green marbles in the entire bag is higher or lower than 30%. In other words, the sample of 50 marbles may not accurately reflect the actual distribution of marbles in the whole bag of 500 marbles. One way to determine the degree of our uncertainty is to calculate a confidence interval.

Precision can be affected by both the sample size and the role of random error, which is variability in the data that cannot be readily explained. A smaller sample size or a significant amount of random error will lead to an imprecise estimate and result in wide confidence intervals. By comparison, a larger sample size or less random error will lead to a more precise estimate and result in more narrow confidence intervals. For example, a relative risk estimate of 5.5 with confidence intervals of 4.1 to 6.7 would be considered to have more weight than a relative risk estimate of 5.5 with confidence intervals of 0.3 to 51.8. In general, narrow confidence intervals indicate higher precision and wide confidence intervals indicate less precision.

In practice, confidence intervals are also used to indicate statistical significance. Remember, if the risk ratio is 1.0, the exposure is not associated with the illness. If the confidence interval for an odds ratio or a risk ratio includes 1.0, it *is not* statistically significant. If the confidence interval does not include 1.0, it *is* statistically significant.

Calculating Confidence Intervals

Epidemiologists often use statistical programs such as Epi Info (http://www.cdc.gov/epiinfo/), SAS (http://www.sas.com/), STATA (http://www.stata.com/), SPSS (http://www.spss.com/), and Episheet (http://www.epidemiolog.net/studymat/) to calculate a confidence interval. (To learn how to calculate confidence intervals by hand, see Giesecke's *Modern Infectious Disease Epidemiology*.[4]) The default is usually a 95% confidence interval, but it can be adjusted to 90%, 99%, or any other level, depending on the desired level of precision. When investigators use a 95% confidence interval, they conclude that the estimated range has a 95% chance of containing the true population value—that is, the true percentage of green marbles in the bag. Let's say that the 95% confidence interval around our 30% point estimate is 17%–43%. This confidence interval tells us that the true percentage of green marbles in the bag is most likely between 17% and 43%. However, there is a 5% chance that this range (17%–43%) does not contain the true percentage of green marbles, or a 5% chance of error.

Epidemiologists are usually comfortable with a 5% chance of error, which is why the 95% confidence interval is so commonly used. However, to reduce the chance of error, investigators might calculate a 99% confidence interval, which has only a 1% chance of error. The trade-off for the reduced risk of error is a wider range in the estimate of the percentage of green marbles, from 17%–43% with a 95% confidence interval to 13%–47% with a 99% confidence interval. If instead investigators were willing to accept a 10% chance of error, they could calculate a 90% confidence interval. In this case, the percentage of green marbles would be 19%–41%.

It is necessary to include confidence intervals with point estimates to provide a sense of the precision of the estimates. A very narrow confidence interval indicates that the estimate is very precise. One way to obtain a more precise estimate is to take a larger sample. If the investigators had taken 100 marbles (instead of 50) from the bag and found 30 green marbles, the point estimate would still be 30%, but the 95% confidence interval would be a range of 21%–39% (instead of the original range of 17%–43%) (Figure 9-1). If they had sampled 200 marbles and found 60 green marbles, the point estimate would be 30%; with a 95% confidence interval, the range would be 24%–36%. The confidence interval becomes narrower as the sample size increases.

To demonstrate how investigators pair measures of association with confidence intervals, we will examine an example from an outbreak of hepatitis A in a restaurant in Pennsylvania.[5] In this case, the exposure of interest is eating salsa at a specific restaurant (or not eating salsa at the restaurant), and the outcome is hepatitis A (or no hepatitis A).

In this study, investigators calculated an odds ratio of 19.6. In other words, the odds of developing hepatitis A among people who ate salsa were 19.6 times that of people who did not eat salsa (Table 9-6). The 95% confidence interval for this estimate was 11.0–34.9, which means there was a 95% chance that the range 11.0–34.9 contained the true odds ratio of hepatitis A among people who ate salsa compared with people who did not eat salsa. The lower bound of the confidence interval was 11.0, which is greater than 1, indicating an association between eating salsa and becoming ill. The investigators observed that people who ate salsa were more likely to become ill than the people who did not eat salsa, which helped them determine the cause of the outbreak.

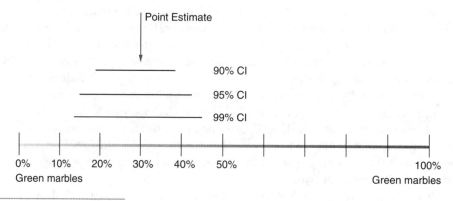

Figure 9-1　Confidence intervals

TABLE 9-6   Calculating an Odds Ratio in an Outbreak of Hepatitis A

	Outcome		
	Hepatitis A	No Hepatitis A	Total
Ate salsa	218	45	263
Did not eat salsa	21	85	106
Total	239	130	369

$$OR = \frac{AD}{BC} = \frac{(218)(85)}{(45)(21)} = 19.6$$

Source: Data from Wheeler C, Vogt TM, Armstrong GL, et al. An outbreak of hepatitis A associated with green onions. *N Engl J Med.* 2005;353:890–7.

Statistical Testing

After investigators have calculated the point estimate and a confidence interval around the point estimate, they use a formal statistical test to determine whether the results are statistically significant. Statistical testing involves two hypotheses: the null (H_0) and alternative (H_A) hypotheses. The null hypothesis states that there is no association between the exposure and the outcome; the alternative hypothesis states that there is an association between the exposure and the outcome.[6]

Analysis of Categorical Data

As noted earlier, a common analysis in epidemiology involves dichotomous variables—such as eating the salsa or not eating the salsa—and uses a 2×2 table to help determine whether Disease X occurs as much among people belonging to one group (an exposed group) as it does among people belonging to another group (an unexposed group). To determine whether those persons who were exposed have more illness than those not exposed, investigators can perform a test of the association between exposure and disease in the two groups.

   A hypothetical example illustrates this testing process. Suppose investigators conducted a retrospective cohort study to determine the source of a *Salmonella* outbreak on a cruise ship. They interviewed all 300 people on the cruise and found that 60 had symptoms consistent with *Salmonella* infection. Questionnaires indicated that many of the case patients ate tomatoes from the salad bar. Table 9-7 shows the number of people who did and did not eat tomatoes from the salad bar.

   One statistical test to determine whether there is a significant difference in the amount of illness between those who ate tomatoes and those who did not is called chi-square (or χ^2_{df}). In this example, the statistical test is testing the null hypothesis that there is no

TABLE 9-7 Sample Cohort Study: Exposure to Tomatoes and *Salmonella* Infection

	Salmonella		
	Yes	No	Total
Tomatoes	41	89	130
No tomatoes	19	151	170
Total	60	240	300

association between tomatoes and *Salmonella* infection—that is, RR = 1. If our example was from a case-control study, the null hypothesis would be that OR = 1. To calculate a basic chi-square value, the data must meet the following conditions:

- The table must have at least 30 observations (people).
- The expected count in each cell of the table must be 5 or more.

To conduct a chi-square test, investigators must calculate the chi-square statistic and its associated degrees of freedom (df). First, investigators calculate the chi-square statistic by comparing the observed data (from their study results) to the data they would expect to see in their data set if there was no association between exposure and disease. To know which data to expect, investigators need to know the size of the population, so they start with the totals from the observed data, as shown in Table 9-8.

These data tell investigators about the overall distribution of people who ate tomatoes and people who became sick. Based on these distributions, the empty cells of the table can be filled in with the expected values, using the totals as weights. A computer program will calculate the expected values, but there is a simple method to calculate them.

$$\text{Expected Value} = \frac{\text{Row Total} \times \text{Column Total}}{\text{Grand Total}}$$

TABLE 9-8 Row and Column Totals for Tomatoes and *Salmonella* Infection

	Salmonella		
	Yes	No	Total
Tomatoes			130
No tomatoes			170
Total	60	240	300

TABLE 9-9 **Expected Values for Exposure to Tomatoes**

| | Salmonella | | |
	Yes	No	Total
Tomatoes	$\dfrac{130 \times 60}{300} = 26$	$\dfrac{130 \times 240}{300} = 104$	130
No tomatoes	$\dfrac{170 \times 60}{300} = 34$	$\dfrac{170 \times 240}{300} = 136$	170
Total	60	240	300

For the first cell, which relates to people who ate tomatoes and became ill:

$$\text{Expected Value} = \frac{130 \times 60}{300} = 26$$

Investigators can use this formula to calculate the expected values for each of the cells, as shown in Table 9-9.

To calculate the chi-square statistic, investigators would use the observed values from Table 9-8 and the expected values calculated in Table 9-9. Using the formula [(Observed – Expected)^2/Expected] for each cell in the table, as in Table 9-10, *investigators* would add these numbers together to find the chi-square statistic. The chi-square statistic for this example is 19.2 (8.7 + 2.2 + 6.6 + 1.7 = 19.2).

Now the degrees of freedom (df) for the chi-square statistic must be calculated. To do so, multiply the number of rows minus one (number of rows – 1) by the number of columns minus one (number of columns – 1).[6] As seen in Table 9-10, there are two categories of exposure to tomatoes (rows) and two categories of *Salmonella* outcome (columns). Using the formula, investigators calculate the df as [(2 – 1) × (2 – 1) = 1]. There is always 1 df for a 2 × 2 table.

TABLE 9-10 **Expected Values for Exposure to Tomatoes**

| | Salmonella | |
	Yes	No
Tomatoes	$\dfrac{(41-26)^2}{26} = 8.7$	$\dfrac{(89-104)^2}{104} = 2.2$
No tomatoes	$\dfrac{(19-34)^2}{34} = 6.6$	$\dfrac{(151-136)^2}{136} = 1.7$

In general, the higher the value of the chi-square statistic, the greater the likelihood that there is a statistically significant difference between the two groups being compared. To be certain, however, investigators look up the P-value (probability value) in a chi-square table.

P-Values

The P-value tells investigators whether an apparent difference between two groups is a statistically significant one—that is, whether we should accept the null hypothesis that there is no association between the exposure and the outcome, or whether we should reject the null hypothesis in favor of the alternative hypothesis, that there is an association between the exposure and the outcome. In our hypothetical cruise ship *Salmonella* outbreak, for example, 32% of the people who ate tomatoes were infected with *Salmonella*, compared to 11% of the people who did not eat tomatoes. Although 32% and 11% *look* different, a statistical test is necessary to confirm that the difference is statistically significant. The P-value tells investigators whether the difference between 32% and 11% is a "real" difference, that the chi-square value of 19.2, with 1 df, is statistically significant.

Many statistical tests provide both a numeric result—such as the chi-square value of 19.2 with 1 df—and a P-value. The numeric result is the test statistic. The P-value is a number ranging from 0 to 1 that indicates the probability of obtaining a given result, under the assumption that the two groups whom investigators are comparing are actually the same. In other words, investigators begin by assuming that there is no difference in outcomes between the groups (null hypothesis), such as the people who ate tomatoes and those who did not. Then they see whether the test statistic and P-value indicate otherwise. A high P-value means that the two groups were not significantly different (accept the null hypothesis). A P-value of 1 indicates that there was no difference at all between the two groups. A low P-value indicates that the probability of observing these results by chance is very small (assuming the groups are actually the same), and it is safe to call the difference between the two groups statistically significant (reject the null hypothesis and accept the alternative hypothesis). Generally, the difference observed is considered statistically significant if the P-value is less than .05. In the cruise ship *Salmonella* outbreak associated with tomatoes, for example, the P-value for the chi-square of 19.2 with 1 df is $P < .0001$, so the difference in *Salmonella* occurrence between exposure groups is statistically significant.

The P-value and the confidence interval are related. If the 95% confidence interval around an RR or OR includes 1 (indicating that the null hypothesis cannot be rejected), the P-value will be greater than .05. If the 95% confidence interval does not include 1 (indicating a rejection of the null hypothesis), the P-value will be less than .05.

Common Statistical Tests for Categorical Data

Investigators can employ a number of statistical tests to obtain a P-value. The best test to use depends on the type of data. Table 9-11 identifies the types of chi-square tests and suggests when to use them.

The most commonly calculated chi-square test is Pearson's chi-square, or the uncorrected chi-square (the chi square calculated earlier for the *Salmonella* outbreak example).

TABLE 9-11 **Statistical Tests for Categorical Data**

Test Type	When to Use
Pearson's chi-square (uncorrected)	Sample size >100 Expected cell counts > 10
Yates chi-square (corrected)	Sample size > 30 Expected cell counts ≥ 5
Mantel-Haenszel chi-square	Sample size > 30 Variables are ordinal
Fisher exact	Sample size < 30 Expected cell counts < 5

If output is simply labeled "chi-square," it is likely that it is actually Pearson's chi-square. A rule of thumb is to use Pearson's chi-square if the sample size is greater than 100.

Following are examples of studies that compared two groups using a chi-square test or Fisher's exact test. In each study, the investigators chose the type of test that best applied to the situation—specifically, the size of the sample. Remember that the chi-square value is used to determine the corresponding *P*-value. Many studies, including the ones described here, report only the *P*-value rather than the actual chi-square value.

- *Pearson (Uncorrected) Chi-Square:* A North Carolina study investigated 955 individuals referred to the Department of Health and Human Services because they were partners of someone who tested positive for HIV. The study found that the proportion of partners who got tested for HIV differed significantly by race/ethnicity (*P* < .001). The study also found that HIV-positive rates did not differ by race/ethnicity among the 610 who were tested (*P* = .4).[7]

- *Yates (Corrected) Chi-Square:* In an outbreak of *Salmonella* gastroenteritis associated with eating at a restaurant, 14 of 15 ill patrons studied had eaten the Caesar salad, while none of 11 well patrons had eaten the salad (*P* < .01). The dressing on the salad was made from raw eggs that were probably contaminated with *Salmonella*.[8]

- *Fisher's Exact Test:* A study of group A *Streptococcus* (GAS) among children attending a daycare program found that 7 of 11 children who spent 30 or more hours per week in the daycare program had laboratory-confirmed GAS, while 0 of 4 children spending less than 30 hours per week in the program had GAS (*P* < .01).[9]

Investigators should be aware that statistical tests such as the chi-square are based on several assumptions about the data, including independence of observations. The assumption of independence means that the value of one observation does not influence the value of another observation. If this assumption is not actually true in the study, then it is incorrect to use the test. Situations in which the chi-square test is not appropriate include repeat observations of the same group of people—such as pre-tests and post-tests—and matched-pair designs in which cases and controls are matched on variables such as age and sex. These situations require special data analysis methods. Most of the situations investigators will face in field epidemiology, however, meet the assumptions of the chi-square test.

Analysis of Continuous Data

Data do not always fit neatly into discrete categories such as "did or did not eat tomatoes," of course. Continuous numeric data, however, can also be of interest in an outbreak investigation. Investigators might want to compare clinical symptoms between groups of patients, such as body temperature of adult patients with that of children. Alternatively, they might want to compare the average age of patients to the average age of nonpatients, or the respiratory rate of those who were directly exposed to a chemical plume to the rate of those who were not exposed. This type of comparison is possible with a test called analysis of variance (ANOVA).

Most of the major statistical software programs will perform ANOVA, but the output varies slightly from program to program. This section discusses the output from Epi Info to introduce the ANOVA test and two other useful tests. Epi Info generates three pieces of information when investigators conduct a test using ANOVA: the ANOVA results, Bartlett's test, and the Kruskal-Wallis test. The next few paragraphs describe how to interpret these tests.

Analysis of Variance Test

When investigators compare the distribution of continuous variables between groups of study subjects, they often require a test that produces a P-value, to determine whether the value of the variable is significantly different between groups. When analyzing continuous data, the null hypothesis states that there is no difference in the means of the outcome among the exposure groups, whereas the alternative hypothesis states that there is a difference in the means of the outcome among the exposure groups. The statistical test used for continuous data differs from the one used for categorical data; instead of the chi-square tests used for categorical data, investigators use a t-test (for comparing continuous data among two groups) or an f-test (for comparing continuous data among three or more groups). ANOVA uses either the t-test or the f-test, depending on the number of groups being compared.

A t-test compares averages between two groups, accounts for the variability in each group, and results in a statistic (t) that has a P-value. For example, when investigators are testing age differences between two groups, if the groups have very similar average ages and a similar "spread" or distribution of age values, the t-statistic will be relatively small and the P-value will not be significant. If the average ages of the two groups are quite different, the *t*-statistic will be larger and the *P*-value will be smaller. If the *P*-value is less than .05, the groups have significantly different ages.

Bartlett's Test

In *t*-tests and *f*-tests, ANOVA assumes that groups being compared have similar *variances*—in other words, the two groups have a similar "spread" of age values. As part of the ANOVA analysis, the software program conducts a separate test to determine whether the variances of the two groups really are comparable, called Bartlett's test for *equality of variance*. The basic assumption for this test is that the variances are comparable. If the *P*-value for the test is larger than .05, indicating the variances are similar, investigators can use the results of their ANOVA. In contrast, if Bartlett's *P*-value is less than .05, the variances in the groups are not the same and they cannot use the results of the ANOVA. In this situation, investigators can use another test in place of ANOVA: the Kruskal-Wallis test.

Kruskal-Wallis Test

If Bartlett's test indicates that the variances between the groups being compared are not similar enough to use ANOVA—that is, the *P*-value of Bartlett's test is less than .05—Epi Info will provide a third test result called the Kruskal-Wallis test. The Kruskal-Wallis test does not make assumptions about the variance in the data, nor does it test averages. It does, however, examine the distribution of the values within each of the groups, resulting in a *P*-value. As with the other statistical tests, if the *P*-value is larger than .05, investigators can conclude that there is not a significant difference between the groups being compared. If the *P*-value is less than .05, there is a significant difference between the groups.

Figure 9-2 summarizes when to use each of these tests for analyzing continuous data.

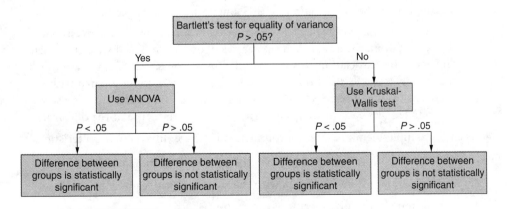

Figure 9-2 Decision tree for analysis of continuous data

Confounding

Although investigators try to minimize sources of bias through good study design, it is always important to consider other exposures or characteristics among the population that may be confusing the exposure–disease relationship (measure of association). This confusion is known as *confounding*. For example, most of the people who became ill in a gastrointestinal outbreak might have been members of the same dinner club, but many club members also might have attended a citywide food festival. Food-handling practices in the dinner club might be blamed for the outbreak when, in fact, food eaten at the festival was the cause—and, therefore, a much larger population was at risk of illness. Membership in the dinner club could be a confounder of the relationship between attendance at the food festival and illness.

Common confounders in epidemiological studies include age, socioeconomic status (SES), and gender. Here are a few examples:

- Children born later in the birth order are more likely to have Down syndrome. This does not mean, however, that investigators can conclude that birth order *causes* Down syndrome. Older women are more likely to have children with Down syndrome. Older women are also likely to be having children who are late in the birth order—it is much more common for a 35-year-old woman to have six children than a 21-year-old woman, for example. The mother's age confounds the association between birth order and Down syndrome: It looks like there is an association when there is not.[10]

- Some studies of hormone replacement therapy (HRT) in women have found no association between HRT use and cardiovascular disease, while others suggest there is an increased risk. Because women of higher SES are more likely to be able to afford HRT, and women of lower SES are generally at higher risk for cardiovascular disease, differences in SES may confound the relationship between HRT and increased risk of cardiovascular disease. This connection becomes apparent only when controlling for SES among study participants.[11]

- In a hypothetical outbreak of gastroenteritis at a restaurant, an investigation found that women were at much greater risk of developing the disease than men. However, this association was confounded by eating salad. Women are much more likely to order salad than men, and the salad was contaminated with the agent that caused disease. Thus the relationship between gender and disease was confounded by salad consumption, which was the true cause of the outbreak.

As these examples demonstrate, confounders must have three key characteristics:

1. A confounder must be associated with the *disease* being studied.
2. A confounder must be associated with the *exposure* being studied.
3. A confounder cannot be a result of the exposure.

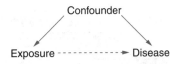

Figure 9-3 Relationship between a confounder and exposure and disease

In other words, the "triangle" shown in Figure 9-3 must be present for confounding to occur.

Controlling for Confounding

To control for confounding, investigators must take the confounding variable out of the picture.

The methods they use to do so include restricting the analysis, stratification, matching, and modeling. When they restrict the analysis, investigators analyze the exposure–disease relationship using only the subset of data within one level of the confounding variable, which requires investigators to ignore much of their data. We will not discuss restriction further here, but rather focus on stratification, matching, and logistic regression; the last of these is the form of modeling used most often in outbreak investigations.

Stratification to Control for Confounding

Stratification can tease out the effects of exposures and confounders by separating the population sample under study into several subsamples according to specified criteria.[2] For example, suppose both a homeless shelter and a soup kitchen have been implicated as the place of transmission in an outbreak of tuberculosis among homeless men. The men were likely to spend time in both places. To determine which site should be prioritized for intervention, investigators could examine the association between the homeless shelter and tuberculosis among men who *did not* go to the soup kitchen, and then examine the same relationship among men who *did* go to the soup kitchen.

In another example, suppose an outbreak has taken place at a reception, and both the cookies and the punch have been implicated in initial analyses. Investigators suspect that one of these food items is confounding the other, but because many people consumed both cookies and punch, they cannot determine the effects without stratifying the data. After investigators conduct a case-control study, the overall data look like Tables 9-12 and 9-13.

Both cookies (Table 9-12) and punch (Table 9-13) have a high odds ratio for illness and a *P*-value that is less than .05. Investigators can stratify to control for confounders and find out which one is really associated with the illnesses.

TABLE 9-12   Odds Ratio for Cookie Exposure in a Foodborne Outbreak

	Cases	Controls	Total
Cookies	37	21	58
No cookies	13	29	42
Total			100

$$OR = \frac{(37 \times 29)}{(21 \times 13)} = 3.93; \ 95\% \ CI: 1.69–9.15$$

$$P = .001*$$

* Exact *P*-values and confidence intervals were calculated in tables with cell sizes less than 5 using SAS 9.13. The chi-square statistical test was applied to detect differences between exposed and unexposed groups and whether they were ill/not ill according to the case definition.

To stratify by punch exposure (Table 9-14), investigators ask the following questions:

- *Among those who did not drink punch,* what is the odds ratio for the association between cookies and illness?
- *Among those who did drink punch,* what is the odds ratio for the association between cookies and illness?

If cookies are the culprit, then there should be an association between cookies and illness, regardless of whether anyone drank punch.

To stratify by cookie exposure (Table 9-15), investigators would ask the questions:

- *Among those who did not eat cookies,* what is the odds ratio for the association between punch and illness?

TABLE 9-13   Odds Ratio for Punch Exposure in a Foodborne Outbreak

	Cases	Controls	Total
Punch	40	20	60
No punch	10	30	40
Total			100

$$OR = \frac{(40 \times 30)}{(20 \times 10)} = 6.00; \ 95\% \ CI: 2.83–2.71$$

$$P = .0004*$$

* Exact *P*-values and confidence intervals were calculated in tables with cell sizes less than 5 using SAS 9.13. The chi-square statistical test was applied to detect differences between exposed and unexposed groups and whether they were ill/not ill according to the case definition.

TABLE 9-14   **Stratification of the Cookie Association by Punch Exposure**

		Did Have Punch	
	Cases	Controls	Total
Cookies	35	17	52
No cookies	5	3	8
Total			60

$$OR = \frac{(35 \times 3)}{(17 \times 5)} = 1.30; \ 95\% \ CI: \ 0.17-7.22$$

$$P = 1.0*$$

		Did Not Have Punch	
	Cases	Controls	Total
Cookies	2	4	6
No cookies	8	26	34
Total			40

$$OR = \frac{(2 \times 26)}{(4 \times 8)} = 1.63; \ 95\% \ CI: \ 0.12-13.86$$

$$P = .63*$$

* Exact *P*-values and confidence intervals were calculated in tables with cell sizes less than 5 using SAS 9.13. The chi-square statistical test was applied to detect differences between exposed and unexposed groups and whether they were ill/not ill according to the case definition.

- *Among those who did eat cookies*, what is the odds ratio for the association between punch and illness?

If punch is the culprit, then there should be an association between punch and illness, regardless of whether anyone ate cookies.

Stratifying allows investigators to examine the two risk factors—cookies and punch—independently. As is evident in Tables 9-14 and 9-15, cookies were not a significant risk factor independent of punch (stratified odds ratios are approximately 1), while punch remained a potential risk factor independent of cookies (the odds ratios were large and *P*-values close to significant). Because stratification essentially decreases the sample size for each calculation, we lose precision. Thus the confidence intervals for stratified estimates are wide.

The epidemiologists and biostatisticians Mantel and Haenszel devised a clever way to control for confounding using stratified analyses. In the example analysis, investigators were left with two stratum-specific estimates of the association between punch and illness: 4.1 and 5.4. The Mantel-Haenszel odds ratio takes an association (such as punch and illness), stratifies it by a potential confounder (such as cookies), and then combines

TABLE 9-15   Stratification of the Punch Association by Cookie Exposure

Did Have Cookies

	Cases	Controls	Total
Punch	35	17	52
No punch	2	4	6
Total			58

$$OR = \frac{(35 \times 4)}{(17 \times 2)} = 4.12; \; 95\% \; CI: 0.52–48.47$$

$$P = .18*$$

Did Not Have Cookies

	Cases	Controls	Total
Punch	5	3	8
No punch	8	26	34
Total			42

$$OR = \frac{(5 \times 26)}{(3 \times 8)} = 5.42; \; 95\% \; CI: < 0.80–40.95$$

$$P = .08*$$

* Exact P-values and confidence intervals were calculated in tables with cell sizes less than 5 using SAS 9.13. The chi-square statistical test was applied to detect differences between exposed and unexposed groups and whether they were ill/not ill according to the case definition.

them by averaging them into a single estimate that is controlled for the stratifying variable. The formula for the Mantel-Haenszel odds ratio is $(\Sigma a_i d_i / T_i) / (\Sigma b_i c_i / T_i)$, where a_i, b_i, c_i, and d_i, represent the cells of each stratified table and T_i is the total number of subjects in each stratified table.[6] This recombined odds ratio is the pooled or *common* odds ratio. Investigators find this technique useful when they have a confounder but want to present only one point estimate.

Matching

In Chapter 7, we noted that investigators may be able to reduce confounding by matching characteristics of cases and controls when they plan an epidemiological study. In cohort studies, they match unexposed persons to exposed persons on the desired characteristics. In case-control studies, they match controls to cases on the desired characteristics.

Generally, investigators must account for matching when they analyze matched data; otherwise, they introduce bias. If investigators select controls to be the same age, gender, and occupation as cases by matching, for example, they are purposefully introducing selection bias into the study. That is acceptable, however, if the matching reduces confounding—as long as investigators account for the matching in the analysis and the matched variables are not exposures of interest.

For example, in a study in a high school where a number of students have reported a strange smell and sudden illness, investigators might test the association between smelling an unusual odor in the school and a set of symptoms (nausea, vomiting, and fainting), and match cases and controls on gender, grade, and hallway. They match on these factors because there is a precedent for an "outbreak" of illness with unusual odors in buildings, for which no defined cause may be identified even after much environmental and epidemiological investigation. Gender is a confounder in such cases because women tend to be more reactive in this type of situation; grade level is a way of controlling for age, because younger and older students may react differently; and matching on hallway controls for the actual odor observed, because students in a hallway with a chemistry classroom may perceive an unusual odor that is different from an odor perceived by students in a hallway near the cafeteria.

Once investigators have matched case-control pairs, they set up the 2 × 2 table differently: they examine pairs in the table, so cases run along one side and controls along the other, and the table cells contain pairs. The general format is shown in Table 9-16.

Cell "e" in Table 9-16 contains the number of matched case-control pairs in which both the case and the control were exposed. It is considered a concordant cell (as is cell "h") because the case and the control have the same exposure status. Cell "f" contains the number of matched case-control pairs in which the case was exposed but the control of the pair was not exposed. It is considered a discordant cell (as is cell "g") because the case and the control have a different exposure status. Because the investigators want to contrast the exposure between cases and controls, only the discordant cells (f and g) provide useful data.

Investigators can easily calculate a chi-square value for matched data—via a method developed by McNemar—from these data using a statistical computing program. The calculation examines discordant pairs and results in a McNemar chi-square value and *P*-value. If the *P*-value is less than .05, investigators can conclude that there is a statistically significant difference in exposure between cases and controls. Investigators can also use the table of discordant pairs to calculate a measure of association. Table 9-17 uses data from the sudden illness outbreak mentioned previously.

TABLE 9-16 **Analysis of Matched Pairs for a Case-Control Study**

		Controls		
		Exposed	Not Exposed	Total
Cases	Exposed	e	f	e + f
	Not Exposed	g	h	g + h
	Total	e + g	f + h	

TABLE 9-17   Sample Data for Sudden Illness in a High School with Controls Matched to Cases on Gender, Grade, and Hallway in the School

Cases		Controls		
		Smell	No Smell	Total
	Smell	6	12	18
	No Smell	4	5	9
	Total	10	17	

Investigators can calculate the odds ratio directly from these data:

$$OR = \frac{(\text{Number of pairs with exposed cases and unexposed cases})}{(\text{Number of pairs with unexposed cases and exposed controls})}$$

$$= f/g = 12/4 = 3.0$$

In this example, the odds of having a sudden onset of nausea, vomiting, or fainting if students smelled an unusual odor in the school were 3.0 times the odds of having a sudden onset of these symptoms if students did not smell an unusual odor in the school, controlling for gender, grade, and location in the school.

An important note about matching: Once investigators have matched on a variable, they cannot use that variable as a risk factor in their analysis. Cases and controls will have the exact same matched variables (because they were chosen purposefully to be that way), so the variables cannot be assessed as risk factors. Investigators should not match on any variable that might be a risk factor; in general, they should match data only if they are sure they have a good reason for doing so.

Logistic Regression

Sometimes simple or stratified analysis tools are not sufficient to obtain an odds ratio that can control for a large number of confounders (provided the sample size is large enough). In such cases, investigators often use logistic regression. The odds ratio produced through this method is known as the "adjusted" odds ratio, because its value has been adjusted for the potential confounders. Some epidemiologists use logistic regression regularly, whereas others find that 2 × 2 tables are all they need.

In a logistic regression, as in a 2 × 2 table, the outcome variable (sick or not sick) and the exposure variable (exposed or not exposed) must both be dichotomous. Other variables are the confounders that investigators want to adjust for; these can be dichotomous, categorical with several levels, or continuous. Logistic regression uses an equation called a logit function to calculate the odds ratio.

In the study described earlier in which both cookies and punch were implicated in initial analyses as the source of an outbreak at a reception, for example, investigators could use logistic regression to clarify the effects without stratifying. The variables are as follows:

- SICK (where the value is 1 if ill, 0 if not ill)
- PUNCH (1 if drank punch, 0 if did not drink punch)
- COOKIES (1 if ate cookies, 0 if did not eat cookies)

In general, the equation would look like this:

$$\text{Logit (OUTCOME)} = \text{EXPOSURE} + \text{CONFOUNDER1} + \text{CONFOUNDER2} + \text{CONFOUNDER3} + \ldots$$

In our example, the outcome is the variable SICK. The exposure is the variable PUNCH, and the confounder is the variable COOKIES. The equation looks like this:

$$\text{Logit (SICK)} = \text{PUNCH} + \text{COOKIES}$$

The computer uses the math behind logistic regression to give the results. It is important to remember that the coefficient calculated by computer programs is often not the odds ratio, but rather the natural logarithm base e (ln) of the odds ratio. To obtain the odds ratio from computer programs, the coefficient must be exponentiated.

- **Logistic equation and odds ratios:** Logit (SICK) = PUNCH + COOKIES
- **Odds ratio for punch:** Odds of disease in those who had punch compared to those who did not have punch (controlled for cookies)
- **Odds ratio for cookies:** Odds of disease in those who had cookies compared to those who did not have cookies (controlled for punch)

Each variable on the right side of the equation (these are dependent variables) will have its own odds ratio. In our example, the odds ratio for *punch* would be the odds of becoming ill if punch were consumed, compared to the odds of becoming ill if punch were not consumed, controlling for *cookies*. If other confounders were included in the equation as dependent variables, the odds ratio for *punch* would also control for those variables. There is also an odds ratio for *cookies*. It represents the odds of becoming ill if cookies were consumed compared to the odds of becoming ill if cookies were not consumed, controlling for *punch*. Each variable on the right side of the equation controls for all other variables on the right side of the equation.

Logistic regression is very useful to epidemiologists, especially when multiple variables could be confounders. If investigators are not sure whether one of several variables is a confounder, they can examine them all at the same time. Two important caveats apply, however:

- Investigators should not put too many variables into the equation. If the sample size is 30 or fewer, the equation should include only one dependent variable. A good rule of thumb is to add one variable to the equation for every

25 observations. Thus, if there are 50 study subjects, investigators could include two dependent variables in the regression model. In the punch and cookies example, there are 200 cases and controls, so there could be as many as eight dependent variables in the regression model to explain the outcome/ observations.

- Investigators cannot control for confounders they did not measure. For example, if a child's attendance at a particular daycare program was a confounder of the *sick–punch* relationship, but investigators do not have data on children's daycare attendance, they will not be able to control for it. (There is always something investigators cannot—or forget to—gather data on, which partly explains why they can never be 100% certain of the results of odds ratio or risk ratio calculations.)

Conditional Logistic Regression

Logistic regression can also account for matching in the analysis of data, using a special method called conditional logistic regression. The computer calculates odds ratios in much the same way as McNemar's test, but the results are "conditioned" on the matching variables. Epi Info can also perform this calculation. Investigators interpret matched odds ratios (MOR) using conditional logistic regression the same way they interpret matched odds ratios calculated from tables.

To see how this works, consider the following example of conditional logistic regression: Investigators conducted a case-control study to identify risk factors for developing typhoid fever (*Salmonella* serotype typhi) in an outbreak affecting more than 10,000 people in Tajikistan in 1996–1997. Cases were culture positive for the organism, and controls were matched to cases by age and neighborhood. Using 2 × 2 tables, investigators associated illness with drinking unboiled water in the 30 days before onset (MOR = 6.5; 95% CI: 3.0–24.0), obtaining drinking water from a tap outside the home (MOR = 9.1; 95% CI: 1.6–82.0), and eating food from a street vendor (MOR = 2.9; 95% CI: 1.4–7.2). When all variables were included in conditional logistic regression analysis to tease out the effects of each factor, controlling for the others, only drinking unboiled water (MOR = 9.6; 95% CI: 2.7–34.0) and obtaining water from an outside tap (MOR = 16.7; 95% CI: 2.0–138.0) were significantly associated with illness. Routinely boiling water in one's home for drinking was protective (MOR = 0.2; 95% CI: 0.05–0.5).[12]

Investigators may never need to use logistic regression in analyzing data from outbreaks or other investigations, but this technique can be extremely helpful in managing confounding or potentially confounding variables. In addition, it can be particularly useful with large data sets and in studies designed to establish risk factors for chronic conditions, cancer cluster investigations, assessments of environmental exposures, and other situations in which numerous confounding factors could obscure the relationships between risk factors associated with disease outcomes. Many software packages, including SAS, SPSS, STATA, and Epi Info, can simplify data analysis using logistic regression.

Effect Measure Modifiers

In some situations, identifying the cause of an outbreak is not as simple as determining whether it was the cookies or the punch that made people ill. Sometimes the degree of association between an exposure and an outcome is different for different subgroups of the population.[3] This occurrence is known as *effect measure modification,* or heterogeneity of effect.[6] Age, gender, and vaccination status are a few examples of variables that can modify the effect between an exposure and the outcome, also known as effect modifiers.

Like confounding, effect measure modification is identified during stratification. However, unlike confounding, in which stratified estimates are similar to one another, effect measure modification leads to differences in stratum-specific estimates. Such differences are often a result of biological differences and, therefore, are of interest to investigators, leading them to question (and investigate) the mechanisms behind the observed differences.[6] Hence the effect measure modification should be described, rather than being adjusted for (as with confounding). When effect measure modification is identified, investigators should present estimates separately for each level or stratum. If gender is an effect modifier, for example, investigators should calculate two odds ratios or risk ratios: one for men and one for women.

When an analysis includes more than just an examination of the crude exposure–outcome association, it is important for investigators first to ascertain whether any of the additional variables are effect modifiers.[6] If an effect modifier is identified, the variable should be stratified by its levels and stratum-specific estimates of the exposure–outcome association should be presented. Once variables have been assessed for effect measure modification, investigators may then examine variables as potential confounders. Note that investigators do not need to assess whether variables identified as effect modifiers are potential confounders; only variables not identified as effect modifiers need be examined for this role.

Planning and Execution of Additional Studies

Sometimes the analytic study does not confirm the hypothesis, and investigators must look anew at their existing data, possibly gather more information from case patients, and generate additional hypotheses. Even if an analytic study confirms the initial hypothesis, investigators may decide to conduct additional studies as part of their mission to control and prevent disease transmission.

For example, in an outbreak of *Salmonella muenchen* in Ohio in 1981, investigators performed a case-control study in which they asked case patients about exposures to many different types of food. When the study failed to reveal any potential food exposure, investigators noticed that all of the case households but fewer than half of the control households included individuals between the ages of 15 and 35 years. This finding prompted them to consider vehicles of transmission that were common among young adults. After additional questioning and a second case-control study, investigators implicated marijuana as the outbreak source. The finding was confirmed by laboratory analysis of the marijuana.[13]

In another situation, such as a hypothetical outbreak of diarrhea on a cruise ship, an initial analytic study might confirm that Norwalk virus caused passengers and crew to become ill. Investigators might follow up this successful study with a second study to determine the effectiveness of an intervention to control the outbreak and prevent future transmission, such as instituting mandatory hand washing for all crew members.

Summary

Analytic epidemiology is how investigators link cause and effect in an outbreak investigation. A few tried-and-true calculations and tests make up the core of the analytic methods investigators use to determine whether their hypotheses are consistent with the data. Outbreak investigators are likely to use Epi Info, SAS, or another statistical program to analyze data. To use these programs successfully, however, they need a basic understanding of measures of association, confidence intervals, P-values, chi-square tests, and ANOVA. Understanding the basics of data analysis—and learning how to construct 2×2 tables—allows investigators to draw conclusions about the hypotheses they have generated in the early stages of the investigation. Sometimes, however, multiple potential exposures or a diverse study population make further analysis of the data necessary. Knowing how to control for confounding using stratification, matched study design, and logistic regression with multiple variables will prepare investigators to be successful when more complex statistical tests are required.

Often the first analytic study confirms the cause of the outbreak. In other situations, the initial hypothesis is wrong, and investigators must generate new hypotheses and conduct additional analytic studies. Sometimes even a successful analytic study leads to additional studies. In subsequent chapters, we will discuss how laboratory, environmental, and traceback studies support descriptive and analytic epidemiological studies in outbreak investigations.

Additional Resources

Simple Interactive Statistical Analysis. http://www.quantitativeskills.com/sisa/statistics/two2hlp.htm

Swinscow TDV. *Statistics at Square One.* 9th ed. London: BMJ Publishing Group; 1997. http://www.bmj.com/collections/statsbk/

Washington State Department of Health. *Guidelines for Using Confidence Intervals for Public Health Assessment.* http://www.doh.wa.gov/Data/Guidelines/ConfIntguide.htm

References

1. Breuer T, Benkel DH, Shapiro RL, et al. A multistate outbreak of *Escherichia coli* 0157:H7 infections linked to alfalfa sprouts grown from contaminated seeds. *Emerg Infect Dis.* 2007;7(6). http://www.cdc.gov/ncidod/eid/vol7no6/breuer.htm. Accessed August 23, 2010.

2. Porta M, ed. *A Dictionary of Epidemiology.* 5th ed. New York: Oxford University Press; 2008.

3. Gregg MB. *Field Epidemiology.* 2nd ed. New York: Oxford University Press; 2002.

4. Giesecke, J. *Modern Infectious Disease Epidemiology.* 2nd ed. London: Arnold; 2002.

5. Wheeler C, Vogt TM, Armstrong GL, et al. An outbreak of hepatitis A associated with green onions. *N Engl J Med.* 2005;353:890-7.

6. Aschengrau A, Seage GR III. *Essentials of Epidemiology in Public Health.* 2nd ed. Sudbury, MA: Jones and Bartlett; 2008.

7. Centers for Disease Control and Prevention. Partner counseling and referral services to identify persons with undiagnosed HIV—North Carolina, 2001. *Morb Mortal Weekly Rep.* 2003;52(48):1181-4.

8. Centers for Disease Control and Prevention. Outbreak of *Salmonella enteritidis* infection associated with consumption of raw shell eggs, 1991. *Morb Mortal Weekly Rep.* 1992;41(21):369-72.

9. Centers for Disease Control and Prevention. Outbreak of invasive group A *Streptococcus* associated with varicella in a childcare center—Boston, Massachusetts, 1997. *Morb Mortal Weekly Rep.* 1997;46(4):944-8.

10. Hecht CA, Hook EB. Rates of Down syndrome at live birth by one-year maternal age intervals in studies with apparent close to complete ascertainment in populations of European origin: A proposed revised rate schedule for use in genetic and prenatal screening. *Am J Med Genet.* 1996;62(4):376-85.

11. Humphrey LL, Nelson HD, Chan BKS, Nygren P, Allan J, Teutsch S. Relationship between hormone replacement therapy, socioeconomic status, and coronary heart disease. *JAMA.* 2003;289(1):45.

12. Centers for Disease Control and Prevention. Epidemic typhoid fever—Dushanbe, Tajikistan, 1997. *Morb Mortal Weekly Rep.* 1998;47(36):752-6.

13. Taylor DN, Wachsmuth IK, Shangkuan Y-H, et al. Salmonellosis associated with marijuana: A multistate outbreak traced by plasmid fingerprinting. *N Engl J Med.* 1982;306:1249.

Chapter 10

Writing an Outbreak Investigation Report

Sarah Pfau
David B. Rice

Learning Objectives
By the end of this chapter, the reader will be able to:

- Describe the purpose of outbreak investigation reports.
- List types of information included in an outbreak investigation report.
- Describe the structure of an outbreak investigation report.

Introduction

One of the final and most important steps of an outbreak investigation is writing an outbreak investigation report. No matter how large or small the outbreak, investigators should always document their work in writing. Depending on the size and complexity of the outbreak, the investigation report might be a brief internal memo or a lengthy article in a peer-reviewed journal. Some reports, such as John Snow's investigations of the London cholera outbreak of 1854[1] and the Centers for Disease Control and Prevention (CDC) report of five cases of *Pneumocystis carinii* pneumonia among previously healthy gay young men in Los Angeles in *Morbidity and Mortality Weekly Report* that marked the start of the HIV/AIDS epidemic in the United States,[2] have become part of public health history. This chapter discusses the function of outbreak investigation reports and their critical components. It concludes by examining the report of an investigation of a multistate outbreak of monkeypox in 2003 that was published in *Morbidity and Mortality Weekly Report*.

Why Communicate Outbreak Investigation Findings?

There are many reasons why it is important for investigators to communicate outbreak investigation findings. A well-written report serves the following purposes:

- Provides a reference for future investigators
- Contributes to the scientific knowledge base of epidemiology and public health

- Provides for discovery of evidence for potential legal issues
- Provides a record of performance
- Presents formal recommendations (providing a blueprint for action) to public health professionals, government officials, and policymakers[3]

Outbreak investigation reports have many audiences and fulfill many functions. Public health officials, for example, review past reports to learn about the type of investigation, questionnaires used, relevant findings, and lessons learned. Epidemiologists regularly review such reports to learn from the mistakes of past investigations and to take advantage of techniques that proved successful. Lawyers use them in outbreak-related litigation. Outbreak investigation reports can also be an important and accurate source of information for journalists covering an outbreak.

An outbreak investigation report can also help prevent the spread or limit the extent of an outbreak across state lines when a source or pathogen is present in the stream of interstate commerce. A published report on a foodborne outbreak in one state, for example, may alert health authorities nationwide to a potentially contaminated food item and trigger heightened surveillance activities. For example, an outbreak investigation in 2003 associated contaminated green onions used in a chain restaurant with an outbreak of hepatitis A in Pennsylvania. Investigators eventually identified more than 500 case patients who had eaten at other chain locations in six other states.[4] An advisory report by the U.S. Food and Drug Administration (FDA) and an article in *Morbidity and Mortality Weekly Report* alerted the public to this problem and helped investigators trace the contaminated green onions back to their source.[5]

Outbreak reports have also helped prevent or detect future outbreaks by providing new insights into disease transmission mechanisms. For example, in 1996, investigators traced an outbreak of Legionnaires' disease to a functioning display model of a whirlpool spa at a retail home improvement store in Virginia. None of the case patients entered the water, but appeared to have been exposed to *Legionellae* merely by walking past the display or spending time in the nearby area and inhaling the pathogen. This finding changed public health professionals' understanding of Legionnaires' disease transmission—and spurred the Virginia Department of Health to issue new recommendations for the maintenance and inspection of display whirlpool spas.[6]

In addition to shifting a disease transmission paradigm, the Virginia Legionnaires' disease outbreak investigation report served as discovery documentation for a civil lawsuit after a subsequent outbreak. In 1999, three years after the outbreak at the Virginia home improvement store, a Legionnaires' disease outbreak at a flower show in the Netherlands resulted in 188 confirmed and probable cases and 21 deaths. An environmental investigation and case-control study of visitors to the show implicated two whirlpool spas at the exhibition as the source of the outbreak. The victims sued the Dutch government for negligence, alleging that public health officials should have formulated new guidelines after the publication of the report on the Virginia outbreak in the 1996 *Morbidity and Mortality Weekly Report*.[7]

When Is the Report Written?

In general, investigators write a report when they complete the investigation, or after they have analyzed the data and laboratory reports. Sometimes, however, they write outbreak reports at various stages of the investigation, updating them as they receive new information or identify additional cases. Some reports include a disclaimer indicating that the investigation is ongoing and that investigators will revise the findings and recommendations as they learn more.

Who Writes the Report?

Generally, a member of the outbreak investigation team will take the lead in writing the investigation report. When multiple departments or agencies work together on an investigation, all participants should approve the final report.

What Are the Types of Reports and Where Do They Appear?

The length and purpose of the outbreak investigation report should reflect the complexity of the investigation and the intended audience. To document the investigation of a single complaint, investigators might simply complete a complaint form, record any actions taken, and recommend any necessary follow-up. Investigators should always remember, however, that a single complaint could be the first indication of a larger problem. A more complex event, such as a large outbreak, may involve people from outside agencies and will require development of a more comprehensive report.

Many outbreak reports are intended only for internal documentation, although an internal report may still be a "public record" under the Freedom of Information Act (FOIA). FOIA is a subsection of the Administrative Procedure Act (specifically, § 552). It requires federal agencies to provide as public information (for inspection and copying, with fees not to exceed the reasonable costs of the information search and duplication of documents) their rules, opinions, orders, records, and proceedings. FOIA provisions require that the head of each agency prepare and make publicly available a guide for requesting records or information.

Nine categories of information are exempt from public disclosure:

1. Classified information or information authorized under an executive order to be kept secret in the interest of national defense or foreign policy

2. Information related solely to an agency's internal personnel and practices

3. Information specifically exempted by statute

4. Privileged or confidential trade secrets and commercial or financial information

5. Inter- or intra-agency letters that would not be available by law unless an agency were in litigation

6. Personnel and medical files whose release would entail a breach of privacy

7. Very specific types of records compiled for law enforcement purposes

8. Reports prepared by, on behalf of, or for a regulatory agency that supervises financial institutions

9. Geological and geophysical information

However, there is an exception to the exception, as is often the case in law. When a record contains *both* exempt and nonexempt information and the nonexempt information is severable, that information must be provided; in this circumstance, the exempt information can simply be removed from the document before releasing it.

Outbreak investigation reports may appear in state publications, on websites, in statewide and national alerts, or in peer-reviewed journals. Even if they do not plan to distribute the report outside of their agency, investigators should thoroughly document the outbreak and the ensuing investigation in writing, so that the report can serve as a resource for future outbreak investigations.

Which Information Should Be Included in an Outbreak Investigation Report?

No matter the size or scope of an outbreak investigation, the report should convey accurate information about individuals affected by the disease and about the investigation process.

The report should include information about outcomes, including the number of:

- Total cases
- Primary and secondary cases
- Healthcare workers infected[8]

The report should summarize the investigation process, including when the following events occurred:

- First clinical observation
- Accurate diagnosis
- Laboratory confirmation
- Identification of the exposure source
- Report to a public health authority
- Report to a law enforcement authority
- Initiation of risk-mitigation activities, post-exposure prophylaxis, public education activities, and risk advice to healthcare workers
- Last reported new case[8]

A study of 116 published articles found that most outbreak investigation reports cover most of the process well, with two notable exceptions: Few document the chronology of the outbreak response with specificity, and few report on the dissemination of information to protect healthcare workers and law enforcement personnel (which is very important in the response to bioterrorism, for example).[8] If report writers carefully include all relevant information, their reports will provide practice-based evidence for safeguarding the public's health, document the performance of the investigation team, and provide benchmarks for training and education.[8]

What Is the Basic Structure of an Outbreak Investigation Report?

The author of an outbreak investigation report should follow a standardized format that comprehensively documents the investigation. Report writers will not be surprised to see parallels between the structure of an outbreak investigation report and the structure of a peer-reviewed journal article. Each standardized section may be as short as two or three sentences, or it may be pages long and very detailed, depending on the complexity of the investigation and the intended audience.

The elements and order of the report are as follows:

1. Summary
2. Introduction and Background
3. Methods
4. Results
5. Discussion
6. Recommendations
7. Supporting Documentation

Summary

The first element—the summary—provides a succinct overview of the investigation. It outlines who was involved, what happened, and where and when the events took place. The summary also succinctly describes the research hypothesis and conclusions. The last sentence should contain key recommendations and describe any action that is ongoing or pending. The summary should be written for a general audience, avoiding or explaining any technical jargon or unfamiliar vocabulary terms. The writers should assume that the summary may be the only part of the report that some people read, so it must be concise yet comprehensive.

Introduction and Background

The introduction and background section describes the outbreak under investigation and provides information about the causative agent. The essential elements of this section are the essential elements of descriptive epidemiology—who became sick, which disease they acquired, when they were exposed and became ill, and where the exposure took place. This section also describes how the outbreak was first reported, lists any steps taken to confirm the outbreak, and names the agencies and individuals who participated in the investigation. Furthermore, it may mention important findings from reports of similar outbreaks in the past.

Methods

The methods section describes how the investigation was conducted, including the methods used for the epidemiological, microbiological, and environmental studies.

- *Epidemiological methods* include the case definition, the means by which the team identified cases, and the study design. If the investigation team conducted a case-control study, for example, the report would describe how the team selected controls, how many controls they chose for each case, and whether they gathered information from study participants through in-person interviews, telephone interviews, or some other means.

- *Microbiological methods* include how investigators collected clinical or environmental samples, where they sent specimens for analysis, and which tests the laboratory performed on the specimens.

- *Environmental methods* include the interviews the team conducted and the risk assessments (such as documenting cooking methods or refrigeration practices) they performed during site visits, if any took place. If investigators undertook a traceback investigation of a food product, they would also describe the methods used in this section.

Results

Like the methods section, the results section is divided into three subsections if appropriate: epidemiological, microbiological, and environmental.

- The *epidemiological results* section summarizes the descriptive epidemiology (the critical who, what, when, and where) and clinical data (such as symptoms of the illness), and concludes with the results of the analytic study.

- The *microbiological results* section describes the results of microbiological or molecular testing, such as serotyping, culture, genotyping, or pulsed-field gel electrophoresis.

- The *environmental results* section describes the results of any risk assessment that investigators undertook as part of the environmental health assessment, such as identifying poor food-handling practices in a restaurant kitchen, and the results of any traceback investigation.

The results section often includes graphs and tables (including epidemic curves), maps of the distribution of cases, and other figures. Well-chosen figures present quantitative results and evidence, highlight trends and relationships among data, clarify complex concepts, and illustrate items or procedures. Any figures included in the report or attached as supporting documents should be "accurate, clear, and concise."[9] An easy-to-understand title, a legend describing any part of the figure that is not self-explanatory, and clearly labeled *x*- and *y*-axes are some of the hallmarks of effective figures. Similarly, map shading or color-coded distinctions often contribute to the effective communication of investigative data. The specifics will vary based on the type of figure and, if the report will be published in a journal, the publisher's style guide. The case study that concludes this chapter contains examples of an epidemic curve and a table that might be included with an outbreak investigation report. Report authors can find detailed guidelines on constructing other figures in reference works such as the *AMA Manual of Style*.

Discussion

The discussion section highlights the hypothesis that was tested in the analytic study and offers new insights into disease origin or transmission. It puts the conclusions of the study in context, details actions that investigators took based on the evidence they did (or did not) find, and explains how the actions protected the public's health.

The discussion section is also where investigators share the lessons they have learned—about the agent involved in the outbreak, for example, or the mechanics of the investigation. Investigators may discuss problems they encountered with sample collection and transportation, or with obtaining the cooperation of other agencies or potential study participants. If the investigation included a case-control study, the authors of the report may discuss whether it was difficult to identify appropriate controls or whether bias (such as selection, misclassification, or recall bias) could have affected the results.

Recommendations

The recommendations section should educate fellow public health practitioners and inform public policy. It explains what has been done or should be done to control the current outbreak (such as improving food-handling procedures or training employees in the proper use of equipment) and describes policy changes that could help prevent a similar outbreak from occurring in the future.

Supporting Documentation

Investigators supply supporting documentation to reinforce the assertions they have made in the report, highlight key information, and provide material that may be useful to future investigators and others with an interest in the investigation. Items frequently attached to reports include the following materials:

- Surveys administered
- Survey data (in electronic and paper versions)

- Copies of communications with those involved in the outbreak
- Menu samples (for a foodborne outbreak)
- Facility inspection reports
- Related reports (such as traceback investigation reports) from any collaborating agencies
- Media communications
- Maps of the site of the outbreak

Case Study: Multistate Outbreak of Monkeypox: Illinois, Indiana, Kansas, Missouri, Ohio, and Wisconsin, 2003

Note: *In 2003, several states, including Illinois, Indiana, and Wisconsin, reported an outbreak of a febrile rash illness to the CDC. Morbidity and Mortality Weekly Report published six reports about this outbreak over four weeks as investigators obtained more information. This case study paraphrases and discusses the first report, which describes the outbreak in five paragraphs followed by an editorial note, references, and supporting tables and photographs.*

Summary

The CDC has received reports that patients have developed a febrile rash illness who had close contact with pet prairie dogs and other animals. A clinic in Marshfield, Wisconsin, identified a poxlike virus by electron microscopy of skin lesion tissue from a patient and isolates of virus isolated from lymph node tissue from the patient's pet prairie dog. Additional testing by the CDC confirmed monkeypox. Initial descriptive epidemic, clinical, and laboratory data, interim infection-control guidance, and new animal import regulations are summarized in this report.

Introduction and Background

By June 10, a total of 53 cases had been identified. Twenty-nine of the case patients (49%) were male. The median age of patients was 26 years (range: 4–53 years). Fourteen patients (26%) were hospitalized. One was a young child with encephalitis.

Investigators were able to obtain clinical information for 30 cases reported in Illinois and Wisconsin. The earliest onset of illness was May 15. Most patients (22, or 73%) became ill with a fever first or had a fever accompanied by the beginning of a papular rash. Many also had respiratory symptoms (16, 64%), lymphadenopathy (14, 47%), and sore throat (10, 33%). The rash typically progressed through several stages; rash and lesions were distributed among the heads, necks, trunks, and extremities of patients. Lesions became ulcerated in some patients, and some patients had generalized rashes.

Methods and Results

Everyone who became ill had contact with animals, and at least two patients reported direct contact with another patient's lesions or ocular drainage. All but two patients reported close contact with prairie dogs. One patient reported contact with a Gambian giant rat, and another had contact with a rabbit that became sick after being exposed to a sick prairie dog at a veterinary clinic.

(continues)

Case Study: Multistate Outbreak of Monkeypox: Illinois, Indiana, Kansas, Missouri, Ohio, and Wisconsin, 2003 (*continued*)

Traceback investigations found that prairie dogs and Gambian giant rats were housed together at a distributor in Illinois, and that the rats traveled from Ghana in April to a wildlife importer in Texas, who then sold them to the Illinois distributor. The actual source of introduction of monkeypox might have been a shipment that contained approximately 800 small mammals of nine different species.

As of June 9, investigators had obtained and tested specimens from 10 patients in Illinois, Indiana, and Wisconsin, of whom nine had DNA sequence signatures specific for monkeypox. A patient who did not have visible skin lesions tested negative by polymerase chain reaction. Four of five patients for whom skin biopsies were available tested positive for orthopox viral antigens by immunohistochemical testing. Of four patients whose skin lesions were evaluated by negative stain electron microscopy, pox viral particles were found in three. Laboratory testing also found monkeypox-specific DNA signatures in a viral isolate derived from the lymphoid tissue of a sick prairie dog belonging to a patient.

Note: *Without delving into specifics about methods (not surprising, given that so many agencies and specialties were involved with the study), the first five paragraphs of this report provide an overview of the investigation, outline the outbreak, and describe the epidemiological, microbiological, and environmental results to that point. Following a list of the professionals from local, state, and federal agencies who contributed to the report—laboratory workers, physicians and infectious disease specialists, public health practitioners, veterinarians, and others—an editorial note provides the rest of the information that is essential to a comprehensive report.*

Discussion and Recommendations

Human monkeypox was discovered in the Democratic Republic of the Congo in 1970, in a region where smallpox had recently been eliminated. It is caused by an orthopoxvirus that is similar to smallpox clinically but is different both biologically and epidemiologically. It has an incubation period of a week to 17 days. It is characterized by fever, headache, backache, and fatigue, followed by a rash that, like smallpox, evolves over 2 to 3 weeks. Unlike smallpox patients, however, most patients with monkeypox develop pronounced lymphadenopathy, or swollen lymph nodes. The disease does not appear to spread easily from person to person. The case-fatality rate in Africa has been approximately 1% to 10%. Death rates have been higher among young children.

Preliminary findings from these investigations point to close contact with infected mammalian pets as the primary route of transmission to humans. Human-to-human contact cannot be ruled out, however. Based on these findings, the CDC has issued interim guidance for patients with suspected monkeypox addressing infection control, exposure management, monitoring of exposed persons, and duration of isolation procedures in healthcare and community settings. Physicians who see patients with unexplained fever, rash, or swollen lymph nodes should ask patients about exposure to unusual or exotic pets, especially small animals such as prairie dogs or

(continues)

Case Study: Multistate Outbreak of Monkeypox: Illinois, Indiana, Kansas, Missouri, Ohio, and Wisconsin, 2003 (*continued*)

Gambian giant rats. When they suspect monkeypox infection, physicians should apply standard, contact, and airborne precautions. Pet owners and veterinarians should follow interim guidelines modeled after human infection-control guidelines with appropriate modifications for home and veterinary settings. To help prevent further transmission of monkeypox among animals, the guidelines also outline the appropriate management of exposed or ill pets.

The potential of monkeypox virus infection and other nonindigenous pathogens makes the introduction of exotic species, such as rodents from Africa, a serious public health threat because of the potential of monkeypox virus infection and other nonindigenous pathogens. Serosurveys have found orthopoxvirus in various healthy rodents and non human primates, and a rope squirrel found with skin lesions in the vicinity of monkeypox cases in the Democratic Republic of the Congo has tested positive for monkeypox virus. Because of the threat, and pursuant to 42 CF 71.32(b), the CDC is implementing an immediate embargo on the importation of all rodents from Africa (Order *Rodentia*.) In addition, pursuant to 42 CF 70.2 and 21 CFR 1240.30, the CDC and the FDA are prohibiting the transportation or offering for transportation in interstate commerce, or the sale, offering for sale, or offering for any other type of commercial or public distribution, including release into the environment, of prairie dogs. The prohibition also applies to additional rodents from Africa: tree squirrels (*Heliosciurus* sp.), rope squirrels (*Funisciurus* sp.), dormice (*Graphiurus* sp.), Gambian giant pouched rats (*Cricetomys* sp.), brush-tailed porcupines (*Atherurus* sp.), and striped mice (*Hybomys* sp.). States may also decide to put in place their own measures to prohibit the importation, sale, distribution, or display of animals that could result in transmission of infectious agents.

Healthcare providers, veterinarians, and public health officials who suspect monkeypox in animals or humans should "report such cases to their state and local health departments." State health departments should contact the CDC Office of Emergency Operations to report suspect cases. A website includes additional information, including an interim case definition.

Supporting Documentation

Note: *An epidemic curve (Figure 10-1) shows the number of persons with monkeypox, by date of first symptom onset, in Illinois and Wisconsin. By the sixth report, the outbreak included 69 cases in six states; the investigators used different shades of the bars in the graph to convey how the case definition changed during the investigation to include suspect, probable, and confirmed cases.*

A photograph of an important clinical feature of the disease (Figure 10-2) is included to help clinicians identify the disease in this and future investigations.

A table (Table 10-1) describes the clinical features of the cases. In the text of the report, the authors note that not all of the cases had clinical information available at the time of the report, so they present information only for the 30 cases for which they had information. It is common to see outbreak reports published with incomplete or evolving data, especially if it is important to provide information about the ongoing investigation immediately to clinicians and the public.

(continues)

Case Study: Multistate Outbreak of Monkeypox: Illinois, Indiana, Kansas, Missouri, Ohio, and Wisconsin, 2003 (*continued*)

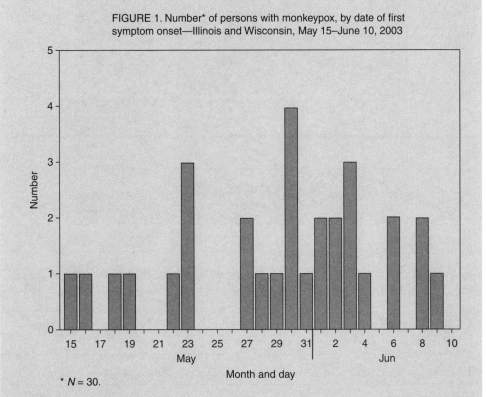

FIGURE 1. Number* of persons with monkeypox, by date of first symptom onset—Illinois and Wisconsin, May 15–June 10, 2003

* *N* = 30.

Figure 10-1   Example of an epidemic curve from a monkeypox outbreak investigation report

Source: Centers for Disease Control and Prevention. Multistate outbreak of monkeypox— Illinois, Indiana, and Wisconsin, 2003. *Morb Mortal Weekly Rep.* 2003;52(23):537–40. http://www.cdc.gov/mmwr/preview/mmwrhtml/mm5223a1.htm

(*continues*)

Case Study: Multistate Outbreak of Monkeypox: Illinois, Indiana, Kansas, Missouri, Ohio, and Wisconsin, 2003 (*continued*)

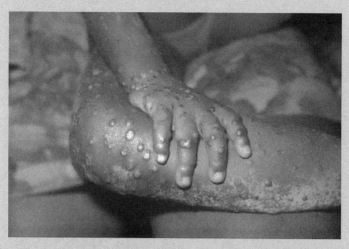

Figure 10-2   Monkeypox lesions on a child

Source: Monkeypox Photos. Centers for Disease Control and Prevention website: http://www.cdc.gov/vaccines/vpd-vac/monkeypox/photos.htm#disease. Accessed June 7, 2011.

TABLE 10-1   **Example of a Table Describing Clinical Features from the Investigation of a Monkeypox Outbreak**

TABLE. Clinical features of persons with monkeypox—Illinois and Wisconsin, 2003*

Clinical features	No. cases	(%)
Rash	25	(83)
Fever	22	(73)
Respiratory†	16	(64)
Lymphadenopathy	14	(47)
Sweats	12	(40)
Sore throat	10	(33)
Chills	11	(37)
Headache	10	(33)
Nausea and/or vomiting	6	(20)

* $N = 30$. As of June 10.
† Includes cough, shortness of breath, and nasal congestion. Data were missing for five patients.

Source: Centers for Disease Control and Prevention. Multistate outbreak of monkeypox—Illinois, Indiana, and Wisconsin, 2003. *Morb Mortal Weekly Rep.* 2003;52(23):537–40. http://www.cdc.gov/mmwr/preview/mmwrhtml/mm5223a1.htm

(*continues*)

Case Study: Multistate Outbreak of Monkeypox: Illinois, Indiana, Kansas, Missouri, Ohio, and Wisconsin, 2003 (*continued*)

Note: *This case study of an outbreak investigation report demonstrates the clear correlation between such reports and risk communication. The CDC published six reports in Morbidity and Mortality Weekly Report related to the monkeypox outbreak to communicate the ongoing investigation findings to the public, as well as to inform physicians about the signs and symptoms of monkeypox. Report authors must decide whether to include an element of risk communication based on the type of investigation and the point at which they write the report. Reports written during an ongoing or multistate investigation often fill a dual role of documentation and risk communication.*

Source: Centers for Disease Control and Prevention. Multistate outbreak of monkeypox—Illinois, Indiana, and Wisconsin, 2003. *Morb Mortal Weekly Rep.* 2003;52(23):537–40. http://www.cdc.gov/mmwr/preview/mmwrhtml/mm5223a1.htm

Summary

Outbreak investigation reports are one of the final and most important steps in an outbreak investigation. They present formal recommendations that can lead to public health actions to halt current outbreaks and prevent future events. Outbreak reports also contribute to the scientific knowledge base of epidemiology and public health and provide for discovery of evidence for potential lawsuits. An outbreak investigation report can also serve as a means of communicating risks, providing the public with information about ongoing investigations and informing physicians about the signs and symptoms of the disease under investigation. Epidemiologists and other public health practitioners regularly review outbreak reports, learning from past mistakes and adopting new techniques to make future investigations more successful.

Outbreak investigation reports generally include information about disease outcomes and the process of the investigation. They follow a basic structure that is similar to the structure of an article in a peer-reviewed journal. The complexity and length of the report depends on the type of investigation, the extent of the outbreak, and the intended audience.

References

1. Snow J. *On the Mode of Communication of Cholera*. 2nd ed. London: John Churchill, New Burlington Street; 1855. http://www.ph.ucla.edu/epi/snow/snowbook.html. Accessed June 29, 2010.
2. Centers for Disease Control and Prevention. Pneumocystis pneumonia—Los Angeles. *Morb Mortal Weekly Rep.* 1981;48(LMRK):77–81.
3. EXCITE: Epidemiology in the classroom. How to investigate an outbreak: Steps of an outbreak investigation. Updated 2004. Centers for Disease Control and Prevention website: http://www.cdc.gov/excite/classroom/outbreak/steps.htm. Accessed June 29, 2010.

4. Centers for Disease Control and Prevention. Hepatitis A outbreak associated with green onions at a restaurant—Monaca, Pennsylvania. *Morb Mortal Weekly Rep.* 2003;52(47):1155-7.

5. Consumers advised that recent hepatitis A outbreaks have been associated with green onions. November 15, 2003. Centers for Disease Control and Prevention website: http://www.cdc.gov/mmwr/preview/mmwrhtml/mm52d1121a1.htm. Accessed June 7, 2011.

6. Centers for Disease Control and Prevention. Legionnaires disease associated with a whirlpool spa display—Virginia, September-October, 1996. *Morb Mortal Weekly Rep.* 1997;46(4):83-86.

7. Den Boer JW, Yzerman PF, Schellekens J, et al. A large outbreak of Legionnaires' disease at a flower show, the Netherlands, 1999. *Emerg Infect Dis* 2002;8(1):37-43.

8. Potter MA, Sweeney P, Iuliano AD, Allswede MP. Performance indicators for response to selected infectious disease outbreaks: A review of the published record. *J Public Health Manage Pract.* 2007;13(5):510-8.

9. American Medical Association. *AMA Manual of Style: A Guide for Authors and Editors.* 10th ed. New York: Oxford University Press; 2009.

Chapter 11

The Public Health Laboratory's Role in Field Epidemiology and Outbreak Investigation

Jeanette K. Stehr-Green
Paul A. Stehr-Green
Amy L. Nelson
Lauren N. Bradley
David B. Rice

Learning Objectives

By the end of this chapter, the reader will be able to:

- Describe the role that the laboratory can play in the investigation of an outbreak or other public health problem.

- Describe the national networks of public health and other types of laboratories, including how they can provide additional resources in the investigation of foodborne outbreaks and bioterrorist attacks.

- Describe the four levels of biosafety at laboratories regulated by the Centers for Disease Control and Prevention.

- List two references that are useful in determining the type of clinical specimen investigators should collect to diagnose an acute infectious disease.

- Discuss special considerations for the collection of clinical specimens—type of specimen, timing of collection, proper conditions during storage and transportation, safety, and information submitted with specimen.

- List equipment used in the collection of food and water samples.

- Describe considerations for interpreting laboratory results of various specimens, including "negative" results.

- Define subtyping.

- Provide four examples of subtyping.

- Discuss how subtyping can be used in public health investigations.

- Interpret subtype results when patients are found to have the same (or indistinguishable) subtypes.

Introduction

Up to this point, this book has focused, almost exclusively, on the epidemiologic investigation of outbreaks and other public health problems. These investigations are actually multifaceted—laboratory, environmental, and behavioral investigations also contribute valuable information. Because laboratories often provide some of the most important pieces of information needed to solve outbreaks and other public health puzzles, investigators must learn to work effectively with laboratories and laboratory investigators.

The public health laboratory's traditional role has centered on isolating causative agents from patients and suspected vehicles of infection, participating in disease surveillance and outbreak investigations, and conducting applied research. Newer technologies such as subtyping have expanded the laboratory's critical role in outbreak investigations by making it possible to use phenotypic or genetic testing to link seemingly unrelated cases. In this chapter, we discuss the national network of public health laboratories, explore the role of laboratories and laboratory investigators in outbreak investigations, and explain how investigators can support the work of the laboratory to bring investigations to a successful conclusion.

A National Network of Laboratories

The United States has an estimated 200,000 private-sector clinical laboratories and a few thousand public health, veterinary, food safety, and environmental testing laboratories.[1] Some laboratories provide only basic water-testing services, others offer more complicated testing involving human samples, and some are able to characterize potential bioterrorism agents. Private laboratories are concerned with the care of individual patients, whereas public health laboratories focus more broadly on the health of entire populations.[1]

Specimen test results that indicate the occurrence of an outbreak could surface at any type of laboratory, so it is critical to link the efforts of laboratories across the United States.[1] A National Laboratory System initiative has been undertaken to create seamless systems within each state for public health surveillance and laboratory support and improvement; until this initiative is fully implemented, state public health laboratories and federal agencies such as the Centers for Disease Control and Prevention (CDC) will continue to work together to coordinate the response to outbreaks and other public health emergencies, such as Hurricane Katrina.[1] The national network of public health laboratories is integrated into the public health system; it provides "surge capacity" when the resources of a state or region are overwhelmed by a natural disaster or other emergency, and it makes sure local jurisdictions, states, and the nation as a whole receive public health laboratory services adequate to their needs.[1]

In many outbreak investigations, epidemiologic investigators can send a clinical/human or environmental specimen to a local laboratory and quickly discover the identity of the pathogen that is causing people to become ill. Some cases, however, require more sophisticated testing. If reports of a related illness come from several different geographic locations, it may be necessary to determine whether all of the patients have been infected by the same strain of the etiologic agent. Moreover, if suspicion arises that a biological or chemical agent has made people ill, investigators will need accurate results as quickly as possible to determine appropriate response measures.

When the demands of an investigation exceed the resources of a local laboratory, the investigation team may call on the national networks that have been established to help with foodborne diseases and bioterrorism or chemical events. Two such networks are described here.

PulseNet

If epidemiologic investigators work with a local or state public health laboratory to identify the cause of a foodborne disease outbreak, the laboratory may connect with PulseNet to determine whether the same strain of the organism that is making people ill in one place is also infecting people at other sites. PulseNet (http://www.cdc.gov/pulsenet/) is a national network of public health and food regulatory agency laboratories coordinated by the CDC. State and local health departments and federal agencies (CDC, U.S. Department of Agriculture/Food Safety and Inspection Service, and the U.S. Food and Drug Administration) make up this network. PulseNet members conduct standardized molecular subtyping (or "fingerprinting") of foodborne disease-causing bacteria by pulsed-field gel electrophoresis (PFGE) to distinguish strains of organisms such as *Escherichia coli* O157:H7, *Salmonella*, *Shigella*, *Listeria*, or *Campylobacter* at the DNA level. They post their results—DNA "fingerprints," or PFGE patterns—to a dynamic database at the CDC, which is available on an on-demand basis to participants so they can compare patterns rapidly.

The Laboratory Response Network

In the late 1990s, public health laboratories began to prepare for the global threats posed by biohazards and biological terrorism. At the time, few such laboratories were able to test for the most virulent biological agents, and those that could used testing methods that were extremely time-consuming.[1] In 1999, the CDC, along with the Federal Bureau of Investigation and the Association of Public Health Laboratories, responded to calls to improve this testing capacity by forming the Laboratory Response Network (http://www.bt.cdc.gov/lrn/). Charged with ensuring an effective laboratory response to bioterrorism, the Laboratory Response Network maintains an integrated network of state and local public health, federal, military, and international laboratories that can respond to bioterrorism, chemical terrorism, and other public health emergencies. The network links local and state public health laboratories with veterinary, agriculture, military, and water- and food-testing laboratories.

The anthrax events of September 2001 provided an early test of the Laboratory Response Network. The network conducted nearly 122,000 work-ups based on environmental samples, and developed a triage system that included initial screening at thousands of sentinel laboratories, confirmatory testing at reference laboratories, and highly sophisticated forensic and epidemiological screening at two national laboratories.[1]

Laboratory Biosafety Levels

The CDC regulates laboratories—hospital, independent, and physician laboratories as well as national, state, and local public health laboratories—based on the agents they handle and the degree of protection they provide to their own personnel, the environment, and the community. CDC regulations cover precautions, special practices, and decontamination procedures for laboratories that work with infectious agents. Based on the degree of hazard that they are equipped to handle, laboratories are divided into four biosafety levels. Biosafety Level 1 (BSL-1) laboratories work with the least dangerous agents and require the fewest precautions; Biosafety Level 4 (BSL-4) laboratories have the strictest methods for handling organisms and deal with agents that are most dangerous to public health.

Following are brief summaries of the four biosafety levels, adapted from the CDC's *Biosafety in Microbiological and Biomedical Laboratories* document.[2]

Biosafety Level 1

BSL-1 laboratories work with well-characterized agents not known to consistently cause disease in healthy human adults. These agents are generally of minimal potential hazard to laboratory personnel and the environment. *Bacillus subtilis, Nigeria gruberi*, infectious canine hepatitis virus, and exempt organisms under the National Institutes of Health (NIH) guidelines are examples of the microorganisms that meet these criteria. BSL-1 laboratories follow standard microbiological practices, which include the following measures:

- Limiting access to the laboratory when experiments or work with cultures and specimens is under way
- Requiring hand washing after handling viable materials, after removing gloves, and before leaving the laboratory
- Forbidding eating, drinking, smoking, handling contact lenses, applying cosmetics, and storing food for human consumption in work areas
- Prohibiting mouth pipetting
- Instituting policies for handling sharp objects such as needles and scalpels
- Minimizing the creation of splashes and aerosols
- Decontaminating work surfaces at least once a day and after any spills
- Decontaminating all cultures, stocks, and other potentially infectious materials before disposal by an effective decontamination method

Biosafety Level 2

BSL-2 laboratories are similar to BSL-1 laboratories and are suitable for work involving agents of moderate potential hazard to personnel and the environment. Microorganisms typically assigned to this containment level include hepatitis B virus, HIV, *Salmonella*, and *Toxoplasma*. Differences of BSL-2 laboratories from BSL-1 laboratories include the former's practices of providing laboratory personnel with specific training in handling pathogenic agents and with supervision by scientists who are competent in handling infectious agents and associated procedures; limiting access to the laboratory when work is being conducted; taking extreme precautions with contaminated sharp items; and conducting certain procedures in which infectious aerosols or splashes may be created in biological safety cabinets or other physical containment equipment.

Biosafety Level 3

BSL-3 laboratories are clinical, diagnostic, teaching, research, or production facilities in which work is done with indigenous or exotic agents that may cause serious or potentially lethal disease to persons who inhale these agents. *Mycobacterium tuberculosis*, St. Louis encephalitis virus, and *Coxiella burnetii* are examples of the agents assigned to this level. The personnel who work in these laboratories have specific training in handling pathogenic and potentially lethal agents, and they are supervised by competent scientists who are experienced in working with these agents. Personnel in BSL-3 laboratories carry out procedures that involve manipulating infectious materials in biological safety cabinets or other physical containment or they wear appropriate personal protective clothing and equipment.

Biosafety Level 4

BSL-4 laboratories work with dangerous and exotic agents that pose a high individual risk of aerosol-transmitted laboratory infections and life-threatening disease that is frequently fatal, for which there are no vaccines or treatments, or a related agent with unknown risk of transmission. These laboratories handle agents with a close or identical antigenic relationship to BSL-4 agents until sufficient data are available either to continue work at this level or to work with them at a lower level of biosafety. The personnel in BSL-4 level laboratories have specific and thorough training in handling extremely hazardous infectious agents; they understand the primary and secondary containment functions of the standard and special practices, the containment equipment, and the laboratory design characteristics. Competent scientists with training and experience working with these agents supervise them.

The laboratory director strictly controls access to BSL-4 laboratories. Each BSL-4 facility is located either in a separate building or in a controlled area in a building that is completely isolated from all other areas of the building. All activities within work areas of BSL-4 laboratories are confined to Class III biological safety cabinets, or Class II biological safety cabinets used with one-piece positive-pressure personnel suits ventilated by a life-support system. Each BSL-4 laboratory has special engineering and design features to prevent microorganisms from being released into the environment.

Many high schools, community colleges, and municipal drinking water treatment facilities have BSL-1 facilities. BSL-2 facilities may be found in local health departments, universities, state laboratories, private laboratories in hospitals or healthcare systems, and industrial laboratories operated by clinical diagnostic companies. Most facilities that conduct infectious disease research have BSL-3 laboratories. They may be located in state health departments, universities, private companies, industry, and federal agencies such as the NIH and the CDC. Currently operational BSL-4 laboratories are located in federal facilities such as the CDC and the U.S. Army Medical Research Institute of Infectious Diseases in Fort Detrick, Maryland, as well as at the Texas Biomedical Research Institute in San Antonio, Texas, and at the University of Texas at Galveston. Additional facilities are planned for federal or academic settings.[3, 4]

Functions of the Public Health Laboratory

Most testing for public health purposes is performed in private laboratories or depends on private laboratories for referral and reporting. Nevertheless, state public health laboratories play an important role in ensuring the availability, quality, and reporting of laboratory testing that takes place in the private sector.[5] In 2002, the Association of Public Health Laboratories developed a list of 11 core functions for state laboratories:

1. Disease prevention, control, and surveillance

2. Integrated data management

3. Reference and specialized testing

4. Environmental health and protection

5. Food safety

6. Laboratory improvement and regulation

7. Policy development

8. Emergency response

9. Public health–related research

10. Training and education

11. Partnerships and communication[5]

Not all state public health laboratories provide all of these functions. As the list of functions suggests, however, these laboratories often play a significant role in outbreak investigations. A public health laboratory may support an investigation through surveillance activities, by conducting initial or confirmatory testing of clinical samples, by analyzing and communicating data from test results, or by testing environmental or food samples. For example, in the case of the multistate outbreak of E. coli O157:H7 discussed in Chapter 4, the Michigan Department of Community Health laboratory confirmed that all of the isolates consisted of E. coli O157:H7, and conducted PFGE subtyping to demonstrate that a number of the isolates had patterns that were indistinguishable, allowing investigators to link cases from different locations.[6]

Traditional Roles of the Laboratory in Public Health Investigations

Determining or confirming that a given pathogen has infected patients is one of the laboratory's traditional roles in public health investigations. Isolating the causative agent from affected individuals is critical for making the best healthcare decisions for the individual patient, and it is as important for implementing appropriate public health control measures as well. For example, isolation of *Mycobacterium tuberculosis* from a patient with symptoms of a lower respiratory tract infection will trigger a chain of healthcare-related activities, including isolation of the patient, skin testing of close contacts, preventive therapy of skin-test-positive persons without clinical signs of disease, and treatment with a combination of antimicrobial agents for those individuals with clinical signs of disease. These activities address the medical treatment of the individual patient, allow for early diagnosis of other cases through contact tracing, and prevent further spread of disease in the community.

Isolating the causative agent from affected individuals can also help epidemiologic investigators identify possible sources of transmission—also known as vehicles—in the community. For example, if the laboratory isolates *Legionella pneumophila*, the bacterium that causes Legionnaires' disease and thrives at temperatures between 25°C and 45°C (77°F and 113°F),[7] from a patient with respiratory failure, epidemiologic investigators might suspect that the source of infection is a hot water system, such as an air-conditioner cooling tower, evaporative condenser, humidifier, or whirlpool spa. In contrast, isolating Sin Nombre virus, which causes hantavirus pulmonary syndrome, suggests that the patient came in contact with rodent feces. Knowing the causative agent may help investigators focus their search for a vehicle of transmission and use their investigation resources wisely.

Isolating causative agents from suspected vehicles is the second role that the laboratory traditionally plays in public health investigations. In this way, the laboratory can provide convincing evidence of the source of an outbreak or other public health problem. For example, laboratory workers provide investigators with good evidence about the source of the problem when they detect botulinum toxin in a can of mushrooms that were eaten by case patients before they became ill, or *E. coli* O157:H7 in a previously unopened package of hamburger meat with the same lot number as hamburger eaten by case patients. Finding the causative agent in a vehicle that is linked to cases of the disease is the *coup de grace* in an outbreak investigation.

The Role of the Laboratory in Public Health Surveillance

Laboratory personnel, along with other healthcare providers, play a critical role in the surveillance of many infectious diseases. In every state, clinical laboratories are required to report the detection of selected infectious agents—*Salmonella*, *Legionella*, measles, human immunodeficiency virus, and others. They are also required to report a few noninfectious agents, such as lead poisoning. These surveillance reports are critical in following disease trends over time and allowing authorities to take appropriate public health actions.

Because they receive specimens from the patients of multiple healthcare providers and usually employ automated data systems, laboratories may be the first to note increases in cases of a disease signaling an outbreak. Furthermore, as discussed later in this chapter, subtyping (tests such as serotyping, antimicrobial susceptibility testing, and PFGE that characterize a microorganism below the species level) allows the laboratory to link seemingly unrelated cases of a disease. If a laboratory identifies the same subtype in a cluster of isolates, the isolates may be related; further investigation can then be undertaken to determine whether the cases have a common source of exposure.

Other Roles of the Laboratory in Public Health Investigations

Another of the laboratory's roles is to help public health practitioners refine definitions of the outcome and exposure of interest in an investigation. A more specific case definition, with laboratory confirmation or special testing, will be more likely to exclude people who do not have the disease associated with an outbreak or who have not been exposed to the pathogen under investigation. Its development will decrease misclassification and increase the study's chances of detecting a difference between the group of interest and the comparison group, if there is a difference.

The laboratory can also conduct studies to confirm or refute the proposed role played by a suspected vehicle, such as a food item, in the disease outbreak and develop methods to detect, control, or eliminate the problem. Identification of the subtype or the causative agent found among cases linked to a suspected vehicle is good evidence that the vehicle is related to the outbreak. To develop effective control measures, laboratory investigators can inoculate the suspected vehicle with the causative agent to determine whether and under which conditions the agent could survive or grow on the vehicle. Through applied research, the laboratory can help to recreate the cause-and-effect pathway, thereby identifying the chain of events that led to the problem in the first place and suggesting ways to control the problem and prevent it from happening again.

The laboratory is a powerful ally for public health personnel. Outbreak investigators may have access to a variety of laboratory investigators whose expertise and guidance can be invaluable. Epidemiologic investigators do not need to become experts on laboratory investigations, but they do need to help laboratory workers by properly collecting specimens and samples.

Collection of Clinical Specimens

The proper collection of clinical specimens is critical to the success of many outbreak investigations. Clinical specimens are samples of bodily fluids or tissues collected from persons who may have been exposed to a causative agent and who may or may not show signs of illness. Samples of blood, sputum, urine, vomit, feces, and occasionally other tissues are all examples of clinical specimens. As discussed in Chapter 4, the outbreak investigation team should include a clinician from the health department or a local medical facility who is trained in the proper collection of these materials from human subjects.

The preferred specimen for testing in an outbreak investigation depends on the causative agent and the test(s) to be performed. For example, measles can be diagnosed by collecting a blood sample and detecting certain antibodies in the serum. (Serum is the clear, yellowish liquid part of the blood that remains after blood cells and clotting proteins have been removed.) Salmonellosis is usually diagnosed by collecting feces and isolating the organism from the stool specimen. Tuberculosis is typically diagnosed by collecting a sputum sample and demonstrating the presence of acid-fast bacilli in stained smears or isolating *Mycobacterium tuberculosis* from a culture.

Because of the necessary level of detail and frequent modifications in recommended procedures, we will not describe the collection of clinical specimens for individual causative agents. We will, however, examine some general considerations on specimen collection (summarized in Table 11-1) that will be valuable to investigators no matter which specimen they are collecting.

First, and foremost, investigators need to determine which specimen needs to be collected and who will do the testing. Before beginning, investigators should be able to answer the following questions:

- Which body fluid or tissue should be collected?
- How much is needed?
- Which kind of container should be used to hold the specimen?
- Is a preservative needed?

TABLE 11-1 Considerations for Collection of Clinical Specimens

- Determine which specimen is needed and who will do the testing.
- Assemble the necessary equipment. Use leakproof containers!
- Collect the specimen during acute illness, unless otherwise specified.
- Follow universal precautions.
- Minimize contamination from external sources.
- Provide the patient with explicit instructions on specimen collection, if appropriate.
- Label the container with identifying information.
- Provide the laboratory with the appropriate information.
- Contact the laboratory to arrange for receipt and testing of the sample.
- Consult with others about the details.

- Should the specimen be refrigerated, frozen, or held at room temperature?
- Who will do the testing? (Not all laboratories can perform all tests.)
- Where will the specimen be sent?
- Are there certain conditions to which the specimen should not be exposed, such as freezing or heat?

The next step is to assemble the equipment needed to obtain the specimen, which can include specimen containers, needles, syringes, sterile scoops, antiseptic, sterile swabs, labeling tape, markers, coolers/refrigerators, and ice packs. The optimal container will vary depending on the agent being tested and the distance, time, and mode of transporting the specimen. In all instances, the container should be of a durable material that, when properly packaged, is leakproof and can withstand the temperature and pressure variations likely to occur during transport. Investigators should also make sure that shipping regulations permit the transport of this type of specimen and that prospective shippers can properly handle the transport.

Unless otherwise instructed, investigators should collect specimens from patients during the acute phase of their illness and as soon as possible after they develop symptoms. There are two good reasons to seek samples promptly. First, patients are more likely to agree to be tested for pathogens while they are ill. Second, some pathogens and toxins remain in the body for only a limited time after onset of illness. (In some cases, however, such as when testing to learn whether a patient has developed antibodies to a pathogen, it may be important to wait before collecting specimens, or to collect specimens at another time.) Equally important, if investigators know or suspect the microbiologic agent that is at fault, they should try to collect specimens before the patient begins medications to treat the infection.

Investigators should always follow universal precautions when collecting specimens:

- Use personal protective equipment as is appropriate to the specimen and the suspected/known disease agent.
- Wear gloves, glasses, and a mask whenever blood or body fluids containing blood are handled and when phlebotomy is being performed.
- Take care to prevent injuries when using and disposing of needles, scalpels, and other sharp instruments.
- Do not recap or remove needles from disposable syringes by hand.
- Do not bend, break, or otherwise manipulate used needles by hand.
- Dispose of needles and sharp equipment in puncture-resistant containers.
- Wash hands carefully after collecting the specimen, even if gloves were worn.[8]

Investigators should take steps to minimize contamination of the specimen from extraneous sources such as hands, body parts, and clothes. This may necessitate swabbing the patient's skin with an antiseptic, draping the area, washing hands, wearing sterile gloves, wearing a sterile gown, or using sterile specimen containers or scoops. If the patient is collecting his or her own urine or stool specimens, investigators should provide the patient with explicit instructions on the collection method.

Before or immediately after collecting a clinical specimen, investigators should label the container with the patient's name or other identifier, the specimen number, and the date of collection. They should provide this information to the laboratory along with the date of onset of symptoms, the requested test(s), and the patient's signs and symptoms. The date of specimen collection allows laboratory investigators to determine the age of the specimen when they receive and process it. Including the date of onset of symptoms along with the date of collection helps laboratory investigators calculate when in the course of the patient's illness the specimen was collected—information they can use to determine the likelihood of isolating the pathogen that caused the illness. Patient signs and symptoms may give the laboratory ideas about the causative agent and indicate tests that should be performed in addition to those requested by the investigators. For example, if the patient has bloody diarrhea, the laboratory may suggest the need to culture specifically for *E. coli* O157:H7 or other Shiga-like, toxin-producing *E. coli*.

If investigators are submitting a number of specimens (or if the specimens will arrive at the laboratory shortly before the weekend or a holiday), they should contact the laboratory to arrange for receipt and testing of the samples. Testing specimens held too long or under improper conditions may jeopardize sample integrity, leading to results that are difficult to interpret or unusable.

The laboratory can provide detailed information about the necessary steps for the proper collection of clinical specimens. Investigators should not expect to remember all of the details, but they should always consult with the laboratory. Investigators might also want to keep on hand a good microbiology text or one of the references cited in the list of additional resources at the end of this chapter. Although some of these references are updated regularly, investigators should remember that rapidly advancing technologies may quickly render any guidelines obsolete. Talking directly with laboratory personnel is always the best course of action.

Collection of Food and Water Samples

Investigators may identify any number of vehicles as the source of outbreaks and other public health problems. This section briefly discusses the necessary equipment and methods typically used to collect samples of two of the most commonly implicated vehicles: food and water. Note that these guidelines are very general, and that specific contaminants (such as organophosphates) or samples (such as chlorinated water) may require special collection techniques.

As with clinical specimens, the outbreak investigation team may include a specialist—either a sanitarian or an environmental health specialist—to collect food and water samples. Whoever does the collection should consult with the testing laboratory before collecting any samples.

The following equipment is often useful in the collection of food and water samples:

- Sterile sample containers—plastic bags, wide-mouth plastic and glass jars with screw caps, bottles
- Sterile and wrapped sample collection implements—spoons, scoops, tongue-depressor blades, spatulas, swabs, knives
- Sterilizing and sanitizing agents—95% ethyl alcohol, sodium or calcium hypochlorite, alcohol swabs
- Refrigerants such as ice packs, insulated containers
- Supporting equipment—fine-point felt-tip marking pen, roll of adhesive or masking tape, waterproof labels/tags, sample forms
- Clothing—disposable plastic gloves, hair restraint, laboratory coat[9]

Before leaving to collect food and water samples, investigators should assemble the necessary equipment so it will be readily available. Putting the items into one carrying bag or box can prevent them from being misplaced or damaged.

Food samples should be collected aseptically with sterile implements such as knives, spoons, or tongs, and placed into sterile jars or sterile plastic bags. A sample weighing 200 to 450 grams (approximately 0.5 to 1 pound) or measuring 200 to 500 mL (approximately 0.5 to 1 pint) in volume should be adequate for most tests. If possible, investigators should submit packaged foods to the laboratory in their original containers or submit the container with the sample. An empty container can be used to detect microleaks, rinsings from these containers can be used to detect microorganisms and toxins, and information on the container can help identify the producer, place, and time of its processing.

Water samples should be collected in sterile bottles. If concentration techniques, such as filtration, are not available, investigators should collect at least 1 liter (approximately 1 quart) for bacteriologic analyses, 5 liters (approximately 1.25 gallons) for viral analyses, and 2 liters (approximately 0.5 gallon) for chemical or physical analysis. When they are able, investigators should obtain "historical" samples that might give an indication of the condition of the water when it was ingested by those who became ill. (Historical samples may be available from bottles in refrigerators, storage tanks, seldom-used taps, and ice in refrigerators.)

Here are some of the guidelines investigators should follow when collecting water samples:

- When collecting a sample from a tap, do not collect samples from hose connections, sprays, or swivel faucets. Uncouple these connections or choose different outlets.
- When taking a sample from a service line, such as the line providing water to the facility or home, allow the water to run to waste for 5 to 10 seconds.
- When taking a sample from a distribution line, such as the water main, open the tap fully and let the water run to waste for sufficient time to empty the service line before filling the sample bottle.

- When collecting samples from water receptacles (storage tanks or wells, for example) and natural bodies of water (rivers, streams, and lakes), hold a 200-mL (0.75-cup) bottle near the bottom and plunge it neck down into the water to a depth of approximately 15 cm (6 in.), turn it right side up, and allow it to fill.

- If collecting water from a large body of water or water course, collect multiple samples from different locations.

Investigators should label both food and water samples with identifying information or a code, and keep a log of the code numbers, date, time of collection, type of sample, and laboratory test to be run. If the food or water samples are not frozen at the time of collection, they should be rapidly chilled to a temperature less than 40°F and kept below this temperature until they can be examined. Samples should not be frozen because certain bacteria die off rapidly during frozen storage. Samples that are frozen when collected, however, should remain so until examined; thawing may cause any bacteria that are present to multiply rapidly. Refrigerated and frozen samples should be transported to the laboratory in insulated containers.

It is helpful to remember that the contaminants in food and water are in a dynamic state. Because their presence and quantity will change with time, samples collected during an investigation may not be representative of those ingested when the problem occurred. In addition to collecting samples for testing, investigators should learn as much as they can about the food or water at the time the problem occurred, handling or treatment of the food or water since that time, and other pertinent information. For example, when they collect food samples, investigators should try to determine how the leftovers were handled after the food was ingested by ill people, including temperatures at which the food was held, how long it stayed at each temperature, and whether and when it came into contact with human hands or environmental surfaces. When collecting samples of drinking water, investigators should look for evidence of water line disruptions, repairs, low pressure that may have allowed backflow, and inadequate chlorination. To help facilitate the interpretation of laboratory results, investigators should also collect information on water temperature, estimated chlorine levels, and estimated chlorine contact time before sampling.

Interpreting Laboratory Results

Epidemiologic investigators should always consult with the laboratory that has tested the specimen for an interpretation of the results and recommendations for follow-up testing. Accurately interpreting laboratory test results involves taking a number of issues into consideration: the characteristics of the test itself—detection thresholds, sensitivity and specificity—and the experience of the testing laboratory; the conditions under which the specimen was collected; the time when the patient's symptoms appeared; and the clinical presentation of the patient. Skilled laboratory investigators can help the investigation team understand and use the test results most effectively.

When reviewing laboratory tests, investigators need to keep in mind the potential errors that can occur during specimen collection and testing, and the limits of what they can learn from test results. Obtaining a positive test result is not the same as confirming the cause of an outbreak or other public health problem. While a positive clinical specimen may help identify the agent of interest, a number of events can affect the interpretation of a positive result:

- The sample might have become contaminated during collection or processing.
- The pathogen might be present on a body surface, but it might not be causing illness.
- The test could have heightened sensitivity or a lack of specificity—for example, cross-reactivity with another related antigen in the sample might cause a positive result.

Similarly, a negative test of a clinical specimen may have alternative explanations beyond the obvious conclusion that the patient does not have the outcome of interest. The specimen may have been improperly collected or mishandled during storage, transport, or processing, leading to the death of any microorganisms present. It may have been collected too late in the course of the illness, when the patient was no longer excreting the pathogen in adequate numbers for detection. Alternatively, it may have been collected too early in the disease course, before the patient's body began producing antibodies in response to the pathogen.

Interpreting Tests of Food and Water Samples

Interpreting tests of food and water samples can be particularly challenging for the laboratory. As noted earlier, the samples collected during an investigation may not be representative of the food or water ingested when the problem occurred. Subsequent handling or processing may have resulted in the death of microorganisms present, multiplication of microorganisms originally present in low levels, or the introduction of new contaminants. If contamination of the food or water was not uniform, the sample collected may have missed the contaminated portion. Finally, because food and water are usually not sterile, the microorganisms isolated from samples may not be the same ones that were responsible for the illness under investigation.

These observations underscore the need to work closely with the laboratory to ensure that the following conditions are met:

- The correct procedures are followed in collecting the specimen.
- The most appropriate test(s) are requested—that is, those designed to detect agents consistent with the patient's symptoms or to be most suitable for the patient's stage of illness.
- The results are considered in the appropriate context, including in relation to the limitations of the test, the quality of the sample, and the capacity of the testing laboratory.
- Further testing, such as confirmatory testing or testing for a different agent, can be considered as necessary.

Subtyping for Epidemiologic Purposes

Subtyping—the identification of strains or groupings of organisms below the species level—takes on a special significance in public health. Laboratories may subtype a variety of organisms for a variety of reasons. For example, subtyping procedures can be used on humans to determine blood type, paternity, and susceptibility to certain diseases, such as the *BRCA1* gene mutation that is associated with an increased risk of breast cancer. In outbreak investigations, the ability of subtyping to trace the lineage of a particular strain of a bacterium or virus and identify isolates with a similar ancestry is especially important. It gives epidemiologic investigators the power to link potentially related cases and to match case patients with the vehicles that infected them.

Laboratories use a number of subtyping methodologies to examine bacteria and viruses, with new techniques being introduced quite frequently. These methodologies are usually classified as "phenotypic" or "genetic." Phenotypic subtyping methods are based on observable attributes of an organism, such as its structure, function, or behavior. Examples of phenotype-based subtyping methods include the following techniques:

- Serotyping—identifying subtypes based on the antibodies that react to them
- Phage typing—identifying subtypes based on the pattern of bacteriophages (viruses that attack bacteria) to which a bacterium is susceptible
- Antimicrobial susceptibility—identifying antibiotics that affect the pathogen

Genetic subtyping methods are based on the composition of the organism's deoxyribonucleic acid (DNA). Genetic-based subtyping methods include these techniques:

- Polymerase chain reaction (PCR)
- PFGE
- Restriction-fragment length polymorphism analysis
- Ribotyping

Figure 11-1 shows how subtyping works. The diagram represents two different strains of bacteria, A and B, each of which has one circular chromosome. The chromosome of strain A is represented as a solid circle and that of strain B as a dotted circle. The circles are different because the two strains have a different DNA composition. The bar code-like images to the side of each strain show the PFGE patterns for that strain; they are based on the DNA composition of the bacteria. Because the DNA compositions of strain A and strain B are different, the PFGE results for the two strains are also different. When the bacteria replicate, the offspring of both strains will resemble the parent and will have the same DNA composition as the parent; their PFGE results will also be the same as their parent. In an outbreak, the bacteria contaminating the vehicle and infecting the cases typically descend from the same parent. Therefore, isolates from all the cases and the vehicle should have the same (or very similar) PFGE patterns.

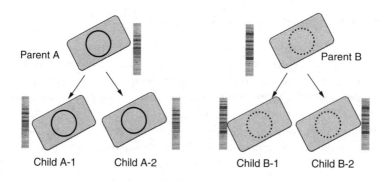

Figure 11-1   Subtyping among related and unrelated strains

Source: Computer-based overview: *E. coli* O157:H7 in Michigan. Modified November 4, 2009. Centers for Disease Control website: http://www.cdc.gov/epicasestudies/computer_ecoli .html. Accessed May 18, 2011.

Subtyping of bacteria and viruses can provide information that can help investigators explore potential outbreaks, provide insight into the source of a problem, integrate surveillance information from different sources, and evaluate interventions. The following sections discuss each of these possibilities.

Explaining Potential Outbreaks by Subtyping

Because outbreaks are typically caused by exposure to a single subtype of a virus or bacterium, routine subtyping of isolates can help detect outbreaks, determine whether cases of the same disease are related, and determine whether a vehicle that is contaminated with a particular agent is related to a particular outbreak caused by the same agent. To highlight the importance of subtyping in outbreak investigations, we will look at three examples, beginning with the outbreak of *E. coli* O157:H7 infection in Michigan discussed in this and earlier chapters:

- More than 60 *E. coli* O157:H7 infections were reported during the month of June 1997 compared to 31 cases in the same period in 1996. None of the cases had obvious epidemiologic linkages to one another, but PFGE results showed that 38 of these initial cases had one indistinguishable pattern. Because similar PFGE patterns would be highly unusual if the cases were random, investigators hypothesized that the cases with the similar pattern were linked but the rest were not. Epidemiologists focused on the cases with the outbreak strain of *E. coli* and identified alfalfa sprouts as the source of the outbreak.[6]

- In 1997, a medical waste treatment worker in Washington state developed tuberculosis. The worker had no known exposures to or risk factors for tuberculosis, which puzzled investigators. Using PCR methods and automated DNA sequencing to identify genetic mutations associated with drug resistance, the laboratory matched the *Mycobacterium tuberculosis* isolate from the worker with an isolate from a tuberculosis case in the community. The worker and the community case had not come in contact with each other, however. When investigators explored further, they found that a tuberculosis culture from the community case was processed by a clinical laboratory that sent contaminated medical wastes to the treatment facility where the infected worker was employed. After examining equipment and the treatment process, investigators concluded that the worker became infected from medical wastes due to equipment failures, insufficient employee training, and inadequacies in respiratory protective equipment at the treatment facility.[10]

- In April and May 1998, 49 cases of infection involving a particular subtype of *Salmonella*, *Salmonella agona,* were reported to the Illinois Department of Public Health. Approximately 1,500 cases of salmonellosis are reported in Illinois each year, so 49 cases over a 2-month period may not have been notable—except that *S. agona* is an uncommon serotype of *Salmonella*. Because only around 20 cases of this serotype might be reported in Illinois in a single year, the detection of 49 cases in 2 months prompted further investigation. Laboratory-based surveillance quickly confirmed that 10 states had experienced increases in the number of their residents with *S. agona* infections. Furthermore, PFGE indicated that many of the *S. agona* isolates tested in those states had the same genetic pattern, suggesting the cases could have a common origin. Investigators traced the outbreak to a contaminated ready-to-eat toasted oats cereal product from a food-processing facility in Minnesota. Without laboratory subtyping, this outbreak might never have been recognized.[11]

Gaining Insight into the Source of a Problem Through Subtyping

Because subtypes of particular bacteria and viruses may be associated with particular vehicles, subtyping can provide insight into the source of an outbreak or other public health problem. For example, *Salmonella* serotype *enteritidis* is commonly associated with unpasteurized eggs and *E. coli* O157:H7 is often associated with foods produced from cattle. Similarly, subtyping may be able to provide useful information about the geographic origin of a disease. For example, sequencing selected genes of the measles virus has allowed investigators to characterize eight distinct genotypes with different geographic distributions. The genotypes labeled "groups 4 and 5" appear to circulate widely in Western Europe, particularly in Germany, Spain, and the United Kingdom, whereas "group 6" viruses have been isolated in the African countries of The Gambia, Cameroon, Gabon, and Zambia. Identifying these genotypes has helped investigators pinpoint the source of sporadic cases of measles, leading to improved measles control measures.[12]

Using Subtyping to Integrate Surveillance Information

Subtyping allows investigators to integrate information from different surveillance sources to obtain a more complex understanding of the reservoirs, modes of transmission, and human illness. For example, by examining *Salmonella* serotypes from surveillance data on poultry, environmental samples, and humans, public health officials in Denmark were able to draw connections between human cases of disease and transovarian transmission of infection among egg-laying chickens. This knowledge, in turn, allowed public health officials to enact new regulations for disinfecting chicken houses and testing eggs and chickens on commercial egg-producing farms that led to a decrease in infections among humans.[13]

Epidemiologic investigators can also use subtyping information to evaluate the effectiveness of interventions and control measures. For example, as early as the 1950s, pet turtles were recognized as a common source of *Salmonella* infection in children. Cases of *Salmonella* serotype *urbana*, *Salmonella* serotype *litchfield*, and *Salmonella* serotype *java* were typically associated with these infections. In the early 1970s, laws were passed that required all turtles sold as pets to be *Salmonella*-free. In 1975, the interstate sale of pet turtles was banned—a move that was effective in decreasing the problem.[14]

As these examples demonstrate, subtyping of bacteria and viruses is a powerful public health tool. It can provide information that is useful in assessing the scope of a public health problem, investigating its source, planning and evaluating interventions, and informing and implementing public health policy. When used wisely, subtyping can help public health practitioners detect outbreaks and direct actions such as the investigation and removal of contaminated foods from the marketplace. Whenever investigators consider subtyping for public health purposes, however, they should keep a number of caveats in mind.

First, a variety of subtyping methods are available, and the usefulness of these methods varies with the microorganism. Because not all laboratories perform subtyping—and those that do might perform only specific subtyping tests—investigators should work closely with the laboratory and other experts to determine the best test to perform and to interpret and use the results properly.

Second, subtyping is an adjunct to epidemiologic investigation and not a replacement for it. Investigators should not consider matching subtypes to be proof of a common exposure, but rather merely confirmation that the isolates share a common ancestry. An epidemiologic investigation is necessary to demonstrate that there is a common source of exposure.

Conversely, identifying nonmatching subtypes of an organism does not mean that cases of a particular disease are not related. Outbreaks can be caused by more than one organism and more than one subtype. When subtypes of isolates do not match, they may still have a common source if food or some other vehicle was contaminated with multiple subtypes of an organism.

Finally, to be most useful, subtyping needs to be performed and interpreted on a routine basis, in real time, so that results are available soon after a case is first detected. Identifying subtypes long after occurrence of a problem does little to aid in the investigation and control of the problem. Investigators need to explore subtyping results while patients can still recall exposures and vehicles of transmission are still available for testing.

Summary

Laboratories and laboratory investigators play a critical role in public health. Epidemiologists rely on laboratories for the isolation of disease-causing agents from patients and suspected vehicles, surveillance of diseases, detection and investigation of outbreaks, and applied research. Likewise, the laboratory relies on public health investigators to collect adequate and appropriate clinical and environmental specimens and provide information that helps in the testing and interpretation of these specimens. Consultation between laboratory workers and investigators during an outbreak investigation is critical to ensure that the proper tests are performed; specimens are properly collected, stored, and transported; and the results are received and correctly interpreted.

The ability to link cases or to match a suspect vehicle with cases through subtyping of bacteria and viruses has added a new dimension to the investigation of outbreaks and other public health problems. However, even with advanced testing, laboratory results alone cannot prove a hypothesis. To reach a well-thought-out conclusion, investigators must compile and interpret epidemiologic information on person, place, and time; complete analytic studies; seek laboratory confirmation of the specific organism or subtype in the suspected vehicle and in case patients; and investigate the place where the suspected vehicle was produced.

Additional Resources

Centers for Disease Control and Prevention. Diagnosis and management of foodborne illnesses: A primer for physicians and other health care professionals. *Morb Mortal Weekly Rep.* 2004;53(RR-04):1–33.

Committee on Communicable Diseases Affecting Man. *Procedures to Investigate Foodborne Illness.* 5th ed. Des Moines, IA: International Association of Milk, Food and Environmental Sanitarians; 1999.

Gregg M. *Field Epidemiology.* 3rd ed. New York: Oxford University Press; 2008.

Heymann DL, ed. *Control of Communicable Diseases Manual.* 19th ed. Washington, DC: American Public Health Association; 2008.

Jenkins WD. *Public Health Laboratories: Analysis, Operations, and Management.* Sudbury, MA: Jones & Bartlett Learning; 2011.

Pickering LK, ed. *Red Book: 2009 Report of the Committee on Infectious Diseases.* 28th ed. Elk Grove Village, IL: American Academy of Pediatrics; 2009.

References

1. Becker S, Perlman EJ. An introduction to public health laboratories. In: Jenkins WD, ed. *Public Health Laboratories: Analysis, Operations, and Management.* Sudbury, MA: Jones & Bartlett Learning; 2011.

2. Centers for Disease Control and Prevention. *Biosafety in Microbiological and Biomedical Laboratories.* 5th ed. HHS Publication No. (CDC) 21-1112. Washington, DC: U.S. Department of Health and Human Services, Public Health Service, National Institutes Health, Centers for Disease Control and Prevention; December 2009. http://www.cdc.gov/biosafety/publications/bmbl5/index.htm. Accessed September 8, 2010.

3. Government Accountability Office. High-containment biosafety laboratories: Preliminary observations on the oversight of the proliferation of BSL-3 and BSL-4 laboratories in the United States. Publication GAO-08-108T. October 4, 2007. http://www.gao.gov/docsearch/abstract.php?rptno=GAO-08-108T. Accessed September 8, 2010.

4. BioDefense: An integrated research facility. Updated 2009. National Institute of Allergy and Infectious Disease website: http://www.niaid.nih.gov/topics/BiodefenseRelated/Biodefense/PublicMedia/pages/faqs.aspx#3. Accessed September 24, 2010.

5. Centers for Disease Control and Prevention. Core functions and capabilities of state public health laboratories. *Morb Mortal Weekly Rep.* 2002;51(RR14):1–8.

6. Centers for Disease Control and Prevention. Outbreaks of *Escherichia coli* 0157:H7 infection associated with eating alfalfa sprouts—Michigan and Virginia, June–July 1997. *Morb Mortal Weekly Rep.* 1997;46(32):741–744.

7. Heymann DL, ed. *Control of Communicable Diseases Manual.* 19th ed. Washington, DC: American Public Health Association; 2008.

8. Centers for Disease Control and Prevention. Perspectives in disease prevention and health promotion update: Universal precautions for prevention of transmission of human immunodeficiency virus, hepatitis B virus, and other bloodborne pathogens in health-care settings. *Morb Mortal Weekly Rep.* 1988;37(24):377–88.

9. Committee on Communicable Diseases Affecting Man, Food Subcommittee. *Procedures to Investigate Waterborne Illness.* 2nd ed. Ames, IA: International Association of Milk, Food, and Environmental Sanitarians; 1996.

10. Johnson, KR, Braden CR, Cairns KL, et al. Transmission of Mycobacterium tuberculosis from medical waste. *JAMA.* 2000;284:1683–8.

11. Centers for Disease Control and Prevention. Multistate outbreak of *Salmonella* serotype *agona* infections linked to toasted oats cereal—United States, April–May 1998. *Morb Mortal Weekly Rep.* 1998;47(22):462–4.

12. Bellini WJ, Rota PA. Genetic diversity of wild-type measles viruses: Implications for global measles elimination programs. *Emerg Infect Dis.* 1998;4(1):29–35.

13. Wegener HC, Hald T, Wong DLF, et al. *Salmonella* control programs in Denmark. *Emerg Infect Dis.* 2003;9(7). http://www.cdc.gov/ncidod/EID/vol9no7/03-0024.htm. Accessed July 1, 2010.

14. Cohen ML, Potter M, Pollard R, et al. Turtle-associated salmonellosis in the United States. *JAMA.* 1998;243(12):1247–9.

Chapter 12

Environmental Health Components of an Outbreak Investigation

Jeanette K. Stehr-Green
Paul A. Stehr-Green
Pia D. M. MacDonald

Learning Objectives
By the end of this chapter, the reader will be able to:

- Define and describe a traceback investigation.
- List the objectives of a traceback investigation.
- Identify the primary sources of information in a traceback investigation.
- Describe the circumstances in which a traceback investigation is most likely to be successful.
- Define and describe an environmental health assessment.
- List sources of information in an environmental health assessment.
- Given a particular outbreak, discuss areas of focus for an environmental health assessment.
- Draw a flow diagram for the production of an item implicated as the source of an outbreak.

Introduction

Chapter 11 explored the role of the laboratory in the investigation of outbreaks and other public health events. In this chapter, we touch on another critical piece of the investigation puzzle: environmental health investigations. Although epidemiologic or microbiologic investigations may implicate a vehicle in an outbreak or other public health problem, environmental health investigations can help investigators determine how and why the implicated vehicle caused the outbreak or health event. This information can be critical to efforts to control the problem and prevent it from happening again.

"Environmental health" is an extensive area of study that includes such topics as air and water pollution, food and waterborne diseases, radiation, toxic substances, and natural disasters. "Environmental health investigation" covers an equally wide territory. This chapter focuses on two specific types of environmental health investigation—the traceback investigation of a vehicle implicated as the source of an outbreak and the environmental health assessment. These types of investigations are common in the practice of public health, and anyone who participates in an outbreak investigation could be called upon to assist in an environmental health investigation. Outbreak investigators should understand the goals, approach, and typical activities involved in each type of investigation and know how to interpret their results. The discussion here begins with traceback investigations because tracebacks may help determine whether—and where—investigators conduct an environmental health assessment.

Traceback Investigations

A traceback investigation is the process used to determine the production and distribution chain of a vehicle implicated during the investigation of an outbreak or other public health problem. Tracebacks can clarify the point at which the implicated item—for example, the food, cosmetic, or medicine that has been identified as the vehicle in an outbreak—may have become contaminated. A traceback investigation identifies the following information:

- Places where the implicated vehicle has been, such as farms, factories, warehouses, stores, and restaurants
- Commonalities among implicated vehicles from different cases in an outbreak, such as being produced at the same plant or transported in the same vehicle

Tracing vehicles to a common location or locations in an outbreak provides investigators with a strong indicator that contamination occurred at or before that point in the production and distribution of the vehicle. The traceback cannot identify the source of the contamination or why it occurred, but it can tell investigators where to look. Further investigation—including inspections of the farms, factories, warehouses, stores, restaurants, or tractor trailers implicated in the traceback investigation—is necessary to identify practices or conditions that may have resulted in the problem and to implement control measures to prevent it from happening again.

A traceback investigation extends backward in time. Investigators begin with information gathered from case patients about the implicated vehicle and work their way back through the people and places involved at all points in the production and use of the vehicle. They speak to employees and gather data from retailers, point-of-service establishments (restaurants, for example), distributors, importers, and producers. Each vehicle implicated in an outbreak has its own unique—and potentially very complex—pattern of distribution. For example, retailers may obtain the product from more than one distributor and may change distributors over time. Distributors may have multiple sources and may supply to other distributors. Producers may be domestic or foreign, and they may sell the same product under different brand names. Figure 12-1 depicts a typical traceback investigation process.

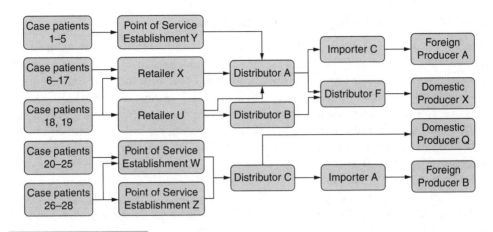

Figure 12-1   Traceback investigation process

The Steps of a Traceback Investigation

Traceback investigations involve extensive detective work resulting in many dead ends and wrong turns, but they typically unfold in three steps:

1. The investigation begins with information gathered from case patients about where and when they purchased the implicated item. If patients still have the original packaging and labels with identifying features, such as lot numbers or the name of the manufacturer, the traceback investigation will go more smoothly. Even so, it is likely to be challenging.

2. The investigation continues at the place where the case patient obtained the item, such as a retail store or restaurant, and expands to encompass distributors. Distributors include the brokers, importers, and other businesses that usually store and/or transport the product or work with other entities to accomplish these activities. Multiple levels of distributors may be involved in the history of a single product.

3. A traceback is complete when investigators identify the producer—the company that supplied, processed, and produced the implicated product—and are able to say with some certainty which batches of the implicated product (e.g., based on the place of production, dates of production, or lot numbers) are affected. As examples given later in this chapter demonstrate, a successful investigation might track an implicated vehicle to an improperly cleaned tanker truck or a contaminated batch of seeds, laying the groundwork for additional investigation and actions to correct the problem.

Conducting a Successful Traceback Investigation

One key to a successful traceback investigation is clearly identifying the implicated product. For commercially packaged commodities—as opposed to such items as fresh fruits and vegetables—the brand name might seem to be an ideal means of identification. In reality, collecting this information is not as easy as it sounds. If the packaging is not available, consumers often do not remember the exact name of the product. This is particularly true if the brand is not well known or the consumer commonly switches sources or brands. Furthermore, one product may be repackaged and distributed under several different or slightly different names.

For example, in April and May 1998, 49 cases of *Salmonella agona* (an uncommon sero-type of *Salmonella*) were reported to the Illinois Department of Public Health. Serotype-specific surveillance confirmed that nine other states had also experienced increases in *S. agona* infection reports. PFGE subtyping indicated that many of the *S. agona* specimens isolated from patients in those states had the same pattern, suggesting that the cases might have a common origin. Although a matched case-control study linked the *S. agona* infections with eating cereal, the case patients all seemed to have eaten different brands of cereal. A traceback investigation revealed that the implicated cereal was produced by a Minnesota company, Malt-O-Meal, under the brand names "Toasted Oats" and "Toasty O's." The cereal was sold in 39 grocery store chains under the individual grocery store's in-house label and packaging, accounting for the different brands of cereal eaten by case patients. At first, it did not appear that the case patients consumed the same cereal—but they actually had.[1]

Even when investigators know the brand name (and read the fine print to determine which brand names are related), they may not have enough information to determine the source of a problem. Most outbreaks result from a temporary problem in the production of the vehicle—a particular batch or lot prepared at a specific time on a specific day. To identify the exact vehicle, investigators need much more detail. In addition to the brand name, gathering the following information is critical:

- Item description
- Where purchased
- When purchased
- Grade
- Color
- Quantity, size, or weight
- Manufacturer
- Supplier
- Lot or batch number
- Date produced

- Date shipped
- Date received
- Sell-by date or code
- Use-by date or code

Furthermore, to determine where the vehicle has been, investigators also may need to know the locations of farms and production facilities, as well as names, dates, times, and quantities of deliveries for suppliers and wholesale customers.

As the Toasted Oats/Toasty O's example suggests, carefully gathering data is critical to the success of a traceback investigation. As they work backward from the restaurant or store where the patient ate or purchased the implicated vehicle, investigators may find it useful to obtain copies of invoices, inventory records, air bills (for air transport) and bills of lading (for trucking), importation documents (such as Customs Form 3461), and other business documentation. Once they have determined where the implicated vehicle most likely became contaminated, they may visit the source of the problem to verify the information already collected, production dates, and the location of the farms or production facilities. The validity of a traceback is highly dependent on proper documentation—receipts and labels are essential. When documentation is incomplete or difficult to interpret, the investigator's job can be very challenging.

To Trace or Not to Trace?

Traceback investigations can be valuable when public health officials seek to control an outbreak and prevent it from happening again. Because they can also be time-consuming and inconclusive, however, such investigations should be undertaken selectively. Investigators should not begin a traceback investigation until they are sure that the vehicle in question is truly implicated in the outbreak and that the source of the contamination resides within the production chain, rather than being due to contamination by the consumer, retailer, or point-of-service establishment.

Before undertaking a traceback investigation, investigators should be able to answer the following questions affirmatively:

- Is there solid epidemiologic evidence linking the outbreak and the implicated product? (Was a controlled study undertaken? Was the selection of subjects and collection of information unbiased? Could confounding account for the association? How likely is it that chance could account for the observed statistical association between a product and an outbreak?)
- Is there historical precedent for the product being contaminated with this organism or a similar organism?
- Is there microbiologic evidence linking the outbreak and the implicated products?

- Does the vehicle have chemical and physical characteristics conducive to the survival and growth of the causative agent?

- Has the investigation ruled out mishandling or environmental contamination of the product by the consumer, retailer, or point-of-service establishment?

- Has the product been commercially distributed in a way that is consistent with the outbreak?

Investigators may also want to consider their likelihood of success before deciding to undertake a traceback investigation. Tracebacks are most likely to be successful when the implicated vehicle is commercially packaged (and has an identifying label), is unusual (such as a dietary supplement), or has a long shelf life (such as frozen hamburger patties). By comparison, traceback investigations of products with a short shelf life, such as fresh fruits and vegetables, and those derived from many sources, such as a blood-clotting factor that is derived from thousands of donors, are often unproductive.

Finally, investigators must weigh the benefits of the investigation. To determine whether the traceback is warranted, they might ask themselves whether the disease is serious, whether exposure is likely to be ongoing, and whether vulnerable populations are at risk. If the disease is likely to lead to death, hospitalization, or permanent disability or if infants, the elderly, or immunocompromised individuals are becoming ill, the traceback investigation might be justified.

Successful tracebacks require coordination among many experts and entities. Most cases will involve local, state, or federal regulatory agencies, including the U.S. Department of Agriculture and the U.S. Food and Drug Administration. Although an epidemiologist may never participate in a traceback investigation, he or she can play a critical role in the success of such an investigation. Traceback investigations require good, solid epidemiological data: A poorly executed epidemiologic study might implicate the wrong vehicle and misdirect subsequent investigations. Good epidemiological work—often beginning with detailed information obtained from case patients about the vehicle during the initial interview—is critical for a successful traceback investigation.

Traceback Investigations: Tanker Trucks and Sprouting Facilities

We conclude this section with two examples of successful traceback investigations.

In 1994, a nationwide outbreak of *Salmonella enteriditis* infections was associated with a particular brand of ice cream. Investigators learned that the ice cream implicated in the outbreak was delivered by truck to the homes of people in 41 states. The tainted ice cream was shipped from multiple warehouses across the country, but it was prepared in a single plant in Minnesota. The implicated plant obtained ice cream pre-mix from two suppliers, which was transported from the pre-mix suppliers to the ice cream plant in tanker trucks. The identification of a common ice cream plant suggested that the ice cream was contaminated with *S. enteritidis* at or before that point in the production of the ice cream, either at the plant, in the tanker trucks that delivered the pre-mix, or in the facility where the pre-mix was prepared. Investigators followed up, focusing on these areas.[2]

In the 1997 multistate outbreak of *E. coli* O157:H7 infections discussed in earlier chapters, a traceback investigation helped investigators determine the source of contaminated alfalfa sprouts that made people ill in Michigan and Virginia. After reviewing information collected from the Michigan case patients through a case-control study, investigators obtained records from the stores and restaurants where the patients had purchased or eaten the sprouts that enabled them to trace the sprouts to a single facility in Michigan (facility A) that likely produced the sprouts implicated in 15 of 16 cases. (In the remaining case, the patient could have eaten sprouts from either facility A or a second facility in Michigan, facility B.) From inventory records obtained at the two sprouting facilities, investigators determined that sprouts grown by facility A prior to the outbreak came from two lots of seed—one from Idaho and one from Australia. (Facility B used a number of different seed lots prior to the outbreak period.)

At this point, investigators learned of a concurrent outbreak of *E. coli* O157:H7 infection in Virginia. The Centers for Disease Control and Prevention (CDC) subtyped the strains from cases from Virginia and identified the same pulsed-field gel electrophoresis (PFGE) pattern as in the Michigan outbreak. A case-control study also linked the Virginia outbreak of *E. coli* O157:H7 infections to alfalfa sprouts.

In Virginia, investigators traced sprouts eaten by 13 patients to a single sprouting facility in Virginia that used a single lot of seed harvested in Idaho—the same lot used by facility A in Michigan. When investigators reexamined the sources of sprouts in Michigan, they found that facility B had sprouted a small number of seeds from the implicated Idaho seed lot during the outbreak period, but had used these seeds for sprouting on only two days. Given that the sprouts eaten by case patients involved multiple home kitchens, restaurants, and grocery stores and three sprouting facilities in two states, investigators concluded that it was likely the problem derived from the lot of seeds from Idaho.[3]

In each of the preceding examples, investigators used a traceback investigation to pinpoint the location where the problem had taken place (Figure 12-2). The investigations did not reveal what caused the problem, however. In both cases, identifying the specific cause of the problem required a detailed environmental health assessment—the subject of the next section.

Environmental Health Assessments

A traceback investigation can reveal the most likely point at which the food, medicine, or other vehicle implicated in an outbreak became contaminated, but it does not identify the actual source of the problem. Rather, it simply tells investigators where to look next. Further investigation and inspection of the restaurants, processing plants, and tanker trucks identified in a traceback investigation are necessary if investigators want to identify practices or conditions that may have resulted in the problem and implement control measures to prevent the problem from happening again. An environmental health study—specifically an environmental health assessment—is often required to determine the root cause of the problem that caused the outbreak.

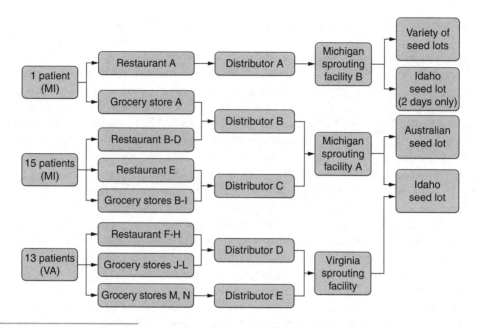

Figure 12-2 Results of a traceback of alfalfa sprouts in Michigan and Virginia for *E. coli* O157:H7 investigation

Source: Adapted from Breuer T, Benkel DH, Shapiro RL, et al. A multistate outbreak of *Escherichia coli* O157:H57 infections linked to alfalfa sprouts grown from contaminated seeds. *Emerg Infect Dis.* 2001;7:977–82.

An environmental health assessment is a systematic, detailed, science-based evaluation of environmental factors that contributed to the transmission of a particular disease in an outbreak or other setting. It is not a general inspection of operating procedures or sanitary conditions like that used for the licensing of an assisted living facility or a restaurant. Rather, it is designed to determine how the causative agent, host factors, and environmental conditions interacted to trigger a specific problem. (The environmental health assessment is unrelated to other public health studies with similar names, such as community environmental health assessments and environmental health impact assessments.)

The environmental health assessment often focuses on the vehicle implicated in an outbreak investigation—for example, a contaminated food item, cosmetics, blood products, or medicine. In some instances, the assessment focuses on the setting in which the problem occurred or, if a specific vehicle has not been implicated, is suspected to have occurred. Examples might be the kitchen in which a meal associated with a foodborne disease outbreak was prepared or an operating room that has been linked to an increased risk of surgical wound infections. In all instances, the goals of an environmental health assessment are to identify any points at which the causative agent could have contaminated the implicated vehicle, determine whether the agent could have survived or remained active at that point, and decide whether conditions were conducive for it to subsequently grow or produce toxins.

Specifically, investigators in an environmental health assessment explore the following elements:

- Possible points of contamination, such as factors that introduce or permit the introduction of pathogenic microorganisms, natural toxins, or other poisonous substances

- Sources of contamination, such as tainted raw materials, an infected person, cross-contamination, and unclean equipment

- Factors that influence contamination, such as breaks in packaging and poor storage practices

- Factors that allow pathogenic microorganisms to survive or fail to inactivate heat-labile toxins that are already present, such as inadequate sterilization or heat-processing of the item, inadequate reheating, or inadequate use of preservatives

- Conditions that allow pathogenic bacteria and fungi to multiply to numbers sufficient to cause illness or that allow toxigenic bacteria and molds to produce toxins, such as inadequate refrigeration, inadequate hot-holding, prolonged anaerobic packaging, and inadequate fermentation

When Should the Environmental Health Assessment Be Undertaken?

The timing of the environmental health assessment depends largely on the specifics of the outbreak and the available information. On the one hand, investigators cannot undertake an environmental health assessment until they have identified the likely setting in which the problem occurred. On the other hand, it is important for investigators to act as quickly as they can, because possible vehicles, such as foods, might be discarded or grow old, and individuals or groups involved in the production, processing, storage, transportation, or preparation of the item might change their practices and procedures as a result of the outbreak. The sooner specimens are collected, for example, the more closely the results will reflect the conditions at the time of the outbreak.

Investigators may go to great lengths to find samples of the food implicated in an outbreak, as in the following case. From October 1997 through October 1998, 16 outbreaks of gastrointestinal illness were reported in Florida, Georgia, Illinois, Indiana, Kansas, North Dakota, and Pennsylvania. All but one outbreak occurred in a school, and approximately 1,700 persons were affected. The predominant symptoms were abdominal cramps (88%), vomiting (62%), headache (62%), and nausea (39%), with only a short incubation period being noted. An etiologic agent was not isolated. Epidemiologic investigations implicated burritos as the source. By the time the investigators in one outbreak had pinpointed the likely source, however, the school cafeteria had discarded the leftover burritos and garbage pick-up had already occurred. Investigators used a forklift to find the burritos at the dump, but they were unable to confirm the cause of the outbreak.[4]

If the source of the problem is unknown, it may be very difficult—and even wasteful—to initiate an environmental health assessment. Investigators may need to wait until the causative agent has been isolated, results from the descriptive epidemiology or hypothesis-generating interviews are available, analytic epidemiologic studies have implicated a specific vehicle, or a traceback investigation has been completed.

Who Should Undertake an Environmental Health Assessment?

Most environmental health assessments are carried out by experts with special training in this field of investigation, such as sanitarians or environmental health specialists. Individuals who have special knowledge about a particular causative agent or vehicle may also contribute their expertise.

Conducting an environmental health assessment requires a good understanding of the causative agent, including where it typically is found, what causes it to grow, and how its growth can be inhibited or the pathogen killed. Whoever carries out the assessment must also understand the factors necessary to cause illness, such as infectious dose and portal of entry. Finally, he or she must have expertise in the implicated vehicle, including how it is produced, processed, and prepared, and how it might facilitate or inhibit the growth of pathogens. A good grasp of this information will allow the investigator to target the likely source of the problem and determine how the causative agent, host factors, and environmental conditions interacted to cause the outbreak (Figure 12-3).

Where Should an Environmental Health Assessment Be Undertaken?

An environmental health assessment should take place where the problem leading to the outbreak occurred. Any location where the suspected vehicle was produced, processed, stored, or used is a possible investigation site, as is any truck or tanker used to transport the vehicle. It may be necessary to investigate a number of sites. Investigators will decide where to focus the assessment based primarily on what they know about the source of the problem. This location may be obvious from information available at the time of the investigation. For example, if an outbreak is associated with a meal served at a banquet, the site

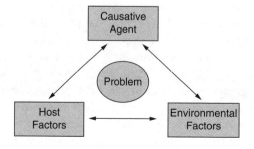

Figure 12-3 The approach of an environmental health assessment

of the assessment is likely to be the kitchen in which the meal was prepared. In contrast, if the outbreak involves cases from across a state or country—or around the globe—it might not be as clear where to start. If they have not done so already, investigators may need to conduct traceback investigations to determine where the problem likely originated.

Conducting an Environmental Health Assessment

The specific activities included in an environmental health assessment will differ based on the causative agent, the suspected vehicle, and the setting. To obtain the information they need, investigators will generally research the implicated product, review written policies and procedures, undertake direct observations and measurements, and conduct interviews with employees and managers. In addition to on-site investigation, they will order laboratory testing of the suspected vehicle, ingredients, or environmental surfaces, and of appropriate specimens from employees or others who have come into contact with the suspected vehicle or the surrounding environment.

To demonstrate the kind of activities that investigators might undertake in an environmental health assessment, we will use the investigation of food implicated in a foodborne disease outbreak as an example. Note that while the activities described in the remainder of this section are specific to investigating a food item implicated in an outbreak, many of these same activities might be used in the investigation of nonfood vehicles.

The environmental health specialist or sanitarian who carries out the assessment will begin by describing the implicated food item and obtaining the recipe for it in writing, if possible. He or she will determine how much of the implicated item was prepared, where the ingredients came from, and what the intrinsic chemical and physical characteristics of the food are (including the expected microbial/toxin content, pH, water content, and sugar content). This information will help establish the likelihood that the causative agent would be able to survive and grow in or on the food item.

Next, the investigator will review every step of the preparation of the implicated food, from receipt of the raw ingredients to the finished product, examining how the ingredients were cleaned and stored and how foods were thawed, cooked, cooled, reheated, served, and transported. He or she will collect leftover samples of the implicated food and ingredients, and swab food preparation surfaces or equipment for cultures or other testing.

Moving from an examination of the food itself to the facility in which the food was prepared, the investigator will inspect the equipment used to prepare the implicated food and consider the floor design of the facility and employee traffic patterns. One determination that the investigator makes during this phase of the assessment is whether there is adequate separation between food preparation activities to prevent cross-contamination.

The assessment continues with interviews of food handlers and managers who are familiar with the food preparation process and facility. The investigator will determine the food preparation schedule, including the date and time of preparation and the person(s) who prepared the implicated food. He or she will ask about standard operating procedures, including policies for sick food handlers and routine food safety education of employees. The investigator will also collect information about the food handlers themselves. It is important to know, for example, whether food handlers use gloves and employ proper hand-washing practices, and whether any of them have been ill recently.

Finally, the investigator will review available records, including the results of past inspections or complaints, worker logs or time cards, and monitoring logs that track conditions such as temperatures in walk-in refrigerators. He or she will collect identifying information about the implicated item or its ingredients, including the brand name; producer; distributor; batch and lot number; dates the implicated item was produced, shipped, and received; and quantities received. This information will help identify the exact source of the food item. It also facilitates traceback of the item, if appropriate.

To summarize the information obtained through an environmental health assessment, environmental health specialists or sanitarians often draw a flow diagram showing each step in the production and use of the vehicle. Investigators can use flow diagrams to verify production activities as they consult different workers and managers. They can also use these aids to help identify possible points of contamination or microbial survival and growth. In the flow diagrams pictured in Figures 12-4 and 12-5, each "operation"—that is,

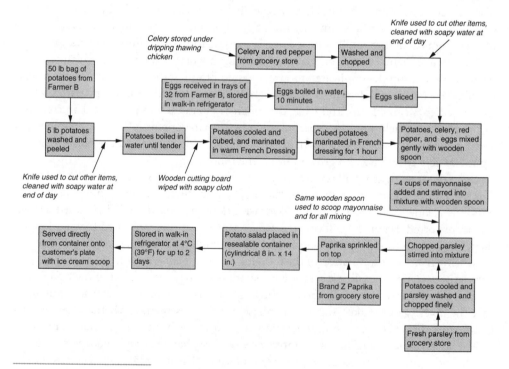

Figure 12-4 Flow diagram for making potato salad

Source: Botulism in Argentina. Centers for Disease Control and Prevention website: http://www.cdc.gov/epicasestudies/computer_botulism.html. Accessed June 7, 2011.

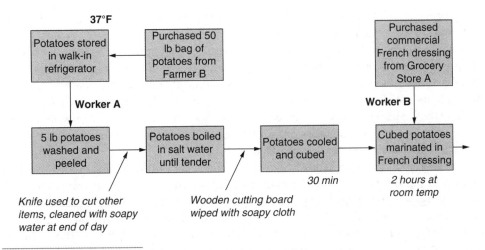

Figure 12-5 Flow diagram for making potato salad (detail)

Source: Botulism in Argentina. Centers for Disease Control and Prevention website: http://www.cdc.gov/epicasestudies/computer_botulism.html. Accessed June 7, 2011.

each detailed step of the process—is represented by a rectangle; arrows indicate the direction of flow. The investigator notes other important information directly on the diagram, including measurements such as temperature and duration of the operation and the name of the person(s) performing the operation.

Important Considerations in Undertaking an Environmental Health Assessment

When incorporating the results of an environmental health assessment into an outbreak investigation, investigators must keep two important points in mind.

First, the presence of factors that allow the causative agent to contaminate the vehicle, survive, and grow may not be sufficient to cause a health problem. If subsequent steps in the production or use of the vehicle eliminate the problem introduced by the factor or reduce it below a critical level, the factor will no longer contribute to a potential problem. For example, if an infected food worker handles a food item with his or her bare hands, the bare-handed contact could be a problem if the food is not cooked after this contact. A pathogen introduced by the contact could survive and multiply sufficiently to cause illness in someone who consumes the food. If the food item is cooked after contact, however, the bare-handed contact would probably not be a problem, because proper cooking will destroy pathogens introduced into the food. This concept is known as the "critical control point" in the food safety world. Critical control points are steps in the preparation of a food item at which action can be taken to prevent or eliminate a food safety problem—if the problem is not resolved at the critical control point, it will not be addressed in subsequent steps in the preparation of the food.

Second, although the primary goal of an environmental health assessment is to identify possible points of contamination, survival, and growth, the assessment will be truly valuable only if investigators identify the "antecedents" that resulted in these conditions. Antecedents are the circumstances behind the problem. They include such factors as inadequate worker education, behavioral risk factors, management decisions, and social and cultural beliefs. Investigators cannot develop effective interventions until they have identified the problem behind the problem.

A fairly typical (if hypothetical) example might be an outbreak of salmonellosis in a small community that was linked to potato salad served at a local restaurant. The environmental health assessment may determine that the potato salad was probably contaminated with *Salmonella* from chicken that was thawing above the potato salad ingredients in the refrigerator. The root of the problem, however, might go deeper than the improper storage of raw chicken. Perhaps the manager of the restaurant replaced several full-time employees with part-time workers. Although the part-time workers have taken a food safety course from the local health department, they lack experience, are not closely supervised, and do not always make good decisions on food-handling practices. To correct the problem, the restaurant management should provide food handlers with education about good food-handling techniques for food prepared in the restaurant's kitchen, including specific instruction on the proper handling of raw chicken, and assign a knowledgeable and experienced employee to provide ongoing oversight of the food-handling activities.

The case of the contaminated ice cream discussed earlier in the chapter is another example of the importance of following up an environmental health assessment with concrete actions to address the root problems. Investigators found no food safety problems at the plant that produced the ice cream and the two suppliers that produced the pre-mix. When they conducted an environmental health assessment of the trucking company that transported the pre-mix, they found that the tanker trucks used to transport the ice cream pre-mix were also used to carry nonpasteurized eggs from egg-breaking plants. Although there were protocols for cleaning and sanitizing the tanker trailers, some were not cleaned at all and some were cleaned inadequately.[2] The investigators believed that stronger regulation and enforcement was necessary to prevent a repeat of this multistate outbreak, and they called on all responsible federal and state agencies to "require that food-grade products be repasteurized after transportation or be transported in dedicated tanker trailers."[2]

Summary

To find the source of an outbreak or other public health problem, investigators need to look back in time and determine what went wrong. Using a traceback investigation as a first step, investigators can locate where problems may have occurred in the chain of production of an implicated vehicle—at the farm, on the production line, in the warehouse, or during transport. Once they have identified the location or locations where the problem took place, they can conduct an environmental health assessment to identify practices or conditions that may have resulted in the problem.

An environmental health assessment provides invaluable insights into the circumstances around an outbreak. It can help investigators identify breakdowns in techniques, problems with system design or operation, or simple human errors that led to the problem underlying the outbreak. This information allows investigators to identify logical points of intervention to stop the problem and prevent future occurrences. More broadly, combining the information from epidemiologic, laboratory, and environmental health studies helps the investigation team complete the picture of an outbreak or other public health problem by putting together characteristics of the agent, host, and environment. Based on this picture, control measures can be implemented more quickly and are more likely to be effective.

References

1. Centers for Disease Control and Prevention. Multistate outbreak of *Salmonella* serotype *agona* infections linked to Toasted Oats cereal—United States, April–May 1998. *Morb Mortal Weekly Rep*. 1998;47:462–4.
2. Hennessy TW, Hedberg CW, Slutsker L, et al. A national outbreak of *Salmonella enteritidis* infections from ice cream. *N Engl J Med*. 1996;334:1281–6.
3. Breuer T, Benkel DH, Shapiro RL, et al. A multistate outbreak of *Escherichia coli* O157:H57 infections linked to alfalfa sprouts grown from contaminated seeds. *Emerg Infect Dis*. 2001;7:977–82.
4. Centers for Disease Control and Prevention. Outbreaks of gastrointestinal illness of unknown etiology associated with eating burritos—United States, October 1997–October 1998. *Morb Mortal Weekly Rep*. 1999;48:210–3.

Chapter 13

Investigating Noninfectious Health Events in Public Health Practice

Jeanette K. Stehr-Green
Paul A. Stehr-Green
Pia D. M. MacDonald

Learning Objectives

By the end of this chapter, the reader will be able to:

- Define a noninfectious disease cluster and give examples of such clusters.
- Compare and contrast noninfectious disease cluster investigations and infectious disease outbreak investigations.
- Describe the public health resources required for investigating a cluster.
- Describe how to plan and conduct a cluster investigation.
- List the entities that should be notified of a cluster reported to the public health department.
- List the information that should be collected during the initial report of a noninfectious disease cluster.
- Explain how the case definition affects investigation of a potential cluster.
- Discuss how to determine the population at risk for a health problem and how it might affect the conclusions in a cluster investigation.
- Discuss the epidemiologic and logistical issues that should be considered when determining the feasibility of an etiologic study.
- List several factors that affect risk perception.
- Discuss issues to consider when dealing with the media.

Introduction

In previous chapters, we have primarily discussed infectious disease outbreak investigations. Sometimes, however, public health practitioners are called upon to investigate a group—or "cluster"— of health events that may be far more difficult to untangle than a typical infectious disease outbreak. Responding to reports of noninfectious disease clusters, and investigating them when appropriate, is a critical public health function.

Sometimes, however, cluster investigations can be difficult or impossible to complete successfully. The health conditions in the alleged cluster may be tenuously linked or not linked at all; the cause or causes may be uncertain; and the exposure or exposures that caused the illness may have taken place years in the past. To complicate matters further, an alleged cluster may draw widespread public attention and bring demands for action, even before proof is gathered that a cluster exists. Only rarely does a cluster investigation result in a scientific breakthrough by linking a specific exposure to a specific disease.

Even in the vast majority of investigations in which no disease-exposure association is found, it is important for public health departments to respond at a certain level to reports of disease clusters and to address public concerns about them. In this chapter, we define and describe noninfectious disease cluster investigations in detail, concluding with a discussion of the importance of communication to a successful response to reports of a cluster.

What Is a Noninfectious Health Event Investigation?

A *cluster* is an unusual aggregation, either real or perceived, of health events reported to the health department.[1] (Even one case of a rare, serious health event can constitute a cluster.) A *cluster investigation* is the systematic, integrated response to a report of a cluster of cases of noninfectious disease and the suspected exposure that caused the disease. Cases in the cluster are linked by time and space—that is, when and where they took place. A cluster can initially be detected through the routine analysis of surveillance data from such sources as cancer registries, birth defects registries, and death certificates. More commonly, however, healthcare providers, patients, parents, or community members are the first to report clusters.[1] The steps of a cluster investigation, which are discussed in detail later in this chapter, include data collection, analysis, interpretation, communication, and action.

Unlike the investigations described in earlier chapters, cluster investigations focus on noninfectious diseases—that is, health events without an obvious infectious cause. Noninfectious diseases vary dramatically in nature. They may include cancers, birth defects, chronic diseases such as multiple sclerosis, and adverse events related to drugs or vaccines. An important focus of cluster investigations is exposures—external factors with which a host comes in contact (e.g., through ingestion, inhalation, or absorption through the skin) that may increase the host's risk of a disease. Potential exposures include industrial chemicals, medications, pesticides, and radioactive materials, among many other substances. Clusters of noninfectious disease are sometimes reported with an exposure that is the suspected cause of the cluster. (Concerns about the exposure are often the driving impetus for reporting the cluster.) The exposure may be human-made or natural, ongoing or historical. In the majority of investigations, the exposure has not previously been shown to be associated with the occurrence of the disease being reported.[1]

In rare but significant instances, cluster investigations have led to important scientific insights. Here are a few examples:

- In the early 1960s, public health officials in several European countries noted a marked increase in the number of infants born with a severe deformity of their limbs called phocomelia. The deformities were linked to maternal use of thalidomide, a sleeping pill and treatment for morning sickness, during pregnancy. The investigation of this cluster had a resounding impact, even in the United States, where the drug was never marketed. Partly as a result of this incident, the United States enacted legislation in 1962 that put into place the rigorous testing now required before a pharmaceutical product can be approved and sold in this country.[2]

- In 1973, healthcare providers diagnosed four cases of angiosarcoma of the liver (a rare disease) among men employed at a B. F. Goodrich plant near Louisville, Kentucky. An investigation ultimately linked the angiosarcomas to high levels of exposure to an organic compound—a vinyl chloride monomer—used in the tire manufacturing process. (The discovery led to further investigations that linked vinyl chloride with cancers that affected the brain, liver, lungs, blood cells, and other organs.) As a result of these investigations, the U.S. government revised the maximum allowable daily exposure to this chemical for workers.[3]

- In 1989, a New Mexico physician reported three patients with a marked increase in a type of white blood cell known as eosinophils and severe muscle pain with no known cause. Public announcement of the cluster led rapidly to reports of similar cases in other states. The newly discovered condition, which was ultimately called eosinophilia-myalgia syndrome, was linked with taking oral preparations of L-tryptophan (a dietary supplement) made by one manufacturer in Japan. The investigation had important implications for the U.S. Food and Drug Administration's (FDA's) regulation of the production and marketing of food supplements.[4]

Other notable investigations of noninfectious disease clusters have occurred as well, but investigations that link a cluster of noninfectious disease to a specific exposure are the exception. Few noninfectious disease cluster investigations have added to our knowledge of the causes of disease or produced a credible explanation of why the disease cluster occurred.[5] Between 1981 and 1988, for example, the Minnesota Department of Health actively responded to more than 400 reports from persons concerned about disease occurrence in their community, school, or workplace. In only one instance, in an occupational setting, was the department able to document an important public health outcome concerning cancer.[6] Other states and federal agencies have reported similar results.[7-9]

Most noninfectious disease cluster investigations fail to come to a satisfactory conclusion for one of several reasons. First, in many cases investigators are unable to confirm a geographic or temporal excess in the number of cases.[1] This happens, at least in part, because many of the noninfectious diseases associated with reported clusters, such as cancers and birth defects, occur fairly commonly in the community; thus the cluster may simply reflect the usual occurrence of the disease. Also, sometimes, the cluster results from confounders—the presence of other factors in the community that account for a seemingly higher rate of occurrence. The older age of a relatively elderly population could explain an apparently high cancer rate, for example. Furthermore, many reported clusters are actually a collection of several different diseases that look alike to the person who reports them, such as a primary tumor of the brain and a tumor that has metastasized to the brain from another organ in the body. Such different diseases typically result from different pathogenic processes; although grouped together in time and space, they are not specifically linked to one another.

Second, even if a noninfectious disease cluster investigation confirms an unusual number of cases of a disease, a number of factors make it unlikely investigators will establish a definitive cause-and-effect relationship between the health event and a supposed exposure. Most clusters involve a small number of cases, which limits the statistical power of studies examining their associations. In addition, investigators are often unable to isolate one potential exposure or cause for investigation. And even if the investigation does point to a causative agent, the long time between exposure to a suspected disease-causing agent and the onset of symptoms makes it very difficult to reconstruct exposure histories among cases.[5]

Finally, identifying the source of a noninfectious disease cluster is difficult because our current knowledge of the causes of many of these diseases remains extremely limited. Controversial theories often link an exposure to a noninfectious disease—one example is the hypothesis that proximity to power lines can cause cancer. Few of these theories have been substantiated, and the causes of the majority of noninfectious diseases remain unknown.[10]

These factors suggest why a noninfectious disease cluster investigation differs considerably from the investigation of an infectious disease. Both types of investigation can confirm case reports, characterize the nature and distribution of reported health events, and determine whether the cases represent an unusual occurrence. The noninfectious disease cluster investigation, however, often ends with these descriptive epidemiology activities, as it rarely provides sufficient information to link a disease and an exposure. If a cluster investigation raises legitimate questions, investigators will almost certainly have to conduct a separate large-scale epidemiologic study to find definitive answers.[1]

There is another critical difference between the investigation of infectious disease outbreaks and noninfectious disease clusters: Noninfectious disease cluster investigations are more likely to be accompanied by expressions of public concern.[1] When news breaks that a public health agency is studying a potential cluster, the public often wants to scrutinize the investigation. People who are concerned about their health and the health of their neighbors are not likely to be satisfied with complex epidemiologic or statistical arguments that fail to confirm the existence or importance of a cluster. The importance of communicating with the media and the public and allaying their fears adds another dimension to these investigations, one that is discussed in some detail later in this chapter.

Noninfectious disease investigations are challenging and multidimensional. Public health practitioners who undertake cluster investigations must carefully and systematically collect and analyze information from multiple sources; at the same time, they must take into account the social dimensions of the investigation and engage members of the community as partners. This raft of responsibilities requires the investigation team to incorporate expertise in communication and education into its efforts, as well as specialized investigation skills.[1]

The Resources Required to Investigate a Noninfectious Health Event

When a public health agency prepares to respond to a report of a cluster of noninfectious disease, it must ensure that the process can proceed smoothly from one level of action to the next. It needs to be able to bring the investigation to a satisfying conclusion when a resolution is reached. In addition, it needs resources equal to the task so that other core agency functions can continue uninterrupted. Having the following organizational components in place can help assure smooth and timely public health responses:

- An internal management system with a locus of responsibility and control
- Written operating procedures for evaluating clusters
- Staff with appropriate skills and knowledge
- Adequate financial and logistical resources
- A process for involving responsible groups and individuals[1]

We will discuss each of these components below.

Internal Management System

An agency needs an internal management system that assures prompt responses to reports of disease clusters. (Not every cluster report has to be investigated, but every report demands a response.) Staff with adequate training and supervision should be designated to receive cluster reports and respond in a timely fashion. If an investigation progresses beyond the initial ascertainment of the cluster, the agency should assign a lead person—a program director, director of environmental health, state epidemiologist, or county health officer, for example—to serve as an identifiable point of responsibility and control for the investigation. In addition to being able to speak for the department, commit resources, and assure action, this person needs to be aware of the potential effects of the investigation on other public health programs in the department.[1]

Written Operating Procedures

Establishing written operating procedures for evaluating clusters—usually referred to as a protocol—enables the public health agency to mount a coordinated and standardized response to all cluster reports and to involve the appropriate entities. A protocol is a set of steps (and decision points) for receiving, processing, and responding to a report of a cluster. The protocol for a cluster investigation describes the information investigators need to collect from the person who initially reports the cluster (and often a data collection form), the persons to be notified of (or involved in) the investigation, criteria for proceeding to the next step of the protocol (or concluding the investigation at that point), and specific actions to be taken at each step. It is particularly important for an agency to use a protocol in cluster investigations because persons who report clusters often talk with more than one contact person within a public health department. Furthermore, in some cases, the agency receiving the report is not the agency that has jurisdiction over the geographic area where the potential cluster occurred. A consistent approach, no matter where the cluster is reported, has clear advantages.[1]

Staff

Investigating a noninfectious disease cluster requires unique scientific skills and finely tuned communication skills. An agency should think about the investigation as a public health surveillance activity focusing on the ongoing collection, analysis, and dissemination of information important to public health practice. Investigators of noninfectious disease clusters usually spend more time looking at patterns of disease occurrence—spatial, temporal, or both—than searching for specific associations between a potential agent and a disease. A variety of statistical techniques are available to detect and characterize patterns of disease in time and space, some of which are shown in Figure 13-1.

Temporal Clustering

- Ederer, Myers, and Mantel test

- Naus' scan test

- Bailar, Eisenberg, and Mantel Test of Temporal Clustering

Spatial Clustering

- Geary contiguity ratio

- Ohno, Aoki, and Aoki test

- Grimson test

Spatial and Temporal Clustering

- Pinkel and Nefzger cell occupancy approach

- Knox 2 × 2 contingency table test

- Barton and David points-on-a-line approach

Figure 13-1 Examples of statistical techniques used to detect patterns

Source: Centers for Disease Control and Prevention. Guidelines for investigating clusters of health events—appendix. Summary of methods for statistically assessing clusters of health events. *Morb Mortal Weekly Rep.* 1990;39(RR-11):17–23.

Staff responsible for cluster investigations should be familiar with these pattern-recognition techniques and know when it is appropriate to use which one.[1]

In addition to epidemiologic and statistical skills, staff involved in cluster investigations should have in-depth knowledge of the noninfectious disease of concern, including its epidemiology, natural history, and diagnosis. They should also be familiar with the relevant scientific and medical literature. If the cluster investigation progresses to an examination of exposures, the investigation team might need skills in environmental or biological sampling, as well as access to laboratories with adequate facilities and experienced staff to analyze and interpret the results.[1]

Communication skills—including communication of the risk inherent in a situation—are also critical in cluster investigations. To communicate effectively, investigators should understand the various ways in which individuals and communities respond to stressful situations and react to uncertainties. They should be able to recognize the source of community suspicions and demands—for example, the community may suspect deliberate delays and cover-ups, and members of the community may demand unrealistic allocations of resources and timelines. Investigators must be aware of and responsive to the fact that the health department must resolve a perceived problem responsibly and sympathetically, even if no underlying community health problem or cluster of disease truly exists. Given the complexity of risk perception, investigators who have skills and experience in risk communications should lead the communications effort, in consultation with the health department's communications team or public relations officer.[1]

Financial and Logistical Resources

Public health agencies cannot ignore reports of clusters despite the likelihood that an investigation will neither demonstrate a clear link between exposure and disease nor fully satisfy a concerned community. When public health officials undertake a cluster investigation, they must develop an approach that manages clusters and maintains community relations without unduly depleting resources.[1]

Involving Responsible Groups and Individuals

The health agency should plan to involve the community in the cluster investigation and should evaluate its communications with key constituencies throughout the investigation. Community residents, citizen groups, health professionals, and state and local government representatives are all important sources of information. They can provide information about the site where suspected exposures took place, demographics, land and natural resource use, environmental contamination, pathways by which humans and animals could have been exposed, health outcomes, and community health concerns.

Involving these groups in the investigation makes health department communications more credible. Communication with a broad audience helps all parties gain a fuller understanding of the situation and recognize any constraints on the investigation, and can help the agency make better decisions. The health department can involve the community in the investigation and decision-making process through many forums, including public hearings, citizen advisory groups, and smaller, more informal meetings. In certain situations, one-to-one communication may work best. The form of involvement will depend on the problem, the setting, and the community.[1]

Given the difficulties inherent in the investigation of noninfectious disease clusters and the resources necessary to investigate them properly, the response to noninfectious disease clusters must be standardized, deliberative, and compassionate.[1] The next section explores the steps an agency can follow to make sure its response to reports of a disease cluster is appropriate and successful.

Basic Steps in Investigating Clusters of Noninfectious Disease

A cluster investigation can be viewed as a series of filters that lead to appropriate responses to a potential problem (Figure 13-2). Each step provides opportunities for collecting and analyzing data and making decisions about whether to take immediate action, proceed to the next step of the investigation, or end the investigation at that point.

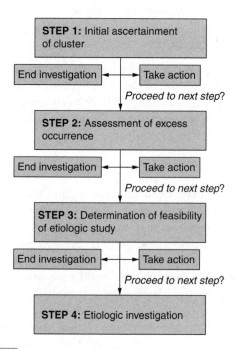

Figure 13-2 Flowchart of a cluster investigation

The four basic steps of a cluster investigation are outlined here:

Step 1: Initial ascertainment of health events and summarization of relevant data

Step 2: Assessment of excess occurrence

Step 3: Determination of the feasibility of an etiologic investigation

Step 4: Etiologic investigation[1]

Although investigators may not follow these steps exactly sequentially, they provide a framework within which to ensure consistency and attention to the appropriate issues. Next, we examine each of the steps in a noninfectious disease cluster investigation in some detail, with examples from real-life investigations.

Step 1: Initial Ascertainment of Health Events and Summarization of Relevant Data

The primary goal of the initial assessment is to gather and summarize the data that are initially available about the cluster, so that investigators can decide whether to close the cluster investigation or proceed to the next step. The information typically collected at this point includes the following items:

- Identifying information from the person reporting the cluster
- Demographic characteristics of case patients in the cluster
- Clinical information for case patients in the cluster
- Identifying information for case patients[1]

The person or persons who report the cluster might be able to provide this information, but it may be necessary to examine medical charts and conduct interviews with case patients or their relatives and/or healthcare providers to learn more. Most public health departments have a standardized form or list of questions to collect this preliminary information.[1]

Investigators should log all cluster reports into the appropriate health department tracking system. The log should include the date, time, reporter identification, health event(s), suspected exposure(s), and geographic area(s). Follow-up contacts should be logged in as well, with a brief note as to their purpose and outcome. Ideally, the log should be cross-referenced and computerized so that other health department staff can easily access the information. Investigators also need to notify the appropriate entities about the cluster. The extent of the notification will largely be based on the nature and magnitude of the cluster, but might include the following entities: other departmental staff, including supervisor, subject-matter experts, and others who might be involved in deciding about further investigation of the cluster; the health department communications team; staff from the local health jurisdiction in which the cluster has occurred, such as the local health officer; and staff from other agencies, such as labor or ecology, who might have jurisdiction or who might provide expertise.[1]

Completing these activities will bring the investigation to its first decision point: Based on examination of the preliminary data, should investigators close out the cluster or investigate further? Further investigation of a documented cluster is indicated if one or more of the following markers is evident:

1. A single and rare disease entity

2. Plausible exposure

3. Plausible clustering[2]

Alternatively, after assessing the preliminary data, investigators may determine that further evaluation is not warranted. Investigators may decide to conclude the investigation if the preliminary data uncovers the following findings:

- Clinically dissimilar health events constituting the perceived cluster
- A plausible alternative cause or causes
- No apparent excess occurrence of health events
- No apparent temporal association with any possible exposure(s)[1]

If investigators decide to terminate the investigation at this point, they should prepare a brief summary report to share with the person or persons who reported the cluster and the appropriate supervisory group at the health department. If further investigation seems to be warranted, they should proceed to Step 2.[1]

If the investigation is halted at this point, it is important to help the person who reported the cluster to understand why. The staff person receiving the report should provide information on usual patterns of the health event involved and known causes, and discuss how this pattern compares with the reported cluster. The following are examples of information that investigators might share at this point:

- Cancer is a common illness, with a one in three lifetime probability. The risk increases with age, and cases among older persons are less likely to be true clusters.
- Major birth defects are less common than cancer, but still occur in 1% to 2% of live births.
- The presence of a variety of diagnoses—different types of cancers, for example— argues against a common origin.
- Because it can take many years for cancer to develop after exposure to a known carcinogen, a person may need to have lived in one place for a substantial length of time to implicate a plausible environmental carcinogen.
- Cases among persons who have died may not be helpful in linking exposure to disease because of the lack of information on exposure and because of possible confounding factors.

- Rare diseases may occasionally "cluster" in a way that is statistically significant, but such an occurrence may be a statistical phenomenon that is not related to a specific exposure.[1]

Step 2: Assessment of Excess Occurrence

The goal of Step 2 is to determine whether the number of cases making up the cluster is greater than expected for a given population during a given time period. This step is divided into two substeps:

- A preliminary evaluation of excess occurrence
- An expanded evaluation of excess occurrence[1]

The preliminary evaluation is designed to provide a quick, rough estimate of the likelihood that a statistically significant excess of cases has occurred. The estimate uses existing data and can often be undertaken in-house. The expanded evaluation, by comparison, is a more thorough and refined analysis that includes a complete description of the epidemiologic and clinical characteristics of the cluster. Undertaking an expanded evaluation often requires investigators to collect new data. If the results of the preliminary evaluation do not indicate an excess of occurrence, the agency should not undertake an expanded evaluation.[1]

Step 2a: Preliminary Evaluation of Excess Occurrence

Evaluating whether an excess of a health event has occurred involves two separate, but related activities: (1) an assessment of available data to determine whether there is a greater than expected number of cases of the disease or health event under investigation and (2) verification of the diagnoses, to assure that a biological basis exists for further investigation. These activities are often interrelated and may occur in parallel. In some circumstances, it may be appropriate to verify the diagnoses before proceeding with the preliminary evaluation of excess occurrence. However, because the preliminary evaluation usually is less expensive and time-consuming, investigators typically begin with this assessment.[1]

Investigators determine whether there is an excess occurrence by comparing observed occurrence and expected occurrence. They begin by identifying the appropriate geographic area and time period in which the cluster will be examined. The geographic area should be large enough to include all persons at risk for the health event, but not so large that it dilutes the occurrence rate by including those who are not at risk. The designated time period should be consistent with the time period during which the supposed exposure took place (if one has been noted) and allow for a long enough latency period that cases should begin to emerge. Selecting the appropriate geographic area and time period is critical because investigators will use these variables to determine the number of cases (numerator) and the population at risk (denominator) for the observed rate of occurrence.[1]

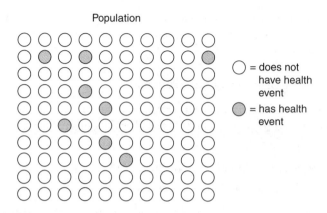

Figure 13-3   Estimating the magnitude of a health event

Figure 13-3 represents this concept graphically. When a "cluster" of health events has been reported and investigators want to estimate the magnitude of the problem (the rate of occurrence), they count the number of people with the health event and the total number of people in the population at risk. The population at risk is defined by the geographic area in which the possible exposure occurred over a designated time period. In Figure 13-3, the white circles represent individuals in the population who do not have the health event and the colored circles represent individuals in the population who have the health event.

If investigators focus solely on the neighborhood immediately surrounding the cases that were reported initially (delineated by the dotted line in Figure 13-4), they will calculate an apparent rate of occurrence of 20%—that is, 7 individuals with the health event out of 35 in the apparent population at risk. If, however, investigators consider the population at risk to be the entire group of 100 circles, as shown in Figure 13-5, the rate of occurrence will be 8%—that is, 8 occurrences of the health event among 100 people.

The second step in determining whether there is an excess of cases is to decide which cases from the reported cluster to include in a preliminary analysis. At this point, investigators usually assume that all reported cases are real, but they might exclude cases if they differ substantially from other cases. Examining the clinical, demographic, and epidemiologic characteristics of cases can help decide which—if any—cases to exclude.[1]

The third step is to determine an appropriate reference population from which to calculate expected rates, one that is comparable to the population in which the cluster has occurred. Typically, investigators use data from a similar geographic area or historical data from the same geographic area where the cluster appears to have occurred. Investigators estimate the expected occurrence rate for the reference population from existing surveillance data (such as cancer registries and birth defect registries) and data from other sources (such as hospital discharge databases and vital statistics records).[1]

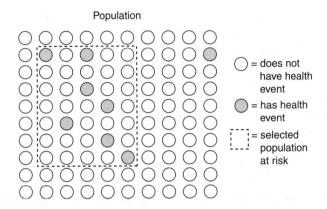

Figure 13-4   Estimating the magnitude of a health event in a specific neighborhood

Finally, investigators compare the observed occurrence rate based on the cluster with the expected rate from the reference population to determine if excess occurrence is present.[1] If the number of cases in the cluster is sufficiently large to calculate meaningful rates (typically five or more cases) and if an appropriate denominator is available, investigators will calculate the occurrence rate for the cluster using chi-square tests or Poisson regression. If the number of health events is too small to permit the calculation of meaningful rates, pooling cases across geographic areas or time may provide sufficient numbers for such calculations. For example, investigators might include cases from adjacent counties in the analysis or examine cases from a five-year period instead of a one-year period. If that is not possible or if denominator data are not available, investigators may use statistical tests that

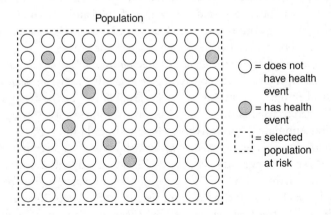

Figure 13-5   Estimating the magnitude of a health event in a larger population

have been developed to assess space, time, or space-time clustering. (See the appendix to the Centers for Disease Control and Prevention's "Guidelines for Investigating Clusters of Health Events" for a brief description of some of these techniques and references to other sources of information.)[11]

Here is an example of the preliminary evaluation of excess occurrence in a noninfectious disease cluster. In 2004, public health officials became aware of a cluster of cases of gastroschisis—a congenital anomaly involving a gap in the abdominal wall—among babies born in Bridgend County Borough, which is located along the coast of South Wales. Risk factors reported in the literature for gastroschisis include young maternal age; exposure to aspirin and decongestants during pregnancy; poor maternal diet; exposure to solvents during pregnancy; and use of tobacco, alcohol, and recreational drugs during pregnancy. An association between gastroschisis and living near landfill sites has also been suggested, although the association could be confounded by the correlation between living near landfill sites with some of the known risk factors already noted.

The cluster of gastroschisis in Bridgend County Borough was first noted by clinicians at the University Hospital of Wales. Data from the Welsh Congenital Anomaly Register also suggested a noticeable rise of gastroschisis in the county. Investigators followed the four steps in their preliminary evaluation of excess occurrence of gastroschisis in Bridgend County Borough.

Step 1: Determine the appropriate geographic area and the time period in which the cluster will be examined. Investigators decided cases would be babies with gastroschisis whose mothers normally resided in Bridgend County Borough. Because reported cases had an expected delivery date during a period of a few months in 2004, investigators selected an expected pregnancy due date during 2004 as the appropriate time period.

Step 2: Determine which cases from the reported cluster will be included in the preliminary analysis. The original line listing is not available, but Table 13-1 shows a reconstructed line listing of cases of gastroschisis known to clinicians at the University Hospital of Wales. Assuming that the diagnoses of gastroschisis were correct, the investigators would have eliminated two of the cases: one with an expected delivery date of 2005 and one whose mother resided in Swansea, a neighboring county, but who received her obstetrical care from a physician in Bridgend County Borough. That left seven cases in the cluster.

Step 3: Determine an appropriate reference population from which to calculate expected rates. Because rates of gastroschisis were reported to be generally higher in Wales than in other parts of the world (ranging from 4.3 to 6.1 per 10,000 live births from 1998 to 2003), investigators decided to use historical data from Bridgend County Borough found in the Welsh Congenital Anomaly Register as the reference population.

Step 4: Compare observed and expected occurrence rates (or other statistics). Based on data from 1998–2003, the average rate of gastroschisis in Bridgend County Borough was 7.9 per 10,000 live births, with the 95% confidence interval ranging from 3.2 to 16.2 per 10,000 live births based on the Poisson distribution. Given the average number of births in the borough, the average rate of gastroschisis translates to an average of 1 case per year, with a maximum expected number of 3. Seven cases of gastroschisis were

TABLE 13-1   Gastroschisis Cases Initially Reported by University Hospital of Wales

Case Number	Expected Date of Delivery	Maternal County of Residence
1	2004	Bridgend
2	2004	Bridgend
3	2005	Bridgend
4	2004	Bridgend
5	2004	Bridgend
6	2004	Bridgend
7	2004	Swansea
8	2004	Bridgend
9	2004	Bridgend

Source: Gastroschisis Investigation Group. Investigation of a cluster of cases of gastroschisis in Bridgend County Borough during 2004. National Public Health Service for Wales, 2004. http://www.wales.nhs.uk/sites3/Documents/719/FinalreportGastroschisisIG.pdf. Accessed May 18, 2011.

included in the Bridgend County Borough cluster. This number was in excess of what was expected—that is, it exceeded the upper bound of the 95% confidence interval for the historical rate of occurrence. The investigators agreed that the occurrence was an important finding that may not have arisen by chance and that further investigation of the cluster was warranted.

Subsequently, investigators tried to establish links between cases and identify environmental factors that might explain the cluster. No specific factors were identified that connected the individuals or that could have explained the cluster. Mothers of cases exhibited a number of risk factors previously described as having an association with gastroschisis, including poor diet, smoking, and taking cold remedies and painkillers. None of these, however, could explain the Bridgend County Borough cluster.[12]

As the Welsh example demonstrates, if the preliminary evaluation suggests a statistically significant excess occurrence, investigators should proceed to the next substep—verification of the diagnosis. If the preliminary evaluation suggests no statistically significant excess and the overall evidence does not suggest an occurrence of potential biologic and public health importance associated with any supposed exposure, the investigation is likely to be terminated. However, investigators may still decide to investigate further if the preliminary evaluation shows no statistically significant excess but the overall evidence suggests an occurrence of potential biologic and public health importance that is plausibly associated with a potential exposure. The decision to proceed at this point should not be based solely on an arbitrary criterion of statistical significance, but rather on the medical literature and the investigating team's judgment.

If the investigation proceeds past the initial evaluation, the next step is to verify the diagnoses of the case patients. It is important to verify the diagnoses of all "cases" according to a clear, consistently applied case definition. If cases are not clearly defined or if they were inconsistently diagnosed, the "cluster" may simply represent a mixture of different health events, likely without a common cause. Depending on the circumstances, the case definition may have been developed prior to the investigation, or it may have been developed or refined based on epidemiologic/demographic and clinical information collected as part of the ongoing investigation. (See Chapter 4 for more on case definitions.)

At this stage of the investigation, investigators might consider a number of approaches to defining a case. For example, they might include multiple diseases or health events in the case definition. This strategy likely will result in a greater number of cases, but if the diseases are not truly related, the broader definition will make it more difficult to hypothesize a unique cause and find an explanation for the cluster. A case definition should include multiple diseases or health events only when consistent scientific information about the presumed causal exposure exists.

Investigators may also try using more than one case definition to identify potential cases. For example, in 1995, the New Jersey Department of Health and Senior Services (DHSS) investigated reports of childhood cancer in Dover Township (including the Toms River section) in southeast New Jersey. Over a number of decades, chemical plants and other area businesses had released industrial pollutants into the Toms River, eventually contaminating the well that provided the township's drinking water. To determine whether an excess occurrence of cancers was present, investigators evaluated all childhood cancers combined, as well as subgroupings of selected childhood cancer types. They identified cancer cases through the New Jersey State Cancer Registry, determined expected numbers of cases based on statewide average annual age and sex-specific numbers for 1979 to 1995, and compared observed and expected numbers by calculating standardized incidence ratios (SIR) and 95% confidence intervals (Table 13-2). The SIR is the ratio of the incident number of cases of a specified condition in the study population to the incident number that investigators would expect to find if the study population had the same incidence rate as a standard population or another group for which the incidence rate is known.[13]

In Dover Township, investigators found excess childhood cancer incidence for all cancers combined and for acute lymphocytic leukemia in females (data not shown). In Toms River, they found excess childhood cancer incidence for all cancers combined, for brain and central nervous system cancers, and for acute lymphocytic leukemia, particularly in female children younger than the age of 5 (Table 13-2). Subsequent studies identified no single factor that was solely responsible for the general elevation in childhood cancer. However, the findings supported the hypothesis that prenatal exposure to township well water between 1982 and 1996 and parental exposure to air emissions from a chemical company were risk factors for leukemia in female children.[14]

The Dover Township/Toms River situation highlights the importance of clarifying the case definition to verify the diagnosis of cases in a cluster. Investigators can take several

TABLE 13-2 Childhood Cancer Incidence in Toms River Census Tracts, 1979–1995, in Children 0–4 Years of Age

Cancer Type	Number Observed	Number Expected	SIR	95% CI
All cancers combined	24	14.4	1.7	1.07–2.49
Brain/central nervous system	4	0.6	7	1.87–17.8
Astrocytoma	2	0.2	8.8	1.00–32.1
Acute lymphocytic leukemia*	4	0.4	9.4	2.52–24.0

*Females only.

Source: Adapted from New Jersey Department of Health and Senior Services. Childhood cancer incidence health consultation: A review and analysis of cancer registry data, 1979–1995, for Dover Township (Ocean County), New Jersey; 1997. http://www.state.nj.us/health/eoh/hhazweb/cansumm.pdf. Accessed September 29, 2010.

CI = confidence interval

steps to determine whether cases meet the case definition, including contacting attending physicians, searching relevant health-event registries, and obtaining copies of relevant pathology reports, laboratory or other diagnostic tests, and medical examiner's reports. In some cases, reexamining biopsy specimens or retesting specimens can provide valuable information. Verifying cases is often a multistep process, involving an initial contact with the attending physician(s) to obtain permission to examine the cases' medical records; investigators also may directly contact case patients or their family members or friends.[1]

Another example, also from New Jersey, illustrates the potential complexity of case verification in a cluster investigation. In 2003, the New Jersey DHSS and the Centers for Disease Control and Prevention (CDC) investigated a reported cluster of patients with Creutzfeldt-Jakob disease (CJD) associated with attendance at the Garden State Park Racetrack in Cherry Hill, New Jersey. The report alleged that from 1988 to 1992, the racetrack served meat that was contaminated with the agent that causes bovine spongiform encephalopathy (BSE), also known as "mad cow disease."

Successfully resolving the case required investigators to make distinctions between the two known forms of CJD and BSE. Classic CJD, which is characterized by rapidly progressive dementia and muscle twitching, is thought to be familial or sporadic in nature and not the result of an outside source of infection. Variant CJD (vCJD), which progresses more slowly than classic CJD and results in a complex of psychiatric/behavioral symptoms, has been associated with clusters and is thought to be acquired through an outside source of infection. Although both forms of CJD are fatal, vCJD is easily distinguishable from classic CJD (see Table 13-3). Strong scientific evidence supports the hypothesis that the agent responsible for BSE in cows is the same agent responsible for outbreaks of vCJD in humans. Classic CJD has not been related to BSE in cows.

TABLE 13-3 Comparison of Classic Creutzfeldt-Jakob Disease and Variant Creutzfeldt-Jakob Disease

Characteristic	Classic CJD	vCJD
Median age at death	68 years	28 years
Median duration of illness	4–5 months	13–14 months
Clinical signs and symptoms	Dementia, early neurologic signs	Psychiatric/behavioral symptoms; painful dysesthesias; delayed neurologic signs
Periodic sharp waves on EEG	Often present	Often absent
Presence of "florid plaques" on pathology	Rare or absent	Present in large numbers
Immunohistochemical analysis of brain tissue	Variable accumulation	Marked accumulation of protease-resistance prion protein

*An electroencephalogram (EEG) is a test that reveals electrical current abnormalities within the brain.

Source: Adapted from Belay E, Schonberger L. Variant Creutzfeldt-Jakob disease and bovine spongiform encephalopathy. Clin Lab Med. 2002;22:849–62.

In the cluster of CJD reported to the New Jersey DHSS, 17 potential cases of CJD were reported among people who had visited the racetrack (Table 13-4). Ten of the 17 potential cases were residents of other states (Pennsylvania, Connecticut, Virginia, Maryland, and Delaware) at the time of diagnosis. The remaining cases were New Jersey residents. All except five of the affected individuals were younger than 60 years of age.

To verify the diagnosis, public health officials contacted healthcare providers of cases (where that information was available) and requested medical records. They also requested tissue from brain biopsy (where available) for review by the National Prion Disease Pathology Surveillance Center (NPDPSC), which provides advanced neuropathologic and biochemical diagnostic services.

Eleven of the 17 patients were determined to be definite or probable classic CJD case patients (Table 13-5). Three patients had no form of CJD, and the diagnosis was unknown for three patients. All of the patients with definite or probable classic CJD were older than the age of 55 at the time of their death. The mean age at the time of diagnosis was 67.4 years, further supporting the diagnosis of classic CJD. None of the patients who had brain tissue submitted for examination at the NPDPSC were documented to have vCJD, the form associated with BSE exposure. None of the patients with classic CJD who were tested for a specific genetic marker that has been associated with vCJD had the marker. Given that patients did not have the variant form of CJD, investigators concluded that it was unlikely that the cases were related to consumption of BSE-contaminated meat or to one another. When investigators examined the occurrence of classic CJD in this cluster,

TABLE 13-4   Line List of CJD Cases

Case Number	Age	Death	State
1	70	1997	New Jersey
2	67	1997	New Jersey
3	70	2002	New Jersey
4	56	2003	New Jersey
5	78	2004	Virginia
6	29	2000	Pennsylvania
7	59	2004	Pennsylvania
8	72	2004	New Jersey
9	59	1997	Pennsylvania
10	83	2000	New Jersey
11	50	2001	Connecticut
12	70	2001	Maryland
13	71	2003	New Jersey
14	68	2003	Pennsylvania
15	72	1995	Pennsylvania
16	61	1995	Pennsylvania
17	69	1995	Delaware

Sources: Adapted from Centers for Disease Control and Prevention. Creutzfeldt-Jakob disease not related to a common venue—New Jersey, 1995–2004. *Morb Mortal Weekly Rep.* 2004:53(Early Release):1–4; Bresnitz EA, Gerwel M. An evaluation of a suspected cluster of Creutzfeldt-Jakob disease (CJD) in New Jersey. New Jersey Department of Health and Senior Services. 2004. http://www.state.nj.us/health/eoh/cjd2004.pdf. Accessed September 28, 2010.

they determined that the number of definite or probable cases was within the estimated normal range and concluded that the evidence did not support the hypothesis of an outbreak or cluster of CJD related to the racetrack.[15,16]

Step 2b: Expanded Evaluation

If investigators determine that a statistically significant excess of cases has likely occurred, the next decision they have to make is whether to undertake additional studies to better define the characteristics of the cluster. Proceeding to Step 2b may require a field investigation involving healthcare providers and the general community.

Expanding the evaluation requires investigators to complete the following tasks:

• Reconsider the initial case definition to determine if it should be more sensitive or more specific

• Establish the most appropriate time and geographic boundaries

TABLE 13-5   Line List of Creutzfeldt-Jakob Disease Cases

Case Number	Tissue Examination	Diagnosis	Other Comment
1	Yes*	Classic CJD[†]	Autopsy
2	Yes	Classic CJD[†]	Autopsy
3	Yes*	Classic CJD[†]	Brain biopsy
4	Yes*	Classic CJD[†]	Autopsy
5	Yes*	Classic CJD[†]	Brain biopsy
6	Yes*	Not CJD	Autopsy
7	Yes*	Not CJD	Autopsy
8	Yes	Not CJD	Autopsy
9	No	Classic CJD	
10	No	Classic CJD	
11	No	Classic CJD	
12	No	Classic CJD	
13	No	Classic CJD	
14	No	Classic CJD	
15	No	Unknown	Under investigation
16	Unknown	Unknown	Under investigation
17	Unknown	Unknown	Under investigation

*Examined by NPDPSC.

[†]Definitive diagnosis (otherwise probable).

Sources: Adapted from Centers for Disease Control and Prevention. Creutzfeldt-Jakob disease not related to a common venue—New Jersey, 1995–2004. *Morb Mortal Weekly Rep.* 2004:53(Early Release):1–4; Bresnitz EA, Gerwel M. An evaluation of a suspected cluster of Creutzfeldt-Jakob disease (CJD) in New Jersey. New Jersey Department of Health and Senior Services. 2004. http://www.state.nj.us/health/eoh/cjd2004.pdf. Accessed September 28, 2010.

- Ascertain all potential cases within the defined time and geographic boundaries
- Identify appropriate database sources for cases and the population at risk, and determine their availability and quality
- Perform an in-depth review of the medical literature and consider whether the supposed association is epidemiologically and biologically plausible
- Assess the likelihood that clustered health events are related statistically, temporally, and physiologically to the supposed exposure or exposures[1]

To make sure that case ascertainment is complete, investigators may need to review additional databases or medical records, or obtain additional information from the community. Although a survey of the community might identify previously unknown cases, investigators generally do not conduct formal surveys until Stage 4 of the investigation process (the etiologic investigation), and they need to be careful not to bias people who might eventually be recruited for such studies. For the same reason, investigators need to be cautious in using the media or other public notification procedures to identify cases at this stage of the investigation.

If investigators find a greater than expected number of cases of disease and compelling evidence cases are associated with the supposed exposure, they should consider whether it makes sense to begin an etiologic study. If they do not confirm an excess number of cases, it is time to prepare a summary report and end the investigation. Even if investigators do confirm an excess number of cases exists, they should conclude the investigation if the cases have no apparent plausible relationship to the supposed exposure, or if the evidence does not suggest an occurrence of potential biologic and public health importance. Most investigations of noninfectious disease clusters end at this step.[1]

Step 3: Determination of the Feasibility of Etiologic Investigation

Before beginning an etiologic study to examine the association between the observed cluster and a particular exposure, investigators must determine the epidemiologic and logistical feasibility of carrying out such a study. First, they must determine the hypothesis to be tested. It should be clearly stated, and include the target population, the health event(s), and the exposure(s) of interest. Next, investigators should consider study designs, comparing the relative strengths and limitations of different methodological approaches, the cost of each design, and the likely utility of the information gained. The team should anticipate well-known methodological and logistical challenges—for example, the sample size, the appropriateness of using previously identified cases, the geographic area and time period concerned, and the selection of comparison/control subjects—and figure out how the investigation might overcome these challenges. The decision should take into account all options for geographic and time analysis, including using cases that were not part of the originally defined "cluster," expanding or using a different case definition, and changing the geographic area or time period.[1]

After investigators have selected a study design, they need to determine which information to collect about case patients and control subjects. Data needs will largely be based on the medical literature about the hypothesized association of the specified health event and the supposed exposure, and are likely to include clinical findings and laboratory test results. Investigators also need to collect data on other known and putative causes of the health event, confounders, and effect modifiers of the health event of concern. The logistics of the data collection and the attendant costs are another important concern.[1]

Determining how to measure (or estimate) the suspected exposure is critical to an etiologic study. Before deciding to proceed to an etiologic study, investigators need to answer these questions:

- If there is no valid measure of exposure to the etiologic agent, how can the study be undertaken?

- Are there clinical or environmental tests for the etiologic agent, or can such tests be developed? How sensitive are these tests?

- Given the time elapsed since exposure to the agent, will the test still be useful?
- If investigators find the supposed agent in the environment, does that mean the agent has been taken up by the body?
- Is the reported exposure history a good predictor of true exposure?[1]

Determining whether the etiologic investigation is logistically and financially feasible might be relatively straightforward. Determining whether the study is likely to be productive, so that the benefits of the study justify the effort, is not so simple. Etiologic studies of clusters of diseases are not likely to be successful unless the disease is extremely rare and the frequency of the disease has suddenly increased. Furthermore, the etiologic agent must be measurable—or at least reliably correlated with some activity or other measurable characteristic—and must leave a physiological response in the bodies of those exposed to it. Investigators also must be able to select an appropriate control group, so levels of exposure must vary within the population.[17]

As they sift through the medical, scientific, and practical questions, investigators also must assess the epidemiologic and policy implications of, and likely community reactions to, doing the study—or not doing it. If an etiologic investigation is feasible and affordable, investigators should proceed. If the investigation is logistically impossible, is prohibitively expensive, or is not likely to affect existing policies or programs despite the results, investigators may decide to forego the investigation and draft a summary report that carefully explains why further investigation is not feasible.[1]

Step 4: Conducting an Etiologic Study

Finally, if investigators have passed "go" on the first three steps, it is time to undertake an etiologic study and examine the association between the exposure of interest and the disease or health event. Such a study requires extensive resources. To be worth the effort and expense, it should generate knowledge about the broader epidemiologic and public health issues that the cluster raised—not merely explain a specific cluster.[1]

Investigators begin the etiologic investigation by writing a formal study protocol that describes the data collection methods to be used and the data elements to be collected. Next, they lay out the detailed steps for data collection, processing, and quality control/assurance, and develop an appropriate plan of data analysis.[1] At this point, study design decisions will be unique to the particular study and further guidance is outside the scope of this book. Reviewing the concepts covered in Chapters 7 and 8 might be helpful to public health personnel who find themselves involved in a noninfectious disease cluster investigation.

Communications

Communications is a critical component of every step of a cluster investigation and the key to a satisfactory outcome, no matter how far the investigation progresses. Communication begins with receipt of the initial report and education of the person(s) reporting the cluster, and continues as the investigation unfolds and information is shared with community groups and the news media. Even after the final report summarizing the investigation and its findings is released, investigators need to communicate the findings of ongoing and completed investigations to all interested parties—public health managers, healthcare providers, members of the general public and the news media, and the broader public health and scientific communities. The presentation and level of detail will vary widely, depending on the intended audience and the purpose of the communication. As noted earlier in the chapter, a cluster investigation may also require specialized expertise, especially in the area of risk communication.

Risk Communication

Public communication about clusters of disease largely revolves around the community's perception of the risk involved. Of course, the risk community members perceive may not necessarily match the estimates of risk produced by mathematical or scientific assessments of a cluster. This divergence may involve more than the health department's failure to communicate the true risk or the community's inability to understand; rather, it likely represents the complicated reactions of people to something they believe has made them, their families, and their neighbors ill or puts them in danger of becoming ill.

Many factors influence risk perception (Table 13-6), some of which may not be rational. Even so, all of these factors help explain why simply conveying the "facts" may not be enough to educate members of the community or allay their fears. Understanding how people perceive risk helps investigators prepare for reactions that may appear irrational and understand how concern can sometimes grow to outrage. Public health officials need to be aware of the factors that influence risk perception and anticipate how they might affect the public's response in any particular situation.

TABLE 13-6   **Factors Influencing Risk Perception**

- Risks perceived to be natural are more accepted than risks perceived to be human-made.
- Risks perceived to be statistical are more accepted than risks perceived to be catastrophic.
- Risks perceived to be generated by a trusted source are more accepted than risks perceived to be generated by an untrusted source.
- Risks perceived to be familiar are more accepted than risks perceived to be exotic.
- Risks perceived to affect adults are more accepted than risks perceived to affect children.

Source: Adapted from Fischoff B, Lichtenstein S, Slovic P, et al. *Acceptable Risk.* Cambridge, UK: Cambridge University Press; 1981.

Given the potentially volatile consequences of risk perception, investigators need to proceed carefully in risk communications. Covello and Allen suggest the following principles for improving the effectiveness of risk communications with the public:

1. Carefully plan communications and constantly evaluate their efforts. Know who the audience is, what their concerns are, how they perceive risk, and whom they trust, and establish measurable objectives and evaluate communication activities based on these objectives.

2. Accept and involve the public as a partner. The goal of communications should be to produce an informed public, not to defuse public concerns or to provide a substitute for real actions. Involve the community at the earliest stage possible, and work toward developing a mutual understanding of the limitations and strengths of available investigation methods.

3. Listen to the public's concerns. Recognize that people's values and feelings are a legitimate aspect of a cluster investigation and that people may convey valuable information when they express their concerns.

4. Be honest, frank, and open. Research shows that public assessment of how much public health officials can be trusted and believed is based on four factors: empathy and caring, competence and expertise, honesty and openness, and dedication and commitment. Trust and credibility are difficult to obtain; once lost, they are almost impossible to regain.

5. Work with other credible sources. Cooperating with sources that the public knows and trusts can help to legitimize the agency's response and improve its credibility in the eyes of the public.

6. Understand and meet the needs of the news media. Working with the media is a primary opportunity to communicate with the public; it is crucial to develop positive relationships with reporters, editors, and producers. (This process is discussed in more detail in the next subsection.)

7. Speak clearly and with compassion, always acknowledging the tragedy of an illness, injury, or death. Empathetic communication may be much more satisfying to the public than well-founded facts and detailed analyses.[18]

Working with the News Media

Working with the news media can help investigators communicate with the public, simply because the news media reach a large proportion of the community on a regular basis. Members of the media know how to get the public's attention and hold it much better than public health officials do. To work effectively with reporters, editors, and producers, investigators must address their needs and understand how they select and present stories. One study of news media coverage of disease clusters found that the media focused on human-interest stories, conflicting information about risk, the parties to blame for the disease, and political implications. The buried chemical wastes in the Love Canal section of Niagara Falls, New York, and open-air testing of nuclear devices at Yucca Flats, Nevada, are examples of stories that engaged the media's interest at all of these levels.[19]

In addition to recognizing what attracts the attention of the media, investigators must recognize that news stories may simplify complex, technical explanations, losing subtle distinctions or qualifications. Greenberg and Wartenberg suggest six strategies that might help investigators gain better control of an interview and influence coverage of the story for the better:

1. Bring two or three main points to an interview, and let the reporter know they are critical to getting it right.

2. Assume that journalists will not have a background in your field.

3. Do not use jargon. Simplify your message so the journalist will not do it for you.

4. Prepare a news release with important risk information—number of cases, types of diseases, research that is under way, a comparison of local rates to state rates, possible environmental causes, possible confounders, and other possible disease outcomes, for example.

5. Stick to what you know and make it clear when you are speculating.

6. Be prepared for personal questions—"Would you allow your child to live in this neighborhood?"—and questions about blame or the political angle of the story.[19]

Summary

Most noninfectious disease clusters result from coincidence and chance, but cluster investigations can still serve a useful purpose, allowing public health practitioners to interact with the community, be responsive to their needs, and learn about exposures of concern. Occasionally, cluster investigations yield new hypotheses about previously unsuspected relationships between diseases and their causes; most cluster investigations, however, fail to produce insights into exposure–disease interactions.

Clusters are usually based on small case numbers and are not readily amenable to epidemiologic analyses. Furthermore, most reported clusters tend to involve health conditions whose usual causes are unknown or little understood. Investigating supposed exposure–disease links satisfactorily can also be very difficult because of the long lag between a supposed exposure and illness or because it is simply not clear what should be investigated. Because cluster investigations can be a drain on scarce public health resources, public health departments must balance the search for knowledge with the need to fulfill ongoing public health responsibilities. Laboratory-based sciences and large epidemiologic investigations are often more effective ways to examine both the small potential risks and the complex biological phenomena associated with clusters of noninfectious health events.

Nonetheless, public health practitioners need to be responsive to threats perceived by the public. When a public health agency responds to reports of noninfectious disease clusters, investigators should balance their duties to address public concerns and use scarce public health resources optimally. Following a stepwise investigation process, such as the four-step process described in this chapter, gives investigators multiple points at which to decide whether to end the investigation or proceed further based on available information. Making the agency's policy of a stepwise investigation process widely known and understood can help win the cooperation and trust of the medical community, the general public, the news media, and other key stakeholders. If investigators take a deliberate and transparent approach when a disease cluster is reported, all stakeholders can follow the investigation. Taking local concern about the cause of the disease cluster seriously without abandoning the prestated investigation process is also important, as is understanding and accommodating the needs of the media. By developing effective methods of communication, maintaining objectivity, and providing leadership for controversial and difficult issues, investigators can bring cluster investigations to a satisfying conclusion.

References

1. Centers for Disease Control and Prevention. Guidelines for investigating clusters of health events. *Morb Mortal Weekly Rep.* 1990;39(RR-11):1–16.
2. Lenz W. Kindliche mißbildungen nach medikament-einnahme während der gravidat [Malformations in children after a drug taken during pregnancy]. *Dtsch Med Wochenschr.* 1961;86:2555–6.
3. Centers for Disease Control and Prevention. Angiosarcoma of the liver among polyvinyl chloride workers—Kentucky. *Morb Mortal Weekly Rep.* 1974;23:49–50.
4. Centers for Disease Control and Prevention. Update: Eosinophilia-myalgia syndrome associated with ingestion of L-tryptophan—United States, through August 24, 1990. *Morb Mortal Weekly Rep.* 1990;39(34):587–9.
5. Cartwright RA. Cluster investigations: Are they worth it? *MJA.* 1999;171:172. http://www.mja.com.au/public/issues/171_4_160899/cartwright/cartwright.html. Accessed September 29, 2010.
6. Bender AP, Williams AN, Johnson RA, et al. Appropriate public health responses to clusters: The art of being responsibly responsive. *Am J Epidemiol.* 1990;132:S48–S52.
7. Blindauer K. *Cancer cluster survey.* Paper presented at Council of State and Territorial Epidemiologists Annual Conference; New York, NY; June 1997.
8. Caldwell GG. Twenty-two years of cancer cluster investigations at the Centers for Disease Control. *Am J Epid.* 1990;132(supp1):43–47.
9. Schulte PA, Ehrenberg RL, Singal M. Investigation of occupational cancer clusters: Theory and practice. *Am J Public Health.* 1987;77:52–6.
10. Thun MG, Sinks T. Understanding cancer clusters. *CA Cancer J Clin.* 2004;54:273–80.
11. Guidelines for investigating clusters of health events—appendix. Summary of methods for statistically assessing clusters of health events. *Morb Mortal Weekly Rep.* 1990;39(RR-11):17–23.
12. Gastroschisis Investigation Group. Investigation of a cluster of cases of gastroschisis in Bridgend County Borough during 2004. National Public Health Service for Wales. 2004.

http://www.wales.nhs.uk/sites3/Documents/719/FinalreportGastroschisisIG.pdf. Accessed May 18, 2011.

13. Porta M, ed. *A Dictionary of Epidemiology*. 5th ed. New York, NY: Oxford University Press; 2008.

14. New Jersey Department of Health and Senior Services. Childhood cancer incidence health consultation: A review and analysis of cancer registry data, 1979–1995, for Dover Township (Ocean County), New Jersey. 1997. http://www.state.nj.us/health/eoh/hhazweb/cansumm.pdf. Accessed August 13, 2008.

15. Centers for Disease Control and Prevention. Creutzfeldt-Jakob disease not related to a common venue—New Jersey, 1995–2004. *Morb Mortal Weekly Rep*. 2004; 53(Early Release):1–4.

16. Bresnitz EA, Gerwel M. An evaluation of a suspected cluster of Creutzfeldt-Jakob disease (CJD) in New Jersey. New Jersey Department of Health and Senior Services; 2004. http://www.state.nj.us/health/eoh/cjd2004.pdf. Accessed September 28, 2010.

17. Rothman KJ. A sobering start for the cluster busters' conference. *Am J Epidemiol*. 1990;132:S6–S13.

18. Covello VT, Allen F. *Seven Cardinal Rules of Risk Communication*. OPA publication 87-020.Washington, DC: U.S. Environmental Protection Agency, Office of Policy Analysis; 1988.

19. Greenberg MR, Wartenberg D. Understanding mass media coverage of disease clusters. *Am J Epidemiol*. 1990;132:S192–S195.

Chapter 14

Forensic Epidemiology Investigations

Sally B. Mountcastle
David B. Rice
Pia D. M. MacDonald

Learning Objectives

By the end of this chapter, the reader will be able to:

- Define forensic epidemiology and describe its role in the courtroom and in public health and law enforcement field investigations of crime sites.
- Cite examples of court cases in which epidemiologists or other public health officials have played a role.
- Cite examples of the use or attempted use of biological agents in criminal or terrorist events.
- Compare and contrast public health and law enforcement investigations.
- Differentiate between overt and covert bioterrorist incidents.
- Discuss the federal laws that govern investigations by public health officials and law enforcement officials.
- Identify key considerations for joint interviewing procedures.
- Describe the two primary criteria under which samples from a public health investigation can be introduced as evidence in a criminal case.
- Compare and contrast concepts of confidentiality in public health investigations and law enforcement investigations.
- Discuss protocols for dealing with the media and handling classified or sensitive information during forensic epidemiologic investigations.

Introduction

In most epidemiological investigations, investigators seek to discover exposure–disease associations caused by naturally occurring phenomena. Sometimes, however, human error may be the culprit in the outbreak—perhaps food is stored improperly or a cooling system is not properly maintained. Although investigators do not usually suspect criminal intent, occasionally public health practitioners and epidemiologists join experts from law enforcement and other fields to investigate deliberate poisonings, bioterrorist events, and

287

other health-related criminal cases. The terrorist attacks of September 11, 2001, and the anthrax attacks that followed made this cooperation more important than ever.

Public health investigations differ from law enforcement investigations in several ways. Although they share the end goal of preserving the public's safety, the means of investigating and achieving that goal differs pursuant to each group's core functions in society. Despite the differences in their approaches and methodologies, however, law enforcement and public health officials face many of the same challenges when investigating suspected bioterrorist events. High concentrations of a toxic or pathogenic agent may have been dispersed and a large primary cohort of people exposed; the agent may have been distributed in a well-traveled area; ill people may be taken to many different hospitals (making it difficult to recognize clusters); a deliberate second attack may affect first responders, among others; widespread panic may occur; and hospitals may become flooded with both sick and nonsick ("worried well") patients looking for treatment, vaccines, or reassurance about their health status. When all participants in the investigation of a suspected bioterrorist event are prepared to respond and can work efficiently and effectively together, they can minimize panic, ensure a rapid response, treat the sick, identify the source, and successfully identify and prosecute those involved in the attack.

This chapter focuses on the branch of epidemiology known as forensic epidemiology. It explores the similarities and differences between epidemiological and law enforcement investigations, and discusses the role of forensic epidemiology in the investigation of suspected bioterrorism and other criminal activities.

Forensic Epidemiology

Forensic epidemiology has traditionally been defined as the use of public health methods in a potential criminal investigation.[1] A classic example comes from the investigation of unexplained deaths in a children's hospital in 1980 and 1981. Epidemiological studies found a strong association between infant deaths and the duty times of a particular nurse, suggesting that a single individual might have injected patients with an overdose of digoxin.[2] Another example is when epidemiologists track the public health consequences of the illegal manufacture of methamphetamine and suggest ways to recognize and properly respond to laboratories where the drug is made, thereby helping responders prevent injuries.[3] Epidemiologists have also been called upon to help resolve disease-related litigation and serve as investigative experts, consulting experts, and expert witnesses in cases involving Agent Orange, Bendectin, diethylstilbestrol (DES), intrauterine contraceptive devices, and swine flu vaccine.[4]

Since the terrorist events of 2001, however, the term "forensic epidemiology" has been used broadly to define field-based investigations of confirmed or suspected bioterrorism attacks in which public health officials collaborate with officials from law enforcement and other agencies. In the 2001 anthrax investigations in the United States, for example, public health and law enforcement investigators worked together at the federal, state, and local levels to identify possible cases of anthrax, describe case and exposure characteristics, and initiate public health interventions to prevent additional people from becoming ill.[5]

Public health is just one of many disciplines that may participate in a field-based forensic epidemiology investigation. Local, state, and federal law enforcement officials;

fire departments; hospitals, health clinics, pharmacies, and laboratories; National Guard and other military units; and state and federal emergency management services may also play roles. In a health-related investigation of an event such as bioterrorism, public health and law enforcement officials fill key roles. Both groups share the goals of protecting the public, preventing or stopping the spread of disease, identifying those responsible for a threat or attack, and safeguarding all people involved in the response and investigative phases. During an investigation, law enforcement can offer criminology expertise, forensic laboratory collaboration, and connections to national and international law enforcement agencies; public health can offer expert medical and laboratory consultation and collaboration with national and international public health organizations.[6]

Examples of Health-Related Criminal or Terrorist Cases

The public is very much aware of the world's vulnerability to health-related criminal events. Table 14-1 offers examples of criminal attacks involving the use of biological agents since 1970. These events, which occurred at sites around the globe, illustrate the range of possible motives for attacks and the types of investigations in which law enforcement and public health might work together. In addition to the criminal acts listed in Table 14-1, perpetrators have injected HIV-contaminated blood into individuals, including one child.[7] Officials have also investigated numerous hoaxes or pretend disseminations of biological weapons. Between 1998 and 2000, for example, at least 105 anthrax hoaxes occurred at U.S. post offices, abortion clinics, high schools, energy plants, congressional offices, and hospitals.[8] Hoaxes are also crimes and take resources to investigate.

TABLE 14-1 **A Sample of Confirmed Use, Probable Use, and Threatened Use (with Confirmed Possession) of Agents Involved in Criminal or Terrorist Events from 1970 to 1997**

Date	Place	Agent Used in Event	Actual or Alleged Event
1997*	New Zealand	Rabbit hemorrhagic disease (RHD) virus	Farmers used RHD virus as an animal control tool.
1996*	Dallas, Texas	*Shigella dysenteriae* type 2	A disgruntled employee used laboratory stock culture to contaminate pastries eaten by lab staff; 12 workers contracted severe diarrheal illness.
1996†	England	*Yersinia enterocolitica*	A man attempted to extort money from British dairies by threatening to contaminate milk.
1990‡	Scotland	*Giardia*	Feces containing Giardia were allegedly placed in a water tank.

(continues)

TABLE 14-1 A Sample of Confirmed Use, Probable Use, and Threatened Use (with Confirmed Possession) of Agents Involved in Criminal or Terrorist Events from 1970 to 1997 (*continued*)

Date	Place	Agent Used in Event	Actual or Alleged Event
1990–1995*	Japan	*Bacillus anthracis*, botulinum toxin, sarin	Aum Shinrikyo, a religious cult, allegedly released toxic agents on several occasions using motor vehicles, a sprayer on a roof, and briefcases or jars in the Tokyo subway system; one attempt (with sarin) was successful in causing injury.
1989‡	Namibia	Cholera, yellow fever virus	The Civilian Cooperation Bureau allegedly contaminated the water supply in a refugee camp.
1985‡*	Mexico	Screwworm	Workers allegedly spread the parasite to protect jobs in an eradication program.
1984*	The Dalles, Oregon	*Salmonella typhimurium*	Members of the Rajneeshee cult put the agent into salad bars at restaurants to influence voter turnout; 751 people became sick.
1984†	New York	*Clostridium tetani*, *Clostridium botulinum*	Two men were convicted of telephone fraud and conspiracy to commit telephone fraud; they were accused of obtaining biological cultures under false pretenses, possibly in an attempt to kill racehorses in an insurance fraud scheme.
1978*	London	Ricin	Bulgarian dissident Georgi Markov was killed by a poison dart filled with *ricin* fired from an umbrella in London.
1977–1980*	Norway	Curacit	A nursing home worker used the agent to kill 22 patients.
1972†	Chicago, Illinois	*Salmonella typhi*	Teenagers plotted to infect the municipal water system.
1970*	Canada	*Ascaris suum* (parasite)	A man infected four roommates, two of whom suffered acute respiratory failure.

*Confirmed use.

†Threatened use (with confirmed possession).

‡Probable or possible use.

Source: Adapted from Carus WS. *Bioterrorism and Biocrimes: The Illicit Use of Biological Agents Since 1900.* Washington, DC: Center for Counterproliferation Research, National Defense University; February 2001. http://www.fas.org/irp/threat/cbw/carus.pdf. Accessed May 20, 2011.

Forensic Epidemiology Investigations

Many public health workers encounter forensic epidemiology through health-related criminal investigations, working side-by-side with law enforcement officials. Because an ordinary public health investigation differs from a law enforcement investigation, however, people in both fields have had to learn how their counterparts conduct investigations.

Some public health officials may be reluctant to share information with law enforcement. They may be concerned that they will be held legally liable for releasing patient information without consent, or they may fear that they will have difficulty obtaining information that will help them identify and control diseases of any type if patients believe they cannot trust public health practitioners to keep medical information confidential.[9] Similarly, some law enforcement officials may not want to share investigation information with public health officials because they are concerned about the safety of confidential informants or the security of classified sources. They may also be worried that if they exchange sensitive information with public health officials, more individuals will know the specifics of the case, thus increasing the likelihood that the inadvertent release of sensitive information will help suspects avoid detection.[9] If these issues can be worked out, preferably in advance of a serious event, representatives of the public health and law enforcement communities can work together to identify criminal events or public health emergencies as early as possible, and to obtain and share critical information as quickly as possible.[9]

Since 2001, the U.S. Congress has passed the Uniting and Strengthening America by Providing Appropriate Tools Required to Intercept and Obstruct Terrorism (USA PATRIOT) Act of 2001 and dozens of other laws to protect citizens and manage bioterrorist and other homeland security events (the Library of Congress lists many of them at http://thomas.loc. gov/home/terrorleg.htm). These laws underpin federal plans to define or clarify terrorist threats and incidents, including bioterrorist events, and coordinate the activities of law enforcement, public health, and other agencies in the event of a threat or actual terrorist incident. For example, the National Response Framework, which in 2008 replaced the earlier National Response Plan, drew authority from the Homeland Security Act of 2002 and numerous other statutes, regulations, executive orders, and presidential directives to establish a comprehensive, national, all-hazards approach to domestic incident response.[10]

In addition to adapting to the federal laws and regulations that apply to bioterrorist and other forensic investigations, public health and law enforcement personnel in many states and localities have held workshops and conducted training sessions and exercises to increase their ability to work together in the case of an outbreak that might be related to bioterrorism. Recognizing the differences and similarities between public health investigations and law enforcement investigations can help the two disciplines work together effectively to protect the public's health and to identify and prosecute individuals responsible for health-related criminal acts. The following subsection discusses some of the points at which public health and law enforcement investigations differ, and describes how personnel from both fields can overcome these differences.

Criminal Intent

Public health investigators usually assume that outbreaks have occurred naturally or via unintentional human error. They look for mistakes in food preparation, changes in the environment, and other unintentional incidents as the cause of an unusual disease occurrence. Their law enforcement counterparts, in contrast, typically become involved when evidence suggests that the outbreak or event is the result of a crime. If the public health community recognizes early on that criminal intent may be involved in a health-related incident, its members can contribute to preserving evidence and solving the crime.

Public health practitioners may be called upon to help investigate two types of criminal activity: covert attacks and overt attacks.[11] In an overt attack, the perpetrator takes responsibility for an action, such as releasing an agent or issuing a threatening communication.[9] An example of an overt attack is the intentional release of sarin nerve agent in the Tokyo subway system in 1995.[11] When an attack is overt, law enforcement officials will likely detect the event first, law enforcement and emergency management teams will be the first responders, and the site will be handled as a crime scene.[11] Public health officials may be asked to help with the threat assessment process and to identify potential public health considerations; they will also be called on if people are ill or preventive health services are necessary.[9]

In a covert attack, no group or individual takes responsibility and the incident may not be initially recognized as a deliberate attack.[11] The large *Salmonella typhimurium* outbreak that took place in 1984 in Oregon is an example of a covert attack: Authorities did not discover until several months after hundreds of people became ill that members of a religious commune had deliberately contaminated restaurant salad bars with the goal of making people ill and affecting voter turnout and subsequently the outcome of local elections.[12] (See the case study near the end of this chapter.) Unlike in an overt attack, primary healthcare providers are likely to be the first to observe and report unusual injuries or illnesses resulting from a covert attack.[13] Public health officials are likely to detect these reports through routine surveillance practices and begin an investigation. The public health response will focus first on diagnosis, medical care, and treatment. Public health officials must notify law enforcement if they suspect that the event may be the result of a criminal act rather than a natural outbreak or source of exposure. Personnel from both disciplines must then work together to determine whether the event involves bioterrorism.[9]

To ensure prompt and proper response to a potential bioterrorist attack, local and state health department officials should have an emergency preparation and response plan in place that includes protocols for notification procedures in the event of a bioterrorist incident. According to the outline for such a plan available on the Centers for Disease Control and Prevention (CDC) website, for example, a local health officer who is informed of a bioterrorist incident or threat would first notify the Federal Bureau of Investigation (FBI) and local law enforcement, and then notify state health department and other response partners according to a pre-established notification list.[14] Furthermore, if state and local public health departments have established good working relationships with their law enforcement counterparts, they are more likely to contact law enforcement early in the investigation, so a threat assessment can begin.[9]

Laws Governing an Investigation

Historically, very different laws have governed public health and law enforcement investigations. These laws represent the historic tension between the police powers written into the U.S. Constitution, which give state actors and government officials, including public health officials, broad latitude to abate public nuisances and regulate other threats to public health, and the Bill of Rights, which enumerates the rights of people accused of crimes.[15] In North Carolina, for example, statutes give health directors the ability to respond quickly to health-related threats, including powers to review medical records, implement control measures, and impose quarantine and isolation.[16] By contrast, law enforcement officials must first obtain a search warrant to investigate a crime. Under normal circumstances, a law enforcement officer can conduct a search and seize a person or property without a search warrant or other authorization only if the person is under arrest, consent to the search is given, or circumstances represent a serious, credible, and "immediate" threat to the public ("exigent circumstances").[16]

Future bioterrorist attacks could force public officials to choose between collecting evidence that will be admissible in court and protecting members of the public.[14] Careful planning, including the involvement of liaison personnel who are cross-trained in the public health aspects of communicable diseases and in law enforcement and criminal investigations, can help public health and law enforcement officials build mutual collaboration and understanding before a biological attack forces them to work together.[9]

Joint Interviewing

Whenever possible, public health and law enforcement personnel should work jointly in teams to conduct interviews with victims and witnesses.[9] Establishing in advance a process for joint interviews can minimize the number of times people are interviewed and allow each interview to reflect the distinct perspectives and needs of law enforcement and public health. Even within joint interviews, however, it may be important for interviewees to have confidential communications with public health officials about specific health-related issues that they might be reluctant to discuss with law enforcement personnel present.[9]

If a joint interview is not possible, the investigator from each discipline should at least be aware of the type of information that his or her counterpart is seeking. Developing lists of the information each team of investigators requires and potential means of acquiring that information can facilitate efficiency and reduce barriers to information sharing.[9]

As noted earlier in this section, both legal concerns and issues of ethics and trust can lead to tension between public health and law enforcement personnel when it comes to interviewing persons who may be victims, suspects, or witnesses in a bioterrorism or other criminal investigation. While both disciplines share broad goals of protecting public health and safety, they are guided by different rules and tasked with different, sometimes conflicting duties. The law enforcement investigator sets out to collect relevant and admissible evidence that will withstand objections in the courtroom, whereas the public health investigator seeks to gather data that will stand up to the scrutiny of subject matter experts and the global scientific community, with the ultimate aim of developing effective control measures.[11] When the two communities work together on an investigation, public health officials may fear that the presence of law enforcement personnel will compromise the collection of sensitive medical information—such as data on illegal drug use—that may be critical to understanding the outbreak, while law enforcement officials may believe that accommodating their public health counterparts will jeopardize their ability to maintain the criminal law standards that will ensure that whoever carried out the crime is punished.[15] Planning and forethought can alleviate the tension and allow law enforcement and public health officials to collaborate effectively on interviews that may have serious implications for both public health investigations and subsequent criminal prosecutions.

Evidence

In a bioterrorism investigation, the need to move rapidly to collect and test samples to save lives can take priority over the normal evidence collection procedures followed by law enforcement officials. In general, however, public health officials can collect and manage specimens so that they can be used later as evidence in a criminal case.[9] Two criteria must be met for information from public health investigations to be used in criminal investigations.

First, investigators must collect and manage the information while maintaining a proper chain of custody so that attorneys can authenticate it and admit it into evidence during trial. A chain of custody is the chronological documentation or paper trail showing the seizure, custody, control, transfer, analysis, and disposition of evidence. Legal protocols require preservation of the chain of custody in a law enforcement investigation: Law enforcement officials are responsible for creating an incident report, maintaining the chain of custody, and transporting a specimen or other piece of evidence to a laboratory or other facility. Law enforcement officials use a special form to document the chronological history of a piece of evidence. This chain of custody form provides the name or initials of the individual who collected the evidence, each person or entity who subsequently had custody of it, the date the item was collected or transferred, the agency and case number, the victim's or suspect's name, and a brief description of the item.[17]

Second, information originating from public health investigations and used for criminal investigations must be obtained as part of a "legitimate public health investigation." For example, laboratory results from food samples taken from a salad bar during the investigation of food poisoning at a social function may be used in a subsequent criminal trial if investigators find that the food was intentionally contaminated. Conversely, food inspectors cannot use their authority to inspect a restaurant's kitchen (an administrative search) as a pretext for searching the lockers of people who work at the restaurant. For information obtained from a search of lockers to be admissible in court, a law enforcement officer would need to have probable cause and obtain a warrant from a magistrate before conducting such a search.[15]

Because careful handling of specimens and other evidence is as important to successful epidemiological investigations as it is to successful criminal investigations, public health officials should also establish a proper chain of custody whenever they collect and process specimens.[15] Persons documented as custodians of the item should be able to testify in court that the item was secure, unaltered, and uncontaminated during the time it was in their custody; they should also be able to describe the procedures used to store, examine, test, and otherwise process the item.[19]

Initial and confirmatory testing of specimens in a suspected criminal or bioterrorism case may involve state health departments and the CDC's Laboratory Response Network as well as state and federal law enforcement laboratories. As health departments develop plans to handle materials that may become part of a forensic epidemiologic investigation, they should ensure that the following tasks are completed:

- Seek CDC guidance
- Establish agreements with law enforcement that specify which circumstances would necessitate specific lab tests for criminal investigations
- Conduct training so that public health practitioners will know when to institute a chain of custody for evidence in a biological incident[9]

Confidentiality

Public health officials are primarily concerned with the confidentiality of patients and their medical records. Under North Carolina statutes, for example, all records containing privileged patient medical information in the possession of the state health department or local health departments are considered confidential and are not matters of public record.[16] Although a person in charge of a healthcare facility may report to the state or local health director any events that may indicate the existence of a case or outbreak of an illness, condition, or health hazard, to the extent possible, personally identifiable information should not be disclosed during this report.

In an outbreak setting, public health officials can contact, interview, and offer testing to all case patients, case contacts, and even contacts who are considered to be suspect cases, but confidentiality must be maintained. As soon as a bioterrorist incident or criminal intent is suspected, however, a law enforcement official may gain access to confidential or protected health information for the purposes of the investigation. At that point, confidentiality concerns apply to the person not only as a patient, but also as a potential witness, informant, or defendant. Law enforcement officials must be concerned about confidentiality in regard to ensuring national security, maintaining the confidentiality of a witness or informant, and preserving the integrity of a case for prosecution.[11]

Because law enforcement officials may request access to clinical samples as part of a criminal investigation, issues of confidentiality may also extend to clinical samples collected from patients. As a public health department develops a plan to work with law enforcement officials, it should research applicable state and federal statutes and establish protocols to comply with the legal requirements to share the information.

Media

The media play an important role in the public reaction to a biological incident. At various points in the investigation, public health and law enforcement personnel will need to share critical information with the media to confirm that something unusual has happened, provide rumor control, convey information about communicable diseases, address the psychological issues of biological terrorism, and reassure the public that the incident is over.[9] To release appropriate messages at appropriate times, and to prevent the untimely release of unauthorized information, public health and law enforcement personnel, including FBI, CDC, and state and local officials, must coordinate their messages through a joint information center. [9] The agencies involved should designate a single point of contact for law enforcement and for public health agencies to coordinate communications with the media.[9]

Classified/Sensitive Information

As participants in a joint law enforcement and public health investigation, public health officials may be required to review classified or sensitive information. Public health officials should consider which personnel should have access to these types of information. Some public health officials should hold security clearances to communicate with law enforcement when necessary, and secure equipment such as phone lines and fax machines should be available for these communications. Some of the concerns of both communities may be addressed through agreements that identify the kinds of information to be shared and establish safeguards to limit unintentional release of information to unauthorized personnel.[9]

Case Study: Bioterrorism Attack in Oregon Using *Salmonella typhimurium*
The first large-scale use of germs by terrorists on U.S. soil took place in 1984, in The Dalles, Oregon, a community of 10,000 in the Columbia River Gorge near Mount Hood. In 1981, the followers of a religious cult called the Rajneeshees bought a remote 64,000-acre ranch 2 hours from The Dalles, the county seat of Wasco County. Over the next few years, the Rajneeshees, who were followers of an Indian man known as the Bhagwan Shree Rajneesh, built a small city named Rajneeshpuram and established their own police force. In 1982, they moved into the neighboring town of Antelope, winning electoral control of the town council and taking over the local school. In 1984, the commune wanted to expand again, and planned to gain electoral control of the county commission and other posts.

On September 9, 1984, employees and customers of Shakey's Pizza in The Dalles began getting ill with stomach cramps, chills, fever, and intense diarrhea and vomiting. The following week, the Wasco-Sherman Public Health Department received complaints from people who had become ill after eating in other restaurants in The Dalles. A pathologist at Mid-Columbia Medical Center determined from a patient's stool that the bacterium making people sick was *Salmonella*. Soon after, the Oregon State Public Health Laboratory in Portland determined the pathogen was *Salmonella typhimurium*, a common agent in food poisoning.

Case Study: Bioterrorism Attack in Oregon Using *Salmonella typhimurium* (continued)

On September 21, a second wave of infection swept through the town. Soon Mid-Columbia's laboratory was overwhelmed, and all 125 of its hospital beds were filled. By the end of the outbreak, nearly 1000 people had reported symptoms; *Salmonella* was confirmed in 751. It was the largest outbreak of its kind in the state's history.

The state asked the CDC and its Epidemic Intelligence Service (EIS) for assistance, and the local health sanitarian recommended that restaurants in the area voluntarily discontinue salad-bar service. More than 20 public health workers from local, state, and national agencies conducted an exhaustive investigation, interviewing hundreds of patients, food handlers, and others who had visited the restaurants. They measured salad-bar temperatures, inspected food-handling practices, visited a dairy farm in Washington state, tested local water systems, and inspected a farm that had suffered from septic-tank malfunctions. Suspect foods from several restaurants were tested. Investigators determined that only people who had eaten from salad bars or had ordered side dishes of mixed salads had gotten sick. They found no common source for the food—the lettuce and other vegetables had come from different suppliers. *Salmonella* was discovered in the milk served with coffee in one restaurant and in the blue cheese dressing served at another, but the dry mix used to prepare the dressing was not infected with *Salmonella*.

Some residents suspected the Rajneeshees of poisoning the townspeople with *Salmonella*. Judge William Hulse, a county commissioner, had become ill after visiting the commune the previous year and had nearly died. He thought a glass of water he had been given had made him ill, but he had no proof and did not file a complaint.

Other officials believed the commune was being unfairly harassed for its members' religious beliefs. The deputy state epidemiologist reported that the investigation "found 'no evidence' to support the hypothesis that the outbreak was the result of deliberate contamination." Federal scientists concurred, saying they had been unable to find the source of the outbreak and that inadequate hand washing on the part of food handlers could have been to blame. Their report said there was "no epidemiologic evidence" of deliberate contamination.

It was not surprising the investigation did not recognize the illnesses in The Dalles as bioterrorism. A CDC official said the public health investigators had been swayed by concerns about bigotry and had been determined not to jump to conclusions. In addition, he noted, the illnesses could easily have been caused by a natural eruption of *Salmonella*.

More than a year later, however, residents of The Dalles would find out that the Rajneeshees had committed bioterrorism in their community. In September 1985, the Bhagwan Shree Rajneesh accused one of the commune's leaders, Ma Anand Sheela, and her allies of several crimes, including trying to kill fellow members who had challenged Sheela's authority, trying to contaminate a water system in The Dalles, and conducting experiments on mice to test poisons that could kill people slowly without detection. Federal and state police formed a joint task force and began an investigation. Eventually, investigators obtained search warrants and entered the ranch. In the laboratory of the commune's medical clinic, Michael Skeels, the director of the Oregon State Public Health Laboratory, found glass vials containing *Salmonella*

(continues)

Case Study: Bioterrorism Attack in Oregon Using *Salmonella typhimurium* (*continued*)

"bactrol disks" that a nurse had obtained from VWR Scientific, a medical supply company in Seattle. The *Salmonella* on the disks, which held germs normally used in diagnostic testing, was tested by the CDC in Atlanta and found to match the strain that had made people ill in The Dalles the previous year.

Federal and state law enforcement agents linked the cult with a variety of crimes, including establishing the largest, most sophisticated illegal electronic eavesdropping system in U.S. history and plotting to kill or sicken 11 people on an "enemies list." The investigation eventually established that a nurse at the clinic had overseen experiments with poisons, chemicals, and bacteria, obtaining dangerous pathogens from the American Type Culture Collection, a private germ bank. An invoice from the company revealed that the cult ordered *Salmonella typhi*, *Salmonella paratyphi*, *Francisella tularensis*, *Enterobacter cloacae*, *Neisseria gonorrhoeae*, and *Shigella dysenteriae*. Several of these pathogens, which were delivered between the two waves of the *Salmonella* outbreak, could have caused even more severe cases of illness than *S. typhimurium*, and almost certainly some deaths.

Because the investigation began more than a year after the poisonings, the cult had ample time to destroy evidence. No pathogens ordered from the germ bank were ever found at the ranch. Public health officials, who would have recognized the significance of the pathogens, did not learn of the orders until years later, but considered both the pathogens and the timing of their arrival at the ranch suspicious. Skeels, the director of the state laboratory, said that several of the pathogens were not necessary in a laboratory the size of the clinic's, and that these bacteria could have been used for terrorism. State and federal investigators eventually concluded that approximately a dozen people were involved in the plot to poison people in The Dalles with *Salmonella*, and that the plot was a by-product of the cult's legal war with the county and its ambition to win the November elections and take control of the county government.

According to sworn affidavits and court testimony in 1985 and 1986, the cult's leadership had come up with the idea of making enough of the 20,000 residents of Wasco County sick that the 4000 members of the commune could sway the election. The cult ordered the bactrol disks and used the bacteria in them to culture and produce large amounts of the bacteria. One cult member testified that she had tested the *Salmonella* on Judge Hulse, giving him tainted water at a restaurant in Antelope and again when he visited the ranch. Prosecutors were able to document poisonings at 4 of the 10 contaminated restaurants and at a supermarket in The Dalles. They also believed the cult had carried out similar attacks in other Oregon cities, including Salem and Portland.

Despite sickening at least 751 people in the fall of 1984 in a test for the planned election attacks (and trying to register as voters some 3000 homeless people whom they had invited to the ranch from New York and other cities), the cult abandoned both the poisonings and the registration schemes. The candidates backed by the Rajneeshees were defeated. In September 1985, Rajneesh was arrested in Charlotte, North Carolina, while trying to flee the country. Other cult leaders were detained by West German police and extradited to the United States. There was no antiterrorism law at the time, so the cultists were charged with violating

Case Study: Bioterrorism Attack in Oregon Using *Salmonella typhimurium* (*continued*)

immigration laws and a product-tampering statute that had been passed in 1982 after the poisoning of Tylenol capsules. Rajneesh received a suspended sentence, paid $400,000 in fines, and left the United States. Two other leaders pleaded no contest to charges of attempted murder, illegal wiretapping, the poisoning of Judge Hulse, causing the *Salmonella* outbreak in The Dalles, and other crimes. They served less than four years in federal prison, and fled the country before Oregon could seek additional remedies against them. Most of the restaurants never recovered, and closed after the outbreaks.

The case received little media attention. Realizing how easily the Rajneeshees had carried out the attacks and not wanting to encourage copycat crimes, public health officials decided not to publish a study about the incident. Nevertheless, as the first large-scale use of germs by terrorists on American soil, the attack was significant, and pointed out many shortcomings in the U.S. system for preventing and responding to bioterrorism. It was very easy for the cultists to obtain pathogens from a germ bank; because it was so small, the Rajneeshees' laboratory did not have to register with the state. The relationship between law enforcement and public health was also problematic. Information was not shared, and it took some time to determine that a crime had been committed. Even to experts, the difference between a germ assault and a natural outbreak is difficult to detect; in both cases, many people become violently ill.

Source: Adapted from Miller J, Engelberg S, Broad W. *Germs: Biological Weapons and America's Secret War.* New York: Simon & Schuster; 2001.

Summary

Public health and law enforcement have conducted joint investigations of many health-related criminal events, and forensic epidemiology has been used in the courtroom for many years. The terrorism events of September 11, 2001, and the anthrax attacks that followed, however, dramatically highlighted the importance of cooperation between the public health and law enforcement communities in the investigation of bioterrorist events. High-level collaboration serves the respective public health and law enforcement objectives of preventing the spread of disease, forestalling public panic, and apprehending those responsible for attacks. The members of both communities require education about how their counterparts conduct investigations and how they can work together. Advance planning, established communication procedures, and mutual awareness and understanding can help public health officials work closely and effectively with law enforcement personnel to protect public safety and punish bioterrorists.

References

1. Goodman RA. *Basics of Public Health/Epidemiologic Investigations for Law Enforcement.* Presented at Forensic Epidemiology Training Course. November 2–5, 2002; Chapel Hill, NC.

2. Buehler JW, Smith LF, Wallace EM, et al. Unexplained deaths in a children's hospital. An epidemiologic assessment. *N Eng J Med.* 1985;313:211–6.

3. Centers for Disease Control and Prevention. Acute public health consequences of methamphetamine laboratories—16 states, January 2000–June 2004. *Morb Mortal Weekly Rep.* 2005;54(14):356–9.

4. Loue S. *Forensic Epidemiology: A Comprehensive Guide for Legal and Epidemiology Professionals.* Carbondale, IL: Southern Illinois University Press; 1999.

5. Jernigan DB, Raghunathan PL, Bell BP, et al. Investigation of bioterrorism-related anthrax, United States, 2001: Epidemiologic findings. *Emerging Infect Dis.* 2002;8:1019–1028.

6. Martinez D. *Law Enforcement and Forensic Epidemiology.* Presented at Forensic Epidemiology Training Course, November 2–5; 2002; Chapel Hill, NC.

7. Centers for Disease Control and Prevention. *HIV/AIDS Surveillance Report, 2004. Vol. 16.* Atlanta: US Department of Health and Human Services, Centers for Disease Control and Prevention; 2005.

8. Carus WS. *Bioterrorism and Biocrimes: The Illicit Use of Biological Agents since 1900.* Washington, DC: Center for Counterproliferation Research, National Defense University; February 2001. http://www.fas.org/irp/threat/cbw/carus.pdf. Accessed May 20, 2011.

9. *Criminal and Epidemiological Investigation Handbook.* 2006. Federal Bureau of Investigation, Centers for Disease Control and Prevention, U.S. Department of Justice, U.S. Army Soldier Biological Chemical Compound. http://www2a.cdc.gov/PHLP/docs/CrimEpiHandbook2006.pdf. Accessed September 14, 2010.

10. National Response Framework. Federal Emergency Management Agency. http://www.fema.gov/pdf/emergency/nrf/nrf-core.pdf. Accessed October 15, 2010.

11. Butler JC, Cohen ML, Friedman CR, et al. Collaboration between public health and law enforcement: New paradigms and partnerships for bioterrorism planning and response. *Emerging Infect Dis.* 2002;8:1152–1156. http://www.cdc.gov/ncidod/eid/vol8no10/02-0400.htm. Accessed May 18, 2011.

12. Torok TJ, Tauxe RV, Wise RP, et al. A large community outbreak of salmonellosis caused by intentional contamination of restaurant salad bars. *JAMA.* 1997;278:389–395.

13. Centers for Disease Control and Prevention. Biological and chemical terrorism: Strategic plan for preparedness and response. *Morb Mortal Weekly Rep.* 2000;RR04:1–14.

14. Protocols: Interim recommended notification procedures for local and state public health department leaders in the event of a bioterrorist incident. Centers for Disease Control and Prevention. Reviewed May 11, 2005. http://www.bt.cdc.gov/EmContact/Protocols.asp. Accessed September 14, 2010.

15. Richards EP. Collaboration between public health and law enforcement: The constitutional challenge. *Emerging Infect Dis.* 2002;8(10):157–1159. http://www.cdc.gov/ncidod/EID/vol8no10/02-0465.htm. Accessed March 31, 2010.

16. NC General Statutes. General Assembly of North Carolina. http://www.ncleg.net/gascripts/Statutes/Statutes.asp. Accessed September 14, 2010.

17. Technical Working Group on Crime Scene Investigation, National Institute of Justice. Crime scene investigation: A guide for law enforcement. January 2000. Available at: http://www.ncjrs.gov/pdffiles1/nij/178280.pdf. Accessed August 31, 2005.

Chapter 15

Geographic Information Systems for Field Epidemiology

Jennifer A. Horney
Rachel Wilfert
Matthew C. Simon
Morgan L. Johnson

Learning Objectives

By the end of this chapter, the reader will be able to:

- Discuss how maps can help present complex information.
- Describe geographic information systems (GIS).
- List ways that GIS are used in public health surveillance and outbreak investigations.
- Cite examples of GIS use in public health surveillance and outbreak investigations.
- Describe how global positioning systems can enhance GIS capabilities.
- Define Community Assessment for Public Health Emergency Response (rapid needs assessments).
- Discuss how GIS can help public health practitioners conduct assessments rapidly and efficiently.

Introduction

Public health practitioners and outbreak investigators have increasingly used geographic information systems (GIS) to help them collect and analyze spatial field data rapidly and effectively. Investigators can use GIS to perform a variety of critical public health functions, including mapping the distribution of infectious diseases, chronic diseases, environmental exposures, and other spatially referenced data; investigating clusters of disease; and exploring proximity to risk factors. GIS can provide necessary information rapidly to local decision makers, thereby improving the efficiency and effectiveness of public health emergency response.

This chapter discusses the traditional uses of mapping in outbreak investigations, surveillance activities, and other public health investigations. It also covers the GIS software programs that are making it faster and easier then ever to enter, store, and analyze spatial data. The chapter concludes with an examination of Community Assessment for Public Health Emergency Response (CASPER) and the ways in which GIS can help the public health community gather and analyze information quickly and efficiently during a natural disaster or other public health emergency.

Maps

Maps have been an important part of understanding and explaining outbreaks and other public health problems since the earliest days of epidemiology, and they remain at the heart of the new technologies discussed in this chapter. The earliest documented field epidemiology study was also the first documented case in which an investigator coupled cartography with epidemiologic analysis. In 1854, Dr. John Snow used maps (Figure 15-1) and

Figure 15-1   John Snow's now-famous map of deaths from cholera in London, 1854

Source: Snow J. *On the Mode of Communication of Cholera.* 2nd ed. London: John Churchill, New Burlington Street; 1855.

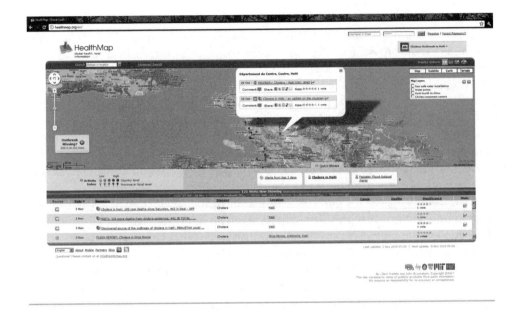

Figure 15-2   The HealthMap website displays the current global state of infectious diseases; shown here is the cholera outbreak in Haiti in the fall of 2010

epidemiological data to trace the source of an outbreak of cholera to a public water pump on Broad Street in London and show that the well had been contaminated by sewage from a nearby cesspit.[1]

A more recent example of the productive use of mapping in epidemiology is HealthMap (www.healthmap.org; Figure 15-2). An online map viewer, HealthMap tracks emerging cases of more than 50 human and animal illnesses worldwide. Created by John Brownstein and Clark Freifield of Harvard Medical School and the Children's Hospital in Boston, the site searches 50,000 websites every hour for signs of outbreak. Accessing global news and health sites, including those operated by the World Health Organization, Google News, and the disease-alert site ProMED-mail, HealthMap automatically extracts, categorizes, filters, and geocodes newly reported cases. During the 2010 cholera outbreak in Haiti, for example, HealthMap used Twitter posts and text messages to map clean water sources. It also integrated cases in near real time using data provided by physicians equipped with iPads and iPhones. Visualizing surveillance data on a user-friendly website facilitates early detection, raises public awareness, and supports situational awareness through the use of current and local outbreak information.[2]

Geographic Information Systems

GIS integrates the disciplines of geography, cartography, statistics, remote sensing, and database technology into tools or applications for storing, manipulating, analyzing, and displaying spatial data. As described throughout this book, epidemiology has three core variables: person, place, and time. Place has always been the most difficult and time-consuming variable to depict.[3] GIS can help overcome this obstacle by displaying spatial data quickly and convincingly. Maps are a widely understood modality for communicating information.[3] GIS takes the traditional map to another level, making it possible for investigators to record, map, and analyze data within a geographical context that facilitates the evaluation of trends, patterns, and other relationships.[4]

GIS includes two types of information: spatial and descriptive. Spatial information includes the points, lines, polygons, or grid cells that populate the map. A set of coordinates such as latitude and longitude are used to describe the location of these features. Descriptive information conveys such data as the population of a city, the percentage who live below the poverty line, or the number of 18-year-olds. Spatial and descriptive information are often stored in two or more different data sets. The ability to relate spatial (or location) information to descriptive (or attribute) information gives GIS its unique power.

When investigators use GIS in infectious disease surveillance and control or in outbreak investigation and response, the technology allows them to optimize data collection, management, and analysis. It can help them select samples for conducting studies, map surveillance data in real time and epidemic dynamics in near real time, and carry out rapid and effective communications. GIS helps answer almost any public health question that has a geographic component, such as the following:

- Which communities should be targeted for a public health intervention, or should serve as a target population for a study involving cardiovascular disease
- When an outbreak of West Nile virus first appeared, in which direction it is spreading, and which areas are most likely to be affected
- How proximity to a treatment center influences the type of breast cancer treatment that a woman chooses

Although GIS is a very useful tool, it does not have all the answers. Investigators who use GIS still must ask the right questions, collect the right data, and know how to interpret an apparent "cluster." Geographically referenced data often contain identifying information, so investigators must also take care to preserve the confidentiality of subjects. Even in aggregated data sets that include only small numbers of events or people, certain data can be linked to individuals.[3] When public health practitioners use GIS to conduct research (at the health department, for example), it may be appropriate to include personal identifiers that are useful to the analysis. If they plan to share or publish maps, however, researchers should exclude any personal identifying information.

GIS Data Models

Two primary GIS data models are used: vector and raster. The type of data model determines how data are represented, stored, and manipulated.

The *vector* model depicts discrete objects in geometric terms as points, lines, and polygons. In the context of public health, points may be used to identify sampling locations, disease cases, or town centers; lines may be used to identify transportation routes, waterways, and other linear features; and polygons may define discrete areas—city or county boundaries or lakes, for example.

The *raster* model is best used for continuous data, such as elevation or temperature, and thematic data, such as vegetation type or temperature. Raster data divide space into a grid of uniformly shaped cells, also called pixels, each of which holds a single value. Common types of raster data include digital aerial photographs, imagery from satellites, and scanned maps.

Digital imagery is geographically referenced or registered to the surface of the Earth and can be collected by satellite or low-flying airplanes. This type of data is referred to as remotely sensed data—an acknowledgment that the information is gathered from a distance, without any direct contact. Remotely sensed data can be used to classify the landscape into different categories (agriculture, developed, vegetated), to describe the type of vegetation cover present, to detect changes over time in the landscape, or to map habitat fragmentation. Epidemiology and infectious disease studies use remote sensing data to determine where environmental conditions are suitable for disease transmission. This effort might include modeling the suitable habitat conditions for disease vectors or creating rainfall, temperature, or humidity surfaces.[5, 6]

Displaying GIS Data

Most GIS software offers the user a good deal of flexibility in displaying and analyzing data. For example, GIS can display disease cases as point locations or express them as a rate per specified geographic area to determine the source of an outbreak. If they want to take a snapshot of the health of the community or preserve the privacy of personal information, however, public health users might choose to summarize the data based on population density, a practice known as "aggregating up." Summarizing data based on population density can, for example, allow investigators to aggregate the number of cases to the county, state, or country level.

In addition to creating sophisticated maps with GIS, investigators can take advantage of spatial analysis techniques. Spatial analysis is the process of manipulating geographically referenced data to extract additional meaning through visualization, exploratory data analysis, and modeling.[7] In malaria-prone regions, for example, spatial analysis has been used to predict the prevalence of the parasite responsible for infection.[8-12] GIS makes it possible to combine ecological, climatic, and topographic variables (e.g., landscape characterizations, land surface temperature, moisture availability, elevation, aspect, slope, soils, tree cover) with data from surveillance activities to create malaria risk maps. Epidemiologic investigators use these maps to help direct limited resources to areas predicted to be at the highest risk, and to add to public health's understanding of the epidemiological processes of malaria.

Spatial Resolution

Spatial resolution, an important consideration as investigators plan to use GIS, refers to the size of the pixel or grid cell being mapped. Different questions require data at different spatial resolutions. When GIS is used to map malaria risk, for example, the spatial resolution of the data plays a key role in the predictive power of the models. If the environmental predictors are fine-scale elements—such as forest edges and small depression areas that often hold water—investigators will likely use high-spatial-resolution aerial photography or satellite imagery. In contrast, if they are testing the hypothesis that broader-scale climate variables (such as elevation) influence disease prevalence, they will likely employ remotely sensed satellite data with a lower or coarser spatial resolution.

The scale of the study or the size of the project study area often will dictate the appropriate spatial resolution. For example, if the investigator is interested in mapping the malaria risk for a single village, he or she will use high-spatial-resolution data (a small cell size of 10 meters or less). If, however, the malaria risk map covers an entire region or country, the investigator will choose coarser resolution data (a large cell size, perhaps up to one kilometer).

Inputting Data into a GIS

To take advantage of any of the techniques described here, users must input spatial and descriptive data into the system. Using existing data sources is the simplest way to do so. Some of the more important data sources include the digital line graphs available from the U.S. Geological Survey and Tiger files from the U.S. Census Bureau. Other types of files are included with GIS software packages. Users can also add point data using a data table with x- and y-coordinates in decimal degrees; convert traditional paper maps into digital format; reformat and import existing spatial data; use address matching, also known as geocoding; and use a device enabled with global positioning system (GPS) software to collect both spatial and descriptive data.

Using GIS in Public Health

To demonstrate how public health practitioners might use GIS to track and analyze the sources and spread of disease, we will use the example of the map layers that individuals might create to help investigate an outbreak of West Nile virus (Figure 15-3). One map layer would show the location of different types of buildings, including enclosures for sentinel species (such as chicken coops and horse stalls), hospitals, and schools, as well as office buildings and dwellings. A second layer would contain the road network that could be used to geocode (apply longitude and latitude values to) infected case patients. A third might include a land-use and land-cover layer (showing the landscape by cover classification—forest land, water, or wetland, for example—or by land use—agriculture or urban, for example). Other useful layers might include a digital elevation model representing the topography or elevation of the landscape and maps showing precipitation, temperature, water features, populations at risk, and the location of physicians who could provide health care in the event of an outbreak.

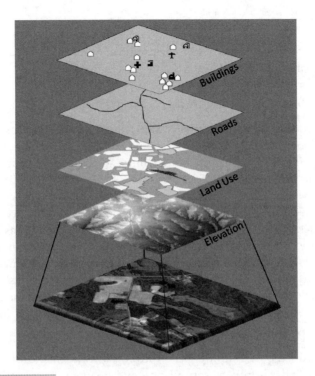

Figure 15-3   Example of possible GIS map layers for an investigation of an outbreak of West Nile virus

Many satellite platforms currently collect data on the surface of the Earth at different spatial and spectral (number of distinct bandwidths of light) resolutions. The most commonly used remote sensing data are provided by the Landsat platform, which collects multi-spectral data at a 30-meter spatial resolution. For large-scale regional studies, MODIS collects data from 36 spectral bands at spatial resolutions from 250 to 1000 meters (m). ASTER is another sensor that is freely available (like MODIS and Landsat), but it collects data upon request across 14 spectral bands at up to 15-m resolution. Higher-resolution data can be obtained from commercial sources such as IKONOS (1 m) or QuickBird (61 cm).

Investigators can do many things with spatial data once they are entered into GIS. In a West Nile virus outbreak, for example, GIS can help maintain surveillance of the locations of case patients and the geographic expansion or variation of the disease. Land cover, elevation, precipitation, and temperature layers can help the user identify areas with environmental conditions ideal for mosquito breeding, which would allow health agencies to undertake preventive measures in those areas. Similarly, because investigators can predict which populations are vulnerable to infection based on their proximity to mosquito breeding habitats, they can use GIS to simulate how an epidemic might evolve given the introduction of infected mosquitoes and birds at various locations. This information can be used to determine where to target interventions or strengthen healthcare resources.

Infectious Disease Surveillance and GIS

Several surveillance programs use GIS to help control or eradicate disease. Three international programs and one in the United States are described here.

WHO Public Health Mapping and GIS Programme

In 1993, the World Health Organization (WHO) and the United Nations Children's Fund (UNICEF) developed the Public Health Mapping and GIS Programme (http://www.who .int/health_mapping/en/) to help eradicate Guinea worm disease, which affects the isolated rural poor in remote parts of Africa that do not have safe water to drink. The program employed GIS to visually depict areas where cases of the disease were concentrated, monitor newly infected or reinfected villages, identify populations at risk, target cost-effective interventions, and track eradication efforts. Since the Guinea worm project was undertaken, GIS and mapping have been greatly expanded to meet the data needs for several disease-control initiatives, including programs to eliminate onchocerciasis (river blindness), blinding trachoma, African trypanosomiasis (sleeping sickness), and lymphatic filariasis (elephantiasis), as well as global initiatives to eradicate poliomyelitis and reduce malaria.

The HealthMapper

WHO developed the HealthMapper (http://www.who.int/health_mapping/tools/ healthmapper/en/index.html), a surveillance and mapping application, to address critical surveillance information needs across infectious disease programs at national and global levels. This program makes it possible to standardize, collect, and update data on epidemiology and interventions, and to display data in the form of maps, tables, and charts. The HealthMapper also packages a database of core baseline geographic, demographic, and health information, including the location of communities, healthcare and education facilities, accessibility by road, access to safe water, and demography. This system currently supports a range of infectious diseases programs in more than 60 countries.

Roll Back Malaria Partnership

Roll Back Malaria (http://www.rollbackmalaria.org/) is a global partnership that helps countries and communities take effective, sustainable action against malaria. To monitor the Roll Back Malaria partnership, WHO developed a GIS program to meet the following needs:

- Strengthen surveillance at the local level for early detection and response to epidemics
- Complement existing national and international health monitoring systems
- Integrate information on community interventions, control interventions, private and public health providers, partner intervention areas, and resources
- Be accessible at different levels

More than 500 partners make up the Roll Back Malaria Partnership, including the governments of countries where malaria is endemic, their bilateral and multilateral development partners, nongovernmental and community-based organizations, foundations, research and academic institutions, and the private sector. By cooperating to strengthen malaria-control efforts at the country level, the partnership works to decrease malaria morbidity and mortality by reaching universal coverage and strengthening health systems.

U.S. West Nile Virus Surveillance

In the United States, the Centers for Disease Control and Prevention (CDC) developed a national surveillance plan for West Nile virus to monitor the geographic and temporal spread of infection, provide current national and regional information on the virus, and identify regional distribution and incidence of other arbovirus diseases. The program (http://www.cdc.gov/ncidod/dvbid/westnile/index.htm) uses GIS software extensively to enhance the federal surveillance system and communicate results to the public. As part of this effort, the CDC combined forces with the U.S. Geological Survey to map the progression of West Nile virus through mosquito, wild bird, horse, and human populations (Figure 15-4) and to track the disease in sentinel species (chickens).

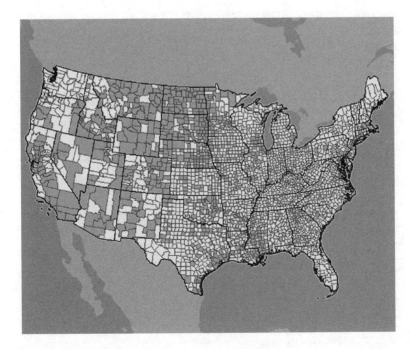

Figure 15-4 U.S. Geologic Survey 2007 West Nile virus surveillance maps (*continues*)

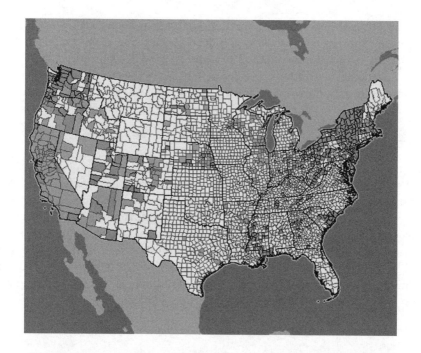

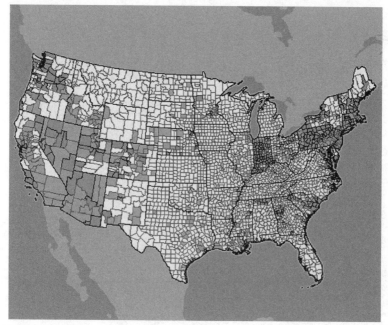

Figure 15-4 *(continues)*

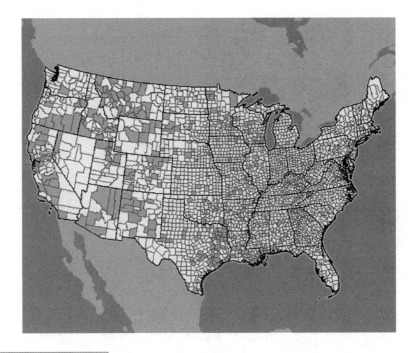

Figure 15-4 (*continued*)

Outbreak Investigation and GIS

In addition to enriching surveillance activities, GIS has enhanced outbreak investigation and response at local, national, and global levels. The examples described in this section illustrate how GIS has been used to strengthen data collection, management, and analysis; develop early warning systems; plan and monitor response programs; and communicate large volumes of complex information simply and effectively to decision makers and the public.

Shigellosis

Investigators used GIS when they studied an outbreak of shigellosis at Fort Bragg, North Carolina, during the summer of 1997. A total of 59 cases of *Shigella sonnei* infection were reported among people who used the healthcare services of the local military hospital and its affiliated clinics. A significant number of those individuals who became ill were children, but the preliminary investigation did not reveal any clear associations with a particular daycare center or common location. The outbreak persisted despite educational campaigns about hand washing and hygiene.

When investigators imported the residential addresses of all of the confirmed shigellosis cases into a GIS and mapped them onto digitized maps of the Fort Bragg housing

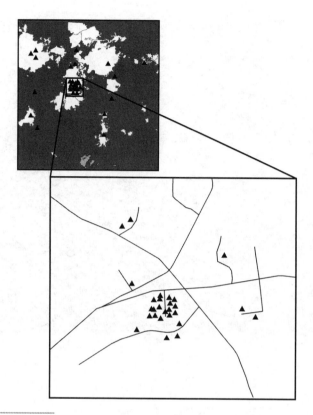

Figure 15-5 GIS display of a neighborhood containing a large cluster of cases of shigellosis

areas, they discovered a cluster of infections on several streets in one particular neighborhood (Figure 15-5). From interviews with case families and neighbors, they learned that affected children played in small communal wading pools in several yards. The pools were removed, home-based information campaigns were initiated, and the spread of the illness was halted.[13]

Using GIS to Track Sexually Transmitted Infections

GIS is also useful for mapping sexually transmitted infections. For example, investigators in Baltimore used the technology to map the distribution of syphilis cases before, during, and after an outbreak, and produced data suggesting that the disease spread outward from two central cores of infection.[14] Researchers at the University of North Carolina at Chapel Hill used GIS to map the distribution of four reportable sexually transmitted infections (chlamydia, gonorrhea, syphilis, and HIV infection) in Wake County, North Carolina, and found clearly defined spatially heterogeneous areas of infection for the different diseases (Figure 15-6).[15]

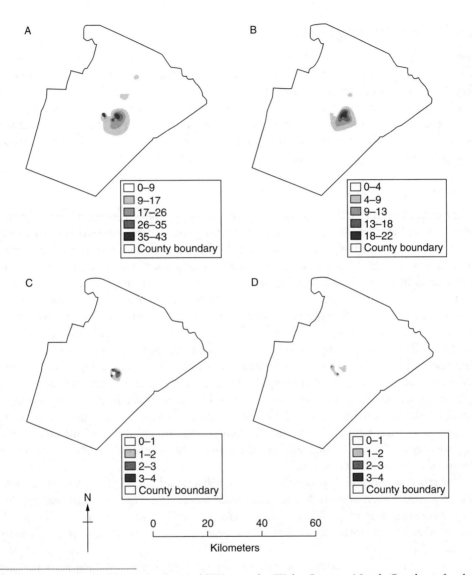

Figure 15-6 Spatial heterogeneity of STI rates for Wake County, North Carolina, for the year 2000: **A.** Chlamydial infection (county average = 4.87/1000). **B.** Gonorrhea (county average = 2.01/1000). **C.** Syphilis (county average = 0.19/1000). **D.** HIV infection (county average = 0.18/1000). Note scale differences between STIs.

Source: Law DCG, Serre ML, Christakos G, Leone PA, Miller WC. Spatial analysis and mapping of sexually transmitted diseases to optimise intervention and prevention strategies. *Sex Transm Infect.* 2004;80:294–299. http://www.ncbi.nlm.nih.gov/pmc/articles/PMC1744854/pdf/v080p00294.pdf.

Global Positioning System

Global positioning system (GPS) technology is a critical tool in outbreak investigations and other public health exercises that require precise identification of research subjects, their locations, and distances to related geographic features. GPS users carry a device that receives signals from up to 12 satellites high above the Earth's surface, allowing them to locate their positions on an electronic map at any given moment. The device calculates the difference between the time each signal is sent and the time it is received, then uses a triangulation technique to determine the user's exact position.

Atrazine Exposure

In one example of how GPS can enhance epidemiological research, investigators employed GPS-enabled handheld technology in a study designed to determine whether there was a relationship between exposure to the herbicide atrazine and proximity to fields where atrazine was applied. When research field staff visited the study area in Illinois to verify the locations of households near selected cornfields, each member of the team was equipped with a Hewlett-Packard iPAQ Pocket PC with a GPS receiver and Environmental Systems Research Institute's (ESRI's) ArcPad software (a type of GIS software used to map applications that allows users to capture, display, and analyze geographic information on handheld devices). The team geocoded the candidate household addresses into a street database and loaded the data onto ArcPad, along with aerial photographs and a street centerline database. Field staff then used GPS and street-name navigation techniques to find the approximate location of the candidate households. When necessary, field staff modified the less accurate original address-matched location of each household to be the actual location based on GPS and the ability to see household rooftops on an aerial map. If they could not see households on the map, they captured a GPS coordinate on the street in front of the household.

Once they had accurately positioned candidate households using GPS, researchers were able to measure each household's distance from a cornfield where atrazine was applied. They were then able to correlate concentrations of atrazine found in each household and in biological samples collected from the occupants with distance from the atrazine source.

Using ArcPad/GPS capabilities instead of paper maps allowed field staff to navigate quickly from household to household and made the household locations much more accurate. The precision of the measurements of household locations and the distances from households to cornfields provided a higher degree of validity during data analysis.[16]

Public health practitioners could easily apply a similar approach to infectious disease surveillance and outbreak investigation and response. In an infectious disease outbreak investigation, for example, the technology could be used to measure the distance from a neighborhood where cases are concentrated to an exposure such as a water source with *Cryptosporidium*. Outbreak investigation and response are time-limited activities: Researchers must act quickly to have the greatest effect. GIS and GPS technology can greatly speed field work, allowing investigations to proceed much more quickly than would be possible if the investigators used traditional mapping methods.

Community Assessments and GIS

The GIS and GPS techniques discussed previously can help investigators conduct rapid needs assessments more thoroughly and efficiently. For example, public health agencies carry out a Community Assessment for Public Health Emergency Response (CASPER) to determine the health status and basic needs of a community in the immediate aftermath of a disaster.[17] Also referred to as rapid need assessment, rapid epidemiologic assessment, and rapid health assessment, CASPER provides the information needed to match a community's emergency needs with the available resources. Early assessment combined with rapid mobilization of resources can significantly reduce the harmful public health consequences of a disaster.[18]

Community assessments can serve the following purposes:

- Provide situational awareness to help establish the extent and possible evolution of an emergency
- Measure the present and potential public health impact
- Determine existing response capacity and identify any additional immediate needs
- Inform priority response actions[17]

Community Assessment Methodology

When investigators conduct a CASPER, they must determine the best way to sample the population being surveyed. To increase efficiency—and because they often do not have a complete listing or census of all households in a given area—investigators may use alternatives to simple random sampling. The WHO Expanded Programme on Immunization (EPI), for example, adapted one method—cluster sampling—to assess levels of immunization coverage.[19]

The EPI method involves a two-stage cluster sample in which investigators sample 30 clusters or primary sampling units from an area of interest and select 7 "points" in each cluster, a strategy referred to as a "30 × 7" survey. Clusters are defined geographical areas—a census block, block group, or tract, for example—and "points" comprise housing units or parcels within that area.[20] This method is easy to implement in the field, requires few resources, and yields reasonably valid and precise estimates (plus or minus 10%).[21] Public health practitioners have adapted two-stage cluster sampling for various purposes over the years (see Table 15-1).[22]

TABLE 15-1 A Brief Timeline of the Use of Two-Stage Cluster Sampling in Public Health

1960s	1970s and 1980s	1990s and 2000s
• Rapid surveys developed as a tool for local health departments to assess community coverage of immunization, population morbidity (diarrheal and respiratory diseases), service coverage, and health service needs	• Adapted by WHO for the Expanded Program of Immunization (EPI) to assess immunization coverage • Modified to provide community-based information to guide the smallpox eradication program in West Africa	• Revised to include community volunteers, incorporation of census data, and random sampling of second-stage participants rather than random start and next nearest neighbor • Adapted by CDC for rapid needs assessment after natural disasters

Modified EPI Cluster Sampling

In 1996, Malilay et al. modified the EPI cluster sampling method to add the ability to estimate the size of the overall post-disaster population and the number of persons with specific needs, and to assess the number of damaged or destroyed housing units. This modified sampling procedure divides the disaster site into mutually exclusive blocks or clusters with well-defined boundaries. (Natural dividers such as street grids or geographical features such as rivers or hills are useful boundaries.) Investigators then use census data, aerial maps, and other data sources to estimate the number of housing units in each cluster. In the first stage, they select a sample of n clusters ($n = 30$ in the EPI method) with "probability proportional to the estimated number of housing units"—in other words, a cluster with more housing units is more likely to be included than one with fewer housing units.[21] In the second stage, investigators choose an equal probability sample of k housing units ($k = 7$ in the EPI method), and conduct an interview at each selected housing unit.

In this modified method, an investigator makes multiple attempts to conduct an interview at a selected housing unit. In the EPI method, by comparison, the interviewer moves to an adjacent housing unit if no one is available to be interviewed at the selected unit.

Investigators using the modified EPI cluster sampling method conduct surveys as soon as possible following the disaster, and they may repeat those surveys over time to assess any changes in the population's needs.[21] First they count all housing units in each sampled cluster, and note any that have been destroyed or damaged. Then they count the people in each selected household, and use these numbers to estimate the size of the overall post-disaster population. The modified method allows investigators to collect more information than does the EPI method.

The CDC has adopted the modified method as the standard for conducting rapid assessments after disasters, and has worked with numerous state and local health departments to conduct post-disaster assessments using this technique. After Hurricane Isabel made landfall on the coast of North Carolina on September 18, 2003, for example, the CDC worked with the North Carolina Division of Public Health to conduct a rapid assessment of the affected population.[22]

Using Rapid Surveys for Community Assessments

Investigators have adapted the rapid survey method used to conduct post-disaster needs assessments for other types of community assessments. For example, epidemiologists at the School of Public Health at the University of California at Los Angeles conducted a small rapid assessment survey in a predominantly Hispanic area of Los Angeles to look at immunization status and related factors. This type of survey may have provided a more representative sample than a telephone survey, given the large percentage (approximately 25%) of respondents who did not have a home telephone number.[23] In North Carolina, county health departments use rapid assessment surveys as part of state-mandated community health assessments.

Federal and state officials also use rapid surveys to assess population vulnerabilities prior to potential catastrophic events as part of preparedness planning.[24] Anticipating that the H1N1 virus would cause a significant number of influenza cases during the winter of 2009–2010, for example, North Carolina officials conducted a rapid assessment to determine whether people in the state's communities had been informed about the vaccine's availability, how they had learned about the vaccine, and whether they intended to be vaccinated.[25]

Role of Geographic Information Systems in Community Assessments

GIS can be a useful tool during community assessments. For example, investigators can use GIS technology to take a more scientific approach when they select households to interview (second-stage randomization). Rather than relying on sequential or systematic sampling, investigation teams can use GIS software to choose households in advance by selecting random points and plotting them on a map for interviewers to follow. Investigators then conduct interviews with a resident of the house located nearest to the random point. This process reduces potential sample selection bias by individual interview teams, although it may be difficult to identify interview subjects if the point is placed in an industrial location or business area where there are no households located nearby.

In field investigations, the GIS technology allows teams to use GPS-based routing rather than paper maps. Interview teams can use GPS-enabled handheld computers that run mobile GIS software to track their whereabouts as they travel through the assessment area, thereby allowing them to easily identify the most efficient route to follow. Paper maps take more time for teams to interpret, are often not as up-to-date as electronic GPS maps, and can be easily misplaced or destroyed, particularly in a disaster assessment situation.

Perhaps most importantly, GIS technology can replace paper surveys with electronic computer-based surveys. Investigators can use GIS-related software to develop electronic surveys and upload them to handheld computers for field deployment. When team members conduct an interview with members of a household, they can enter data on their handheld computers rather than writing down every response. Teams that conduct surveys with handheld devices do not have to carry around stacks of paper that, aside from being cumbersome, might be lost or damaged during the assessment. No one has to enter the data manually from paper surveys into an electronic database. Instead, investigators simply upload data from the handheld computers to a central computer, where the GIS software swiftly merges the data into one large database. If assessment teams are deployed to the field to conduct interviews, they can upload their data to a server via a wireless Internet hotspot.

Thus handheld computers with GIS technology reduce data entry time and minimize the errors that may occur when data from paper surveys are entered into an electronic database. Rapid data entry makes it possible to analyze results quickly to guide public health response activities.

Getting Geographic Information Systems into the Field

Incorporating new computer-based technologies in local public health practice can present challenges. Agencies must dedicate funds to purchase computer equipment and software licenses, and training is required to use these tools correctly and effectively. Nevertheless, the potential gains in data quality and timeliness and the elimination of double data entry make spatial analysis and electronic field data collection attractive to state and local public health agencies. While the initial expenditure for mobile GIS/GPS technology may seem considerable, the long-term investment may significantly enhance public health preparedness and public health functions overall.[26]

Summary

The spread of disease—especially infectious disease—is unavoidably spatial.[27] Infection moves from individual to individual following a network of contacts within a population through local or even global transmission. As public health agencies have increasingly discovered, the capacity of GIS to capture geospatial information is ideally suited for infectious disease surveillance and control. GIS also equips epidemiologic investigators to meet the demands of outbreak investigation and response. Its combination with GPS technology allows users to collect both spatial and descriptive data and download those data to a central database.

Rapid assessments have become an essential component of efficient disaster relief operations. Such assessments, particularly with the incorporation of GIS technology, allow public health officials working under intense time pressures to identify and prioritize areas of need and target resources appropriately. Investigators can use rapid assessment methods in post-disaster settings as well as in other areas of public health that require population-based surveys.

GIS Resources

There are many providers of GIS software in the public health sector, and many resources for GIS users. Three of the commonly used packages are listed here:

- Environmental Systems Research Institute (ESRI) is the largest vendor. It produces ArcGIS, a collection of GIS software products for spatial analysis, data management, mapping, and mobile GIS (http://www.esri.com/).

- GRASS GIS (Geographic Resources Analysis Support System) is free, open-source GIS software for spatial analysis, data management, image processing, and more (http://grass.itc.it/).

- The CDC offers Epi Info/Epi Map (http://www.cdc.gov/epiinfo/). The CDC's Resources for Creating Public Health Maps page also has links to sites with geographic boundaries, data, and public health and GIS overviews.

There are many sources of free GIS data available online. For projects within the United States and at a local scale, states are often the best source for free GIS data. National data sets such as aerial and satellite imagery, elevation, and land cover are available from the U.S. Geological Society (USGS) Cumulus Portal for Geospatial Data. A wide variety of data, including demographic data such as census data, is available for free in the United States at the GeoData.gov website. For international projects, ESRI offers worldwide satellite imagery, topographic maps, and street map data to ArcGIS users. The Earth Resources Observation and Science (EROS) Center is the best source to determine which remote sensing products, both commercial and free, are available for a particular study area.

Additional Resource

More information about sampling for public health assessments is available from the University of North Carolina Center for Public Health Preparedness and the North Carolina Public Health Regional Surveillance Team 5 at http://nccphp.sph.unc.edu/PHRST5/.

Further Readings

- Melnick AL. *Introduction to Geographic Information Systems in Public Health*. Gaithersburg, MD: Aspen Publishers; 2002.

- Cromley EK. *GIS and Public Health*. New York: Guilford Press; 2002.

- Moore DA, Carpenter TE. Spatial analytical methods and geographic information systems: Use in health research and epidemiology. *Epidemiol Rev*. 1999;21(2):143–60.

References

1. Snow J. *On the Mode of Communication of Cholera.* 2nd ed. London: John Churchill, New Burlington Street; 1855. http://www.ph.ucla.edu/epi/snow/snowbook.html.
2. Brownstein JS, Freifield CC, Reis RY, et al. Surveillance sans frontières: Internet-based emerging infectious disease intelligence and the HealthMap Project. *PloS Med.* 2008:5(7):1019–24.
3. Melnick AL, Fleming DW. Modern geographic information systems: Promise and pitfalls. *J Pub Hlth Mgmt Prac.* 1999;5(2):viii–x.
4. What is GIS? Environmental Systems Research Institute. http://www.esri.com/what-is-gis/index.html. Accessed May 19, 2010.
5. Emch M, Ali M, Root ED, Yunus M. MBBS spatial and environmental connectivity analysis in a cholera vaccine trial. *Soc Sci Med.* 2009;68(4):631–7.
6. Maxwell SK, Meliker JR, Goovaerts P. Use of land surface remotely sensed satellite and airborne data for environmental exposure assessment in cancer research. *J Exposure Sci Environ Epidemiol.* 2010;20:176–85.
7. Clarke KC, McLafferty SL, Tempalski BJ. On epidemiology and geographic information systems: A review and discussion of future directions. *Emerg Infect Dis.* 1996;2(2):85.
8. Beck LR, Rodriguez, MH, Dister SW, et al. Remote-sensing as a landscape epidemiologic tool to identify villages at high-risk for malaria transmission. *Am J Trop Med Hyg.* 1994;51(3):271–80.
9. Haque U, Magalhaes RJS, Reid HL, et al. Spatial prediction of malaria prevalence in an endemic area of Bangladesh. *Malar J.* 2010;9:120.
10. Kitron U. Landscape ecology and epidemiology of vector-borne diseases: Tools for spatial analysis. *J Med Entomol.* 1998;35(4):435–45.
11. Omumbo J, Ouma J, Rapuoda B, et al. Mapping malaria transmission intensity using geographical information systems (GIS): An example from Kenya. *Ann Trop Med Parasitol.* 1998;92(1):7–21.
12. Saxena R, Nagpal BN, Srivastava A, et al. Application of spatial technology in malaria research and control: Some new insights. *Indian J Med Res.* 2009;130(2):125–32.
13. McKee KT, Shields TM, Jenkins PR, et al. Application of a geographic information system to the tracking and control of an outbreak of shigellosis. *Clin Infect Dis.* 2000;31:728–33.
14. Law DCG, Bernstein KT, Serre ML, et al. Modeling a syphilis outbreak through space and time using the Bayesian maximum entropy approach. *Ann Epidemiol.* 2006;16:797–804.
15. Law DCG, Serre ML, Christakos G, et al. Spatial analysis and mapping of sexually transmitted diseases to optimise intervention and prevention strategies. *Sex Transm Infect.* 2004;80:294–9.
16. Allpress JLE, Curry RJ, Hanchette CL, et al. A GIS-based method for household recruitment in a prospective pesticide exposure study. *Int J Health Geogr.* 2008;7(1):18.
17. Centers for Disease Control and Prevention. Community Assessment for Public Health Emergency Response (CASPER) toolkit. 2009. http://emergency.cdc.gov/disasters/surveillance/pdf/casper_toolkit_508%20compliant.pdf. Accessed September 23, 2010.
18. Lillibridge SR, Noji EK, Burkle FM. Disaster assessment: The emergency health evaluation of a population affected by a disaster. *Ann Emerg Med.* 1993;22:1715–20.
19. World Health Organization. *Rapid Health Assessment Protocols for Emergencies.* Geneva, Switzerland: World Health Organization; 1999.
20. Frerichs RR. Rapid surveys. Department of Epidemiology, School of Public Health, University of California, Los Angeles. Updated May 26, 2008. http://www.ph.ucla.edu/epi/rapidsurvey.html. Accessed September 23, 2010.
21. Malilay J, Flanders WD, Brogan D. A modified cluster-sampling method for post-disaster rapid assessment of needs. *Bull World Health Organ.* 1996;74(4):399–405.

22. Centers for Disease Control and Prevention. Rapid community health and needs assessments after Hurricanes Isabel and Charley—North Carolina, 2003-2004. *Morb Mortal Weekly Rep.* 2004;53:840-2.

23. Frerichs RR, Shaheen MA. Small-community-based surveys. *Annu Rev Public Health*. 2001;22: 231-47.

24. Horney J, Snider C, Gammons L, Ramsey S. Factors associated with hurricane preparedness: Results of a pre-hurricane assessment. *J Natural Dis*. 2008;3(2):143-9.

25. Centers for Disease Control and Prevention. Intent to receive influenza A (H1N1) 2009 monovalent and seasonal influenza vaccines—two counties, North Carolina, August 2009. *Morb Mortal Weekly Rep.* 2009;58(50):1401-5.

26. Horney J, Ramsey S, Smith M, et al. Implementing mobile GIS/GPS technology in North Carolina to enhance public health preparedness: Evaluation of associated trainings and exercises. Under review at *Disaster Medicine and Public Health Preparedness*.

27. Holmes EE. Basic epidemiological concepts in a spatial context. In: Tilman D, Kareiva P, eds. *Spatial Ecology: The Role of Space in Population Dynamics and Interspecific Interactions*. Princeton, NJ: Princeton University Press; 1997:111-36.

Chapter 16

Special Considerations

Michelle R. Torok
Laura C. Alexander
Pia D. M. MacDonald

Learning Objectives
By the end of this chapter, the reader will be able to:

- Describe the Incident Command System (ICS) and explain how it can be used in outbreak investigations.
- List ICS command staff positions and the four major sections of the ICS.
- Cite examples of how ICS has been used for public health outbreak investigations.
- Define partner notification and describe its uses in sexually transmitted infection and tuberculosis cases.
- Identify the key characteristic of cluster interviewing, and differentiate cluster interviewing from traditional partner notification interviewing.
- List three methods for partner notification.
- Discuss legal and confidentiality issues related to contact tracing/partner notification.

Introduction

Throughout this book, we have outlined the steps of an outbreak investigation. We have described additional investigations that might be conducted in support of outbreak investigations, such as environmental investigation; special situations that may require extensive cooperative with law enforcement and other agencies, such as bioterrorism; and some of the resources that are available to outbreak investigators, such as public health laboratories and geographical information systems. Anyone who has read this far should be well equipped to undertake his or her first outbreak investigation, preferably under the guidance of an experienced investigator. Nevertheless, the scope of an investigation can vary greatly, as can the specialized knowledge required to bring it to a successful conclusion. This chapter focuses on two resources that may be useful in outbreak investigations with special considerations.

As mentioned earlier in this book, an outbreak investigation can be a simple affair, in which a single individual wraps up an investigation with a phone call or two, or a far more complicated venture, which involves many health department personnel as well as individuals from several other agencies. When an investigation is large or requires intensive collaboration, investigators can benefit from the organizational and operational structure provided by the Incident Command System (ICS). This chapter discusses ICS first, and then presents two case studies of investigations that benefited from implementing an ICS.

Likewise, investigations that involve certain infectious diseases, such as sexually transmitted infections (STIs) and tuberculosis, may require investigators to take extra measures to locate as many infected persons as possible and encourage them to be tested, make behavioral changes to protect their health, and identify others who may be infected. Such investigations, known as contact tracing, may require special interviewing skills as well as an understanding of state and federal laws covering confidentiality and the legal authority of partner notification. This chapter concludes with a section that describes contact tracing and considers how it might be involved in an outbreak investigation.

The Incident Command System

The Incident Command System (ICS) was created to organize personnel and resources from multiple jurisdictions in a coordinated and efficient response to a health crisis. ICS is a standard incident management system that is used by public health organizations, as well as fire fighters, police, emergency management, and medical teams. It is required by law to be used by all federal, state, local, and tribal governments.[1]

ICS was created in the 1970s following a disastrous wildfire in California. The fire burned for 13 days, and was responsible for 16 deaths and the destruction of 700 buildings.[1] Although the fire was eventually contained, problems with communication and coordination during the response contributed to the high level of destruction. In response, Congress required the U.S. Forest Service to devise a system to organize coordinated responses to disasters—and ICS was born.[1] ICS has evolved over time, and is now used for organizing countless events, including responses to terrorist attacks and natural disasters, and even large festivals or parades. More recently, health professionals have used ICS to respond to disease outbreaks and other situations that involve cooperation with fire, police, or emergency management agencies. The discussion here primarily focuses on the use of ICS for outbreak investigations.

ICS offers many benefits to public health. It easily organizes the response to a disease outbreak, eliminating concerns about what to do first and who does which task. It also makes cooperating with other agencies outside of public health easier by requiring that all partners work together in the same system, under the same plan. Furthermore, ICS is fully scalable: It can be used for a small outbreak of illness following a wedding reception or a huge multistate outbreak of *Salmonella* infection.

Characteristics of ICS

An ICS organizes the individuals involved in responding to a disease outbreak or health event into specific groups. The person leading the response is called the incident commander; this individual has authority for the response as a whole. Different persons can serve as the incident commander during the course of an event. Typically, the first person told about a disease outbreak is the first incident commander. As the outbreak changes and evolves, another individual at the health department (such as the health director or public health epidemiologist) or at a partnering agency might be designated as incident commander. It is important that the incident commander demonstrates strong leadership during the response, and is able to provide purpose, direction, and motivation for the other responders.

Below the incident commander in the ICS hierarchy are positions that make up the command staff. They include the public information officer, who communicates with the media and creates all news releases, announcements, and educational materials for the public; the safety officer, who is responsible for ensuring the safety of the responders; and the liaison officer, who coordinates with other relevant agencies or groups. Many different people within a health department can fulfill these roles during an outbreak. For instance, a health educator may be well suited to serve as the public information officer as long as he or she has training in working with the media, whereas an environmental health specialist or county safety officer could act as the safety officer.

The incident commander and the command staff combine to form the ICS command staff. One of the most important jobs of the command staff is to determine the incident objectives. These objectives are based on the following goals:

1. Saving lives

2. Stabilizing the public health event

3. Preserving property[2]

In addition to the ICS command staff, other responders or investigators can be organized as needed for the response. Most ICS situations include an operations section, a planning section, a logistics section, and a finance/administration section (see Figure 16-1). Each of these sections has a section chief who manages the group and who reports to the ICS command staff. Together, the section chiefs form the general staff. In addition, each section can be further broken down into divisions, groups, or branches, as necessary.

The operations section is usually the first section created, and is typically responsible for completing the tasks necessary to bring the situation under control. In an outbreak investigation, the operations section might interview case patients or distribute antibiotics to protect exposed people. During the investigation, the other sections will perform their assigned tasks, but their primary obligation is to support the operations section.

The planning section is responsible for using the incident objectives created by the command staff to write an incident action plan. This incident action plan outlines the activities that will be completed during the outbreak investigation. It specifies what the investigators want to accomplish, who is responsible for what, how they will communicate

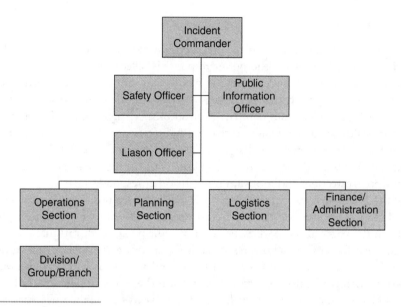

Figure 16-1 ICS organization chart

Source: Adapted from *ICS in Action: Using the Incident Command System in Public Health Outbreak Investigations* [Training Program on DVD], North Carolina Center for Public Health Preparedness, University of North Carolina Gillings School of Global Public Health; 2009.

with one another, and what they will do if someone becomes injured. The command staff often uses standardized forms to create the incident action plan, such as an organization assignment form, a communications plan form, and a medical plan form.

The logistics section is charged with providing the resources that the operations section investigators need to complete their objectives, such as clipboards and pens for interviewing case patients, food for investigators, and transportation. Not every investigation will require a finance/administration section. If its inclusion is necessary, however, this section can monitor and allocate the money needed to carry out the investigation.

In addition to establishing a standardized way of organizing people and assigning roles, ICS specifies how people should work together. Using a concept called span of control, ICS dictates that no one can manage more than seven people directly, and preferably no more than five. Furthermore, each person reports to and receives instructions from only one supervisor—a concept called unity of command. ICS also provides guidance about how people should talk to one another, requiring all responders involved to speak in common terminology. For example, law enforcement personnel should not say "10-4" when they mean "okay" or "10-9" when they want something repeated. Using common terminology also means that public health investigators should avoid using jargon that others might not be familiar with, such as "line lists" or "epi curves."

While the terms and forms and intricacies of ICS might seem overwhelming, the system becomes easier to understand with practice. Most importantly, ICS is a tool investigators can use to organize an outbreak investigation or other public health event, especially when they are working with other agencies or partners.

Case Study: ICS in an Outbreak of West Nile Virus in New York

In the summer of 2008, 20 people in Nassau County, New York, were diagnosed with West Nile virus. While West Nile virus infection is seen fairly regularly in Nassau County, 20 cases occurring in one season was abnormally high, and indicated an outbreak was occurring. To respond to the outbreak and implement effective control measures, officials at the Nassau County Department of Health (NCDOH) activated their ICS.

The first order of business was to assign individuals to the roles of incident commander, other command staff, and section chiefs. During the outbreak, NCDOH partnered with several other organizations, including the Department of Public Works and the Office of Emergency Management. NCDOH staff filled the roles of incident commander, public information officer, liaison officer, safety officer, operations section chief, and administration section chief. A member of the Public Works Department served as the logistics section chief, and the planning section chief was from Emergency Management.

Once the roles were assigned, meetings began, and were held twice a day. The primary objective of the response was to spray pesticide to kill adult mosquitoes carrying West Nile virus. To achieve this goal, the team decided that the logistics section and the planning section would determine how to implement the spraying both on the ground and from the air, hire a plane to perform the aerial spraying, use geographic information systems (GIS; see Chapter 15) to create a map of the areas to spray, and purchase the appropriate pesticide.

Meanwhile, the public information officer created a public notification system to notify people who lived in the spray area, as well as numerous other groups, including local governments, managers of water systems, school systems, and hospitals. The public notification system consisted of an emergency-alert phone system that could automatically make calls, faxes, announcements on local radio, and interviews with local media. The public information officer also set up a toll-free phone line to answer questions from the community, and posted pertinent information about the scheduled spraying on the NCDOH website.

The pesticide spraying was scheduled to take place on Thursday, September 4, 2008. The phone system was activated the night before, with 236,000 calls being made to inform residents and businesses of the plan. However, as Thursday progressed, the weather worsened due to Hurricane Gustav, with winds rising above the 10 miles-per-hour limit necessary to ensure effective aerial spraying. The command staff met and decided to postpone the spraying, despite all the preparations that had been made. The communications team under the public information officer notified the public that the spraying operation had been canceled. Over the next several days, a second major storm, Hurricane Hanna, made landfall, and again forced NCDOH and its partners to put mosquito control plans on hold. The ICS structure remained intact during these postponements.

(continues)

Case Study: ICS in an Outbreak of West Nile Virus in New York (*continued*)

When the hurricane threat passed, the team members were able to resume their ICS duties. By September 9, it seemed possible to schedule an aerial spraying, so the ICS team contacted the public with the new information. The spraying was completed the following day with successful results.

After the outbreak was over, NCDOH reported that ICS helped the department carry out an effective response to the increase in West Nile virus cases. Specifically, this system allowed NCDOH to clarify roles with partnering agencies, reduce duplication of information disseminated during the event, and successfully notify the public about the scheduled and rescheduled pesticide spraying.

Source: Adapted from Adams EH, Scanlon E, Callahan JJ 3rd, Carney MT. Utilization of an Incident Command System for a public health threat: West Nile virus in Nassau County, New York, 2008. *J Public Health Manag Pract.* 2010;16(4):309–315.

Case Study: ICS in a *Shigella* Outbreak in Western North Carolina

In the fall of 2007, several children in a large daycare center in western North Carolina developed diarrhea, which was later confirmed to be shigellosis. The daycare center, which was the largest in western North Carolina, was located on the Qualla Boundary where the Eastern Band of the Cherokee live. Concerned that the outbreak might spread, the health officer for the tribe activated the ICS. Incident command was located at the Health and Medical Division on the Qualla Boundary, and the health officer became the incident commander. Health directors from two of the adjoining counties, as well as community health nurses and hospital staff, joined the response and were assigned roles in ICS.

The incident commander held briefings twice a day, and insisted that representatives from all pertinent organizations be in attendance, including daycare personnel, emergency management, tribal groups, and local health departments. Between 30 and 40 people frequently attended the meetings. New information on case definitions, treatment, confirmed lab reports, and new case patients to be investigated was disseminated through the meetings, and dictated the actions of the teams that evening and the next day. Everyone left the meetings with the most current information available.

A public information officer was assigned, and communicated a single, clear message to the media. An environmental health specialist from one of the local health departments served as the safety officer. She developed protocols to ensure the safety of the responders as well as isolation plans for daycare centers that divided the healthy and sick children to keep the outbreak from spreading, while allowing the facilities to remain open.

Within a month, no new cases of shigellosis had developed, and the outbreak ended. The investigators credited ICS with facilitating good communication, limiting redundancy of tasks, allowing the group to operate quickly, and saving resources during the outbreak. The ICS structure also allowed the leaders of all of the groups involved to get to know one another, which will enable them to form effective partnerships in the future.

Source: Adapted from *ICS in Action: Using the Incident Command System in Public Health Outbreak Investigations* [Training Program on DVD]. North Carolina Center for Public Health Preparedness, University of North Carolina Gillings School of Global Public Health; 2009.

Additional Resources Related to ICS

More information on the ICS is available from the Federal Emergency Management Agency's ICS Resource Center (http://training.fema.gov/EMIWeb/IS/ICSResource/index.htm).

Contact Tracing

Contact tracing, sometimes called "partner notification" in the context of sexually transmitted infections (STIs), is another method used to control outbreaks. In contact tracing, persons with a new diagnosis or report of a communicable disease (index patients) are usually interviewed by trained public health professionals called disease intervention specialists. Disease intervention specialists, sometimes referred to as DIS, attempt to identify persons whom the index patient may have exposed (contacts or partners) to notify those individuals of their possible exposure and to encourage testing and prophylaxis or treatment. The index patient and his or her contacts are also offered services in addition to testing and treatment, such as counseling and referrals to medical, psychosocial, and/or prevention resources; these combined services are called "partner services programs."[3] The short-term aims of contact tracing are to identify persons who were exposed to the disease and to provide treatment or prophylaxis, while the long-term goals of partner services programs include improved clinical, public health, and cost outcomes.[3,4]

Use in Outbreaks

Health departments routinely use contact tracing for outbreaks of tuberculosis. Contact tracing may also be used for outbreaks of measles and other respiratory diseases as well as hepatitis.[5–9] In addition, these systems have been studied to prepare for possible bioterrorist acts such as smallpox.[10,11] Partner notification is often used for outbreaks of syphilis and HIV infections, and may be used in outbreaks of other STIs such as gonorrhea and chlamydia.[12,13]

Voluntary Participation, Informed Consent, and Confidentiality

Although the details of contact tracing may vary by health department or state, all programs should emphasize voluntary participation, informed consent, and confidentiality.[3,14,15] Specific federal and state laws concerning patient confidentiality protect index patients and contacts and should be considered when developing partner services programs.[3,5] In addition to meeting legal obligations, programs that maintain confidentiality have another benefit: Studies have shown that patients are more likely to participate with contact tracing if they believe confidentiality will be maintained.[3] Moreover, lapses in confidentiality could cause personal problems for the patient.[3] Specific examples of maintaining confidentiality include training all staff, such as disease intervention specialists and administrative personnel, who may be involved in contact tracing; taking steps to ensure neighbors or household members do not know the purpose of a contact investigation visit, phone call, or letter; and conducting interviews in a private setting, in person.[3,5]

Training for Contact Tracing

Contact tracing requires a variety of skills, and adequate training ensures that disease intervention specialists are capable of performing their duties. For example, persons performing contact tracing must be familiar with clinical and epidemiological information about the disease they are investigating. They must also know how to encourage testing and treatment, take patient histories effectively, elicit partner contact information, refer patients to various support services, and counsel individuals on high-risk behavior and disease prevention. These tasks must be performed in a confidential and trust-building manner, despite the fact that patients may not be motivated to cooperate with the investigation.

Furthermore, disease intervention specialists frequently face logistical challenges. They may need to find a homeless contact based only on information about the shelter that person frequents, or locate a prostitute contact knowing only the individual's street name and physical description. Dealing with safety issues, such as working in a crack house or a neighborhood known for violence, is often also part of their job.[3]

Disease intervention specialists receive training through their place of employment and may attend conferences on contact tracing that utilize lectures and role-playing. The Centers for Disease Control and Prevention (CDC) also offers a self-study module, and other online resources are available.[14,16] Hands-on field observation and supervision with an experienced disease intervention specialist mentor is highly valuable, and learning how to stay safe on the job is a critical part of training.[3]

Contact Tracing Interviews

The disease in question, as well as the nature of the outbreak, dictates the interview plan. However, several interview steps commonly occur in traditional contact tracing.

Pre-Interview Analysis

Health department, physician, hospital, and jail or prison records may be used to learn about medical and psychosocial issues unique to the patient. For example, data on sexual orientation, history of domestic violence, and psychiatric issues could be useful for planning the interview. The time period of infectiousness should also be estimated to determine when the patient might have exposed others.[3]

Initial Interview

The goals of the initial interview include collecting additional data on clinical symptoms to better determine the period of infectiousness, obtaining missing patient data that are needed to perform the investigation, identifying contacts and obtaining contact information, determining the frequency and duration of potential contact exposures, and locating where the patient spent time during the period of infectiousness, including places of residence, work, school, and recreation.[3,16] Developing rapport with the patient is also an important part of the initial interview.[3,16]

Re-Interview

Disease intervention specialists often need to re-interview index patients. During the initial interview, the patient may be too ill or overwhelmed by the new diagnosis to provide the necessary information, or he or she may not yet trust the disease intervention specialists.[3,16] Therefore, one or more re-interviews may be required to elicit additional contact information after establishing a good relationship during the initial interview, or to verify that the index patient has received the needed clinical follow-up.[3,16]

Site Visit

Site visits may be performed, especially in the context of respiratory disease outbreaks.[16] Visiting places where the index patient spent time during the period of infectiousness can be useful for the investigation and may identify other potentially exposed individuals. For example, the physical layout of a location might provide clues about where transmission was likely to occur.

Additional Contact Tracing Techniques

Clustering and Cluster Interviewing

Clustering and cluster interviewing are contact tracing techniques that are used to identify additional cases.[3] Clustering entails asking the index patient about uninfected persons in his or her social network who might be at high risk for the disease. Cluster interviewing involves contacting the uninfected partners or social contacts of the index patient and eliciting information about their own high-risk contacts. Although the effectiveness of clustering and cluster interviewing for case finding has not yet been determined, these techniques are sometimes used in outbreak investigations.[3,17]

Social Network Analysis

Social network analysis is another tool for identifying additional cases that can be used in conjunction with traditional case-finding methods.[3] It involves gathering information from interviews or existing records about relationships (such as social, sexual, and drug-using connections) and the locations where they take place. Social network information can be analyzed using network analysis software to create diagrams and to statistically evaluate the network.[18-20]

Internet-Based Notification

Research has shown that certain populations, such as men who have sex with men, may engage in high-risk sexual behaviors with anonymous partners they find on the Internet.[21] Internet partner notification systems have been developed and evaluated in an attempt to reach these partners who may otherwise be unidentifiable.[21,22]

Responsibility for Contact Notification

Generally, there are four ways to notify contacts of their potential exposure:[3]

- Provider referral most often involves notification by disease intervention specialists, but may also be performed by clinicians or HIV counselors, for example.
- In self-referral, the patient takes responsibility for notification and referral to support services.
- In contract referral, the patient agrees to notify and refer all contacts within a certain time period. If the patient fails to do so, the provider may then perform notification and referral.
- Dual referral occurs when the patient and provider notify contacts together.[3]

Due to limited health department resources and the varied circumstances in which contact notification is required, novel forms of notification—such as treating sex partners of persons infected with STIs without services such as clinical confirmation or health education—have also been developed.[23]

Examples of Contact Tracing in Outbreak Investigations

In January 2005, a woman visited the Ashtabula County Health Department in Ohio to have a tuberculin skin test as part of a pre-employment physical. The skin test was positive, and the woman subsequently developed active tuberculosis, as indicated by chest radiograph and a positive sputum smear. Once the patient was diagnosed with active disease, public health nurses interviewed her to obtain information about her contacts, all of whom tested negative for tuberculosis. When additional cases of tuberculosis were reported to the health department in March 2005, contact investigation of these patients uncovered a source patient who had some connection to all of the patients who tested positive, including the woman who tested positive in January. He had been experiencing symptoms for the previous 4 years; although various medical professionals had suspected he had tuberculosis, none had treated the patient or notified the health department. The complete contact investigation uncovered 7 skin test conversions after testing 87 exposed contacts.[24]

In 2007, a child from Japan imported and spread measles at a large 10-day international youth sporting event. The outbreak was controlled through case finding, contact tracing, isolating patients, and administering post-exposure prophylaxis. Contact tracing efforts included for 1,250 individuals in 8 states and identified 7 cases that were epidemiologically linked to the index case.[7]

Example of Partner Notification in STI Outbreaks

In the summer of 1999, the San Francisco Department of Public Health learned of two cases of early-stage syphilis. Both patients had met most of their sexual partners through the same Internet chat room. When investigators interviewed the patients, they discovered that these individuals did not have any identifying information about many of these sexual partners other than their Internet screen names. This issue required that investigators modify the traditional partner notification process. They sent notification e-mails to the screen names and requested a reply. Partners who responded were advised to undergo medical evaluation. Through contact tracing and efforts to increase community awareness of the syphilis cluster, investigators ultimately identified seven Internet chat room–related cases of syphilis.[25]

Legal Authority for Partner Notification

The legal authority for partner notification of STIs resides with the states.[3] The legal authority for mandatory disease reporting is derived from state law. States may have slightly different organizational structures and approaches to partner notification depending on their laws. All 50 states require that certain diseases be reported to the appropriate state or local health department, although the list of reportable diseases varies by state.

Confidentiality

In addition to state and federal confidentiality laws, each public health department has specific confidentiality guidelines and legal regulations that investigators are required to follow. Maintaining patient confidentiality about disease status throughout the entire process is imperative. Not only does this practice promote a trusting relationship between the investigator and the patient, but it is required by law to protect the privacy of the patient. To this end, investigators should always attempt to interview cases and partners in a private setting. They should try to notify partners on a face-to-face basis, and should never reveal the identity of the original case patient to a partner. Investigators should not mention the disease when they leave verbal or written messages for the patient, nor should they provide confidential information to others such as spouses, friends, or family members. Furthermore, documentation of the investigation is confidential material and must be treated as such.

Summary

Sometimes special considerations complicate an outbreak investigation. When an outbreak is large and involves several jurisdictions, or when it is necessary to identify and provide services to individuals who may be difficult to identify and reach, tools such as ICS and contact tracing can help investigators bring the investigation to a successful conclusion.

Although developed in response to a devastating wildfire, ICS can be a useful tool for an outbreak investigation team, especially if the investigation requires the cooperation and coordination of multiple agencies. ICS can provide a chain of command, establish protocols for planning and operations, and ensure smooth communications among agencies and between investigators and the public.

Contact tracing may be a critical component of an investigation into an outbreak of an infectious disease such as HIV, syphilis, or tuberculosis. Although specific contact tracing procedures differ by state, the goals of contact tracing and partner notification are to intervene in the transmission of an infectious disease, educate patients and their contacts, encourage testing when appropriate, and provide treatment when needed. The provider or the patient may contact partners and others who might have been exposed, or the provider might reach an agreement with the patient to contact partners if the patient has not done so within a specified time period. When a patient is unable or unwilling to identify partners, cluster interviewing can uncover additional cases of the disease in question. In addition to training in how to trace contacts and conduct interviews, investigators who carry out contact tracing and partner notification must be aware of and follow state laws and department guidelines covering confidentiality and the legal authority to notify contacts.

References

1. NIMS and the Incident Command System. Federal Emergency Management Agency. November 23, 2004. http://www.fema.gov/txt/nims/nims_ics_position_paper.txt. Accessed September 3, 2010.
2. Public Health Regional Surveillance Team 6. *Incident Command System Practicum.* Presented at the National Association of County and City Health Officials Public Health Preparedness Summit; February 20, 2009.
3. Centers for Disease Control and Prevention. Recommendations for partner services programs for HIV Infection, syphilis, gonorrhea, and chlamydial infection. *Morb Mortal Weekly Rep.* 2008;57(RR09):1–63.
4. Hogben M. Partner notification for sexually transmitted diseases. *Clin Infect Dis.* 2007;44(suppl 3):S160–S174.
5. Centers for Disease Control and Prevention. Essential components of a tuberculosis prevention and control program: Recommendations of the Advisory Council for the Elimination of Tuberculosis. *Morb Mortal Weekly Rep.* 1995;44(RR11):1–16.
6. Centers for Disease Control and Prevention. Infectious disease and dermatologic conditions in evacuees and rescue workers after Hurricane Katrina—multiple states, August–September, 2005. *Morb Mortal Weekly Rep.* 2005;54:1–4.
7. Chen T-H, Kutty P, Lowe LE, et al. Measles outbreak associated with an international youth sporting event in the United States, 2007. *Pediatr Infect Dis J.* 2010;29:794–800.
8. Tortajada C, de Olalla PG, Pinto RM, et al. Outbreak of hepatitis A among men who have sex with men in Barcelona, Spain, September 2008–March 2009. *Euro Surveill.* 2009;14(15):19175. http://www.eurosurveillance.org/ViewArticle.aspx?ArticleId=19175. Accessed October 2, 2010.
9. Vogt TM, Perz JF, Van Houten CK Jr, et al. An outbreak of hepatitis B virus infection among methamphetamine injectors: The role of sharing injection drug equipment. *Addiction.* 2006;101(5):726–30.
10. Eichner M. Case isolation and contact tracing can prevent the spread of smallpox. *Am J Epidemiol.* 2003;158(2):118–28.
11. Porco TC, Holbrook KA, Fernyak SE, et al. Logistics of community smallpox control through contact tracing and ring vaccination: A stochastic network model *BMC Public Health.* 2004;4:34 http://www.biomedcentral.com/1471-2458/4/34/. Accessed October 2, 2010.

12. Du P, Coles FB, Gerber T, et al. Effects of partner notification on reducing gonorrhea incidence rate. *Sex Transm Dis.* 2007;34(4):189–94.

13. Kohl KS, Farley TA, Ewell J, et al. Usefulness of partner notification for syphilis control. *Sex Transm Dis.* 1999;26(4):201–7.

14. Centers for Disease Control and Prevention. Guidelines for the investigation of contacts of persons with infectious tuberculosis. *Morb Mortal Weekly Rep.* 2005;54(RR15):1–37.

15. Passin WF, Kim AS, Hutchinson AB, et al. A systematic review of HIV partner counseling and referral services: Client and provider attitudes, preferences, practices, and experiences. *STD.* 2006;33(5):320–8.

16. Self-study modules on tuberculosis: Module 6: Contact investigations for tuberculosis. Centers for Disease Control and Prevention. Reviewed July 1, 2010. http://www.cdc.gov/tb/education/ssmodules/module6/ss6contents.htm. Accessed October 2, 2010.

17. Gerber AR, King LC, Dunleavy GJ, et al. An outbreak of syphilis on an Indian reservation: Descriptive epidemiology and disease-control measures. *Am J Public Health.* 1989;79:83–5.

18. Seña AC, Muth SQ, Heffelfinger JD, et al. Factors and the sociosexual network associated with a syphilis outbreak in rural North Carolina. *Sex Transm Dis.* 2007;34(5):280–7.

19. De P, Singh AE, Wong T, et al. Sexual network analysis of a gonorrhoea outbreak. *Sex Transm Infect.* 2004;80(4):280–5.

20. McElroy PD, Rothenberg RB, Varghese R, et al. A network-informed approach to investigating a tuberculosis outbreak: Implications for enhancing contact investigations. *Int J Tuberc Lung Dis.* 2003;7(12 suppl 3):S486–S493.

21. Mimiaga MJ, Fair AD, Tetu AM, et al. Acceptability of an Internet-based partner notification system for sexually transmitted infection exposure among men who have sex with men. *Am J Public Health.* 2008;98(6):1009–11.

22. Centers for Disease Control and Prevention. Using the Internet for partner notification of sexually transmitted diseases—Los Angeles County, California, 2003. *Morb Mortal Weekly Rep.* 2004;53(6):129–31.

23. Schillinger JA, Hogben M. Partner notification for gonorrhea: Time for new ideas. *Sex Transm Dis.* 2007;34(4):195–6.

24. Kettunen CM, Sunmonu Y, Hodgkinson AL, et al. Contact investigation of a case of active tuberculosis in the community. *Am J Infect Control.* 2007;35(6):421–4.

25. Klausner JD, Wolf W, Fischer-Ponce L, et al. Tracing a syphilis outbreak through cyberspace. *JAMA.* 2000;284(4):447–9.

INDEX